走向未来

Chinese for Tomorrow

新中文教程

A New Five-Skilled Approach

课本第一册

Simplified Character Textbook, Volume 1

何文潮、焦晓晓、邵秋霞、李克立

Wayne He, Dela Jiao, Qiuxia Shao,
Christopher M. Livaccari

CHENG & TSUI COMPANY
Boston

Copyright © 2008 by Wayne He, Dela Jiao, Qiuxia Shao, and Christopher M. Livaccari

16 15 14 13 12 11 10 09 08   1 2 3 4 5 6 7 8 9 10

Published by
Cheng & Tsui Company, Inc.
25 West Street
Boston, MA 02111-1213 USA
Fax (617) 426-3669
www.cheng-tsui.com
"Bringing Asia to the World"™

Simplified Character Edition
ISBN 978-0-88727-568-5

Library of Congress Cataloging-in-Publication Data

Chinese for tomorrow : a new five-skilled approach : textbook volume one / He Wenchao ... [et. al] = [Zou xiang wei lai : xin Zhong wen jiao cheng : ke ben di yi ce / Wayne He ... et. al]
    p. cm.
  Parallel title in Chinese characters.
  ISBN 978-0-88727-568-5 (pbk.)
  1. Chinese language--Textbooks for foreign speakers--English. I. He, Wayne. II. Title: Zou xiang wei lai.
PL1129.E5C417 2007
495.1'82421--dc22

                            2006049166

This Project has been partially funded by the China National Office for Teaching Chinese as a Foreign Language, （中国国家对外汉语教学领导小组办公室） The Department of East Asian Studies, and Curriculum Development Challenge Fund, New York University

Printed in Canada

CONTENTS

▶ 第二课 **Lesson 2** 我和我家 **My Family and I**   **63**

▶ 第五课 **Lesson 5**　去买东西 **Going Shopping**　　　　　**161**

▶ 第六课 **Lesson 6**　乘车 **Transportation**　　　　　**197**

▶ 第十课 **Lesson 10** 天气 **The Weather**   **355**

PUBLISHER'S NOTE

The Cheng & Tsui Chinese language Series is designed to publish and widely distribute quality language learning materials created by leading instructors from around the world. We welcome readers' comments and suggestions concerning the publications in this series. Please contact the following members of our Editorial Board, in care of our Editorial Department (e-mail: editor@cheng-tsui.com).

Professor Shou-hsin Teng, Chief Editor

> Graduate Institute of Teaching Chinese as a Second Language
>
> National Taiwan Normal University

Professor Dana Scott Bourgerie

> Department of Asian and Near Eastern Languages
>
> Brigham Young University

Professor Samuel Cheung

> Department of Chinese
>
> Chinese University of Hong Kong

Professor Ying-che Li

> Department of East Asian Languages and Literatures
>
> University of Hawaii

Professor Timothy Light

> Department of Comparative Religion
>
> Western Michigan University

VOLUME 1 OVERVIEW

Lesson	Objectives	Selected Language Points (Textbook)†	Grammar Points (Grammar Book)
Introduction to the Chinese Language	1. Learn how to pronounce Chinese. 2. Understand the basics of the Chinese writing system. 3. Begin typing Chinese on a computer.		
Lesson 1 打招呼 **Greetings**	1. Say and respond to basic greetings. 2. Introduce yourself and others.	1. 吗 questions 2. Adjectives used as verbs	1. Sentence with 是 2. Question with 吗 3. Sentence with 有 4. Cardinal numbers under 100 5. Measure words
Lesson 2 我和我家 **My Family and I**	1. Introduce family members. 2. Talk about occupations.	1. The complement of degree 2. Plural forms in Chinese 3. Use of the adverbs 不 and 都 4. The 是……的 construction	1. A-not-A questions 2. Usage of adjectives 3. Adverb 都 4. Sentences with 在 5. Ordinal numbers 6. Questions with 好吗 or 对不对
Lesson 3 约时间 **Making Appointments**	1. Make appointments. 2. Extend, accept, and decline invitations.	1. Tag questions such as "……, 怎么样?", and "……, 好吗?" 2. The complement of result 3. Pivotal sentences	1. Telling time 2. Years, months, dates and weekdays 3. Time words 4. Numbers in daily life usage 5. Money expressions 6. The particle 呢

† This chart lists only the language points that students are required to master. These points are marked by an asterisk in the Language Use Notes in each lesson.

Pronunciation	Character Writing and Computer Input	Customs & Culture
Introduction to Mandarin Chinese pronunciation	Introduction to the Chinese Writing System Computer Input in Chinese	
Understand the "tone sandhi" rules for pinyin.	Understand the basic form and structure of Chinese characters. Use the computer to type a few sentences (3–5) introducing yourself to your teacher.	**中国人的名字 Chinese Names** Test Your Knowledge: Match these names to their owners.
Review and practice the pinyin system, including the "neutral tone" and the "er" sound.	1. Learn basic Chinese radicals. 2. Use the computer to type 5–6 sentences introducing your family.	**中国人的家庭称呼** **Chinese Family Relationships** Test Your Knowledge: Make a family tree.
Review and practice the pinyin system, including spelling rules and syllable separation marks.	1. Understand the basic strokes and stroke order of Chinese characters. 2. Write a core group of characters (5) by hand. 3. Use the computer to type 5–6 sentences about what you like to do in your spare time.	**中国的少数民族** **China's Ethnic Minorities** Test Your Knowledge: Identify these regions and ethnic minorities in China.

Lesson	Objectives	Selected Language Points (Textbook)†	Grammar Points (Grammar Book)	
Lesson 4 学中文 **Learning Chinese**	1. Talk about Chinese language studies. 2. Ask questions about language study.	1. Using 在, both to indicate an action in progress and as a preposition meaning "in" or "at" 2. The uses of 一点儿, 就 and 会 3. A-not-A questions	1. Question words 2. Topic-comment sentences 3. Pivotal sentences 4. The particle 吧 5. Usage of 的 6. Alternative question with 是……还是	
Lesson 5 去购物 **Going Shopping**	1. Ask for prices, bargain, and purchase items. 2. Return and exchange items.	1. 比 2. 的 3. 要是 4. 什么的 5. 等 6. 除了…… 以外, 还……)	1. The particle 得 2. Auxiliary verbs 能, 会, and 可以 3. Auxiliary verbs 要 and 想 4. Auxiliary verbs 得 and 应该 5. Imperative sentences	
Lesson 6 乘车 **Transportation**	1. Talk about public transportation. 2. Tell how to get to a destination by public transportation.	1. 是……还是…… 2. 要看 3. 又……又…… 3. 有的……有的 …… 4. 差不多 5. 左右	1. The particle 了 2. Rhetorical questions 3. The particle 地 4. Sentences with 是……的 5. The conjunction 因为……所以	
Lesson 7 旅行 **Travel**	1. Make travel plans. 2. Book, purchase and change airline tickets.	1. 先……再…… 2. 过 (verb) 3. 怎么 + 这么/那么 4. 多 (adverb) 5. 得 (děi, aux. verb) 6. 只好	1. Past experience with 过 2. Changes in near future with 了 3. Progressive aspect or ongoing action 4. Continued action or situation with 着 5. Simultaneous actions with 一边……一边	

† This chart lists only the language points that students are required to master. These points are marked by an asterisk in the Language Use Notes in each lesson.

Pronunciation	Character Writing and Computer Input	Customs & Culture
	1. Write a core group of characters (5) by hand. 2. Use the computer to type 6–7 sentences about the difficulties and pleasures of learning Chinese.	**读书与科举考试制度** **Education and the Legacy of the Imperial Examination System** Test Your Knowledge: Who is the "Number One Scholar"?
	1. Write a core group of characters (5) by hand. 2. Use the computer to type 6–7 sentences about your experiences shopping in a street market.	**中国的货币与购物** **Chinese Money and Shopping** Test Your Knowledge: Where to go shopping?
	1. Write a core group of characters (5) by hand. 2. Use the computer to type 7–10 sentences describing the public transportation system in your city.	**中国的交通** **Transportation in China** Test Your Knowledge: How will you get there?
	1. Write a core group of characters (8) by hand. 2. Use the computer to type a paragraph (8–10 sentences minimum) about your plans for Thanksgiving break.	**欣赏京剧** **Enjoying and Appreciating Beijing Opera** Test Your Knowledge: How well do you know these famous Chinese novels?

Lesson	Objectives	Selected Language Points (Textbook)†	Grammar Points (Grammar Book)
Lesson 8 邮局和银行 **At the Post Office and Bank**	1. Send mail at the post office. 2. Deposit and withdraw money at the bank.	1. Adj. + 是 + Adj. 2. 就是/可是 3. 只要 4. The 把 sentence 5. 原来 6. Topic-Comment sentence	1. Comparisons 2. Questions with 多 3. The complement of result 4. Simple directional complements 5. The adverb 就 for emphasis
Lesson 9 生病 **I Am Sick**	1. Communicate with a doctor. 2. Describe symptoms. 3. Understand instructions on taking medicine.	1. 就是 meaning "only" 2. 来 meaning "come and do" 3. 一下 4. 有没有 (A-not-A question) 5. 什么 as a general referral 6. The complement of frequency 7. 或者 8. 不用 9. Different uses of 了	1. Duration of time 2. The complement of frequency 3. Compound directional complements 4. 一……就 5. The conjunction 不但……而且
Lesson 10 天气 **The Weather**	1. Talk about the weather. 2. Read and understand the weather forecast. 3. Describe the climate of a particular place.	1. Rhetorical questions 2. 害得 3. 被 used passively 4. 比较 5. 吧 in a question 6. 是……还是…… 7. 不如	1. Potential complements 2. 把 sentences 3. 被 sentences 4. The conjunction 连……都/也 5. The conjunction 虽然……但是

† This chart lists only the language points that students are required to master. These points are marked by an asterisk in the Language Use Notes in each lesson.

Pronunciation	Character Writing and Computer Input	Customs & Culture
	1. Write a core group of characters (8) by hand. 2. Use the computer to type a paragraph (8–10 sentences minimum) about a past experience at the post office or bank.	**中国的邮局、电话和互联网** **Post, Phone and Internet Services in China** Test Your Knowledge: Which service should you use?
	1. Write a core group of characters (8) by hand. 2. Use the computer to type an essay (200 characters, 10 sentences minimum) talking about an experience seeing a doctor.	**中医和中药** **Traditional Chinese Medicine** Test Your Knowledge: How would you treat these patients?
	1. Write a core group of characters (8) by hand. 2. Use the computer to type an article (200 characters minimum, 10 sentences minimum) talking about the climate where you live.	**二十四节气** **The 24 Solar Terms** Test Your Knowledge: Can you identify the solar term for these events?

PREFACE FOR TEACHERS

Welcome to *Chinese for Tomorrow*, a uniquely effective approach to Chinese language learning that takes full advantage of the possibilities offered by computer technology. This series is projected to cover three years of instruction corresponding to a six-semester sequence of college or high school Chinese. Using what we call the "Computer Chinese" or "CC" method, we treat computer input of Chinese characters as both a language learning tool, and as a fifth language skill, along with the more traditionally defined ones of speaking, listening, reading, and writing. With the computer as an integral part of a first-year Chinese program, we can rapidly speed the process of language acquisition and greatly reduce the "pain-gain" ratio for students. The greatest obstacle for teachers hoping to use the computer method right now is the lack of appropriate material. *Chinese for Tomorrow* fills this gap, and represents an important step in bringing Chinese language teaching into the digital age. Our new approach to teaching Chinese has proven highly effective and engaging to our students during five years of field-testing at New York University, and we hope to offer its advantages to you through this material.

"Computer Chinese:" A New Approach to Learning the Chinese Language

Our "Computer Chinese (CC)" method starts out by emphasizing the use of pinyin to teach students how to write Chinese characters on the computer. This allows students to use the language in a practical and engaging way very early on in their studies, and to solidify their pinyin and pronunciation skills from the start. During the first year of study, in addition to teaching computer input, we also explain the components of Chinese characters and offer exercises for writing a specially selected number of characters by hand. This serves as preparation for the more focused and intense teaching of handwriting that occurs later, after students have built a solid foundation in the spoken language.

Computer Chinese integrates computer input and handwriting instruction.

We integrate computer input and handwriting instruction as complements, each supporting the other to help students read and write Chinese. We have found that using a computer for input and selection of characters can greatly increase students' learning efficiency and knowledge retention at the beginning stages. The major difference between our approach and traditional approaches is that our course allows students to learn how to write Chinese characters by hand gradually over a period of three years, instead of all at once in the first year of study, when they are still struggling to grasp the basics of the language.

Chinese teachers have long recognized the high degree of student anxiety that comes with learning Chinese characters, and this has forced many to de-emphasize literacy skills for lower-level students and to focus instead on speaking and listening skills by writing only in pinyin. This approach may have some merits in the short run, but it does not get around the very real fact that Chinese books, newspapers, magazines, and even street signs, are written in Chinese characters, and that pinyin is a phonological tool, not a writing system in itself.

Computer Chinese uses the computer as a study tool, not just a word processing system.

Before the widespread use of Chinese language computer technology, there was simply no other way for students to master characters but to write each one over and over again, stroke by stroke. Now, however, it is possible to use the computer as a study tool, and not just as a word processing system. *Chinese for Tomorrow* addresses the most formidable hurdle facing beginning Chinese language learners by allowing them to write (type) in pinyin and see those words displayed as Chinese characters. In this way, students can use pinyin for the task for which it was intended—as a phonological tool—and not as a substitute for writing characters. With this in mind, we analyzed existing Chinese language curricula and studied the feasibility of applying computer technology to teaching, and found definitively that using the computer to input Chinese is the best method of teaching Chinese to beginning learners. The book you are holding in your hands is a systematic, structured approach to learning Chinese based on these findings.

Computer Chinese improves students' vocabulary retention and language ability.

Through our teaching and testing experience in the Chinese language program at New York University, we have found that students using the CC method learn on average twenty more new words per class than those using more traditional methods. While developing this curriculum over five years of teaching, we found that our experimental group using the CC approach achieved higher rates of accuracy in vocabulary tests (93.22 percent vs. 76.12 percent in the control group) and better performance on reading comprehension tests (98.08 percent vs. 92.51 percent) than students in the control group using more traditional methods. Moreover, after one semester of training, essays written by CC students were judged equal to or better than essays written by students trained for three semesters in the traditional manner, assessed with regard to accuracy in grammatical expression (97.44 percent for the CC students vs. 94.83 percent for traditional students) and ability to use different word types (358 word types [CC] vs. 238 word types [traditional]). Students who used the computer to learn vocabulary items simply processed them more quickly and remembered them better. The validity of this approach is also supported by the findings of the Penless Chinese Research Project funded by the U.S. Department of Education and led by Professor Ping Xu of Baruch College, City University of New York, and Professor Theresa Jen of the University of Pennsylvania.[1]

Computer Chinese speeds the process of language learning and reduces psychological barriers.

There are several advantages to our new approach. First, learning to input pinyin is much like inputting English—if you can say it, you can write it. In addition, the CC method reduces the number of characters learned incorrectly; indeed, one of the most frequent errors made by students is learning to write a character incorrectly (one too many or one too few strokes) and not realizing that it is incorrect. The computer will tell you immediately, and bypass this type of error altogether. Another key advantage of this new system is that it integrates reading and writing; if you want to write a Chinese character correctly, you must first learn to read and spell it correctly. The method saves time, as beginning students only need to recognize Chinese characters, and do not need to learn to write them stroke by stroke, rapidly increasing their reading ability. Using an online Chinese language dictionary makes looking up words incredibly easy, and online dictionaries include pinyin for each character, giving even first year students the ability to read a wide range of material and surf the Internet in Chinese. Finally, our approach increases students' ability to write. Lower-level students generally do not know how to write enough characters to assemble a decent composition, but after learning computer input, even first year students can begin to write compositions—and what they are writing is characters, not just pinyin. But perhaps the most important advantage of computer input is that it removes the psychological barrier that Chinese is difficult to learn and increases the confidence of students, thus reducing the number of students who are likely to drop Chinese before they reach even the second semester of study.

How We Address Some Common Concerns about the CC Approach.

Concerns that have been raised regarding our new method are (1) how to choose appropriate Chinese software; (2) whether or not writing by hand should be taught at all; and (3) how to assess students' learning.

---

[1] For more information on the Penless Chinese Research Project, see www.penlesschinese.org. Also see Xu, Ping and Theresa Jen, Eds,. *Hanzi jiaoxue yu diannao keji*. Taipei: Linking Press, 2005.

Software.

There are many Chinese word processing software packages on the market. The most recent versions of Microsoft® Windows® operating systems have a number of Chinese language input methods, and many instructors use these. Macintosh® computers also now come equipped with built-in Language Kits. Using these input methods saves teachers the trouble of finding an add-on software program and getting funding to buy a site license. (See Appendix 2 for basic instructions on how to set up your computer to type in Chinese using the latest versions of Windows and Macintosh operating systems.) From the perspective of teaching effectiveness, we prefer NJStar Chinese Word Processor (NJSTAR-CWP). Some of its functions are especially designed for Chinese language instructors and learners, such as the ability to add pinyin to character texts, hear sounds while typing, look up words in an online dictionary, control tone input and use a mouse as a pen for writing characters. Another option is the "Penless Chinese" software program, which can be freely downloaded at **http://www.penlesschinese.org**. If these Chinese software programs are not available to you, you can use the Internet to input Chinese, and you can look up words with the help of online dictionaries and translation programs. Some useful sites are listed on the companion web site for *Chinese for Tomorrow*, hosted at **www.cheng-tsui.com.**

CC versus handwriting.

As to the question of whether or not to teach handwriting at all, we think that computer typing and handwriting can and must complement one another in the process of learning Chinese. Indeed, it must be emphasized that computer typing and handwriting are two distinct language skills, both of which serve the same purpose—written communication. Writing Chinese characters by hand helps students develop an appreciation for the ways in which characters are structured and helps many students to recognize and remember new words. In this course we concentrate on the CC approach during the first two years of study, handwriting only a limited number of characters selected by frequency of use (5–10 per lesson). In the third year, students will then be ready to make a smooth transition to an emphasis on handwriting. Teachers who wish to emphasize handwriting more than this (or less than this) can use their own discretion in deciding what combination of the CC method and handwriting will be best for their students. For example, a teacher could use 90 percent CC and 10 percent handwriting in teaching (or vice versa); 50 percent CC and 50 percent hand writing, or even 100 percent CC, depending on the teaching goals, student learning styles, curriculum design, and available equipment.

Testing.

It is important that students be tested using the computer. Since they are being trained with the computer, it makes sense that they should be tested in this way. If a computer cannot be accessed in the classroom, then students can be given an electronic exam in the school computer or language lab, or can be tested via Blackboard Academic Suite™ or other web-based classroom tools. Alternatively, teachers can upload exams to the Internet and restrict access by setting up passwords.

You design your new curriculum simply by developing an understanding of the CC approach, selecting the appropriate computer software and hardware, and utilizing the material offered in this textbook. The key features of this book are discussed below.

Key Features of Chinese for Tomorrow

This course is new and different in a number of important ways:

The series teaches language that is useful, interesting, natural, and relevant to daily life.

This is the guiding philosophy of our approach. Many popular Chinese language textbooks being used today are based on traditional approaches, which overemphasize grammar. In such textbooks, the readings, topics and vocabulary words are limited to those that incorporate the grammar points, and students often find themselves learning artificial language just for the sake of practicing a particular grammar structure. We insist on the language presented being natural, commonly used, and interesting. We accomplish this by presenting grammar in a separate, companion grammar book, thus freeing students and teachers to focus on the most relevant, useful language in the textbook. Topics in the textbook are appropriate for the particular needs of senior high school and university students, and students enjoy using the phrases they have learned in familiar situations. We introduce a number of commonly used expressions, including exclamations and fillers, such as ah (啊), ya (呀), and na (那). Several new expressions that have become common in China are also included, such as "Hollywood blockbuster" (美国大片) or dadi (打的) for "taking a taxi." If you know what dǎdī (打的) means, then dīgē (的哥) or dījiě (的姐) will be readily understandable. Young people in China often use such expressions, and introducing them assures learners that they are learning the most current, colorful, and useful language.

Textbook lessons introduce the language succinctly and clearly, and a companion grammar book explains grammar in detail.

The teaching of grammar has long been one of the most difficult challenges facing foreign language teachers. We take the view that new language can be acquired quickly and effectively without detailed grammatical explanation, but that a deep understanding of the language and its principles is crucial for developing a "feel" for the language and the way it works. We therefore offer our companion grammar book, which contains a systematic explanation of the basic grammatical principles of Mandarin Chinese.

The grammar book is based on the principle that the most effective way to teach a foreign language to adolescents and adults is by means of a two-track approach. One of these is the communicative approach, which is situational and builds competency in terms of using the target language to negotiate a wide range of topics and situations. The second approach is that of deeper knowledge and analytical understanding of the grammatical, phonological, and pragmatic systems of the language. The textbook follows the first track, the communicative approach, and the grammar book the second track.

For example, in a given lesson in the textbook, a student may be asked to learn how to say a small set of numbers, but as preparation for future growth, the student must also understand the workings of the number system and how to say all the numbers from one to one hundred. While the student may not be able to say all the numbers immediately, he or she will eventually gain mastery of the counting system. It makes sense to concentrate on the small set of numbers in the textbook lesson, but include the counting system in the grammar book.

The companion grammar book has been designed to give teachers and students maximum flexibility and allow them to cover grammar at a pace that works best for their particular program. Students can study the grammar book together with the *Chinese for Tomorrow* textbook if they would like to have a better understanding about the grammar points introduced in the textbook. In addition, students using textbooks other than *Chinese for Tomorrow* can study this grammar book as an independent reference book because the grammar points discussed here are the most basic grammar points that every student is expected to know.

If you are teaching this book as part of the curriculum, we suggest teaching the relevant grammar points simultaneously with each corresponding lesson of the textbook. For example, if you are spending two weeks on Textbook Lesson 1, you might spend one full day or two half-days during that two-week period to cover the relevant grammar points discussed in the Grammar Book. Please see the suggested sample syllabi in the *Chinese for Tomorrow* Teacher's Manual for more detailed suggestions.

The textbook and the grammar book are closely connected. What students learn in the textbook is reinforced in the grammar book, and vice versa. Here are some specific ways in which the two books complement each other:

Vocabulary

The vocabulary used in corresponding lessons of the textbook and grammar book connects the two books. For example, the vocabulary introduced in Lesson 1 of the textbook is repeated and reinforced in Lesson 1 of the grammar book, to allow students and teachers to cover both books simultaneously in the same course.

Cross References

In the textbook, notes to the dialogues and passages refer to the points explained in the grammar book and indicate the lessons in which they can be found. In the grammar book, we also provide sample sentences selected from the textbook and explain certain grammar points by analyzing these sentences. It is important to note that the language items introduced in a given textbook lesson may or may not be covered in exactly the same lesson in the grammar book. In the textbook, vocabulary and sentence structures are presented in the order that students are likely to encounter them in their daily lives. In the grammar book, however, grammar items are presented in order of difficulty—the grammar items that are easiest to grasp are presented first. This two-track design is intentional, and it helps to strengthen students' language skills by providing broader exposure to language patterns and more repetition of vocabulary. For example, students may get a brief exposure to the use of the particle 了 "le" in Textbook Lesson 1, but may not learn 了 in detail until Grammar Book Lesson 6. This is because students will encounter 了 fairly early on in Chinese communication, but may not be ready to understand the range of uses of 了 until later. The grammar book serves to reinforce what was learned in textbook lessons, explain the new usage of familiar words at increasing levels of difficulty, and strengthen students' grasp of grammar.

Exercises

In the grammar book exercises, we provide at least one piece of conversation similar to what was introduced in the corresponding lesson in the textbook, but focusing on new grammar items explained in the grammar book. This way, the students can practice using the new grammar items in situations similar to the ones introduced in the textbook.

Large numbers of new vocabulary items are introduced in each lesson.

Because ordinary textbooks are written with the assumption that students must learn to write each and every character by hand, the amount of new words taught is severely limited. Most beginning textbooks commonly used in the United States introduce just over 20 new words per lesson, and a bit more in later lessons. More demanding textbooks introduce over 30 or so new words per lesson. *Chinese for Tomorrow* introduces 50–60 new words per lesson. This number is based upon our experience using the Computer Chinese method.

Students can learn how to speak, understand, and recognize vocabulary items in a relatively short period of time.

Based on current research, in order for students to reach limited proficiency, they need to know about 2,500 Chinese characters. In order to reach a working proficiency, they need to know about 3,500. And to reach fluency they need to know 5,000 to 6,000 characters. It takes far too long to get there by learning only 20 or 30 words per lesson. With our Computer Chinese method, students can learn one-third to one-half more words per lesson than students using traditional methods, and can therefore progress much more quickly.

The design of the texts focuses on the transition from single character words to compounds.

All existing Chinese learning materials introduce vocabulary items (single-character words or compound words). The traditional way of memorizing vocabulary items one by one according to their English meaning puts a serious limit on the amount of vocabulary a student can master. In *Chinese for Tomorrow*, we introduce a more effective way to build vocabulary: we present a range of specially designed activities that allow students to practice distinguishing characters with similar sounds and structures. In addition to the compound words we introduce as vocabulary items in each lesson, we select about 5–10 commonly used single characters that appear in those compounds. We ask students to study and practice these 5–10 characters, using online or traditional dictionaries to explore the range of compound words the characters can be used to form. When selecting these characters, we focused on the top 200 most commonly used characters by frequency-of-usage ranking[2] and the "A Level" characters tested on the HSK Chinese Proficiency Exam.[3] There are many homophones and many

---

[2] The frequency-of-usage ranking is an important reference for selecting the most commonly used vocabulary in standard Mandarin Chinese. We mainly use the frequency of usage information from two computer programs: Chinese TA and NJStar.

[3] The HSK Chinese Proficiency Exam is the official standardized test of Chinese as a second language developed in the People's Republic of China. Its vocabulary program is divided into four levels. Level A is the lowest of the four, and it includes the most commonly used 800 characters.

characters with similar shapes in Chinese, and these can be very confusing for students. The more time students spend seeing how words and characters they are learning relate to other words they have learned or will soon learn, the stronger their vocabulary will become.

The series includes a diversity of practice activities.

One of the special features of our approach is the diversity of practice activities and exercises that we offer. The student textbook and grammar book present both in-class and out-of-class exercises. Additional in-class communicative activities can be found in the teacher's manual.

Exercises and texts are designed to reinforce previously learned knowledge. In addition to such traditional standards as sentence structure and reading comprehension exercises, we offer specialized computer-based activities and computer input exercises, as well as a full range of tasks that address listening, conversation, recognizing Chinese characters, and writing characters by hand. There are exercises for everything that is covered, providing the student with ample opportunity to truly digest the contents of the texts, to use the language that has been learned, and to maximize communicative competence.

There are also exercises that extend the student's learning to language not specifically taught in the text. For example, each lesson's Reading Exercises are divided into two parts: one a "controlled vocabulary" section that uses language very close to that presented in the text, and the other section an "open" range of simple jokes, stories, and other material that go beyond the limits of the text and test students' ability to guess a word or phrase's meaning from context.

Previously learned language is continuously re-introduced.

In addition to introducing large amounts of new vocabulary, each lesson incorporates much previously introduced material, in order to reinforce students' mastery of earlier material. Vocabulary items from previous lessons are used in the listening, speaking, typing and other exercises in the textbook and grammar book. The textbook offers relatively concise grammatical explanations with an emphasis on communication, while the grammar book explains language points in more detail. The examples and exercises in the grammar book use vocabulary words that have been introduced in the textbook. The emphasis throughout is on continuity, so that students can constantly review and build on the language learned previously.

Chinese for Tomorrow has been developed to conform to ACTFL National Standards[4] and AP and HSK testing material.

Chinese for Tomorrow is firmly grounded in the "Five Cs" of the National Standards for Foreign Language Learning in the 21st Century: Communication, Culture, Connections, Comparisons, and Communities. This set of material is also an effective tool for preparing students for the Advanced Placement Chinese Language and Culture exam, and has been prepared with the AP course description in mind. In writing and designing the textbook and grammar book, we have used the HSK Chinese Proficiency Test Program as the central guide (中国汉语水平考试大纲), particularly with regard to the selection of vocabulary items and grammar points. The material contained in this book utilizes a wide variety of approaches, including both the communicative approach and more traditional methodologies. We employ many different techniques to help make Chinese learning more fun, interesting, systematic and practical for use in real life situations.

Topics integrate cultural knowledge and language learning.

Chinese for Tomorrow allows students of all backgrounds and nationalities to make observations about life in China and to make some cultural comparisons.

In the Notes on Language Usage, we point out some specific uses of the language that reflect Chinese culture, such as the use of the term "老师," greetings, responses to compliments, etc. Chinese and English are very different languages with very different traditions and cultural contexts. There is often no "one-to-one" translation between words or expressions in the two languages. Learning to appreciate these subtle differences is one of the great joys of learning another language and discovering another culture. This text presents Chinese conversations in their most natural contexts. We show students not only how to put sentences together, and we offer useful observations and hints to students about how to use their newly acquired Chinese words and expressions in the ways most appropriate to the culture.

In each lesson's Chinese Customs and Culture section, we provide important cultural material related to the topics presented in the texts. In Lesson 1, for example, we explain how Chinese names are given to children and, in Lesson 2, we introduce Chinese family life and family relationships. These sections are written completely in English, contain engaging and useful activities, and serve to help students build a deeper knowledge of Chinese cultural life. Some people with excellent language skills fail to attain real access to daily life in China because they fail to understand and internalize the

---

[4] For more information about the American Council on the Teaching of Foreign Language, and the Standards for Foreign Language Learning in the 21st Century, visit **www.actfl.org**.

subtleties of the culture. We hope that the sections on cultural knowledge will help students avoid this problem.

Chinese for Tomorrow Sets a New Standard

Chinese for Tomorrow fills the need in Chinese teaching for an effective and engaging computer-based learning method, and is the first systematically developed set of material in this area. We hope you enjoy teaching with this course and we welcome your feedback. Please send all comments and suggestions to us, in care of **editor@cheng-tsui.com.**

The authors

March 2007, New York

PREFACE FOR STUDENTS

· ·

This book is unlike earlier attempts to teach Chinese in that it introduces computer input methods that make the process of learning Chinese more efficient and rewarding. Traditional approaches to language learning are centered on four skills: reading, writing, speaking, and listening. We add a fifth, computer input, to meet the needs of today's learners. The computer allows you to maximize your progress and to gain a solid grounding in what is now the fastest-growing medium for written communication in Chinese—the computer. Whether typing a letter, writing a report, or sending an email to a friend, you will need to know how to use a computer to write in Chinese. Typing Chinese on a computer simply involves entering pinyin—or the English letters that represent the sounds of the Chinese word you wish to write—and then selecting the appropriate character from a list that your computer software will generate automatically. Thus, as you are learning Chinese computer input, you will also be gaining a strong knowledge of pinyin, which will help you perfect your pronunciation of Chinese.

In this course you will also learn how to write Chinese characters with a pen, pencil, or brush, but because it takes careful study and attention to detail, we teach handwriting gradually over a period of three years. While many teachers spend great amounts of time early on in their Chinese courses teaching students how to write by hand, we ask you to begin with computer input of Chinese characters, which will allow you to first build a strong foundation in the spoken language while getting used to writing Chinese characters by hand more gradually. You will focus on character recognition and will be able to start putting sentences together on your computer screen almost immediately. In this way, you will have more time to spend expanding your vocabulary, practicing speaking, and studying the structure of the language. Please see the Preface for Teachers for a more comprehensive explanation of the Computer Chinese method.

Using the computer will greatly boost your efficiency as a learner, and will make the process more fun and, ultimately, more rewarding. The Introduction to the Chinese Language will lead you through the basics and get you started using Chinese right away by typing it on your computer. Current versions of Windows® and Macintosh® operating systems already have a built-in capability for Chinese word processing, so it's incredibly easy to get started. See Appendix 2 for basic instructions on how to set up your computer to type in Chinese. Then turn to the Introduction to start learning!

We would like to say 欢迎 huānyíng (welcome) to you as you begin this course, and we hope you enjoy the fascinating journey on which you are embarking.

THE STRUCTURE OF EACH LESSON

Volume 1 of *Chinese for Tomorrow* includes three parts: an Introduction to the Chinese Language, 10 lessons with exercises, and appendices.

The Introduction to the Chinese Language is further divided into three parts: (1) pinyin; (2) characters; and (3) computer input. We first introduce the Chinese pronunciation system, with a focus on pinyin as the foundation of the CC approach. To make learning pinyin fun, we introduce words for some foreign brand-name products that are currently popular in China. The Introduction briefly explains the nature of Chinese characters, and then moves to an explanation of computer typing skills. Most of the pinyin exercises and typing practice exercises in the Introduction are selected from the first few lessons. In this way, from the very beginning, students will be used to acquiring a wide range of new vocabulary quickly and efficiently.

Each lesson in this textbook contains two dialogues and one prose passage, which is either a narrative text that summarizes what happens in the dialogues, or a reading related to the topics discussed in the dialogues. These are called the "texts," and each is presented in two forms: first in pinyin with characters, and second as a characters-only text. New Words lists and Notes on Language Usage associated with each text are presented, followed by English translations of the texts.

In the first three lessons, a special section on Learning Pinyin introduces some pinyin rules, such as tone changes and spelling rules. The first three lessons also include a section on Learning Chinese Characters. In Lesson 3, we begin to teach students how to write a small number of characters by hand: five characters each in Lessons 3–6 and eight characters each in Lessons 7–10. These characters are used as the basis for vocabulary-building exercises that let students practice forming compound words based on single characters they have learned.

This section is followed by four distinct exercise sections: Exercises for Listening and Speaking, Exercises for Computing and Learning Characters, Exercises for Understanding the Texts, and Supplementary Reading Exercises, (divided into "Controlled Vocabulary" and "Open Vocabulary" readings). The "Exercises for Computing and Learning Characters" can be completed by students in the computer lab; the other exercises can be done in or out of class, orally or with a computer. The "Supplementary Reading Exercises" focus on reviewing and reinforcing material introduced in the dialogues, and on developing the four language skills. The teacher can decide which items are done in class and which are done as homework according to the class schedule, the students' progress and the particular needs of the program. Each lesson concludes with a Chinese Customs and Culture section.

ACCOMPANYING MATERIAL

In addition to this textbook, the *Chinese for Tomorrow* series includes a teacher's manual, a companion grammar book, and online resources.

The teacher's manual is an important resource for teaching. It presents sample syllabi, extra classroom activities, sample quizzes and tests, and answer keys to the exercises in the textbook.

The grammar book provides a systematic explanation of the basic grammatical principles of Mandarin Chinese, and should be taught concurrently with the textbook.

The *Chinese for Tomorrow* online resources are located at **www.cheng-tsui.com** and include

1) audio files for the pronunciation section of the Introduction and for the listening and speaking exercises,

2) electronic versions of the dialogues, narratives, and readings for each lesson,

3) electronic versions of the supplementary reading exercises,

4) interactive texts and word lists,

5) flashcards for all the vocabulary words in the word lists, and

6) links to other web sites with information and tools for students using the Computer Chinese method.

Students can study the interactive texts on the computer by moving the cursor over a word or sentence to see its meaning or pinyin pronunciation, or to hear its sound. The electronic versions of the reading comprehension exercises allow students to use an online dictionary to help them read and understand the stories. The flashcards are a great way for students to reinforce their recognition of Chinese characters at home, on the bus or train, or wherever they may be.

ACKNOWLEDGMENTS

During the writing of this book, we received support, assistance and encouragement from many people. Their comments, suggestions, and inspiration have been invaluable to us.

We are grateful to our many friends and colleagues who reviewed the book and encouraged us to develop this new approach to teaching Chinese. We would especially like to thank Dr. Yu Feng (冯禹) of Harvard University, whose insights and constructive advice made the book possible. Weijia Huang (黄伟嘉), author of the popular intermediate Chinese textbook Chinese Language and Culture, reviewed the Chinese texts and gave us a number of critical suggestions. Dr. Tianwei Xie (谢天蔚) of the State University of California, Long Beach; Dr. Ping Xu (徐平) of Baruch College, City University of New York; Dr. John Yu (俞志强) of Baruch College, City University of New York; Dr. Claudia Ross (罗云) of the College of the Holy Cross; Dr. Dongdong Chen (陈东东) of Seton Hall University, Dr. John Jinghua Yin (印京华) of the University of Vermont and Dr. Martha Gallagher (王莅文) of the U. S. Military Academy all reviewed some or all of the manuscript and provided valuable input. We also want to thank the anonymous reviewers of the textbook and grammar book, whose constructive and critical feedback ensured the books' high quality.

Miss Chiung-Li Wei (魏琼丽), our intern teacher, collaborated with us in field- testing the material in this book and contributed many original suggestions. Jianwei Cai (蔡建伟) designed and made the interactive texts, making learning the lessons easier and more fun. Kathryn Taylor contributed line art that brings our text to life. William Moy designed the eye-catching online flashcards and glossary that are such important tools for students. Xiaolin Zhang (张小琳) collected the foreign brand names introduced in the pronunciation section of the Introduction, and made important contributions to that section of the text. Mark Candella and Fan He took the beautiful photos that appear throughout the book. Eva Wen contributed the instructions on how to set up Chinese input on computers. We would also like to thank the twenty students of Elementary Chinese I from the Spring 2005 semester at New York University (NYU), whose class was the first to use the completed book, and who gave us extraordinary feedback, suggestions, and insights.

We would like to thank the Department of East Asian Studies at NYU for its encouragement and administrative support. Our special thanks go to Professor Moss Roberts, former chair of the Department, who gave us critical support and encouragement; and Miss Alejandra Beltran, who provided constant administrative assistance. We also owe our thanks to the Humanities Computing Group of NYU Information Technology Services (ITS) and the ITS Faculty Technology Services Center, for their valuable technical support. We would like to thank the team at Cheng & Tsui, especially the President, Jill Cheng, and our fabulous editor, Kristen Wanner; as well as the rest of the staff, for their continued confidence and support.

We would like to conclude by thanking our families and friends, whose love and support form the very foundation of this project. Wayne He (何文潮) thanks his wife Ming and son Fan, for their loving care and wholehearted support. Dela Jiao (焦晓晓) thanks her husband John and son Dany for their endurance, understanding and constant support. Qiuxia Shao (邵秋霞) thanks her friend and colleague Stella Lee for her helpful ideas during the project. Chris Livaccari (李克立) thanks his wife Jisu Kim for her patience and unflagging moral support, his parents Dom and June Livaccari, and his sister Stephanie.

ABBREVIATIONS OF GRAMMAR TERMS

Adj	Adjective
Ad	Adverb
AV	Auxiliary Verb
CE	Common Expression
Conj	Conjunction
Int	Interjection
M	Measure Word
N	Noun
Neg	Negation
NP	Noun Phrase
Num	Numerals
O	Object
Par	Particle
PN	Proper Noun
Pron	Pronoun
Prep	Preposition
PW	Place Word
QW	Question Word
QP	Question Particle
S	Subject
TW	Time Word
V	Verb
VC	Verb plus Complement
VO	Verb plus Object

INTRODUCTION TO THE CHINESE LANGUAGE

qiān lǐ   zhī xíng shǐ yú zú xià

千   里   之   行， 始   于 足 下

The Chinese have a saying that a journey of a thousand miles begins with the first step. We hope you will enjoy your first steps as a student of Chinese and the journey upon which you are embarking. Above you see the Chinese characters for this phrase, along with romanized symbols called "pinyin." Pinyin forms the basis of the computer input method we will use in this course, and will be your first tool for pronouncing Chinese. You will notice that there is a symbol above most of the vowels in the pinyin words above. These symbols are called diacritic marks, and they represent the tone of the word. There are four tones (first, second, third, or fourth) in Mandarin Chinese, and these four tones indicate the pitch of one's voice when pronouncing the words.

In this Introduction, we will introduce the Chinese pronunciation system, the Chinese writing system, and the use of computers to type Chinese. The pronunciation system includes three major components of the sound system of standard modern Mandarin Chinese: (1) the tones, (2) the initials, and (3) the finals. The introduction to the Chinese writing system provides a brief explanation of the structure of Chinese characters. It also compares Chinese computer input with Chinese handwriting in order to suggest a new and uniquely effective way of learning Chinese. Some common, useful expressions will also be introduced in the exercises found within each section.

Pinyin is the first step toward computerized Chinese, so let's begin together by learning the pronunciation system and pinyin. We invite you to savor and enjoy the experience of learning Chinese. 祝您成功！zhù nín chénggōng (Good luck!)

The Chinese Pronunciation System

▶ **SECTION 1:**
Introduction to Mandarin Chinese Pronunciation

First let us get acquainted with some terms we will use in teaching Mandarin Chinese pronunciation.

A. **Mandarin Chinese:** The Mandarin Chinese language you are learning is the official spoken language used in the People's Republic of China. Mandarin Chinese is one of approximately 500 dialects spoken by the Han people, who make up about 92 percent of the Chinese population. While 500 dialects sounds like an overwhelming number, the Chinese language actually falls into eight major dialect categories: 1) Mandarin, the dialect of northern China; 2) Wu dialect, the dialect spoken south of the lower reaches of the Yangtze River; 3) Hunan dialect; 4) Jiangxi dialect; 5) Hakka dialect; 6) the dialect of southern Fujian; 7) the dialect of northern Fujian and 8) Cantonese. Unlike Cantonese, which has been the major Chinese dialect familiar in the West, standard Mandarin Chinese is based on the pronunciation of the Beijing area, the grammar of northern China, and the vocabulary of modern vernacular literature. It is known in Chinese as Pǔtōnghuà, which means "common language." Outside the Mainland, especially in Taiwan, Mandarin Chinese is called Guóyǔ, literally "national language," and Huáyǔ, an ethnic designation, in countries such as Singapore. Learners of Mandarin Chinese should know that although the spoken forms of Chinese differ radically from dialect to dialect, they all share the same characters and formal written language.

B. **Chinese Pinyin:** Pinyin is a system for marking the pronunciation of Chinese characters; it is essentially a phonetic representation of Chinese in the Roman alphabet. The words written in italics in this Introduction—words such as "Pǔtōnghuà", "Guóyǔ" and "Huáyǔ"—are written in pinyin with tone marks, rather than Chinese characters. Since Chinese has not had an alphabet for most of its history, the way to mark pronunciation used to be very complicated. It was only in 1918 that a set of symbols called "Zhùyīn Fúhào" was created to mark the pronunciation. The use of Zhùyīn Fúhào helped Chinese people learn their own language, although it did not make it much easier for people without a Chinese background. Efforts have been made by people inside and outside China to resolve this problem, and they have achieved some degree of success. The Wade-Giles System was created with Herbert Giles's Chinese-English dictionary in 1912. It was the main system of transliteration in the English-speaking world for most of the twentieth century. In 1928, another set of symbols based on the letters of the Roman alphabet and referred to as Chinese Romanization was adapted and used mainly for teaching Chinese overseas. Thirty years later in 1958, a new set of romanized symbols called "Hànyǔ Pīnyīn" was implemented nationwide in China and has been used ever since. Hànyǔ Pīnyīn has become the international standard of Chinese pronunciation and has served as a bridge for connecting China with the outside world. The letters of the Roman alphabet have been adopted as pinyin symbols. Twenty-five out of the 26 letters are used as phonemes in Chinese pinyin with the exception of the letter "v," which is only used in imported words and expressions. A new letter "ü" is added to the alphabet as a major vowel in the pronunciation of Chinese.

C. **Tones:** Chinese is a tonal language, and the pitch of one's voice while speaking Chinese is referred to as "tone." In Mandarin Chinese, there are four tones (first, second, third and fourth) plus a fifth one called "neutral tone" with no stress. Syllables with neutral tone are pronounced more lightly, and their pitch depends on the preceding syllable.

D. **Phoneme:** A phoneme is the smallest recognizable speech sound. Each pinyin letter is the equivalent of one phoneme, such as [b], [p], [m], [f] and [a], [o], [e]. Just as a word in English is made up of letters, a pinyin word is made up of phonemes.

E. Syllable: A Chinese syllable is a speech sound that may or may not have a concrete meaning. It is the most natural speech unit and is usually composed of what are called "initials" and "finals," plus a tone mark. Generally, all Chinese characters are one-syllable units. There are about 400 syllables in Mandarin Chinese.

F. Initials: Similar to consonants in English, initials are phonemes such as [b], [p], [m] and [f] that always appear at the beginning of a syllable. For example, the sound [bi] contains the initial [b] and the final [i]; the sound [ma] contains the initial [m] and the final [a]. Some initials, such as [zh], [ch] and sh] consist of two consonants. There are 21 initials in the Chinese language.

G. Finals: Finals are speech sounds that consist of vowels such as [a], [o], [e], [i], [u] and [ü], or vowels combined with one of the two nasal sounds [n] or [ng], such as [an] and [ang]. There are 37 finals in modern Mandarin Chinese.

H. Zero Initials: Zero initials are syllables that do not contain an initial. There are two types of zero initials in Mandarin Chinese. The first type, referenced above, consists of simple finals or combinations of two or more vowels and nasal sounds that can stand alone to form a syllable, e.g., [a], [o], [e], [ai], [an], [ou], [en], [ang], etc. The second type consists of the semi-vowels [w] and [y] that are used to form syllables when vowels such as [i], [u], [ü] and their combinations stand alone. They are called zero initials because, technically speaking, they are part of the finals. For example: [yi], [wu], [yan], [yong], etc.

qiān	lǐ	zhī	xíng	shǐ	yú	zú	xià
千	里	之	行，	始	于	足	下

In the passage quoted at the beginning of this Introduction, you saw eight Chinese characters. The pronunciation of each character is indicated by a pinyin syllable directly above each character. Here, the syllables contain an initial plus a final, as in lǐ, where [l] is the initial and [i] is the final, or in xíng, where [x] is the initial and [ing] is the final. In the syllable shǐ, the initial is [sh] and the final is [i].

liàn xí
练   习

▶ Exercises

....

I. Study the following pinyin words and separate initials from finals.

	Pinyin	Chinese	English	Initial	Final
1.	mā	妈	mother	_____	_____
2.	zì	字	word, character	_____	_____
3.	nǐ	你	you	_____	_____

4. chī   吃   eat   _____   _____

5. chū   出   go out, come out   _____   _____

II. Study Questions for Section 1

1. What are Mandarin Chinese and Cantonese? Where are they spoken?

2. What is pinyin? What do pinyin words look like?

3. What is a syllable? What are the components of a syllable?

4. How many tones are there in Mandarin? What are they?

5. What are initials and finals? How do they differ?

Useful Expressions

Characters	Pinyin	English
1. 你好！	Nǐ hǎo!	Hi! Hello!
2. 早上好！	Zǎoshang hǎo!	Good morning!
3. 再见！	Zài jiàn!	Goodbye!

Classroom Expressions

Characters	Pinyin	English
1. 老师好！	Lǎoshī hǎo!	Hello, teacher!
2. 同学们好！	Tóngxué hǎo!	Hello, students!
3. 上课！	Shàng kè!	Class begins!
4. 下课！	Xià kè!	Class is over!

▶ SECTION 2:
Finals, Initials and Tones

A. Finals

In modern Mandarin Chinese pronunciation, there are 37 finals grouped into categories according to the way they are pronounced and their phonetic properties. These categories are simple finals, compound finals, and special finals. A simple final is a single vowel. Let's first have a look at the six simple finals listed below.

Simple Finals					
a	o	e	i	u	ü

There are three factors that help distinguish the different ways to pronounce the finals.

1. the position of the tongue in the mouth (front or back)
2. the height of the tongue in the mouth (high or low)
3. the shape of the lips (round or straight)

Below is a short explanation of how each simple final is pronounced. For your convenience, we include some examples of similar English sounds. Please keep in mind that the English sound is not always an accurate pronunciation of the Chinese sound. Please be sure to listen to the sound files and watch your teacher pronounce each sound as you practice.

a: a central vowel. The tongue remains low, mouth wide open. This sound is similar to the "a" in the American English word "father."

o: a semi-high back vowel. The back of the tongue is raised slightly towards the soft palate of the mouth. This sound is similar to the "o" in the American English word "for."

e: an un-rounded, semi-high vowel. This means that the lips are not rounded, and the tongue is raised slightly. The position of the tongue is similar to the position when the English sound "uh" is pronounced, but the lips are spread as if you were smiling slightly. This sound is similar to the American English "e" in "her."

i: an un-rounded front vowel. The position of the tongue is high and towards the front of the mouth, and the lips form a straight line. This sound is similar to the "ee" in the English "fee." (But when [i] occurs after [z], [c], [s], or [zh], [ch], [sh], [r], it is written as [-i] and pronounced quite differently.)

u: a rounded high back vowel. The tongue is raised high at the back of the mouth, and the mouth protrudes into a small round shape. This sound is similar to the "u" in the American English "flu."

ü: a rounded high front vowel. The position of the tongue is similar to that of [i], but with a round mouth. There is no equivalent sound in American English, so you should listen to this sound carefully on the audio recording.

B. Initials

There are 23 initials in Mandarin Chinese. Two of them, [w] and [y], are special initials usually categorized as "semi-vowels." Most textbooks currently used outside China introduce 21 initials, but we include [w] and [y] here. The initials are listed in the following chart.

▶ Table 1. Initials

Group #	Initials			
1	b	p	m	f
2	d	t	n	l
3	g	k	h	
4	j	q	x	
5	zh	ch	sh	r
6	z	c	s	
7	y	w		

Please note, the initials are arranged according to their phonetic properties and should be memorized exactly in the order given.

Since most of the initials are not resonant enough to be heard by themselves, for the purpose of pronouncing the initials in Table 1, vowels such as [o], [e], [i] and [-i] are added in Table 2 to help produce the sounds.

▶ Table 2. Initials combined with vowels

🔊 *Listen to the sound files and watch your teacher pronounce each sound as you practice.*

Group #	Initials				Added Vowels
1	bo	po	mo	fo	o
2	de	te	ne	l	e
3	ge	ke	he		e
4	ji	qi	xi		i
5	zhi	chi	shi	ri	(-i)
6	zi	ci	si		(-i)
7	ya	wa			a

Beginning learners may have trouble producing the sounds in Groups 5 and 6. A tip for practicing the sounds in Group 5 is to try to add the [r] sound after each initial. In other words, instead of [zhi], [chi], [shi], treat them like [zhr], [chr], [shr]. In pronouncing the Group 6 [zi], [ci] and [si] sounds, try your best to withhold the [-i] sound. Otherwise they will sound like Group 4: [ji], [qi], [xi].

C. Tones

Every learner of Chinese is struck early on by how important tones are in pronouncing the language accurately. Each and every Chinese syllable has a tone, whether it is first, second, third, fourth, or neutral. The same syllable with a different tone usually indicates a distinct word with a distinct meaning. The most frequently quoted example is the syllable "ma" with three different tones, as seen in the tongue twister "māma qí mǎ, mǎ màn, māma mà mǎ." (Mother is riding a horse. The horse is slow. Mother is scolding the horse). While [mā] with a first tone is "mother," [mǎ] with a third tone is "horse" and [mà] with a fourth tone is "to scold." The same syllable with a second tone [má] means "hemp" and with a neutral tone [ma] is a question particle. Such examples of words that are the same syllable with different tones are many.

While every Chinese syllable has a tone, not every tone-syllable combination is used in the language. For example, the sound [an] has particular meanings when pronounced in first, third or fourth tones. The sound [an] pronounced with second tone, however, does not form a meaningful word in Chinese. So you can see that tones are essential to a word's meaning; if you don't know a word's tone, you won't know its meaning.

The four tones are indicated by the diacritical marks that appear over the main vowel of a spelled syllable (see the table below). Tone marks are placed directly above the main vowel in each syllable. You'll see that all syllables contain at least one vowel, but many syllables contain more than one vowel. Where there is more than one vowel, the tone mark is placed over the main vowel. The main vowels are identified according to the order of the simple finals, ranked in the following manner: [a] [o] [e] [i] [u] [ü], with [a] being the most resonant and [ü] the least. For example, in the syllable "xia," the tone mark is placed over [a], not [i].

▶ Table 3. Tones and tone marks

Tone	Tone Mark	Example Using Tone Mark
First	‒	mā
Second	´	má
Third	ˇ	mǎ
Fourth	`	mà

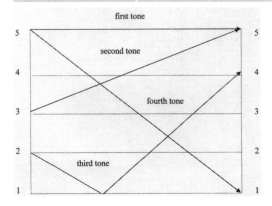

Four tones

The diagram to the left shows graphically the five levels of voice range.

As you can see above, the range of a person's voice is divided into levels one to five, with five representing the highest pitch. There are high, upper middle, middle, lower middle and low levels. The lines in the diagram indicate the levels of pitch.

The importance of getting the tones right simply cannot be overemphasized at the beginning stages of learning Chinese, since they form the basis for so much of Chinese pronunciation and the production of meaningful speech. At the same time, learners should not be frustrated by the difficulty of getting the tones exactly correct, as many foreign speakers of Chinese with less than perfect tones function beautifully in the language. Of course, the closer attention to tones, the easier it will be for others to listen to and understand you. Always keep this in mind: 熟能生巧 Shú néng shēng qiǎo (Practice makes perfect).

liàn xí

练 习

▶ Exercises

....

I. Listen to the sound files and practice saying the pinyin syllables, which are initials combined with simple finals.

Group 1: b, p, m, f (In this group, the initials [b], [p], [m], and [f] cannot combine with [e]).

bā	bá	bǎ	bà		pā	pá	pǎ	pà
mā	má	mǎ	mà		fā	fá	fǎ	fà
bō	bó	bǒ	bò		pō	pó	pǒ	pò
mō	mó	mǒ	mò		fō	fó	fǒ	fò
mē	mé	mě	mè		bī	bí	bǐ	bì
pī	pí	pǐ	pì		mī	mí	mǐ	mì
bū	bú	bǔ	bù		pū	pú	pǔ	pù
mū	mú	mǔ	mù		fū	fú	fǔ	fù

Group 2: d, t, n, l

dā	dá	dǎ	dà		tā	tá	tǎ	tà
nā	ná	nǎ	nà		lā	lá	lǎ	là
dē	dé	dě	dè		tē	té	tě	tè
nē	né	ně	nè		lē	lé	lě	lè
dī	dí	dǐ	dì		tī	tí	tǐ	tì
nī	ní	nǐ	nì		lī	lí	lǐ	lì
dū	dú	dǔ	dù		tū	tú	tǔ	tù

nū	nú	nǔ	nù		lū	lú	lǔ	lù
nǘ	nǘ	nǚ	nǜ		lǖ	lǘ	lǚ	lǜ

Group 3:   g, k, h (In this group, the initials [g], [k] and [h] can only combine with [a], [e] and [u].)

gā	gá	gǎ	gà		kā	ká	kǎ	kà
hā	há	hǎ	hà		gē	gé	gě	gè
kē	ké	kě	kè		hē	hé	hě	hè
gū	gú	gǔ	gù		kū	kú	kǔ	kù
hū	hú	hǔ	hù					

Group 4:   j, q, x (In this group, [j], [q] and [x] can only combine with [i] and [ü].)

jī	jí	jǐ	jì		qī	qí	qǐ	qì
xī	xí	xǐ	xì		jū	jú	jǔ	jù
qū	qú	qǔ	qù		xū	xú	xǔ	xù

Group 5:   zh, ch, sh, r (The special final [-i] after [zh], [ch], [sh] and [r] is silent.)

zhā	zhá	zhǎ	zhà		chā	chá	chǎ	chà
shā	shá	shǎ	shà		zhē	zhé	zhě	zhè
chē	ché	chě	chè		shē	shé	shě	shè
rē	ré	rě	rè		zhī	zhí	zhǐ	zhì
chī	chí	chǐ	chì		shī	shí	shǐ	shì
rī	rí	rǐ	rì		zhū	zhú	zhǔ	zhù
chū	chú	chǔ	chù		shū	shú	shǔ	shù
rū	rú	rǔ	rù					

Group 6:   z, c, s (The special final [-i] after [z], [c] and [s] is silent.)

zā	zá	zǎ	zà		cā	cá	cǎ	cà
sā	sá	sǎ	sà		zē	zé	zě	zè
cē	cé	cě	cè		sē	sé	sě	sè
zī	zí	zǐ	zì		cī	cí	cǐ	cì
sī	sí	sǐ	sì		zū	zú	zǔ	zù
cū	cú	cǔ	cù		sū	sú	sǔ	sù

Note: The final [o] can only appear after [b], [p], [m] and [f], and [ü] can be only used after [n], [l], [j], [q] and [x].

II. Listen to the sound files and try to distinguish the tone differences. Then practice saying the syllables out loud.

Group 1: first vs. second

bā—bá	gā—gá	shā—shá	bō—bó	pō—pó	fō—fó
mē—mé	nē—né	lē—lé	pī—pí	mī—mí	tī—tí
bū—bú	fū—fú	lū—lú	nǖ —nǘ	qū—qú	xū—xú

Group 2: first vs. third

dā—dǎ	fā—fǎ	chā—chǎ	bō—bǒ	pō—pǒ	mō—mǒ
dē—dě	tē—tě	kē—kě	dī—dǐ	mī—mǐ	nī—nǐ
pū—pǔ	shū—shǔ	tū—tǔ	nǖ —nǚ	lǖ —lǚ	jū—jǔ

Group 3: first vs. fourth

mā—mà	hā—hà	zhā—zhà	bō—bò	pō—pò	mō—mò
hē—hè	lē—lè	rē—rè	bī—bì	dī—dì	lī—lì
kū—kù	zhū—zhù	chū—chù	lǖ —lǜ	jū—jù	xū—xù

Group 4: second vs. third

má—mǎ	ná—nǎ	shá—shǎ	dé—dě	shé—shě	cé—cě
pí—pǐ	lí—lǐ	jí—jǐ	qí—qǐ	xí—xǐ	nú—nǔ
shú—shǔ	zú—zǔ	cú—cǔ	lǘ —lǚ	jú—jǔ	xú—xǔ

Group 5: second vs. fourth

zá—zà	shá—shà	lá—là	dé—dè	gé—gè	ké—kè
bǐ—bì	dí—dì	lí—lì	qí—qì	xí—xì	hú—hù
chú—chù	tú—tù	lú—lù	lǘ —lǜ	jú—jù	xú—xù

Group 6: third vs. fourth

bǎ—bà	lǎ—là	gǎ—gà	pǒ—pò	mǒ—mò	fǒ—fò
mě—mè	gě—gè	kě—kè	pǐ—pì	bǐ—bì	qǐ—qì
bǔ—bù	fǔ—fù	lǔ—lù	nǚ—nǜ	lǚ—lǜ	qǔ—qù

 III. Listen to the sound files as the speaker reads the following pairs of syllables made of initials and single finals. Try to distinguish the difference between initial sounds, and then practice saying the sounds.

Group 1: b vs. p

| bā—pā | bō—pō | bī—pī | bū—pū |
| bá—pá | bó—pó | bí—pí | bǔ—pǔ |

Group 2: d vs. t

| dà—tà | dè—tè | dì—tì | dù—tù |
| dǎ—tǎ | dé—té | dǐ—tǐ | dū—tū |

Group 3: g vs. k

gā—kā	gē—kē	gū—kū	gé—ké
gǎ—kǎ	gě—kě	gǔ—kǔ	gù—kù

Group 4: n vs. l

nā—lā	nē—lē	nī—lī	ná—lá
nǐ—lǐ	nà—là	nè—lè	nì-lì
nǔ—lǔ	nǎ—lǎ	ní—lí	nú—lú
nǎo—lǎo	niè—liè	nèi—lèi	nuò—luò

Group 5: l vs. r

lē—rē	lú—rú	lě—rě	lǔ—rǔ
lè—rè	lù—rù	lì—rì	lǚ—lǚ
luò—ruò	lóu—róu	lèi—rùi	lěi—ruǐ

Group 6: z, c and s

zā—cā	cā—sā	zá—cá	zà—sà
zé—cè	zū—cū	sù—cù	zi—ci

Group 7: zh, ch and sh

zhí—chí	chì—shì	zhā—shā	chá—zhá
shé—zhé	chè—zhè	chú—shú	zhǔ—chǔ

Group 8: z vs. zh

zá—zhá	zé—zhé	zǔ—zhǔ	zì—zhì
zǎ—zhǎ	zè—zhè	zú—zhú	zù—zhù

Group 9: c vs. ch

cā—chā	cè—chè	cū—chū	cī—chī
cǎ—chǎ	cù—chù	cǐ—chǐ	cǎo—chǎo

Group 10: s vs. sh

sā—shā	sè—shè	sù—shù	sì—shì
sǎ—shǎ	sū—shū	sě—shě	sī—shī

Group 11: w vs. h

wā—hā	wú—hú	wǔ—hǔ	wà—hà
wǒ—huǒ	wò—huò	wá—huá	wèi—huì

IV. Listen to the sound recording. Practice saying the following tongue twisters with correct tones.

1. Māma qí mǎ, mǎ màn, māma mà mǎ. （妈妈骑马，马慢，妈妈骂马。）Mother rides a horse. The horse is slow. Mother scolds the horse.

2. Sì shì sì, shí shì shí, shísì shì shísì, sìshí shì sìshí. （四是四，十是十，十四是十四，四十是四十。）Four is four. Ten is ten. Fourteen is fourteen. Forty is forty.）

V. Read the following pinyin syllables and separate initials from finals.

Pinyin	Character	English	Initial	Final
1. mā	妈	mother	_____	_____
2. zǐ	子	child	_____	_____
3. nǐ	你	you	_____	_____
4. shī	师	teacher	_____	_____
5. bù	不	no	_____	_____
6. zhè	这	this	_____	_____
7. kè	课	class	_____	_____
8. yī	一	one	_____	_____
9. chī	吃	eat	_____	_____
10. gè	个	[a measure word]	_____	_____
11. bà	爸	father	_____	_____
12. qù	去	go	_____	_____

VI. The following words are selected from the first few lessons in this book. Listen the sound recording and practice saying the words out loud. Pay attention to the initials and finals they contain.

Group 1: Initials b, p, m, f

bà (爸, father)　　bàng (棒, good)　　běi (北, north)　　péng (朋 friend)
piàn (片, slice)　　pīn (拼, spell)　　méi (没, not)　　mèi (妹, younger sister)
míng (名, name)　　fāng (方, square)　　fǎ (法, law)　　fù (付, pay)

Group 2: Intitials d, t, n, l

dà (大, big)　　diàn (电, electricity)　　dōu (都, all)　　dēng (灯, light)
tài (太, too)　　tiào (跳, jump)　　nǎ (哪, which)　　nán (男, male)
nín (您, you)　　lǎo (老, old)　　lèi (累, tire)　　liú (流, flow)

Group 3: Initials g, k, h

guì (贵, expensive)	guǎn (馆, shop)	guǎi (拐, turn)	gēn (跟, and)
kāi (开, open)	kàn (看, look)	kě (可, but)	kuài (快, fast)
hǎo (好, good)	hěn (很, very)	hóng (红, red)	huā (花, spend)

Group 4: Initials j, q, x

jiā (家, home)	jiàn (见, see)	jiào (叫, call)	jiù (就, then)
qǐ (起, up)	qǐng (请, please)	qiú (球, ball)	qù (去, go)
xiǎng (想, think)	xiǎo (小, small)	xīn (新, new)	xué (学, study)

Group 5: Initials zh, ch, sh, r

zhè (这, this)	zhēn (真, real)	zhōng (中, middle)	cháng (常, often)
chū (出, out)	chī (吃, eat)	shàng (上, up)	shí (十, ten)
shēng (生, born)	ràng (让, let)	rén (人, people)	róng (容, contain)

Group 6: Initials z, c, s

zài (在, at)	zěn (怎, how)	zuì (最, best)	zuò (坐, sit)
cái (才, just)	cān (餐, food)	cóng (从, from)	cì (次, times)
sàn (散, spread)	sān (三, three)	suǒ (所, place)	suàn (算, count)

Group 7: Final a

bà (爸, father)	dà (大, big)	wā (挖, dig)	fā (发, distribute)
kǎ (卡, card)	lā (拉, pull)		

Group 8: Final o

mō (摸, touch)	bō (播, broadcast)	wǒ (我, I)	fó (佛, buddha)
pò (破, broken)	pó (婆, grandma)		

Group 9: Final e

è (饿, hungry)	gē (哥, elder brother)	hē (喝, drink)	kè (课, class)
rè (热, hot)	zhè (这, this)		

Group 10: Final i

shí (时, time)	xí (习, study)	yī (衣, clothes)	zhǐ (只, only)
zì (字, character)	cì (次, times)		

Group 11: Final u

fù (付, pay)	dù (肚, belly)	chū (出, out)	bǔ (补, make up)
zú (足, feet)	shū (书, book)		

lǜ (绿, green)   nǚ (女, female)   jù (句, sentence)   yú (鱼, fish)

xū (需, need)   qǔ (取, get)

VII. Study Questions

1. What are the six simple finals in Mandarin Chinese? Practice reading them aloud and writing them in correct order.

2. What are the 23 initials? Practice reading them aloud and writing them in correct order.

3. How many tones are there in Mandarin Chinese? How do we mark them?

4. What are the differences in pronunciation between the four tones?

Useful Expressions

Characters	Pinyin	English
1. 好久不见，你好吗？	Hǎojiǔ bújiàn. Nǐ hǎo ma?	Long time no see. How are you?
2. 我很好，你呢？	Wǒ hěn hǎo, nǐ ne?	I'm fine, what about you?
3. 不错，谢谢。	Bú cuò, xièxie!	Not bad, thanks!
4. 请问您贵姓？	Qǐng wèn nín guìxìng?	What is your name? (polite)
5. 你叫什么名字？	Nǐ jiào shénme míngzi?	What is your name? (informal)

Classroom Expressions

Characters	Pinyin	English
1. 请听我说。	Qǐng tīng wǒ shuō.	Listen to me, please.
2. 跟我说。	Gēn wǒ shuō.	Repeat after me.

▶ **SECTION 3:**
Compound Finals and Special Finals

Generally speaking, the combinations of two or more vowels, or one or two vowels with a nasal sound such as [n] or [ng], are called "compound finals."

🔊 *Listen to the sound files and watch your teacher pronounce each sound as you practice.*

Group#	Combination of Two or More Vowels			
1	ai	ei	ao	ou
2	ia	ie	iao	iou
3	ua	uo	uai	uei
4	üe			

🔊 *Listen to the sound files and watch your teacher pronounce each sound as you practice.*

Group #	Combination of One or More Vowels with Nasal Sounds				
1	an	en	ang	eng	ong
2	ian	in	iang	ing	iong
3	uan	uen	uang	ueng	
4	üan	ün			

In addition to the above compounds, there are two "special finals": the first is the tongue tip final [-i], which appears after a limited number of initials, namely: [zh], [ch], [sh], [ri] and [z], [c], [s]. In this book, we write the special vowel as [-i] to distinguish it from [i]. The second special final is the retroflexed final [er], which always stands alone as a syllable and never combines with any initials to form syllables.

When you pronounce the compound finals, try to achieve a "glide" of sounds as you move from one vowel to the next. There is always one final (the main final) that is pronounced more resonantly than the other vowel or vowels.

liàn xí

练 习

▶ Exercises

· ·

I. Listen to the sound recording and practice saying the pinyin words out loud. The words in this group are monosyllabic words with compound finals made of two or more vowels.

Group 1: ai, ei, ao, ou
_____

bái (白, white)	cài (菜, vegetable dish)
zài (再, again)	chāi (拆, tear open)
bēi (杯, cup)	péi (陪, accompany)
měi (美, pretty)	lèi (泪, tear; teardrop)
dào (到, arrive)	nǎo (脑, brain)
lǎo (老, old)	hǎo (好, good)
dōu (都, all)	tóu (头, head)
hòu (后, back)	yǒu (有, have; there is)

Group 2: ia, ie, iao, iou*
_____

jiā (家, family; home)	jiǎ (甲, first)
jià (价, price)	xià (下, below; down)
yá (牙, tooth)	yě (也, also; too)
biǎo (表, surface; outside)	piào (票, ticket)
xiào (校, school)	jiāo (教, teach)
liù (六, six)	jiǔ (九, nine)
niú (牛, ox; cow)	qiū (秋, autumn)

*Note that the sound "iou" is actually spelled as "iu."

Group 3: ua, uo, uai, uei*
_____

guā (瓜, melon)	huā (花, flower; blossom)
huà (话, word; talk)	wā (蛙, frog)
duō (多, many; much)	guó (国, country; state)
zuò (做, make; produce)	shuō (说, speak; talk)
guài (怪, strange; odd)	kuài (块, piece; lump)
kuài (筷, chopsticks)	huài (坏, bad; ruin)
duì (对, answer; reply)	tuì (退, move back)
guì (贵, expensive; costly)	huì (会, meeting; gathering)

*Note that the sound "uei" is actually spelled as "ui."

Group 4: üe*

yuè (月, the moon; month)   yuē (约, make an appointment)

yuè (乐, music)   xué (学, study)

*Note that except when combined with l or n, the "ue" sound is written without an umlaut.

II. Listen to the sound recording and practice saying the pinyin words out loud. The words in this group are monosyllabic words with compound finals made of vowels and nasal sounds.

Group 1: an, en, ang, eng, ong

bān (班, class)   màn (慢, slow; postpone)

fàn (饭, meal)   nán (难, difficult; hard)

běn (本, book)   mén (门, door)

gēn (跟, follow; and)   hěn (很, very)

máng (忙, busy)   shàng (上, upper; up)

zhāng (张, a surname)   táng (糖, sugar)

téng (疼, ache; pain)   lěng (冷, cold; cold in manner)

zhèng (正, straight; upright)   chéng (城, city wall; city; town)

dōng (冬, winter)   dǒng 懂, understand; know)

tóng (同, same; alike)   lóng (龙, dragon)

Group 2: ian, in, iang, ing, iong

biān (边, side; margin)   miàn (面, face)

tiān (天, sky; heaven)   nián (年, year)

lín (林, forest; woods)   xìn (信, letter; mail)

nín (您, you)   xīn (心, heart)

yáng (阳, the sun)   yàng (样, kind; type)

xiǎng (想, think; miss)   xiàng (象, appearance; look as if)

bìng (病, ill; sick)   míng (明, bright; light)

qǐng (请, ask; invite)   xìng (姓, surname; family name)

xiōng (兄, elder brother)   duǎn (短, short; lack)

Group 3: uan, uen*, uang, ueng*

guǎn (馆, of service trades; shop)   huàn (换, exchange)

wán (玩, play; have fun)   wǎn (晚, evening; late)

wén (文, writing; language)   wèn (问, ask; inquire)

dùn (顿, a measure word for a meal)   lùn (论, discuss; talk about)

wáng (王, king; a surname)   wàng (忘, forget; neglect)

guāng (光, light; ray)   huáng (黄, yellow)

yuán (原, primary; original) yuàn (院, courtyard)

yùn (运, motion; movement) jūn (军, armed forces)

*Note that the sound "uen" is actually written as "un" or "en," and the sound "ueng" is actually written as "eng."

III. Listen to the sound recording, then practice saying the pinyin words out loud. The words in this group are initials combined with compound finals.

kāimén (开门, open the door) hǎojiǔ (好久, long time)

Měiguó (美国, America) guìxìng (贵姓, what's your name? [formal])

chīfàn (吃饭, eat a meal) Zhōngguó (中国, China)

xiàkè (下课, class is over) huānyíng (欢迎, welcome)

cāntīng (餐厅, cafeteria) xīnshēng (新生, new student)

huílai (回来, come back) cānjiā (参加, join, attend)

chūchāi (出差, on a business trip) gàosu (告诉, to tell)

Zhōngwén (中文, Chinese language) liúlì (流利, fluently)

lǎojiā (老家, hometown) xiànzài (现在, now)

yímín (移民, immigrant, emigrant) xuéxí (学习, study, learn)

yīsheng (医生, doctor) xiǎngjiā (想家, homesick)

jiàoshòu (教授, professor) Yīngwén (英文, English)

qǐngjiào (请教, ask for advice) hùxiāng (互相, each other)

bāngzhù (帮助, help) guǎngchǎng (广场, public square)

diànnǎo (电脑, computer) xiàtiān (夏天, summer)

yǒumíng (有名, well known) dǎsuàn (打算, plan, intend)

jìhuà (计划, plan) xuéxiào (学校, school)

dìfāng (地方, place) zhīdào (知道, know)

shāngxuéyuàn (商学院, business school) Huáyì (华裔, foreign citizen of Chinese origin)

IV. Listen to the sound recording, then practice saying the pinyin words out loud. The words in this group are zero initials and semi-vowels.

Group A: Zero Initials. The finals [a, o, e] and their combinations stand alone as syllables.

àiguó (爱国, patriotic)	ānquán (安全, safe, secure)	ángguì (昂贵, very expensive)
àoqì (傲气, arrogance)	ōuzhōu (欧洲, Europe)	èsǐ (饿死, starve to death)
ēnrén (恩人, benefactor)	érzi (儿子, son)	ǒurán (偶然, accidental)

Group B: The semi-vowels [y] and [w] are used to help finals [i, u, ü] and their combinations form syllables.

yīnwèi (因为, because)	yīngxíong (英雄, hero)	wūzi (屋子, room)
yánsè (颜色, color)	yángguāng (阳光, sunlight)	wèishénme (为什么, why)

V. Listen to the sound recording and try to say the tongue twisters out loud. Pay attention to correct tones.

1. Chī pútao bù tǔ pútao pí, bù chī pútao dào tǔ pútao pí.

   吃葡萄不吐葡萄皮，不吃葡萄倒吐葡萄皮。

   Eat grapes without spitting out the skin. Stop eating grapes to spit out the skin.

2. Rìtou rè, shài rénròu, shài de rénròu hǎo nánshòu.

   日头热，晒人肉，晒得人肉好难受。

   The sun is hot, shining upon human bodies, making people suffer.

 VI. Listen to the sound recording and read the poems out loud.

1. The Geese, by Luo Bin-Wang 骆宾王 (Tang dynasty)

Yǒng É
咏鹅
The Geese

É, é, é,
鹅，鹅，鹅，
The geese! The geese! The geese!

qū xiàng xiàng tiān gē,
曲项向天歌。
Sing towards the sky with curved necks.

bái máo fú lü shuǐ,
白毛浮绿水，
White plumage floating in green waters,

hóng zhǎng bō qīng bō.
红掌拨清波。
Red paddles stirring up clear ripples.

2. A Counting Song (A Children's Nursery Rhyme)

Shùzì Gē
数字歌
A Counting Song

Yī qù èr sān lǐ,
一去二三里，
I went two or three *li*,

shān cūn sì wǔ jiā,

山村四五家，

saw four or five households in a mountain village,

értóng liù qī gè,

儿童六七个，

with six or seven children,

bā jiǔ shí zhī huā.

八九十枝花。

and eight, nine, ten flowers.

VI. The following words are simple and compound finals selected from the first few lessons in this book. Listen to the sound files and practice saying the words out loud. Pay attention to the initials and finals listed in each group.

Group 1: Finals ai, ei, ao

āi (哎, hey)	chāi (差, business)	dài (代, generation)	hái (还, still)
hēi (黑, black)	lèi (累, tired)	měi (美, pretty)	wèi (位, place)
bāo (包, bag)	dāo (刀, knife)	gào (告, tell)	hǎo (好, good)

Group 2: Finals ia, ie, iao, iou*

xià (下, down)	jiā (家, home)	jià (价, price)	bié (别, other)
jié (节, festival)	jiè (介, introduce)	xiǎo (小, small)	diào (掉, drop)
biǎo (表, form)	qiú (球, ball)	liú (流, flow)	jiù (就, then)

*Note that the sound "iou" is actually spelled as "iu."

Group 3: Finals ua, uo, uai, uei*

huà (化, change)	guà (挂, hang)	huá (华, China)	duō (多, many)
guó (国, country)	huǒ (火, fire)	huài (坏, bad)	shuài (帅, handsome)
kuài (快, fast)	huí (回, return)	duì (对, toward)	shuì (睡, sleep)

*Note that the sound "uei" is actually spelled as "ui."

Group 4: Final üe*

yuè (月, month)	xué (学, study)	quē (缺, lack)	nüè (虐, cruel)
lüè (略, brief)			

*Note that except when combined with l or n, the "ue" sound is written without an umlaut.

Group 5: Finals an, en, ang, eng, ong

bàn (半, half)	gǎn (感, feel)	fǎn (反, in reverse)	hěn (很, very)
mén (门, door)	rèn (认, recognize)	ràng (让, let)	shàng (上, up)

wǎng (网, net)	zhèng (证, certificate)	péng (朋, friend)	lěng (冷, cold)
hóng (红, red)	gòng (共, total)	kōng (空, empty)	

Group 6: Finals ian, in, iang, ing, iong

miàn (面, face)	pián (便, cheap)	qián (钱, money)	yīn (音, sound)
xìn (信, letter)	jìn (近, enter)	liáng (凉, cool)	xiǎng (想, think)
qiáng (墙, wall)	yīng (英, hero)	xìng (姓, surname)	míng (名, name)
xiōng (兄, elder brother)		qióng (穷, poor)	yòng (用, use)

Group 7: Finals uan, uen, uang, ueng*

zhuǎn (转, turn)	wǎn (晚, late)	guǎn (馆, shop)	zhǔn (准, accurate)
kùn (困, difficult)	xún (寻, seek)	huáng (黄, yellow)	chuáng (床, bed)
guǎng (广, wide)	wēng (翁, old man)		

*Note that the sound "ueng" is actually spelled as "eng."

VII. Study Questions for Section 3

1. How are compound finals formed?

2. Which finals can stand alone as syllables, and which finals cannot?

3. What do we do when finals beginning with [i], [u] and [ü] stand alone as syllables?

Useful Expressions

Characters	Pinyin	English
1. 对不起。	Duì bu qǐ.	Sorry / Excuse me.
2. 沒关系。	Méi guānxi.	It doesn't matter.
3. 别客气。	Bié kèqi.	You are welcome.

Classroom Expressions

Characters	Pinyin	English
1.听懂了吗？	Tīng dǒng le ma?	Do you understand?
2.听懂了。	Tīng dǒng le.	Yes, I understand.
3.沒懂。（不懂）	Méi dǒng. (Bù dǒng.)	No, I don't understand.
4.老师，请您再说一次，好吗？	Lǎoshi, qǐng nín zài shuō yícì, hǎo ma?	Teacher, could you say it again, please?

Pinyin Review Exercises

 I. Reading Practice

Group A: Most Chinese words are composed of two characters. Read aloud the following two-character words selected from this book. Listen to the sound recording to check your pronunciation.

xīngqī (星期, week)	Zhōngguó (中国, China)	cāntīng (餐厅, cafeteria)	yīshēng (医生, doctor)
Yīngwén (英文, English)	pīnyīn (拼音, pinyin)	chāoxiě (抄写, copy)	fāngfǎ (方法, method)
bāngzhù (帮助, help)	shēngrì (生日, birthday)	zhīdào (知道, know)	chīfàn (吃饭, eat)
shíjiān (时间, time)	fájīn (罚金, fine)	yímín (移民, immigrant)	niánlíng (年龄, age)
huílái (回来, return)	xuéxí (学习, study)	méiyǒu (没有, not have)	péngyou (朋友, friend)
niúnǎi (牛奶, milk)	liúlì (流利, fluent)	Měiguó (美国, America)	míngzi (名字, name)
xǐhuān (喜欢, to like)	xiǎngjiā (想家, miss home)	lǎoshī (老师, teacher)	jiǔbā (酒吧, bar)
lǎoxiāng (老乡, person from the same hometown)		huáyì (华裔, foreign citizen of Chinese origin)	

Group B: Some Chinese words and phrases are composed of three characters. Read aloud the following three-character words and phrases selected from this book.

diànyǐngyuàn (电影院, movie theater)	duì bu qǐ (对不起, sorry)	hùliánwǎng (互联网, internet)
hòuzhěnqū (候诊区, waiting area)	huìyuánzhèng (会员证, membership ID)	jùlèbù (俱乐部, club)
lādùzi (拉肚子, diarrhea)	lǚxíngshè (旅行社, travel agency)	liúxuéshēng (留学生, foreign student)
luòtāngjī (落汤鸡, soaked)	méiguānxi (没关系, it doesn't matter)	qǐ míngzi (起名字, give a name)
shōujiànrén (收件人, addressee)	tǐyùguǎn (体育馆, gym)	wèishénme (为什么, why)

xǐfàyè

(洗发液, shampoo)

xǐyīfěn

(洗衣粉, detergent)

xiànjīnjī

(现金机, cash machine)

xìnyòngkǎ

(信用卡, credit card)

yǒuyìsi

(有意思, interesting)

Group C: Some Chinese words and phrases are composed of four characters. Read aloud the following four-character words and phrases selected from this book.

xiōngdì jiěmèi

(兄弟姐妹, siblings)

tèkuài zhuāndì

(特快专递, express mail)

shàngtù xiàxiè

(上吐下泻, vomit and diarrhea)

pàomò sùliào

(泡沫塑料, foam plastics)

méiyǒu yìsi

(没有意思, not interesting)

háojiǔ bújiàn

(好久不见, long time no see)

gōnggòng qìchē

(公共汽车, bus)

chūzū qìchē

(出租汽车, taxi)

chāojí shìchǎng

(超级市场, supermarket)

bújiàn búsàn

(不见不散, [If we] do not see [each other], [we] should not leave.)

Group D: Can you read the following short sentences selected from the first three lessons?

1. Nǐ jiào shénme míngzi?

   你叫什么名字？(What is your name?)

2. Qǐng wèn nín guìxìng?

   请问您贵姓？(May I ask your family name?)

3. Kuài qù cāntīng chīfàn ba.

   快去餐厅吃饭吧。(Hurry to the dining hall to eat.)

4. Xiǎo Zhào gěi wǒ qǐ le yī ge Zhōngwén míngzi.

   小赵给我起了一个中文名字。(Xiao Zhao gave me a Chinese name.)

5. Tā yǒu yī ge Zhōngguó péngyǒu.

   他有一个中国朋友。(He has a Chinese friend.)

6. Nǐ shì Zhōngguórén ma?

   你是中国人吗？(Are you Chinese?)

7. Wǒmen míngtiān qù kàn diànyǐng ba.

   我们明天去看电影吧。(Let's go to a movie tomorrow.)

8. Wǒ shì zài Měiguó zhǎngdà de.

   我是在美国长大的。(I grew up in America.)

9. Gēge shì zhōngxué lǎoshī.

哥哥是中学老师。(My brother is a middle school teacher.)

II. Foreign Words and Brand Names in Chinese

Since the 1980s, many foreign commodities and businesses have entered Chinese people's lives. In this part, we will practice pinyin with these foreign names. Answer keys for this part can be found in Appendix 1.

Group A: Listen carefully to these names of fast food chains. Put tone marks over the correct syllables and write their English meanings.

Characters	Pinyin	English
1. 麦当劳	Maidanglao	_____
2. 汉堡王	Hanbao Wang	_____
3. 肯德基	Kendeji	_____
4. 比萨屋	Bisawu	_____
5. 塔可钟	Takezhong	_____
6. 赛百味	Saibaiwei	_____
7. 星巴克	Xingbake	_____
8. 扒房	Pa Fang	_____
9. 温蒂	Wendi	_____
10. 星期五	Xingqiwu	_____

Group B: Listen carefully to these food names and try to write down what you hear in pinyin. (Don't forget the tone marks!)

Pinyin	English	Characters
1. _____	sandwich	三明治
2. _____	hamburger	汉堡包
3. _____	pizza	比萨饼
4. _____	chocolate	巧克力
5. _____	cheese	芝士（乳酪）
6. _____	hot dog	热狗
7. _____	croissant	牛角包

8.	_____	salad	沙拉
9.	_____	sardine	沙丁鱼
10.	_____	fillet	腓力
11.	_____	cookie	曲奇

Group C: Listen carefully to these names of beverages and try to write the names in pinyin based on their English pronunciations.

English	Pinyin	Characters
1. Sprite	_____	雪碧
2. Fanta	_____	芬达
3. 7-Up	_____	七喜
4. coffee	_____	咖啡
5. Coca-Cola	_____	可口可乐
6. Pepsi	_____	百事可乐
7. chocolate milk	_____	巧克力奶
8. yogurt	_____	优格
10. whisky	_____	威士卡
11. brandy	_____	白兰地

Group D: The following are brand names of shoes and clothes. Can you figure out the English based on the pinyin spellings?

English	Pinyin	Characters
1. _____	Nàikè	耐克
2. _____	Ruìbù	锐步
3. _____	Adídásī	阿迪达斯
4. _____	Biāomǎ	彪马
6. _____	Lǐwéi	李维
7. _____	Jìfánxī	纪梵希
8. _____	Lùyìwēidēng	路易威登
9. _____	Wéiduōlìyà Mìmì	维多丽亚秘密

10._____	Tiěfūní	铁芙尼
11. _____	Xiábùshì	暇步士

Group E: Listen carefully to the names of cosmetics and add initials to form complete pinyin words.

English	Pinyin	Characters
1. Avon	_____ǎ_____āng	雅芳
2. Mary Kay	_____éi_____ín_____ǎi	玫琳凯
3. Maybelline	_____ěi_____ǎo_____ián	美宝莲
4. Lancôme	_____án_____òu	兰蔻
5. L'Oreal	Ōu_____ái_____ǎ	欧莱雅
6. Clinique	_____iàn_____ì	倩碧
7. Elizabeth Arden	_____ī_____ì_____ā_____ái _____ǎ_____ùn	伊丽莎白雅顿
8. Chanel	_____iāng_____ài'er	香奈儿
9. Estee Lauder	_____ǎ_____ī_____án_____ài	雅诗兰黛
10. Almay	Ào_____ěi	傲美
11. Christian Dior	_____ē_____ǐ_____ī_____īng _____í'ào	克里斯汀迪奥

Group F: Listen carefully to the skin care and health products, and add finals to form complete pinyin words.

English	Pinyin	Characters
1. Crest	J_____j_____sh_____	佳洁士
2. Colgate	G_____l_____j_____	高露洁
3. Pert	P_____r_____	飘柔
4. Pantene	P_____t_____	潘婷
5. Head & Shoulders	H_____f_____s_____	海飞丝
6. Lux	L_____sh_____	力士
7. Dove	Du_____f_____	多芙
8. Hazeline	X_____sh_____l_____	夏士莲
9. Pond's	P_____sh_____	旁氏
10. Safeguard	Sh_____f_____j_____	舒肤佳

11. Pampers	B_____ b_____ sh_____	帮宝适
12. Kleenex	Sh_____ j_____	舒洁
13. Johnson & Johnson	Q_____ sh_____	强生
14. Victoria's Secret	W_____ d_____ l_____ y_____ m_____ m_____	维多丽亚秘密

Group G: Match English with the correct pinyin words. The Chinese characters are included for your reference.

English	Pinyin	Characters
1. T-shirt	(A) tǎnkè	T 恤衫
2. tank	(B) shāfā	坦克
3. cartoon	(C) Wò'ěrmǎ	卡通
4. email	(D) tīxùshān	伊妹儿
5. sofa	(E) wǎngbā	沙发
6. Internet cafe	(F) Yíjiā	网吧
7. Wal-Mart	(G) Fěnsī	沃尔玛
8. Ikea	(H) yīmèi'er	宜家
9. Tiffany	(I) kǎtōng	铁芙尼
10. Fans	(J) Tiěfūní	粉丝

The Chinese Writing System

A. Hànzì 汉字

A script is a set of symbols used to record spoken language. 汉字 Hànzì (Chinese characters) are the written symbols used to record the Chinese language, originally spoken by the Han people.

There are two major kinds of written languages in the world: alphabetic and non-alphabetic writing. In alphabetic writing, words are written using symbols (or letters) that indicate how a word is pronounced; for example, the word "cat" in English is written with the symbols "c," "a" and "t." Chinese uses a non-alphabetic system in which syllables are represented by characters that give few clues as to how the word should be pronounced. There are many legendary stories about the creation of the original Chinese script. One of the most popular myths is that Chinese writing originated from pictures in the time of Emperor 黄帝 Huángdì. He ordered 仓颉 Cāngjié, a scholar in his administration, to record history in writing. It was said that 仓颉 Cāngjié first drew pictures of objects and then simplified them by reducing the number of lines, making the first pictographs. These scripts derived from pictures were later called 象形字 Xiàngxíngzì (pictographs) by the Han lexicographer 许慎 Xǔ Shēn in the year 100 A.D. when he completed the first comprehensive Chinese dictionary. This dictionary not only defined words but also explained their etymology.

Pictographs were useful in representing objects that are tangible and concrete, such as animals, plants, natural phenomenon, or body parts. But not all the concepts or things can be represented clearly in pictures. As the Chinese language developed, other ways of forming characters were invented. Looking at the history of Chinese writing more broadly, the following six methods, as classified by Xu Shen, were used to create Chinese characters: 象形 Xiàngxíng (Pictographs); 指事 Zhǐshì (Ideographs); 会意 Huìyì (Associative Compounds); 形声 Xíngshēng (Determinative-Phonetic Characters); 假借 Jiǎjiè (Phonetic Loan Characters); 转注 Zhuǎnzhù (Mutually Explanatory Characters). For details about each method, please see below.

B. Types of Character Formation

1. 象形 (Xiàngxíng) Pictographs

Characters in this category are derived from drawings of actual objects or from interpretations of visual images. Examples:

日 rì (the sun): a round circle with a black dot in it is how the people in ancient times thought of the sun.

羊 yáng (sheep): taken from the shape of the head of a sheep with two horns.

2. 指事 (Zhǐshì) Ideographs (also called "Self-Explanatory" or "Indicative" Characters)

Characters in this category represent simple abstract concepts. They are usually formed by combining one pictograph and one abstract symbol to indicate a new meaning. Examples:

一 yī (one)   二 èr (two)   三 sān (three)

上 shàng (above, up)   下 xià (lower, below)

In both 上 and 下, there is a horizontal line indicating a boundary. The vertical line clearly shows the direction represented by the character (up for 上 and down for 下).

3. 会意 (Huìyì) Associative Compounds

Characters in this category are basically formed by combining two pictographic symbols to represent a new meaning. Examples:

从 cóng: follow (two persons, one following the other)

众 zhòng: many, numerous, a crowd

The character 从 cóng is formed by two persons walking one after the other to indicate the concept of "to follow." The simplified character 众 zhòng is made of three persons indicating the idea of "many people."

Another example is the character 明 míng (bright) with a 日 (sun) and a 月 (moon), indicating brightness.

灾 zāi (disaster), with the two elements 水 (water) and 火 (fire) in traditional form, shows people's fears about these natural phenomenon.

These first three kinds of characters represent the features of the earliest and simplest Chinese writing. But such characters make up only a small percentage of the characters used today. As civilization developed, the need arose for conveying more abstract concepts in writing, and a fourth method of creating characters called 形声 "xíngshēng" or "Determinative-Phonetic Characters" appeared. Today, there are approximately 56,000 characters in the Chinese language, and each of them is a one-syllable speech unit that includes the three basic elements of sound, shape and meaning. Almost 90 percent of modern Chinese characters belong to the "Determinative-Phonetic" category of characters.

4. 形声 (Xíngshēng) Determinative-Phonetic Characters

Characters in this category are picto-phonetic characters with one part a determinative, conveying meaning (called 形旁 xíng páng) and a phonetic part (called 声旁 "shēng páng) to show pronunciation. This method essentially combines two pre-existing characters to form a new meaning. Examples:

妈 mā (mother): the left part is 女 nǚ (female) and the right part is 马 mǎ for the pronunciation.

饭 fàn (meal): the left side is 食 shí (to eat) and the right part is 反 fǎn indicating the sound.

In most determinative-phonetic or phonetic compounds, the left part indicates the meaning, while the right part gives the pronunciation. But this is not always the case. In some characters, the right part or the top part may show the meaning, such as in the character 飘 piāo (float), where the right part is "a wind that makes things float in the air." In the character 雾 wù (fog), the top portion refers to rain, or the moisture that makes fog.

There are also examples of determinative-phonetic characters with the bottom part indicating the meaning, as in 想 xiǎng (to think); or the inner part determining the meaning, as in 问 wèn (to ask); or outer part conveying the meaning, as in 园 yuán (a garden).

5. 假借 (Jiǎjiè) Phonetic Loan Characters

As the ancient Chinese tried to devise characters for words using the methods discussed above, it became obvious that certain concepts are very difficult to depict using pictures, such as the personal pronouns 你 nǐ (you) and 我 wǒ (me). A common practice at the time was to borrow a character with the same or similar sound that was close in meaning, and to use it to express the idea. As a result, some characters were created purely on the basis of sound similarity. Examples:

来 lái: to come

我 wǒ: me, I

6. 转注 (Zhuǎnzhù) Mutually Explanatory Characters

Characters in the last category are actually those created by using part of one existing character to make a new one with a similar pronunciation. They are also called "derivative" characters. These characters reflect natural language development and differences in dialect. Examples:

老 lǎo: old or aging

栲 kǎo: a noun in Classical Chinese that also means "to live to an old age", or "the dead."

Mutually explanatory characters are the most controversial and the least common way to form characters. Because they are vaguely defined, they are also likely to cause confusion. Scholars in the field of Chinese linguistics differ widely over what should be included in this category and it is often omitted in their works.

Writing Chinese characters is one of the basic skills required for learning the language. One must first recognize the shape of the character, know how to read it, and make associations with their verbal knowledge in order to be fully literate. Even in the computerized Chinese classroom, in which characters are typed rather than "drawn" by hand, it is still important to understand the structure of Chinese characters in order to recognize and distinguish them. In Lessons 1-3 of this book we will introduce the fundamentals of character structure, radicals, basic strokes and stroke order. In the rest of this Introduction, we will focus on learning the basics of computer input, in order to begin typing characters immediately.

Computer Input in Chinese

There are different ways to input Chinese characters. Typing pinyin is the best way for students to input Chinese. The Windows® XP operating system comes equipped with Chinese input capability; you can set it up in Control Panel, Regional & Language Options. Macintosh® users can set up their computers to type in Chinese by activating the built-in Chinese Language Kit. (See Appendix 2 for basic instructions on how to set up your computer to type in Chinese.) You can also use any of the available Chinese software programs that utilize pinyin input methods. If you do not have a Chinese software program, you can type Chinese online and copy and paste to an English word processing program such as Microsoft Word. (See the *Chinese for Tomorrow* web site at **www.cheng-tsui.com** for a list of software programs and useful web links.)

Students should feel free to choose their own software to complete the typing tasks in this book. However, we strongly recommend that all students become familiar with the Microsoft Pinyin IME (MSPY), which is based on Hanyu Pinyin. This is because most standardized tests of Chinese, such as the Advanced Placement Chinese Language and Culture Test, require students to use this method on computer-based writing tests.

In this section, we introduce some basic training for typing Chinese. The chart lists some of the basic typing functions you will be performing. An explanation of each function follows the chart.

A. Basic Typing Functions

	Function	Example of What You Type	Example of What You See on Your Screen	Example of Your Final Text
1.	Typing Chinese characters	xue ["to study"]	1 学 2 雪 3 血 4 ⋯	1 学
2.	Typing Chinese characters with tone marks	xue2 ["to study"]	1 学 2	1 学
3.	Typing Chinese words	xuexi yingwen ["to study English"]	1 学习 1 英文 2 血洗	1 学习英文
4.	Mixing Chinese with English	My Chinese name is Zhang Xuewen.	My Chinese name is 张学文.	

1. Typing Chinese Characters

There are different input methods; you should choose "standard pinyin input." When you type a pinyin syllable and then hit the space bar, the computer generates a list of characters corresponding to the pinyin syllable you have just typed. These characters all share the same pinyin spelling, but may have different tones. You use your cursor or the arrow key (or sometimes a number depending on the software program), to choose the correct character from the list that appears on your screen.

2. [Typing Chinese Characters with Tone Marks]

For the purpose of teaching tones, and also to shorten the list of characters, some software programs like NJStar and the Penless Chinese software (www.penlesschinese.org) allow you to type in numbers after pinyin syllables to indicate tones, for example, you can type lao3 for 老 and shi1 for 师. We encourage beginners to use this function. For details, you should read the manual of the particular software package that you are using.

3. [Typing Chinese Words]

Most single Chinese characters are also words. In this book, we call them single-character words. Many words are compound words, composed of two, three or four characters. If you know a word, you can type the pinyin syllables together, rather than typing the first syllable first, choosing a character, and then typing the second syllable. This way, you can type more quickly and choose words more accurately.

4. [Mixing Chinese with English]

If you need to mix Chinese with English, you can toggle the language input button of your program back and forth between Chinese and English.

B. Special Punctuation and Letters

There are a few important punctuation marks and one special letter in Chinese. You need to know how to type them.

Period	∘
Comma	,
Slight pause mark	、
Special letter	ü

1. **Period.** The Chinese period is a small circle, instead of a dot. Usually if you choose Chinese punctuation on the "Settings" menu of your Chinese word processing program, you will get it when you hit the period key.

2. **Comma.** The Chinese comma is used in the same way as the English comma, and typed by hitting the comma key.

3. **Slight pause mark.** In Chinese this is called 顿号 (dùnhào) and it is written differently than a comma. There is no such punctuation in English. It is used to separate a list of things or examples. You should check the manual of the particular software package that you are using for instructions. Sometimes it is represented by "\".

4. **Words with "ü" sound.** Because there is no such sound in English, you cannot find this letter on your keyboard. Usually it is represented by "v" or "uu." Different Chinese programs have different ways to type these special codes. You should find out how to type them with the specific software that you use.

C. Using an Online Dictionary

The dictionary and translation functions that come with many software programs are convenient tools for students. Some programs allow you to use the dictionary or translation function to find Chinese words based on their English meanings. This function is helpful for students writing compositions. You should check the manual of the particular software package that you are using for this function. If you do not have these functions in your program, go to the Chinese for Tomorrow web site at www.cheng-tsui.com for a list of useful web sites.

Typing Practice

1. Type your Chinese name.

For example: If you type "wang2 xiao3 nian2," you should get 王小年.

2. Type the following characters from the textbook.

Lesson 1

hǎo   wǒ   xìng   wáng   shì   jiào

You should get these words:

好   我   姓   王   是   叫

Lesson 2

shuō   de   rén   zài   cháng   yě

You should get these words:

说   得   人   在   长   也

3. Type the following words from the textbook.

Lesson 1

lǎoshī míngzì chīfàn zàijiàn zhōngguó péngyǒu

You should get these words:

老师   名字   吃饭   再见   中国   朋友

Lesson 2

zěnme (how; why) yéye (grandfather) yīshēng (doctor) dàxué (university) jiàoshòu (professor) Yīngwén (English)

You should get these words:

怎么   爷爷   医生   大学   教授   英文

4. Check the English meaning of the words that you typed in the previous section and make a word list.

5. Look up these English words in a dictionary and then type them in Chinese characters.

good student teacher why help left

You should get these words:

好   学生   老师   为什么   帮助   左

6. Type the following sentences with mixed Chinese and English.

My Chinese name is Zhāng Xuéwén.

I am Tom, shì Měiguó liúxuéshēng.

You should get these words:

My Chinese name is 张学文.

I am Tom, 是美国留学生.

7. *Type the following sentences, paying attention to the special codes.*

A. Chinese Period

Wǒ jiào Gélín, shì Měiguó liúxuéshēng.

Tā cái dào Niǔyuē, Yīngwén bù hǎo.

You should get these sentences:

我叫格林，是美国留学生。

他才到纽约，英文不好。

B. Slight Pause Mark

Gélín yǒu hěn duō Zhōngguó péngyǒu, yǒu Xiǎo Wén, Wáng Xiǎonián, Huáng Fāng, Wáng Jiāshēng hé Zhāng Xiǎomèi.

You should get these sentences:

格林有很多中国朋友，有小文、王小年、黄方、王家生和张小妹。

C. ü

Lǚ xiānshēng de dà nǚér xǐhuān chuān lǜsè de nǚshì máoyī.

Lǚkè Lǚ Xiānshēng de xiǎo nǚ'ér bù xǐhuān chuān lǜsè de nǚshì máoyī.

You should get these sentences:

吕先生的 大 女儿 喜欢 穿 绿色 的 女式 毛衣。

(Mr. Lü's older daughter likes to wear green "female-style" sweaters.)

旅客 吕先生的 小 女儿 不 喜欢 穿 绿色 的 女式 毛衣。

(Passenger Lü's younger daughter does not like to wear green "female-style" sweaters.)

liàn xí

练 习

▶ Exercises

· ·

Typing Words

1. Type the following words:

a. lǎoshī	b. míngzi	c. Měiguó	d. jiàoshòu
e. yīngwén	f. qìchē	g. dǎqiú	h. wǎnhuì

You should get these words. Type them again, paying attention to their English meanings.

a. 老师 (teacher)   b. 名字 (name)   c. 美国 (America)   d. 教授 (professor)

e. 英文 (English)   f. 汽车 (car)   g. 打球 (play ball)   h. 晚会 (evening party)

Typing Sentences

1. Xiǎo Wén gěi tā qǐ le gè Zhōngwén míngzi.

2. Māma shì yīshēng, bàba shì dàxué jiàoshòu.

You should get these sentences:

小文给他起了个中文名字。

Xiao Wen gave him a Chinese name.

妈妈是医生，爸爸是大学教授。

[My] mother is a doctor; [my] father is a college professor.

Typing a Dialogue

Gélín: Lǎoshī, qǐng wèn nín guì xìng?

Wáng Lǎoshī: Wǒ xìng Wáng. Nǐ shì xīn xuéshēng ma?

Gélín: Shì, wǒ shì Měiguó liúxuéshēng.

You should get this dialogue:

格林：老师，请问您贵姓？

(Green: Professor, may I ask your (honorable) surname?)

王老师：我姓王。你是新学生吗？

(Professor Wang: My surname is Wang. Are you a new student?)

格林：是，我是美国留学生。

(Green: Yes, I am an American student.)

dì yī kè
第 一 课

LESSON 1

dǎ zhāo hu
打 招 呼
Greetings

▶ **Objectives:**

1. To say and respond to basic greetings
2. To introduce yourself and others

duì   huà   yī
对   话   （一）

DIALOGUE 1

nǐ   hǎo
你   好

▶ **Hello**

....

shēng   cí
生   词

New Words

	Chinese	Pinyin	Part of Speech	English
1.	你好	nǐ hǎo	CE	hello, hi
	你	nǐ	Pron	you
	好	hǎo	Adj	good; fine; well
2.	老师	lǎoshī	N	teacher
3.	请	qǐng	V	please
4.	问	wèn	V	ask
5.	您	nín	Pron	you (polite)
6.	(您)贵姓	guìxìng	CE	What is your honorable surname?
7.	我	wǒ	Pron	I; me
8.	姓	xìng	V/N	surname; family name
9.	王	Wáng	PN	a surname
10.	是	shì	V	to be; yes

11.	新	xīn	Adj	new
12.	学生	xuésheng	N	student
13.	吗	ma	Par	(a particle used for making questions)
14.	叫	jiào	V	call; to be named
15.	什么	shénme	QW	what
16.	名字	míngzi	N	(given or full) name
17.	格林	Gélín	PN	Green (a name), a standard translation of the English surname
18.	美国	Měiguó	PN	the United States of America
19.	留学生	liúxuéshēng	N	foreign student
20.	欢迎	huānyíng	V	welcome
21.	吃饭	chīfàn	VO	eat; have a meal
	饭	fàn	N	cooked rice or other cereals; meal
22.	了	le	Par	(an aspectual particle)
23.	没有	méiyǒu	Ad	not, not have
24.	快	kuài	Adj	fast; quickly; hurry up
25.	去	qù	V	go
26.	餐厅	cāntīng	N	dining room; restaurant, dining hall
	餐	cān	N	food; meal
27.	吧	ba	Par	(here, a particle used for making suggestions)
28.	再见	zàijiàn	CE	goodbye

pīn yīn kè wén
拼 音 课 文

🔊 **Text with Pinyin**

▶▶▶

When reading the text below, try to identify compound words and phrases by underlining them. For example:

kuài qù cān tīng chī fàn ba, zài jiàn
快 去 餐 厅 吃 饭 吧，再 见。

- -

gé lín: nǐ hǎo!
格 林： 你 好！

wáng lǎo shī: nǐ hǎo!
王 老 师：你 好！

gé lín: lǎo shī, qǐng wèn nín guì xìng?
格 林： 老 师，请 问 您 贵 姓？

wáng lǎo shī: wǒ xìng wáng. nǐ shì xīn xué shēng ma?
王 老 师：我 姓 王。你 是 新 学 生 吗？
nǐ jiào shén me míng zi?
你 叫 什 么 名 字？

gé lín: shì, wǒ jiào gé lín, shì měi guó
格 林： 是，我 叫 格 林，是 美 国
liú xué shēng.
留 学 生。

wáng lǎo shī: huān yíng, huān yíng. nǐ chī fàn le ma?
王 老 师：欢 迎，欢 迎。你 吃 饭 了 吗？

gé lín: méi yǒu.
格 林： 没 有。

wáng lǎo shī: kuài qù cān tīng chī fàn ba, zài jiàn.
王 老 师：快 去 餐 厅 吃 饭 吧，再 见。

gé lín: zài jiàn.
格 林： 再 见。

hàn　zì　kè　wén
汉　字　课　文
🔘 **Text in Chinese Characters**

▶▶▶

格林：　　你好！

王老师：　你好！

格林：　　老师†，请问您贵姓？

王老师：　我姓王。你是新学生吗？你叫什么名字？

格林：　　是，我叫格林，是美国留学生。

王老师：　欢迎，欢迎。你吃饭了吗？

格林：　　没有。

王老师：　快去餐厅吃饭吧，再见。

格林：　　再见。

◀◀◀

†Note: The underlined words and expressions are explained in the "Notes on Language Usage" section below.

yǔ　yán　yīng　yòng　zhù　shì
语　言　应　用　注　释
Notes on Language Usage

> About this section:
>
> (1) While this section includes some grammatical explanations, it is primarily intended to provide the cultural, social, and linguistic background necessary to understand and appreciate the texts. For more complete and systematic explanations of grammar, please see the companion grammar book.
>
> (2) Items marked with an asterisk are those that students must master before moving on to the next lesson.

1. 老师

In China, all teachers from kindergarten through university are addressed as *lǎoshī*. Since our book involves a university setting, we often translate 老师 as "professor," though it may also be used to refer to other kinds of teachers. Please note the difference in word order between Chinese and English forms of address. In Chinese we say "王老师", with the surname preceding the title "teacher." But in English we say "Professor Wang", with the job title preceding the surname. Similarly, Chinese surnames always precede given names. For example, in the name 文国新，文 is the surname. In English, of course, we would say Guoxin Wen.

2. 请问您贵姓？ **May I ask your honorable surname?**

贵 means "expensive; valuable; noble." It is used to make this question especially polite.

3. 什么

什么 is a question word corresponding to the English "what."

For example:

你 吃 什 么？

Nǐ chī shénme?

我 吃 美 国 饭。

Wǒ chī Měiguófàn.

What are you eating?

I am eating American food.

(For details, please see Grammar Book I, Lesson 4.)

4. 你吃饭了吗？ 没有。 **Have you eaten your meal? No.**

In this sentence, 了 is an aspectual particle, which means that it indicates the completion of an action.

For example:

A: 你 吃 饭 了 吗？

　　Nǐ chīfàn le ma?

B: 吃 了。or 没 有 (吃)。

　　Chī le. or Méiyǒu chī.

A: Have you eaten (your meal)?

B: Yes, I have. or No, I haven't.

(For details, please see Grammar Book I, Lesson 6.)

The negative form is 没有 + verb. 了 is not used in the negative sentence.

For example:

我 出 差 了。

Wǒ chūchāi le.

I went on a business trip.

我 没 有 出 差。

Wǒ méiyǒu chūchāi.

I did not go on a business trip.

5. 你吃饭了吗？ **Have you eaten your meal?**

你吃饭了吗？ Although it is a question in Dialogue 1, here it can also be used as a greeting. In China, 你好 is used mostly in formal situations. Acquaintances do not often use 你好! as a greeting. They use such greetings as （你）吃饭了吗？ and （你）去哪儿？ (Where are you going?) to show concern or a close relationship.

*6. 吗

吗 is a question particle. It is used to ask about or verify a fact.

For example:

你 是 新 学 生 吗？

Nǐ shì xīn xuésheng ma?

Are you a new student?

你 有 中 文 名 字 吗？

Nǐ yǒu Zhōngwén míngzi ma?

Do you have a Chinese name?

(For details, please see Grammar Book I, Lesson 1.)

7. 吧

吧 is a particle used in making suggestions and requests.

For example:

去 吃 饭 吧。

Qù chīfàn ba.

Let's go eat.

老 师，给 我 起 个 中 文 名 字 吧。

Lǎoshī, gěi wǒ qǐ ge Zhōngwén míngzi ba.

Professor, give me a Chinese name, please.

(For details, please see Grammar Book I, Lesson 4.)

* Language usage notes marked with an asterisk are those that students must master before moving on to the next lesson.

duì   huà   èr
对   话   （二）

DIALOGUE 2

wǒ   yǒu   zhōng wén   míng zì   le
我   有   中   文   名   字   了

▶ **I have a Chinese name now**

shēng   cí
生   词

🔘 **New Words**

	Chinese	Pinyin	Part of Speech	English
1.	好久不见	háojiǔ bùjiàn	CE	long time no see
2.	很	hěn	Ad	very
3.	出差	chūchāi	V	be away on official business; be on a business trip
4.	才	cái	Ad	just
5.	回来	huílai	V	return; come back
	回	huí	V	return; back
	来	lái	V	come
6.	这	zhè/zhèi	Pron	this
7.	位	wèi	M	(a measure word for people)
8.	谁	shéi	QW	who
9.	他	tā	Pron	he
10.	的	de	Par	(a structural particle)
11.	中国	Zhōngguó	PN	China

12.	朋友	péngyou	N	friend
13.	文国新	Wén Guóxīn	PN	Guoxin Wen (a name)
14.	小	xiǎo	Adj	small; little; young
15.	给	gěi	Prep	for, to
16.	起名字	qǐ míngzi	VO	to give a name
17.	个	gè	M	(a measure word used for counting objects, people, etc.)
18.	中文	Zhōngwén	N	the Chinese language
19.	张学文	Zhāng Xuéwén	PN	Xuewen Zhang (a name)
20.	哦	ò	Int	(indicates realization or recollection)
21.	要	yào	AV	must; should; will; be going to
22.	上课	shàngkè	V	attend class; go to class; give a lesson
	课	kè	N	class, lesson
23.	一会儿	yīhuìr	CE	a little while; in a moment
24.	见	jiàn	V	see; catch sight of

pīn yīn kè wén
拼　音　课　文

🔊 **Text with Pinyin**

▶▶▶

When reading the text below, try to identify compound words and phrases by underlining them.

For example:

kuài qù cān tīng chī fàn ba, zài jiàn.
快　去　餐　厅　吃　饭　吧，再　见。

- -

gé lín:　　　nín hǎo, wáng lǎo shī. hǎo jiǔ bù jiàn,
格　林：　　您　好，王　老　师。好　久　不　见，
　　　　　　nín hǎo ma?
　　　　　　您　好　吗？

wáng lǎo shī: hěn hǎo. wǒ chū chāi le, cái huí lai.
王 老 师：很 好。我 出 差 了，才 回 来。
zhè wèi shì shéi?
这 位 是 谁？

gé lín: wáng lǎo shī, tā shì wǒ de zhōng guó
格 林： 王 老 师，他 是 我 的 中 国
péng you, jiào wén guó xīn.
朋 友，叫 文 国 新。

wáng lǎo shī: xiǎo wén, nǐ hǎo.
王 老 师：小 文，你 好。

wén guó xīn: wáng lǎo shī hǎo.
文 国 新：王 老 师 好。

gé lín: xiǎo wén gěi wǒ qǐ le yī ge
格 林： 小 文 给 我 起 了 一 个
zhōng wén míng zi, jiào zhāng xué wén.
中 文 名 字，叫 张 学 文。

wáng lǎo shī: zhè ge míng zi hěn hǎo. Ò, yào
王 老 师：这 个 名 字 很 好。哦，要
shàng kè le, yī huìr jiàn.
上 课 了，一 会 儿 见。

gé lín: yī huìr jiàn
格 林： 一 会 儿 见。

hàn zì kè wén
汉 字 课 文

🔘 **Text in Chinese Characters**

▶▶▶

格林： 您好，王老师。好久不见，您好吗？
王老师： 很好。我出差了，才回来。这位是谁？
格林： 王老师，他是我的中国朋友，叫文国新。
王老师： 小文，你好。

文国新： 王老师好。

格林： 小文给我起了一个中文名字，叫张学文。

王老师： 这个名字很好。哦，要上课了，一会儿见。

格林： 一会儿见。

yǔ   yán   yīng yòng zhù   shì
语   言   应   用   注   释
Notes on Language Usage

1. 你好吗？

Although the literal meaning of this phrase is "how are you?" it is used as a greeting in Chinese only when you haven't seen someone for a long time. It should not be used in situations where you see someone on a regular basis.

2. 小文

Chinese speakers like to put 老 (old) and 小 (young, little) before a person's surname to show their close relationship and their place in a hierarchy (older people are called 老 and younger people 小).

*** 3.** 这个名字很好。 **This name is very good.**

In Chinese, adjectives are often used as verbs. So, you do not need 是 (meaning "is") in this sentence.

> *For example:*
>
> 餐 厅 的 饭 很 好。
>
> Cāntīng de fàn hěn hǎo.
>
> The food in the dining hall is very good.
>
> (For details, please see Grammar Book I, Lesson 2.)

有空

xù   shù

叙   述

▶ **Narration**

· ·

shēng   cí

生   词

🔘 **New Words**

	Chinese	Pinyin	Part of Speech	English
1.	看见	kànjian	V	see
2.	告诉	gàosu	V	tell
3.	有	yǒu	V	have

pīn   yīn   kè   wén

拼   音   课   文

🔘 **Text with Pinyin**

▶▶▶

When reading the text below, try to identify compound words and phrases by underlining them.

For example:

kuài	qù	cān	tīng	chī	fàn	ba,	zài	jiàn.
快	去	餐	厅	吃	饭	吧，	再	见。

· ·

gé	lín	shì	měi	guó	liú	xué	shēng.	tā	kàn	jiàn	chū
格	林	是	美	国	留	学	生。	他	看	见	出

chāi	huí	lái	de	wáng	lǎo	shī,	gào	su	wáng	lǎo	shī,	tā
差	回	来	的	王	老	师，	告	诉	王	老	师，	他

yǒu	yī	gè	zhōng	guó	péng	yǒu,	jiào	wén	guó	xīn.	xiǎo	wén
有	一	个	中	国	朋	友，	叫	文	国	新。	小	文

gěi	tā	qǐ	le	yī	gè	zhōng	wén	míng	zi,	jiào	zhāng	xué
给	他	起	了	一	个	中	文	名	字，	叫	张	学

wén.
文。

◀◀◀

hàn zì kè wén

汉 字 课 文

Text in Chinese Characters

▶▶▶

格林是美国留学生。他看见出差回来的王老师，告诉王老师，他有一个中国朋友，叫文国新。小文给他起了一个中文名字，叫张学文。

◀◀◀

▶ English Translations of the Texts

Dialogue 1   Hello

Green:	Hello.
Professor Wang:	Hello.
Green:	Professor, may I ask your surname?
Professor Wang:	My surname is Wang. Are you a new student? What's your name?
Green:	Yes, I'm called Green. I'm an American student.
Professor Wang:	Welcome, welcome. Have you eaten your meal?
Green:	No.
Professor Wang:	Hurry up to the cafeteria to have your meal. Goodbye.
Green:	Bye.

Dialogue 2   I have a Chinese name now

Green:	Hello, Professor Wang. Long time no see. How are you?
Professor Wang:	Very well. I was on a business trip, and just came back. Who is this gentleman?
Green:	He is my Chinese friend, Guoxin Wen.
Professor Wang:	Hello, Xiao Wen.
Guoxin Zhao:	Hello, Professor Wang.
Green:	Professor Wang, Xiao Wen gave me a Chinese name, Xuewen Zhang.
Professor Wang:	This name is very good. Oh, it's time for class. See you in a moment.
Green:	See you in a moment.

Narration

Green is an American student. He sees Professor Wang, who has just come back from a business trip. He tells Professor Wang he has a Chinese friend who is called Guoxin Wen. Xiao Wen gives him a Chinese name, Xuewen Zhang.

xué   pīn   yīn

学   拼   音

🔊 Learning Pinyin

Tone Sandhi

In Mandarin Chinese, the tone of a syllable can change under certain conditions. For example, when two syllables normally pronounced in the third tone, such as nǐ and hǎo, are spoken in succession, as in ní hǎo 你好, the pitch of the first syllable changes from third tone to a level between the second and third tones (often called a "half third tone"). Linguists call this phenomenon of tonal change "tone sandhi."

The most frequently heard tone sandhi occur with 1) two third tone syllables, 2) the numbers yī, qī and bā, and 3) the negation word bù.

1. Two third tone syllables occurring in succession.

> ***For example:***
>
> xiǎojiě → xiáojiě   zhǎnlǎn →zhánlǎn

2a. When yī is used alone or appears at the end of an expression, it is a first tone.

> ***For example:***
>
> shíyī → eleven   pǎo dì yī → run in first place

But when it combines with a fourth tone it becomes a second tone.

> ***For example:***
>
> yíyàng →the same   yí cì → one time

When it combines with all other tones, it is a fourth tone:

> ***For example:***
>
> yì tiān →one day   yì nián→ a year   yì diǎnr → a little

2b. The only change in the tone of the numbers qī and bā occurs when they combine with a fourth tone syllable.

> ***For example:***
>
> qí gè rén → seven people
>
> bá bàng ròu → eight pounds of meat

In modern Mandarin Chinese, the changes of pronunciation with qī and bā are no longer as important and therefore not emphasized in teaching.

3. The rules for pronouncing bù are similar to the rules for pronouncing yī. When used alone or before words in the first, second, and third tones, bù is pronounced in the fourth tone:

bù shuō → won't tell   bù wánr → don't play   bù hǎo → not good

However, when it combines with a fourth tone, bù becomes a second tone:

bú pà → not afraid   bú lèi → not tired

Note: In this book, we write pinyin words with their base tones. You should learn to adjust your pronunciation according to the tonal changes when you speak in Chinese.

Practice: Read the following aloud and adjust your pronunciation according to the tonal changes.

1. Two or three third tone syllables occurring in succession

kěyǐ (can, may)   xiǎojiě (miss)

xiǎngqǐ (remember)   yǒnggǎn (brave)

fěnbǐ (chalk)   hǎishuǐ (sea water)

hǎo lǐngdǎo (good leader)   xiǎo zǔzhǎng (group leader)

2. Tone changes with yī and bù

dàxiǎo bùyī (different in size)   yībèizi (all one's life)

yīxīn yīyì (wholeheartedly)   yīmú yīyàng (exactly the same)

bùdà bùxiǎo (the right size)   yīshì wúchéng (accomplish nothing)

bùwén bùwèn (show no concern)   yījǔ liǎngdé (kill two birds with one stone)

▶ Nanjing University.

xué   hàn   zì

学　汉　字

Learning Chinese Characters

The Basic Form and Structure of Chinese Characters

A Chinese character is written in the frame of a square and is made up of one or more components. The following are some examples of Chinese characters analyzed by components. Note that no matter how many components it is composed of, each character takes up the same amount of space within the frame.

one component:

女 nǔ → female

子 zǐ → son

不 bù → no, not

two components:

女 nǔ + 子 zǐ = 好 hǎo →good

three components:

不 bù + 女 nǔ + 子 zǐ = 孬 nāo→bad

立 lì + 日 rì + 心 xīn = 意 yì→ meaning

four components:

日 rì + 刀 dāo + 口 kǒu + 火 huǒ = 照 zhào→shine

more than four:

亡 wáng + 口 kǒu + 月 yuè + 贝 bèi + 凡 fán = 赢 yíng→win

Many people believe that Chinese characters are pictographs. But this is simply not the case. Writing a Chinese character is not like drawing a picture. There are a number of special rules that must be followed. The chart below illustrates the basic components of Chinese characters. Some characters can be divided into two, three or more components, while others cannot be divided at all: we call these "single body" characters. The various character structure types, their forms, and examples of each type are illustrated in the chart below.

Name of Basic Structure	Form	Example Characters	Breakdown of Example Characters by Components
独体 Single body	∣	白 bái 大 dà	白 大
左-右 Left-right	‖	他 tā 好 hǎo	亻 + 也 → 他 女 + 子 → 好
左-中-右 Left-middle-right	⫴	谢 xiè 咖 kā	讠 + 身 + 寸 → 谢 口 + 力 + 口 → 咖
上-下 Top-bottom	═	早 zǎo 音 yīn	日 + 十 → 早 立 + 日 → 音
上-中-下 Top-middle-bottom	≡	贵 guì 意 yì	中 + 一 + 贝 → 贵 立 + 日 + 心 → 意
左右对称 Symmetrical	◆∣◆	坐 zuò 小 xiǎo	人 人 + 土 → 坐 亅 → ∣ → 丶 → 小
全包围 Enclosure 半包围 Half enclosure	口 冂	回 huí 间 jiān	囗 + 口 → 回 门 + 日 → 间

tīng shuō liàn xí

听　说　练　习

▶ Exercises for Listening and Speaking

· ·

一、完成对话。*(1. Work with a partner to complete the dialogues.)*

A: Nǐ hǎo!

B: _____

A: Qǐng wèn nín guì xìng?

B: _____

A: Nín jiào shénme míngzi?

B: _____

A: Qǐng wèn nín shì lǎoshī ma?

B: _____

A: Nín qù cāntīng chīfàn ma?

B: _____

A: Wǒ yào qù cāntīng, zài jiàn.

B: _____

🔘 二、听对话，回答问题。*(2. Listen to the conversation on the audio recording and answer the questions.)*

1. What is A going to do?

   _____

2. Is B going?

   _____

3. What is the name of A's Chinese friend?

   _____

4. What is Xiao Wen going to do?

   _____

🔘 三、先听对话，然后两人一组朗读。 *(3. Listen to the following conversation without looking at the book, and then read it aloud in pairs, first by following the pinyin, then by following the characters.)*

A: Wáng Lǎoshī, hǎojiǔ bùjiàn, nín hǎo ma?

B: Hěn hǎo.

A: Xiǎo Wén gěi wǒ qǐ le yí ge Zhōngwén míngzi.

B: Jiào shénme?

A: Jiào Zhāng Xuéwén.

B: Zhège míngzi hěn hǎo.

A:　　Lǎoshī, nín qù shàngkè ma?

B:　　Wǒ qù shàngkè, zàijiàn.

A:　　Zàijiàn.

甲†：　王老师，好久不见，您好吗？

乙†：　很好。

甲：　小文给我起了一个中文名字。

乙：　叫什么？

甲：　叫张学文。

乙：　这个名字很好。

甲：　老师，您去上课吗？

乙：　我去上课，再见。

甲：　再见。

†In Chinese, people use the characters 甲 (jiǎ) and 乙 (yǐ) to represent the speakers in a dialogue, just as English speakers use "A" and "B."

四、角色表演。*(4. Role Play.)*

1. Introduce yourself (A) to your new Chinese professor (B). Tell him/her your Chinese name and that you are an American student. Politely ask his/her surname and if he/she has eaten.

2. You (A) meet Professor Wen (B). Say to him "Long time no see, how are you?" Also tell Professor Wen that your Chinese friend Wang gave you a Chinese name, Ming Wang. Professor Wen says it is a good name and tells you to go to Chinese class.

diàn nǎo yǔ　hàn zì　liàn xí
电　脑　与　汉　字　练　习

type / email / print.

▶ **Exercises for Computing and Learning Characters**

· ·

一、打出下面段落。*(1. Type the following passage.)*

　　我有个中国朋友叫小文，他问我："吃饭了吗？"我说："没有。"我以为 (yǐwéi, think) 他要请我吃饭，可是 (kěshì, but) 他说 (shuō, say)："快去吃吧。""吃饭了吗？"也是打招呼 (dǎ zhāohu, greet somebody)。

二、把下面拼音句子打成汉字。*(2. Type the following pinyin sentences and select the appropriate characters from the list that appears on your computer screen.)*

1. Lǎoshī, qǐng wèn nín guìxìng?

_____

2. Nǐ shì xīn xuésheng ma? Nǐ jiào shénme míngzi?

_____

3. Hǎojiǔ bújiàn. Nín hǎo ma?

_____

4. Xiǎo Wén gěi wǒ qǐ le yī gè Zhōngwén míngzi, jiào Zhāng Xuéwén.

_____

三、圈出正确的汉字。*(3. Circle the correct character to fill in the blanks.)*

1. 你是美 ___ (困、图、团、国、帼) 留学生吗？

2. 老师问我 ___ (持、痴、吃、叨、叱) 饭了没有。

3. 我的名 ___ (自、字、子、宁、宇) 是王中久。

4. 我不是中国人，我是美国留 ___ (穴、觉、宵、赏、学) 生。

四、把汉字分成部件。*(4. Test your understanding of character structure by dividing the following characters into their component parts.)*

Example: 吗—> 口 马

1. 字 —> _____ 宀 子

2. 吃 —> _____ 口 乞

3. 问 —> _____ 门 口

4. 您 —> _____ 亻 尔 心

5. 姓 —> _____ 女 生

kè wén liàn xí
课　文　练　习

▶ Exercises for Understanding the Texts

· ·

一、根据课文回答问题。*(1. Answer the questions orally based on this lesson's dialogues and text.)*

1. 格林是谁 (shéi, who) ？Who is Green?

2. 他从哪儿 (nǎr, where) 来？Where is he from?

3. 他吃饭了吗？Has he eaten yet?

4. 他去哪儿吃饭？Where will he eat?

5. 王老师从哪儿回来？Where did Wang Laoshi come back from?

6. 他的中国朋友叫什么名字？What is Green's Chinese friend's name?

7. 格林的中文名字叫什么？What is Green's Chinese name?

8. 谁给格林起的中文名字？Who gave Green his Chinese name?

▶ The Shanghai University campus.

二、完成对话。 *(2. Complete the dialogues orally.)*

1. A: 请问您贵姓？

    B: _____ 。

2. A: 你吃饭了吗？

    B: _____ 。

3. A: 好久不见。您好吗？

    B: _____ 。

4. A: _____ 。

    B: 这个名字很好。

三、先填空，再朗读段落。 *(3. Fill in the blanks with the numbers corresponding to the correct Chinese characters, and then read the paragraph aloud.)*

1 吧　2 贵　3 了　4 问　5 吗

　　格林看见王老师。他＿＿王老师："请问您＿＿姓？"王老师问他："你吃饭了吗？"格林说没有，王老师说："快去餐厅吃饭吧，再见。"

四、作文 *(4. Composition)*

Use the computer to write a few sentences (3-5) in Chinese introducing yourself to your teacher.

五、翻译 *(5. Translation)*

Translate the following sentences orally in class. Then type your translations in Chinese using the words and phrases provided.

1. My name is Guoxin Wen. May I ask what your surname is? (贵)

2. My surname is Wang. Call me Wang laoshi. (叫，吧)

3. I am Tom (汤姆, tāngmǔ), I'm an American student. (叫)

4. Have you eaten (yet)?

5. Hurry to the dining hall to eat. (快，吧)

6. Long time no see. How are you?

7. Fine.

8. I have a Chinese friend called Xiao Wen. （叫）

9. My teacher gave me a Chinese name called Xuewen. （起名字，叫）

10. I have a Chinese name. （有）

bǔ　chōng yuè　dú　liàn　xí
补　充　阅　读　练　习
▶ **Supplementary Reading Exercises**
. . . .

zhè　ge　bù　néng chī
这　个　不　能　吃

▶ **This Is Not Edible**

Using the word list, see if you can understand the joke below. Then answer the questions that follow.

shēng　cí
生　詞
New Words

<table>
	Chinese	Pinyin	Part of Speech	English
1.	这个	zhège	CE	this
2.	不能	bù néng	CE	cannot
3.	餐馆	cānguǎn	N	restaurant
4.	可是	kěshì	Conj	but
5.	我们	wǒmen	Pron	we
6.	认识	rènshi	V	know; recognize
7.	字	zì	N	character
</table>

8.	指	zhǐ	V	point at
9.	菜单	càidān	N	menu
10.	说	shuō	V	say
11.	服务员	fúwùyuán	N	waiter; waitress

Pinyin Text

Wǒ hé Gé Lín méi qù cāntīng chīfàn, wǒmen dào yí gè Zhōngguó cānguǎn chīfàn. Kěshì wǒmen bù rènshí zì. Gé Lín zhǐ le zhǐ càidān shuō: "wǒmen chī zhège." Fúwùyuán shuō: "ò, zhège bù néng chī, shì wǒmen cānguǎn de míngzi."

Chinese Character Text with Pinyin

wǒ	hé	gé	lín	méi	qù	cān	tīng	chī	fàn,	wǒ	men
我	和	格	林	没	去	餐	厅	吃	饭，	我	们

dào	yí	gè	zhōng	guó	cān	guǎn	chī	fàn.	kě	shì	wǒ	men
到	一	个	中	国	餐	馆	吃	饭。	可	是	我	们

bù	rèn	shí	zì.	gé	lín	zhǐ	le	zhǐ	cài	dān	shuō:	"wǒ
不	认	识	字。	格	林	指	了	指	菜	单	说:	"我

men	chī	zhè	ge."	fú	wù	yuán	shuō:	"ò	zhè	ge	bù	néng
们	吃	这	个。"	服	务	员	说:	"哦，	这	个	不	能

chī,	shì	wǒ	men	cān	guǎn	de	míng	zi."
吃，	是	我	们	餐	馆	的	名	字。"

Chinese Character Text

我和格林没去餐厅吃饭，我们到一个中国餐馆吃饭。可是我们不认识字。格林指了指菜单说："我们吃这个。"服务员说："哦，这个不能吃，是我们餐馆的名字。"

Questions

1. Where did Ge Lin and the writer eat?

2. Why did Ge Lin point at the menu?

3. Why couldn't they eat this?

► A sculpture on the Nanjing University campus.

zhōng guó　wén　huà　xí　sú
中　国　文　化　习　俗

Chinese Customs and Culture

. . . .

zhōng　guó　rén　de　míng zì
中　国　人　的　名　字

▶ Chinese Names

Many Chinese people believe that a child's name will determine his or her future. Accordingly, giving one's child an auspicious name is an undertaking of major importance for most Chinese. Most Chinese names are made up of three characters; the first of these is always the family name. Many people believe that the importance of the family in China is reflected in the placing of the family name first. The second or third character of the name is often used to indicate one's place in a generation. That is, all members of the same generation in one family will share the same second or third character. Traditionally, these characters were chosen by the heads of a family, often taken from poems or other literary sources, and then written into the family genealogy to be used by their descendants. For example, in the famous classical Chinese novel *Dream of the Red Chamber* (also translated as *The Story of the Stone*), the girls of the 贾 (Jiǎ) family are named 贾元春 (Jiǎ Yuán-chūn), 贾探春 (Jiǎ Tàn-chūn), and 贾迎春 (Jiǎ Yíng-chūn). Here, 贾 (Jiǎ) is the family name, 春 (Chūn) indicates that they are all sisters of the same generation, and the second character is the girl's personal name.

Although most Chinese names have three characters, there are some exceptions. Because some Chinese family names have two characters, such as 司马 (Sīmǎ), 诸葛 (Zhūgě), and 欧阳 (Ōuyáng), there are instances of four-character names, like 司马相如 (Sīmǎ Xiàngrú), a famous classical writer. There are also cases in which children are given one-character personal names. This is especially true of the period after the One-Child Policy came into effect in 1979. Since most Chinese children born after 1979 do not have siblings, their parents gave them one-character personal names. This has created a significant problem of large numbers of people having the same name. One newspaper reported that some popular names, like 王涛 (Wáng Tāo), are shared by thousands of people. And according to *The China Press* (Sept. 13, 2006), the name 陈洁 (Chén Jié) was shared by 3,937 people in Shanghai.

Female names often contain characters with the 女 (nǚ, female) radical, or characters related to plants and flowers, beauty, lovely ornaments, or symbols of femininity. In most (but not all) cases, a Chinese person's gender can be determined from his or her name.

Some parents give their children the name of famous figures from history, hoping that their child will inherit that person's nobility or greatness. Chinese names also often reflect social, political and cultural changes. For example, during the Cultural Revolution, many people took such names as 卫东 (Wèidōng, meaning "defending Chairman Mao"), and 向阳 (Xiàngyáng, meaning "following the sun"); 东 is part of Chairman Mao's name, and 阳 is the sun, used here also to refer to Chairman Mao, who was considered "the sun shining over China."

Some parents go so far as to impose their own wishes onto their children via the names they choose. For example, when they want to have financial success, they may name their son 招财 (Zhāocái) meaning "expecting fortune."

In the past women in China used to add their husband's surname before their own and use the word 氏 (shì) meaning "family name" at the end. But this custom has fallen out of practice in Mainland China, where married women no longer change their names in order to show equality between men and women. In Taiwan, Hong Kong and some other Chinese-speaking communities, women keep their own names after marriage, but they still add the husbands' surname before their own, so that people will know they are married women.

▶ Test Your Knowledge: Match these names to their owners.

To test your understanding of Chinese names, can you find out the names of the four people below? Match the names with the pictures and then explain why you chose that name for the figure in the picture. (Answers can be found at the end of the exercise.)

Names:

A: 张爱丽

   Zhāng Àilì (surname/love/ beauty)

B: 王卫国

   Wáng Wèiguó (surname/ defending/country)

C: 胖胖

   Pàngpang (fat/fat)

Picture 1   Picture 2   Picture 3   Picture 4

D: 张王婉蓉

   Zhāng Wáng Wǎnróng (husband's surname / maiden name / graceful / hibiscus, or another name for lotus)

1_____ 2_____ 3_____ 4_____

Answers:

1=C   This is a nickname for a cute and chubby baby or child.

2=A   This is a girl's name, indicating a love of beauty.

3=B   This is a name for a boy or man whose parents hope he can devote himself to the cause of defending his country.

4=D   This is a name for a married woman.

wǒ hé wǒ jiā
我 和 我 家
My Family and I

▶ **Objectives:**

1. To introduce family members
2. To talk about occupations

duì huà yī

对 话 （一）

DIALOGUE 1

huá yì xué shēng

华 裔 学 生

▶ **A Chinese-American Student**

··

shēng cí

生 词

New Words

	Chinese	Pinyin	Part of Speech	English
1.	王小年	Wáng Xiǎonián	PN	Xiaonian Wang (a name)
2.	啊	a	Par	(a tone softener)
3.	怎么	zěnme	Ad	how; why
4.	啦	la	Par	(a tone softener)
5.	说	shuō	V	speak; say
6.	得	de	Par	(a particle used after a verb)
7.	流利	liúlì	Adj	fluent; smooth
8.	华裔	huáyì	N	foreign citizens of Chinese origin
9.	人	rén	N	human being; man; person; people
10.	就是	jiùshì	CE	that is...
11.	生	shēng	V	give birth to; be born
12.	老家	lǎojiā	N	native place; old home
13.	在	zài	Prep	at

14.	哪儿	nǎr	Pron	where
15.	第三	dì-sān	Num	third
16.	代	dài	N	generation; era
17.	移民	yímín	N	emigrant; immigrant
18.	长	zhǎng	V	grow
19.	大	dà	Adj	big; large; great
20.	爷爷	yéye	N	grandfather; grandpa; a respectful form of address for an elderly man
21.	奶奶	nǎinai	N	grandmother; grandma; a respectful form of address for an elderly woman
22.	从	cóng	Prep	from; through
23.	广东	Guǎngdōng	PN	Guangdong province (formerly called "Canton")
24.	也	yě	Ad	also
25.	可是	kěshì	Conj	but; yet; however
26.	爸爸	bàba	N	papa; dad; father
27.	妈妈	māma	N	mom; mother
28.	都	dōu	Ad	all; both
29.	北京	Běijīng	PN	Beijing (formerly called "Peking")
30.	们	men	Par	(a plural marker for pronouns and some animate nouns)
31.	工作	gōngzuò	V/N	work; job
32.	那	nà/nèi	Pron	that; (a discourse connector)
33.	老乡	lǎoxiāng	N	person from the same hometown; fellow villager
34.	去	qù	V	go

pīn yīn kè wén
拼 音 课 文

Text with Pinyin

▶▶▶

When reading the text below, try to identify compound words and phrases by underlining them. For example:

kuài qù cān tīng chī fàn ba, zài jiàn.
快 去 餐 厅 吃 饭 吧，再 见。

zhōng guó xué shēng: qǐng wèn, nǐ shì zhōng guó rén ma?
中 国 学 生： 请 问，你 是 中 国 人 吗？

wáng xiǎo nián: shì a. zěn me la?
王 小 年： 是 啊。怎 么 啦？

zhōng guó xué shēng: nǐ de zhōng wén zěn me shuō de
中 国 学 生： 你 的 中 文 怎 么 说 得
bù liú lì?
不 流 利？

wáng xiǎo nián: wǒ shì huá yì xué shēng,
王 小 年： 我 是 华 裔 学 生，
yǒu rén jiào wǒ ABC.
有 人 叫 我 ABC。

zhōng guó xué shēng: shén me shì ABC?
中 国 学 生： 什 么 是 ABC？

wáng xiǎo nián: jiù shì American Born Chinese.
王 小 年： 就 是 (American Born Chinese)
zài měi guó shēng de zhōng guó rén.
在 美 国 生 的 中 国 人。

zhōng guó xué shēng: nǐ de lǎo jiā zài nǎr?
中 国 学 生： 你 的 老 家 在 哪 儿？

wáng xiǎo nián: wǒ shì dì sān dài yí mín,
王 小 年： 我 是 第 三 代 移 民，
zài měi guó zhǎng dà. wǒ de yé ye,
在 美 国 长 大。我 的 爷 爷、

奶奶 是 从 中 国 广 东 来
nǎi nai shì cóng zhōng guó guǎng dōng lái
美 国 的。
měi guó de.

中 国 学 生： 我 的 老 家 也 在 广 东，
zhōng guó xué shēng: wǒ de lǎo jiā yě zài guǎng dōng,
可 是 爸 爸、妈 妈 都 在
kě shì bà ba, mā ma dōu zài
北 京 工 作。
běi jīng gōng zuò.

王 小 年： 那 我 们 是 老 乡 了。
wáng xiǎo nián: nà wǒ men shì lǎo xiāng le.
我 们 去 吃 中 国 饭 吧。
wǒ men qù chī zhōng guó fàn ba.

汉 字 课 文
hàn zì kè wén
Text in Chinese Characters

中国学生：请问，你是中国人吗？

王小年： 是啊。怎么啦？

中国学生：你的中文怎么说得不流利？

王小年： 我是华裔学生，有人叫我ABC。

中国学生：什么是ABC？

王小年： 就是 (American Born Chinese) 在美国生的中国人。

中国学生：你的老家在哪儿？

王小年： 我是第三代移民，在美国长大。我的爷爷、奶奶是从中国广东来美国的。

中国学生：我的老家也在广东，可是爸爸、妈妈都在北京工作。

王小年： 那我们是老乡了。我们去吃中国饭吧。

yǔ   yán   yīng   yòng zhù   shì
语　言　应　用　注　释
Notes on Language Usage

1. 啊

啊 softens the tone of one's speech, making it less strong and less direct. It is used at the end of a sentence to show agreement.

*2. 说得不流利

得 + adjective is called a "complement of degree" in grammar terminology. The complement indicates the degree or nature of the action. In this case it answers the question, "How does he speak?" with the complement "not fluently." (For details, please see Grammar Book I, Lesson 5.)

3. 华裔

This term is used to refer to people of Chinese ancestry born in foreign countries. In the United States, they are also called 美 měi (America) 籍 jí (citizenship) 华人 huárén (Chinese).

4. 哪儿

哪儿 meaning "where" is used in spoken Chinese. 哪里 also means "where," but it is used both in written and spoken Chinese.

*5. 我的爷爷、奶奶是从中国广东来美国的。

My grandparents came to America from Guangdong, China.

The 是……的 construction is used here to emphasize a place, specifically the place from which the speaker's grandparents came. In the sentence 格林是在中国学习中文的 (Green learned Chinese in China), the same construction highlights the place where Green learned Chinese.

(Please see Grammar Book I, Lesson 6 for notes on how to use the 是……的 construction.)

*6. 都

都 means "all" or "both." It is positioned after the subject, which must be a plural number.

For example:

格林和王小年都学中文。

Gélín hé Wáng Xiǎonián dōu xué Zhōngwén.

Both Green and Xiaonian Wang study Chinese.

(For details, please see Grammar Book I, Lesson 2.)

▶ A family photo.

7. 那

那 does not mean "that" here. Rather, it is a transition word used to connect the two sentences.

*8. 们

们 is a suffix used for pluralizing personal pronouns and nouns, as in 我们，你们，他们，老师们，学生们，朋友们.

duì huà èr

对 话 (二)

DIALOGUE 2

wǒ hěn xiǎng jiā

我 很 想 家

▶ I Miss Home

....

shēng cí

生 词

New Words

	Chinese	Pinyin	Part of Speech	English
1.	想家	xiǎngjiā	VO	be homesick; miss home
	想	xiǎng	V	think; miss
	家	jiā	N/M	family; home; (a measure word for stores and businesses)
2.	做	zuò	V	do; make
3.	呢	ne	Par	(a question particle)
4.	医生	yīshēng	N	doctor
5.	大学	dàxué	N	university
6.	教授	jiàoshòu	N	professor
7.	口	kǒu	M	(a measure word for people)
8.	哥哥	gēge	N	(elder) brother
9.	和	hé	Conj	and
10.	妹妹	mèimei	N	younger sister; sister

11.	纽约大学	Niǔyuē Dàxué	PN	New York University, NYU
12.	开	kāi	V	open; open up; run; drive
13.	馆	guǎn	N	a place of accommodation for guests; a shop (often used in compound words)
14.	兄弟姐妹	xiōngdì jiěmèi	N	brothers and sisters
15.	上学	shàngxué	V	go to school; attend school
16.	中学	zhōngxué	N	middle school
17.	不	bù	Ad	no; not
18.	跟	gēn	Conj/Prep	and; with; follow
19.	学习	xuéxí	V	study
	学	xué	V/N	study, subject of study
20.	电脑	diànnǎo	N	computer
21.	商学院	shāngxuéyuàn	N	business school
	学院	xuéyuàn	N	college; academy; institute
22.	会计	kuàijì	N	accounting; bookkeeper; accountant
23.	纽约	Niǔyuē	PN	New York
24.	英文	Yīngwén	N	English (language)
25.	请教	qǐngjiào	V	ask for advice; consult
26.	可以	kěyǐ	AV	can; may
27.	互相	hùxiāng	Ad	mutual; each other
28.	帮助	bāngzhù	V	help; assist
29.	教	jiāo	V	teach; instruct

pīn yīn kè wén
拼 音 课 文
Text with Pinyin

▶▶▶

zhōng guó xué sheng: 中 国 学 生 ：	wǒ hěn xiǎng jiā. 我 很 想 家 。
wáng xiǎo nián: 王 小 年 ：	nǐ bà ba mā ma dōu shì zuò shén 你 爸 爸 妈 妈 都 是 做 什 me de ne? 么 的 呢 ？
zhōng guó xué sheng: 中 国 学 生 ：	mā ma shì yī shēng, bà ba shì dà 妈 妈 是 医 生 ， 爸 爸 是 大 xué jiào shòu. nǐ ne? 学 教 授 。 你 呢 ？
wáng xiǎo nián: 王 小 年 ：	wǒ men jiā yǒu wǔ kǒu rén. bà ba, 我 们 家 有 五 口 人 。 爸 爸 、 mā ma, yī ge gē ge hé yī ge 妈 妈 、 一 个 哥 哥 和 一 个 mèi mei. bà ba, mā ma kāi le yī 妹 妹 。 爸 爸 、 妈 妈 开 了 一 jiā zhōng cān guǎn. 家 中 餐 馆 。
zhōng guó xué sheng: 中 国 学 生 ：	wǒ méi yǒu xiōng dì jiě mèi. nǐ gē 我 没 有 兄 弟 姐 妹 。 你 哥 ge hé mèi mei dōu shàng xué ma? 哥 和 妹 妹 都 上 学 吗 ？
wáng xiǎo nián: 王 小 年 ：	tā men bù dōu shàng xué, gē ge shì 他 们 不 都 上 学 ， 哥 哥 是 zhōng xué lǎo shī, mèi mei gēn wǒ dōu 中 学 老 师 ， 妹 妹 跟 我 都

电囵

请教
教授

互相 助

LESSON 2 ▶ My Family and I **71**

zài niǔ yuē dà xué xué xí. wǒ xué
在 纽 约 大 学 学 习。我 学
diàn nǎo. mèi mei zài shāng xué yuàn xué
电 脑。妹 妹 在 商 学 院 学
kuài jì xué.
会 计 学。

zhōng guó xué shēng: wǒ cái dào niǔ yuē, yīng wén bù hǎo,
中 国 学 生： 我 才 到 纽 约，英 文 不 好，
yǐ hòu yào duō qǐng jiào nǐ.
以 以 要 多 请 教 你。

wáng xiǎo nián: wǒ men kě yǐ hù xiāng bāng zhù. nǐ
王 小 年： 我 们 可 以 互 相 帮 助。你
kě yǐ jiào wǒ xué zhōng wén.
可 以 教 我 学 中 文。

zhōng guó xué sheng: nà tài hǎo le.
中 国 学 生： 那 太 好 了。

hàn zì kè wén
汉 字 课 文
Text in Chinese Characters

中国学生： 我很想家。

王小年： 你爸爸妈妈都是做什么的呢？

中国学生： 妈妈是医生，爸爸是大学教授。你呢？

王小年： 我们家有五口人。爸爸、妈妈、一个哥哥和一个
妹妹。爸爸、妈妈开了一家中餐馆。

中国学生： 我没有兄弟姐妹。你哥哥和妹妹都上学吗？

王小年： 他们不都上学，哥哥是中学老师，妹妹跟我都在
纽约大学学习。我学电脑。妹妹在商学院学会计学。

中国学生：　我才到纽约，英文<u>不</u>好，以后要多请教你。

王小年：　　我们可以互相帮助。你可以教我学中文。

中国学生：　那太好了。

◀◀◀

yǔ　yán　yīng　yòng zhù　shì
语　言　应　用　注　释
Notes on Language Usage

Homewrk pg 20
Gram 25
32, 59
11 AM

1. 呢

When used at the end of a question, this word softens the tone of the question. But in the phrase 你呢, it means "how about you?"

For example:

格林是美国留学生，你呢？

Gélín shì Měiguó liúxuéshēng, nǐ ne?

Green is an American student; how about you?

格林去餐厅吃饭，小文呢？

Gélín qù cāntīng chīfàn, Xiǎo Wén ne?

Green is going to eat in the cafeteria; how about Xiao Wen?

(For details, please see Grammar Book I, Lesson 3.)

*2. 不都

不都 means "not all" or "not both." In the sentence 他们不都上学, the speaker 王小年 means "they do not both go to school." His sister goes to school, but his brother does not. (For details, please see Grammar Book I, Lesson 2.)

*3. 不

不 is an adverb used for negation. It is placed right before the word it negates.

For example:

我不是美国留学生。

Wǒ bù shì Měiguó liúxuéshēng.

I am not an American student.

这个名字不好。

Zhège míngzi bù hǎo.

This name is not good.

(For details, please see Grammar Book I, Lesson 1.)

xù shù

叙 述

▶ **Narration**

....

shēng cí

生 词

🔘 **New Words**

Chinese	Pinyin	Part of Speech	English
学校	xuéxiào	N	school; educational institution

pīn yīn kè wén

拼 音 课 文

🔘 **Text with Pinyin**

▶▶▶

wáng	xiǎo	nián	shì	huá	yì	dà	xué	shēng,	zài	měi	guó
王	小	年	是	华	裔	大	学	生,	在	美	国

shēng,	měi	guó	zhǎng.	wáng	xiǎo	nián	de	bà	ba,	mā	ma	kāi
生,	美	国	长。	王	小	年	的	爸	爸、	妈	妈	开

zhōng	cān	guǎn.	gē	ge	shì	zhōng	xué	lǎo	shī,	mèi	mei	gēn
中	餐	馆。	哥	哥	是	中	学	老	师,	妹	妹	跟

wáng	xiǎo	nián	zài	niǔ	yuē	dà	xué	xué	xí.	wáng	xiǎo	nián
王	小	年	在	纽	约	大	学	学	习。	王	小	年

de	zhōng	wén	bú	tài	hǎo.	yī	tiān,	wáng	xiǎo	nián	zài	xué
的	中	文	不	太	好。	一	天,	王	小	年	在	学

xiào	jiàn	dào	yī	ge	zhōng	guó	xué	sheng,	nà	gè	xué	sheng
校	见	到	一	个	中	国	学	生,	那	个	学	生

de	mā	ma	shì	yī	shēng,	bà	ba	shì	dà	xué	jiào	shòu.
的	妈	妈	是	医	生,	爸	爸	是	大	学	教	授。

tā	cái	dào	niǔ	yuē,	yīng	wén	bù	hǎo.	tā	gēn	wáng	xiǎo
他	才	到	纽	约,	英	文	不	好。	他	跟	王	小

nián	xué	yīng	wén,	wáng	xiǎo	nián	gēn	tā	xué	zhōng	wén.
年	学	英	文,	王	小	年	跟	他	学	中	文。

◀◀◀

xù   shù

叙   述

▶ **Narration**

. . . .

hàn   zì   kè   wén

汉   字   课   文

Text in Chinese Characters

▶▶▶

王小年是华裔大学生，在美国生，美国长。王小年的爸爸、妈妈开中餐馆。哥哥是中学老师，妹妹跟王小年在纽约大学学习。王小年的中文不太好。一天王小年在学校见到一个中国学生，那个学生的妈妈是医生，爸爸是大学教授。他才到纽约，英文不好。他跟王小年学英文，王小年跟他学中文。 ◀◀◀

▶ **English Translations of the Texts**

. . . .

Dialogue 1: My Family and I

Chinese student:	May I ask, are you Chinese?
Xiaonian Wang:	Yes. Why?
Chinese student:	How come your Chinese is not fluent?
Xiaonian Wang:	I'm an American student of Chinese origin. Some people call us "ABCs."
Chinese student:	What's an "ABC?"
Xiaonian Wang:	It's an "American Born Chinese," a Chinese person who was born in the United States.
Chinese student:	Where's your hometown?
Xiaonian Wang:	I'm a third generation Chinese. I grew up in America. My grandfather and grandmother came to America from Guangdong, China.
Chinese student:	My hometown is also in Guangdong. But my father and mother both work in Beijing.
Xiaonian Wang:	So, we are *lǎoxiāng* (people from the same hometown). Shall we go have some Chinese food?

Dialogue 2: I Miss Home

Chinese student:	I miss home.
Xiaonian Wang:	What do your parents do?

Chinese student: My mother is a doctor. My father is a college professor. How about you?

Xiaonian Wang: There are five people in my family. Dad, Mom, an elder brother and a younger sister. My parents run a Chinese restaurant.

Chinese student: I don't have brothers and sisters. Are your brother and sister both going to college?

Xiaonian Wang: No, they are not. My brother is a middle school teacher. My sister and I both study at New York University. I am studying computer science. My sister is studying accounting at the business school.

Chinese student: I just came to New York, and my English is not very good. I will ask you to teach me later on.

Xiaonian Wang: We can help each other. You can teach me Chinese.

Chinese student: That's great.

Narration

Xiaonian Wang is an American student of Chinese origin who was born and grew up in America. Xiaonian's father and mother run a Chinese restaurant. Xiaonian's elder brother is a middle school teacher. Xiaonian's sister studies at New York University with him. Xiaonian's Chinese is not very good. One day Xiaonian meets a Chinese student at school. The student's mother is a doctor, and his father is a college professor. The student has just arrived in New York. His English is not good, so he learns English from Xiaonian, and Xiaonian learns Chinese from him.

xué pīn yīn
学　拼　音

🔘 Learning Pinyin

The Neutral Tone

In some Mandarin Chinese words, certain syllables are pronounced so lightly that they lose their original tone and are pronounced without a tone. This is called "qīng shēng" or "neutral tone." Syllables with neutral tones are not written with tone marks. Neutral tones can help distinguish the meaning or part of speech of a word or expression. For example, the word shàng 上 in shàngxué 上学 and shàngbān 上班 is a verb when it is used in the fourth tone. However, in zǎoshang 早上 (morning), the same syllable is written without a tone mark because it is part of a noun. Neutral tones can also indicate a change in part of speech from noun to adjective. For instance, the phrase dìdào 地道 with a fourth tone means "tunnel," while dìdao 地道 with a neutral tone means "authentic." Another example is dàyì 大意, which means "the general idea of a piece of writing" as a noun, while dàyi 大意 with no tone mark over yi is an adjective meaning "careless." Although the two characters that make up the written form of these two expressions are exactly the same, their meaning depends on the tone in which they're pronounced.

The [Er] Sound

When Mandarin Chinese is spoken by native speakers from northern China, especially people from Beijing, an [er] sound is often heard at the end of certain words and expressions. Very often, putting an [er] after a syllable, usually a noun, shows the speaker's positive feelings, such as 小孩 xiǎo háir (a little child); 金鱼 jīn yúr (a goldfish); 小田 Xiǎo Tiánr ("Little Tian," a way to call a younger colleague named Tian). This change can also serve a grammatical function. Sometimes, when the [er] sound is added to a verb or an adjective, the word becomes a noun. For example, the original meaning of 盖 gài is "to cover," but 盖儿 gàir means "a cover" or "a lid" after an [er] sound is added. The adjective 亮 liàng means "bright," but if an [er] sound is added, it becomes 亮儿 liàngr, the noun for "light." Since the [er] sound is used to vary the natural flow of speech, and sometimes to indicate a change in part of speech, it should not be used excessively.

Practice: Read the following words aloud, paying special attention to changes in pronunciation.

▶ **A statue of Confucius in New York City's Chinatown.**

PINYIN

A. The Neutral Tone (The second syllable in the following words is unstressed and pronounced lightly and quickly.)

bàba (father)	māma (mother)	gēge (older brother)
jiějie (older sister)	dìdi (younger brother)	mèimei (younger sister)
tāmen (they)	háizi (child)	shénme (what)
péngyou (friend)	kuàiji (accountant)	xuésheng (student)
wūli (in the room)	wàitou (outside)	shàngbian (above)
chūqu (go out)	jìnlai (come in)	zhàn qilai (stand up)
qīngchu (clear)	dìdao (authentic)	piàoliang (beautiful)
xiǎngxiang (consider)	kànkan (have a look)	
pǎo bu dòng (cannot run)	kàn yi kàn (have a look)	
hǎo de hěn (very good)	ná zhe shū (holding a book)	

B. The [Er] Final

yīhuìr (a little while)	rénr (person)	shuǐr (water)
fànguǎnr (restaurant)	yì bāor chá (a bag of tea)	wánr (to play)
bǐjìběnr (notebook)	nǎr (where)	míngr (name)

xué hàn zì

学 汉 字

Learning Chinese Characters

Basic Chinese Radicals

A radical is the basic component of a written character. Radicals are useful for learners of Chinese because they often reveal something about the basic meaning of a character. Radicals are also used in organizing dictionaries, indexes, etc., in Chinese publications. A radical can be as simple as one stroke, such as 一 or 乙, or as complicated as 鼠 or 龟. All Chinese characters are made up of one or more radicals. Most radicals are, in fact, independent characters or words that have their own meanings, and these are referred to as 独体字 dútǐzì (single-body characters).

A majority of characters in Chinese are formed when a radical combines with a phonetic element. The radical often gives some hint as to the meaning of the character, while the phonetic element indicates its pronunciation. In a character made up of two or more components, the radical is usually the portion on the left, or the part that remains if the phonetic element is removed. For example, in the character 湖 hú meaning "lake," 氵 (sān diǎn shuǐ) is the radical meaning "water" and 胡 (hú) indicates the pronunciation.

Traditionally there are 214 radicals in the Chinese language, but after simplification of character forms, the total number of modern radicals has increased to 227. Most dictionaries published outside of Mainland China include about 178–188 radicals. Being able to recognize radicals will give you an advantage in learning to recognize, read, and handwrite characters, as well as in using dictionaries. The following is a list of the most frequently used radicals. These radicals are all single-body characters.

	Character	Pinyin	English	Examples of Characters Containing the Radical
1.	力	lì	power	动 (move), 助 (help), 努 (exert effort)
2.	口	kǒu	mouth	吃 (eat), 叫 (call), 吹 (blow)
3.	囗	wéi	enclose	四 (four), 回 (return), 国 (country)
4.	土	tǔ	earth, dirt	坐 (sit), 在 (at), 地 (the earth)
5.	大	dà	big, large	天 (sky), 夫 (husband), 太 (too)
6.	女	nǚ	female	妈 (mother), 姐 (sister), 奶 (grandma)
7.	子	zǐ	son	孙 (grandson), 孩 (child), 学 (study)
8.	寸	cùn	inch	对 (right), 封 (seal), 导 (lead)
9.	小	xiǎo	little, small	少 (young), 尚 (still), 尖 (tip)

10. 山	shān	mountain	仙 (immortal), 岳 (mountain), 岭 (ridge)
11. 工	gōng	labor, work	左 (left), 差 (difference), 功 (achievement)
12. 弓	gōng	bow	弯 (bend), 张 (spread), 引 (guide)
13. 心	xīn	heart	您 (you), 忠 (loyal), 意 (meaning)
14. 日	rì	sun	时 (time), 春 (spring), 星 (star)
15. 月	yuè	moon, month	服 (clothes), 朝 (dynasty), 期 (period)
16. 木	mù	wood	林 (forest), 村 (village), 李 (plum)
17. 水	shuǐ	water	池 (pond), 汁 (juice), 河 (river)
18. 火	huǒ	fire	灯 (light), 炉 (stove), 炒 (stir fry)
19. 田	tián	field	男 (male), 界 (border), 留 (remain)
20. 目	mù	eye	睡 (sleep), 看 (look), 睛 (eye)

tīng shuō liàn xí
听 说 练 习

▶ Exercises for Listening and Speaking

....

一、完成对话。**(1. Work in pairs to complete the dialogue.)**

A: Xiǎo Wáng, nǐ de Zhōngwén zěnme shuō de bù liúlì?

B: _wo shi ABC_

A: Shénme shì ABC?

B: _Jiu shi zai mei guo sheng de zhong guo ren._

A: Nà nǐ de lǎojiā zài nǎr?

B: _zai zhong guo beijing_

A: Tài hǎo le, wǒmen shì lǎoxiāng le, wǒ yě shì cóng Běijīng lái de. Qù chī Zhōngguó fàn ba.

B: _____

🔵 二、听对话，回答问题。*(2. Listen to the conversation and answer the questions.)*

1. Who are the members of B's family?

baba ~~hi~~ mama

2. Does B have any brothers?

mei you

3. Does A have any brothers?

yi ge ge gi

4. Are A's parents both doctors?

bu dui

5. In B's family, who is a professor?

ta de baba

🔵 三、先听对话，然后两人一组朗读。*(3. Listen to the following conversation without looking at the book, and then read it aloud in pairs, first by following the pinyin, then by following the characters.)*

Jiǎ: Qù zhōngcānguǎn chīfàn ba.

Yǐ: Qù nǎ jiā zhōngcānguǎn?

Jiǎ: Wǒ bàba, māma kāi le yī jiā zhōngcānguǎn.

Yǐ: Nǐ jiā hái yǒu shéi?

Jiǎ: Wǒ hái yǒu yī ge gēge hé yī ge mèimei.

Yǐ: Tāmen dōu shì xuésheng ma?

Jiǎ: Wǒ gēge shì zhōngxué lǎoshī. Mèimei yě zài Niǔyuē Dàxué xuéxí.

Yǐ: Tā xué shénme?

Jiǎ: Tā xué kuàijì hé Zhōngwén.

Yǐ: Hěn hǎo.

Jiǎ: Yǐhòu wǒ yào duō qǐngjiào nǐ Zhōngwén.

Yǐ: Wǒ yě gēn nǐ xuéxí Yīngwén.

Jiǎ: Nà tài hǎo le.

甲：去中餐馆吃饭吧。

乙：去哪家中餐馆？

甲：我爸爸、妈妈开了一家中餐馆。

乙：你家还有谁？

甲：我还有一个哥哥和一个妹妹。

乙：他们都是学生吗？

甲：我哥哥是中学老师。妹妹也在纽约大学学习。

乙：她学什么？

甲：她学会计和中文。

乙：很好。

甲：以后我要多请教你中文。

乙：我也跟你学习英文。

甲：那太好了。

四、角色表演 *(4. Role Play)*

A is a Chinese student who has just arrived in New York from China. He meets B (his classmate). They introduce themselves to each other and talk about their family members: what their names are, what they are doing, and who is studying at college or teaching at school. They agree to help each other learn Chinese and English.

diàn nǎo yǔ hàn zì liàn xí

电 脑 与 汉 字 练 习

▶ Exercises for Computing and Learning Characters

一、打出下面段落。*(1. Type the following passage.)*

王小年的朋友叫王小年ABC。他问爸爸、妈妈是什么意思 (yìsi, meaning)，他们说就是华裔美国人。他们的老家在中国，那里都是中国人。中国人都会说很流利的中文。

二、把下面拼音句子打成汉字。*(2. Type the following pinyin sentences and select the appropriate characters from the list that appears on your computer screen.)*

1. Nǐ de Zhōngwén zěnme shuō de bù liúlì?

2. Wǒ shì dì-sān dài yímín, zài Měiguó zhǎngdà.

3. Māma shì yīshēng, bàba shì dàxué jiàoshòu.

4. Mèimei gēn wǒ dōu zài Niǔyuē Dàxué.

5. Tā de bàba, māma kāi Zhōngcānguǎn.

三、圈出正确的汉字。**(3. Circle the correct character to fill in the blanks.)**

1. 你是美国 ___ （八、几、人、入、九）吗？

2. 老师不是 ___ （花、华、毕、伞、卉）裔。

3. 我的老师是在美国 ___ （华、长、张、千、九）大的。

4. 我的老 ___ （加、宁、宇、家、宗）不在美国，在中国。

5. 我哥哥在商学___ （完、原、院、愿、陀）___ （校、叫、教、救、赦）电脑。

四、读生字，找出偏旁部首。**(4. The characters in each of the following groups share a radical. Read the characters and write the shared radicals.)**

Example: 这 迎　shared radical: 辶

1. 那 都 院　shared radical: 阝

2. 姐 妹 妈 奶　shared radical: 女

3. 啊 哪 口 和　shared radical: 口

五、把汉字分成部件。**(5. Test your understanding of character structure by dividing the following characters into their component parts.)**

Example: 吗—> 口 马

1. 教—> 孝 攵

2. 想—> 木 目 心

3. 请—> 讠 圭 月

4. 妈—> 女 马

5. 爸—> 父 巴

kè   wén   liàn   xí
课   文   练   习

▶ Exercises for Understanding the Texts

一、根据课文回答问题。*(1. Answer the questions orally based on the text.)*

1. 王小年是中国学生还是美国学生？
   Is Xiaonian Wang a Chinese or American student?

2. 王小年的中文说得怎么样？
   How is Xiaonian Wang's spoken Chinese?

3. 他的老家在哪儿？那个中国学生呢？
   Where is his hometown? Where is the Chinese student's hometown?

4. 那个中国学生的爸爸、妈妈做什么？
   What do the Chinese student's father and mother do?

5. 王小年的家有几口人？他们都是谁？
   How many people are there in Xiaonian Wang's family? Who are they?

6. 他们家谁在纽约大学学习？
   Which member of their family is going to New York University?

7. 王小年和中国学生怎么互相帮助？
   How do they help each other?

 二、完成对话。*(2. Complete the dialogues orally.)*

1. A: 请问你是哪国人？

   B: 我是美国人

2. A: 你有华裔朋友吗？他们是谁？

   B: 我有一个华裔朋友，他是王小年

3. A: 你的老家在哪儿？

   B: 我的老家在广东

4. A: <u>你爸爸妈妈都是做什么的呢？</u>_____。

   B: 我爸爸、妈妈不都是大学教授。

5. A: 我有两个妹妹和两个哥哥，你呢？

   B: <u>我有一个哥哥和两个妹妹</u>_____。

三、先填空，再朗读段落。*(3. Fill in the blanks with the numbers corresponding to the correct Chinese characters, and then read the paragraph aloud.)*

1 哪儿 2 在 3 不都 4 都 5 都 6 都不 7 得 8 华裔

　　王小年是<u>华裔</u>大学生，<u>在</u>美国生，美国长。他的中文说<u>得</u>不流利。他的爸爸、妈妈开中餐馆。他不知道他的老家在<u>哪儿</u>。哥哥和妹妹<u>都</u>跟他在纽约大学学习。可是他们<u>都不</u>是华裔，他们在学校<u>不都</u>学中文，<u>都</u>学日文 (Rìwén, Japanese)。

四、作文 *(4. Composition)*

Use the computer to write a few sentences (5-6) in Chinese introducing your family.

五、翻译 *(5. Translation)*

Translate the following sentences orally in class. Then type your translations in Chinese using the words and phrases provided.

1. How come your Chinese is not fluent? (得)

2. My grandfather and grandmother came to America from Guangdong, China. (是……的)

3. So, we are from the same hometown. Let's go have some Chinese food. (那，吧)

4. I just came to New York. My English is not very good.

5. They are not both going to college. My brother is a doctor. (不都)

6. We can help each other.

7. My sister is studying at New York University's business school.

8. What do your parents do? (呢)

9. My mother is a middle school teacher. My father is a college professor.

10. I am a third generation immigrant. I grew up in America. (是……的)

bǔ chōng yuè dú liàn xí
补　充　阅　读　练　习

▶ **Supplementary Reading Exercises**

···

wǒ nǐ tā tā
我、 你、 他 （她）

▶ **Me, You, Him/Her**

Using the word list, try to understand the joke below. Then answer the questions that follow.

shēng cí
生　词

New Words

	Chinese	Pinyin	Part of Speech	English
1.	第一天	dì yī tiān	CE	the first day
2.	指	zhǐ	N/V	finger; point at
3.	着	zhe	Par	(a particle indicating an action in progress)
4.	女生	nǚshēng	N	female student
5	女同学	nǚ tóngxué	N	female classmate
6.	今天	jīntiān	N	today
7.	生气	shēngqì	V	get angry
8.	昨天	zuótiān	N	yesterday
9.	胡说	húshuō	N/V	nonsense; talk nonsense

Pinyin Text

Wénwén dì yī tiān shàngxué, xué le sān gè zì: wǒ、
nǐ、tā(tā). Lǎoshī shuō: "Wǒ, wǒ shì nǐ de lǎoshī."
Tā zhǐ zhe Wénwén shuō: "Nǐ, nǐ shì wǒ de xuéshēng."
Tā zhǐzhe yī ge nǚshēng shuō: "Tā, tā shì nǐ de nǚ
tóngxué."

Wénwén huí jiā gàosu tā bàba: "Wǒ jīntiān xué le
sān gè zì. Wǒ, wǒ shì nǐ de lǎoshī. Nǐ, nǐ shì wǒ de
xuéshēng." Tā zhǐzhe tā māma shuō: "Tā, tā shì nǐ de nǚ
tóngxué."

▶ New York's Chinatown.

Bàba tīng le hěn shēngqì, tā shuō: "húshuō! Wǒ, wǒ shì nǐ bàba. Nǐ, nǐ shì wǒ érzi. Tā, tā shì nǐ
māma."

Dì èr tiān lǎoshī wèn: "Zuótiān wǒmen xué le shènme?" Wénwén shuō: "Zuótiān xué le sān ge zì.
Wǒ, wǒ shì nǐ bàba. Nǐ, nǐ shì wǒ érzi." Tā zhǐzhe nàge nǚshēng shuō: "Tā, tā shì nǐ māma." Lǎoshī
tīng le……

Text with Pinyin

wén	wén	dì	yī	tiān	shàng	xué,	xué	le	sān	ge	zì:
文	文	第	一	天	上	学，	学	了	三	个	字：

wǒ,	nǐ,	tā	tā.	lǎo	shī	shuō:	"wǒ,	wǒ	shì	nǐ	de	lǎo
我、	你、	他	（她）。	老	师	说：	"我，	我	是	你	的	老

shī."	tā	zhǐ	zhe	wén	wén	shuō:	"nǐ,	nǐ	shì	wǒ	de	xué
师。	他	指	着	文	文	说：	"你，	你	是	我	的	学

shēng."	tā	zhǐ	zhe	yī	ge	nǚ	shēng	shuō:	"tā,	tā	shì	nǐ
生。	他	指	着	一	个	女	生	说：	"她，	她	是	你

de	nǚ	tóng	xué."
的	女	同	学。"

wén	wén	huí	jiā	gào	su	tā	bà	ba:	"wǒ	jīn	tiān
文	文	回	家	告	诉	他	爸	爸：	"我	今	天

xué	le	sān	gè	zì.	wǒ,	wǒ	shì	nǐ	de	lǎo	shī.	nǐ,
学	了	三	个	字。	我，	我	是	你	的	老	师。	你，

nǐ	shì	wǒ	de	xué	shēng."	tā	zhǐ	zhe	tā	mā	ma	shuō:
你	是	我	的	学	生。	他	指	着	他	妈	妈	说：

"tā,	tā	shì	nǐ	de	nǚ	tóng	xué."	bà	ba	tīng	le	hěn
"她，	她	是	你	的	女	同	学。"	爸	爸	听	了	很

shēng qì, tā shuō: "hú shuō! wǒ, wǒ shì nǐ bà ba. Nǐ,
生 气，他 说："胡 说！我，我 是 你 爸 爸。你，
nǐ shì wǒ ér zi. tā, tā shì nǐ mā ma."
你 是 我 儿 子。她，她 是 你 妈 妈。"
dì èr tiān lǎo shī wèn: "zuó tiān wǒ men xué le
第 二 天 老 师 问："昨 天 我 们 学 了
shèn me? wén wén shuō: "zuó tiān xué le sān gè zì. wǒ,
什 么？"文 文 说："昨 天 学 了 三 个 字。我，
wǒ shì nǐ bà ba. nǐ, nǐ shì wǒ ér zi." tā zhǐ
我 是 你 爸 爸。你，你 是 我 儿 子。"他 指
zhe nà ge nǚ shēng shuō: "tā, tā shì nǐ mā ma." lǎo
着 那 个 女 生 说："她，她 是 你 妈 妈。"老
shī tīng le ....
师 听 了……

Chinese Character Text

　　文文第一天上学，学了三个字：我、你、他（她）。老师说："我，我是你的老师。"他指着文文说："你，你是我的学生。"他指着一个女生说："她，她是你的女同学。"

　　文文回家告诉他爸爸："我今天学了三个字。我，我是你的老师。你，你是我的学生。"他指着他妈妈说："她，她是你的女同学。"

　　爸爸听了很生气，他说："胡说！我，我是你爸爸。你，你是我儿子。她，她是你妈妈。"

　　第二天老师问："昨天我们学了什么？"文文说："昨天学了三个字。我，我是你爸爸。你，你是我儿子。"他指着那个女生说："她，她是你妈妈。"老师听了……

Questions

1. How did the teacher explain 我，你，他？

2. How did the father explain 我，你，他？

3. Why was the child wrong?

zhōng guó wén huà xí sú

中 国 文 化 习 俗

Chinese Customs and Culture

zhōng guó rén de jiā tíng chēng hū

中 国 人 的 家 庭 称 呼

▶ **Chinese Family Relationships**

The Chinese have a very complicated system of family titles. Unlike in English, in Chinese, an "uncle" is not just an "uncle." There are different words for your father's older and younger brothers, your mother's brothers, and uncles by marriage. These titles are very important, as they help Chinese people find their places in the hierarchy of relationships that are so critical to family and social life in China. What follows is a list of the most important family relationships. Of course, Chinese family relationships can get very complicated – if you have more than one family member of the same relationship, you need to address them according to their birth order, status and seniority relative to yours. For example, if I have three older brothers, I call the oldest as 大哥 (dàgē, first older brother), then the second oldest 二哥 (èrgē, second older brother) and the third 三哥 (sāngē, third older brother). If I have three younger sisters, I can use 大妹 (dàmèi, first younger sister), 二妹 (èrmèi, second younger sister) and 三妹 (sānmèi, third younger sister). 三妹 can also be called 小妹 (xiǎomèi) if she is youngest of your younger sisters. After studying the following relationships, please try and fill in your own family tree below.

Grandparents' Generation

Father's father: 爷爷 yéyé

Father's mother: 奶奶 nǎinǎi

Mother's father: 外公 wàigōng

Mother's mother: 外婆 wàipó

Parents' Generation

Father: 爸爸 bàba

Father's older brother and his wife: 伯父 bófù、伯母 bómǔ

Father's younger brother and his wife: 叔叔 shūshu、婶婶 shěnshen

Father's sister and her husband: 姑妈 gūmā、姑夫 gūfū

Mother: 妈妈 māma

Mother's brother and his wife: 舅舅 jiùjiù、舅母 jiùmǔ

Mother's sister and her husband: 姨妈 yímā、姨夫 yífū

Your Generation

Myself: 我 wǒ

Elder brother: 哥哥 gēge

Younger brother: 弟弟 dìdi

Elder sister: 姐姐 jiějie

Younger sister: 妹妹 mèimei

Father's brother's son:
堂哥 tánggē、堂弟 tángdì

Father's brother's daughter:
堂姐 tángjiě、堂妹 tángmèi

Father's sister's son: 表哥
biǎogē、表弟 biǎodì

Father's sister's daughter:
表姐 biǎojiě、 表妹 biǎomèi

Mother's brother's son: 表哥 biǎogē、表弟 biǎodì

Mother's brother's daughter: 表姐 biǎojiě、表妹 biǎomèi

Mother's sister's son: 姨哥 yígē、姨弟 yídì

Mother's sister's daughter: 姨姐 yíjiě、姨妹 yímèi

Children's Generation

Son: 儿子 érzi

Daughter: 女儿 nǚér

Nephew: brother's son 侄子 zhízi

Niece: brother's daughter 侄女 zhínǚ

Nephew: sister's son (addressor is male) 外甥 wàishēng

Niece: sister's daughter (addressor is male) 外甥女 wàishēngnǚ

Grandchildren's Generation

Son's son: 孙子 sūnzi

Son's daughter: 孙女 sūnnǚ

Daughter's son: 外孙 wàisūn

Daughter's daughter: 外孙女 wàisūnnǚ

► **Test Your Knowledge:** Make a family tree. (Answers can be found at the end of the exercise.)

Instructions: There are four levels in the tree, indicating the four generations. The uppermost level is the grandparents' generation, the second the parents' generation, the third your own generation, and the fourth your children's generation. Place the characters or pinyin for the appropriate family relationships in the circles to complete the tree. Make sure that those more closely related to you are placed closer to you. In terms of organization, place relatives from your father's side to the left of "myself," and relatives from your mother's side to the right of "myself."

1. 奶奶 nǎinai
2. 爸爸 bàba
3. 弟弟 dìdi
4. 伯母 bómǔ
5. 外婆 wàipó
6. 表哥 biǎogē
7. 外甥 wàishēng
8. 舅舅 jiùjiù
9. 姐姐 jiějie
10. 妈妈 māma
11. 堂妹 tángmèi
12. 侄女 zhínǚ

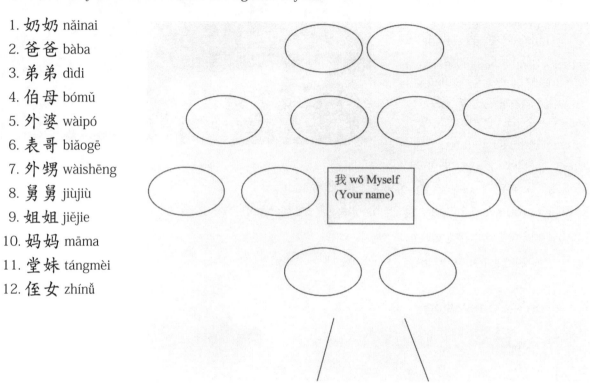

我 wǒ Myself
(Your name)

Answers:

Level One: 1, 5

Level Two: 4, 2, 10, 8

Level Three: 11, 3, 9, 6

Level Four: 12, 7

dì sān kè

第 三 课

LESSON 3

yuē shí jiān

约 时 间

Making Appointments

▶ **Objectives:**

1. To make appointments
2. To extend, accept and decline invitations

duì   huà   yī
对   话   （一）

DIALOGUE 1

kàn   diàn   yǐng
看   电   影

▶ **Going to a Movie**

shēng   cí
生   词

🔘 **New Words**

	Chinese	Pinyin	Part of Speech	English
1.	王家生	Wáng Jiāshēng	PN	Jiasheng Wang (a name)
2.	张小妹	Zhāng Xiǎomèi	PN	Xiaomei Zhang (a name)
3.	明天	míngtiān	TW	tomorrow
4.	看	kàn	V	see; look at; watch; read
5.	电影	diànyǐng	N	film; movie; motion picture
6.	到	dào	V	arrive; reach
7.	大片儿	dàpiānr	CE	well-known movie (especially referring to American movies)
	片	piān/piàn	N/M	a flat, thin piece (here refers to a movie 电影片); (a measure word for a slice)
8.	嘿	hēi	Int	hey
9.	真	zhēn	Ad	true; real; genuine; really
10.	棒	bàng	Adj	(colloquial) good; excellent; awesome

11.	大华电影院	Dà Huá Diànyǐngyuàn	PN	Dahua Movie Theater
12.	电影院	diànyǐngyuàn	N	cinema; movie theater
13.	坐	zuò	N	sit; travel by (a car, plane, vehicle, etc.)
14.	路	lù	M	road; route
15.	公共汽车	gōnggòng qìchē	N	public bus
	公共	gōnggòng	Adj	public; common; communal
	汽车	qìchē	N	automobile; motor vehicle; car
16.	下	xià	V/Adj	get off; exit; below; down; under
17.	站	zhàn	N	stand; (bus or train) stop; station
18.	出	chū	V	go out; come out
19.	北	běi	N	north
20.	门	mén	N	entrance; door; gate; valve
21.	往	wǎng/wàng	Prep	in the direction of; toward
22.	左	zuǒ	N	left, the left side; the left
23.	拐	guǎi	V	turn
24.	第二	dì-èr	Num	second
25.	十	shí	Num	ten
26.	字	zì	N	word; character
27.	路口	lùkǒu	N	crossing; intersection
	口	kǒu	N	mouth; opening; entrance
28.	红绿灯	hónglǜdēng	N	traffic light; traffic signal
	红	hóng	Adj	red

	绿	lǜ	Adj	green
	灯	dēng	N	lamp; lantern; light
29.	旁边	pángbiān	N	side; by; next to
30.	几	jǐ	QW	how many; a few; several; some
31.	点	diǎn	N	drop (of liquid); spot; dot; point; o'clock
32.	怎么样	zěnmeyàng	CE	how about
33.	下午	xiàwǔ	TW	afternoon
34.	不见不散	bùjiàn bùsàn	CE	(If we) do not see (each other), (we) will not leave.
	散	sàn	V	break up; disperse

pīn   yīn   kè   wén
拼   音   课   文
● **Text with Pinyin**
▶▶▶

As you read, underline the compound words and phrases, as below:

kuài   qù   cān   tīng   chī   fàn   ba,   zài   jiàn.
快   去   餐   厅   吃   饭   吧， 再   见 。

(Two freshmen at a Chinese college)

wáng jiā shēng: zhāng xiǎo mèi,   wǒ   men   míng   tiān   qù   kàn
王 家 生：   张   小   妹，我   们   明   天   去   看
                       diàn   yǐng   ba.
                       电   影   吧。

zhāng xiǎo mèi: shén   me   diàn   yǐng?
张   小   妹：   什   么   电   影？

wáng jiā shēng: xīn   dào   de   měi   guó   dà   piānr.
王 家 生：   新   到   的   美   国   大   片   儿。

zhāng	xiǎo	mèi:	hēi,	zhēn	bàng!	zài	nǎr?				
张	小	妹：	嘿，	真	棒！	在	哪	儿	？		

wáng	jiā	shēng:	dà	huá	diàn	yǐng	yuàn,	zuò	shísì	lù	gōng	gòng
王	家	生：	大	华	电	影	院，	坐	14	路	公	共
			qì	chē	zài	dà	xīn	lù	xià	chē.		
			汽	车	在	大	新	路	下	车。		

zhāng	xiǎo	mèi:	shísì	lù	chē	zhàn	zài	nǎr?	
张	小	妹：	14	路	车	站	在	哪	儿？

wáng	jiā	shēng:	chū	běi	xiào	mén,	wǎng	zuǒ	guǎi,	zài	dì	èr
王	家	生：	出	北	校	门，	往	左	拐，	在	第	二
			ge	shí	zì	lù	kǒu,	hóng	lǜ	dēng	páng	biān.
			个	十	字	路	口，	红	绿	灯	旁	边。

zhāng	xiǎo	mèi:	wǒ	men	jǐ	diǎn	qù?
张	小	妹：	我	们	几	点	去？

wáng	jiā	shēng:	xià	wǔ	sì	diǎn,	zěn	me	yàng?
王	家	生：	下	午	四	点，	怎	么	样？

zhāng	xiǎo	mèi:	hǎo,	míng	tiān	xià	wǔ,	shísì	lù	chē	zhàn,
张	小	妹：	好，	明	天	下	午，	14	路	车	站，
			bù	jiàn	bù	sàn.					
			不	见	不	散。					

wáng	jiā	shēng:	zài	jiàn!
王	家	生：	再	见！

◀◀◀

hàn zì kè wén
汉 字 课 文
🔘 **Text in Chinese Characters**

▶▶▶

(Two freshmen at a Chinese college)

王家生： 张小妹，我们明天去看电影吧。

张小妹： 什么电影？

王家生： 新到的<u>美国大片儿</u>。

张小妹： 嘿，真棒！在哪儿？

王家生： 大华电影院，坐<u>14路</u>公共汽车，在大新路下车。

张小妹： 14 路车站在哪儿？

王家生： 出北校门，往左拐，在第二个十字路口，红绿灯旁边。

张小妹： 我们几点去？

王家生： 下午四点，<u>怎么样</u>？

张小妹： 好，明天下午，14路车站，<u>不见不散</u>。

王家生： 再见！

◀◀◀

yǔ yán yīng yòng zhù shì
语 言 应 用 注 释
Notes on Language Usage

1. 美国大片

This means an "American blockbuster" movie. 片 here refers to 电影片 (film). The word 片 usually refers to flat and thin things. It has two pronunciations, piān and piàn. Piān is used in spoken Chinese to refer to movies and photographs. It is often followed by an [er] final sound. For example: 片子 (piānzi, film; movie), 相片儿 (xiàngpiānr, photograph), 动画片儿 (dònghuàpiānr, animated cartoon), etc. Piàn is used more generally and can refer to other things. For example: 卡片 (kǎpiàn, card), 贺年片 (hèniánpiàn, New Year's card), 照片 (zhàopiàn, photograph), 药片 (yàopiàn, medicine tablet), 明信片儿 (míngxìnpiàn, postcard), 电影片 (diànyǐngpiàn, movie), 电视片 (diànshìpiàn, TV program), 故事片 (gùshìpiàn, feature movie) 等. Piàn can also be used as a measure word, as in 一片面包 (yīpiàn miànbāo, a slice of bread).

2. 14路公共汽车

路 has many meanings, but here refers to the route number of the bus. In Taiwan, the word 号 (hào) is used instead of 路 to refer to a route number.

*3. 下午四点，怎么样？**How about 4:00 p.m.?**

"……，怎么样？means "how about...?"

For example:

在 14 路 公 共 汽 车 站 见，怎 么 样？

Zài 14 lù gōnggòng qìchē zhàn jiàn, zěnmeyang?

How about meeting at the Route 14 bus stop?

去 中 餐 馆 吃 饭，怎 么 样？

Qù zhōngcānguǎn chīfàn, zěnmeyang?

How about going to the Chinese restaurant to eat?

4. 不见不散

This set phrase is used when you have set up a time to meet someone and want to tell that person not to leave until you show up. The phrase can be literally translated as "(If we) do not see (each other), (we) will not leave."

For example:

明 天 下 午 两 点 酒 吧 门 口 见，不 见 不 散。

Míngtiān xiàwǔ liǎngdiǎn jiǔba ménkǒu jiàn, bùjiàn bùsàn.

See you in front of the bar at two tomorrow afternoon. Don't leave until we see each other.

duì   huà   èr
对   话   （二）

DIALOGUE 2

wǒ   bù   qù
我   不   去

▶ **I Am Not Going**

....

shēng   cí
生   词
🔘 **New Words**

	Chinese	Pinyin	Part of Speech	English
1.	约翰	Yuēhàn	PN	John (a name)
2.	苏珊	Sūshān	PN	Susan (a name)
3.	对不起	duìbuqǐ	CE	I'm sorry; sorry, excuse me; I beg your pardon
4.	喜欢	xǐhuān	V	like; love; be fond of
5.	体育馆	tǐyùguǎn	N	gym
6.	打	dǎ	V	play; strike; hit; break
7.	球	qiú	N	ball; the globe; anything shaped like a ball
8.	太	tài	Ad	excessively; too
9.	累	lèi	Adj	tired; fatigued; weary
10.	生日	shēngrì	N	birthday
11.	晚会	wǎnhuì	N	an evening of entertainment; evening party
12.	没(有)意思	méiyǒu yìsi	CE	not interesting

有意思	yǒuyìsi	Adj	interesting
意思	yìsi	N	meaning; idea
13. 酒吧	jiǔbā	N	bar
酒	jiǔ	N	alcoholic drink; wine; liquor; spirits
吧	bā	N	bar
14. 玩儿	wánr	V	play; have fun; amuse oneself
15. 喝	hē	V	drink; drink liquor
16. 年龄	niánlíng	N	age
17. 算了	suàn le	CE	let it be; let it pass; forget it
18. 睡觉	shuìjiào	V	sleep
19. 男	nán	Adj	man; male
20. 跳舞	tiàowǔ	V	dance

pīn   yīn   kè   wén
拼   音   课   文
🔘 **Text with Pinyin**

▶▶▶

(Two freshmen at an American college)

yuē hàn: sū shān, míng tiān wǒ men qù kàn diàn yǐng ba.
约   翰： 苏   珊， 明   天   我 们 去 看 电   影 吧。

sū shān: duì bu qǐ, wǒ bù xǐ huān kàn diàn yǐng.
苏   珊： 对 不 起， 我 不 喜 欢   看 电   影。

yuē hàn: nà wǒ men qù tǐ yù guǎn dǎ qiú ba.
约   翰： 那 我 们 去 体 育 馆   打 球 吧。

DIALOGUE 2

| sū | shān: | dǎ | qiú | tài | lèi | le. |
| 苏 | 珊: | 打 | 球 | 太 | 累 | 了。 |

yuē	hàn:	nà	wǒ	men	qù	wáng	xiǎo	nián	de	shēng	rì
约	翰:	那	我	们	去	王	小	年	的	生	日
		wǎn	huì,	zěn	me	yàng?
		晚	会,	怎	么	样?

| sū | shān: | nà | duō | méi | yì | sī. |
| 苏 | 珊: | 那 | 多 | 沒 | 意 | 思。 |

| yuē | hàn: | qù | jiǔ | bā | wánr, | hǎo | ma? |
| 约 | 翰: | 去 | 酒 | 吧 | 玩 儿, | 好 | 吗? |

sū	shān:	bù	qù,	wǒ	men	hái	méi	dào	hē	jiǔ	de
苏	珊:	不	去,	我	们	还	沒	到	喝	酒	的
		nián	ling.
		年	龄。

| yuē | hàn: | nà | suàn | le, | nǐ | zài | jiā | shuì | jiào | ba. |
| 约 | 翰: | 那 | 算 | 了, | 你 | 在 | 家 | 睡 | 觉 | 吧。 |

sū	shān:	bù,	wǒ	yào	gēn	wǒ	de	nán	péng	yǒu	qù
苏	珊:	不,	我	要	跟	我	的	男	朋	友	去
		tiào	wǔ.
		跳	舞。

▶ Friends relaxing in the park.

hàn zì kè wén
汉 字 课 文

🔊 Text in Chinese Characters

▶▶▶

(Two freshmen at an American college)

约翰： 苏珊，明天我们去看电影吧。

苏珊： 对不起，我不喜欢看电影。(1)†

约翰： 那我们去体育馆打球吧。

苏珊： 打球太累了。(2)

约翰： 那我们去王小年的生日晚会，怎么样？

苏珊： 那多没意思。(3)

约翰： 去酒吧玩儿，好吗？

苏珊： 不去，我们还没到喝酒的年龄。(4)

约翰： 那算了，你在家睡觉吧。

苏珊： 不，我要跟我的男朋友去跳舞。   ◀◀◀

† The numbers in parentheses here are used to indicate the four exchanges in this dialogue that are dealt with in the note on refusal strategies below.

yǔ yán yīng yòng zhù shì
语 言 应 用 注 释

Notes on Language Usage

1. 那我们去体育馆打球吧。 **Then how about playing ball at the gym?**

那 as introduced in Lesson 2 means 那么，or "then." It is called a "discourse connector," and it is used to connect what has been said previously with a new situation or suggestion.

For example:

你 不 喜 欢 跳 舞，那 我 们 去 看 电 影 吧。

Nǐ bù xǐhuān tiàowǔ, nà wǒmen qù kàn diànyǐng ba.

You don't like dancing. Then let's go to see a movie.

你 有 中 文 名 字 了？那 我 就 不 叫 你 的 英 文 名 字 了。

Nǐ yǒu Zhōngwén míngzi le? Nà wǒ jiù bù jiào nǐ de Yīngwén míngzi le.

You've got a Chinese name? Then I will not use your English name.

2. 打球太累了。 **Playing ball is too tiring.**

了 is used at the end of a sentence to emphasize a feeling or tone, and in this usage it has no specific meaning.

For example:

太 好 了！

Tài hǎo le!

That's great!

太 有 意 思 了！

Tài yǒuyìsi le!

It's very interesting!

*3. 去酒吧玩儿，好吗？ **How about going to a bar (to have fun)?**

好吗 (Is it OK?) is a tag question. The first part is a suggestion, and 好吗 is used at the end of the sentence to ask the other person's opinion regarding that suggestion.

For example:

我 们 没 到 喝 酒 的 年 龄，不 要 去 喝 酒，好 吗？

Wǒmen méi dào hējiǔ de niánling, bu yào qù hējiǔ, hǎo ma?

We are not yet of drinking age. So let's not go drinking, OK?

我 有 中 文 名 字 了，叫 我 中 文 名 字，好 吗？

Wǒ yǒu Zhōngwén míngzì le, jiào wǒ Zhōngwén míngzi, hǎo ma?

I have a Chinese name now. So use my Chinese name, OK?

(For details, please see Grammar Book I, Lesson 2.)

4. 我们还没到喝酒的年龄。 **We are not yet of drinking age.**

In this sentence, 没(有) is used to negate the verb. The meaning is that we have not yet reached the age. 没(有) as a negation word is used to indicate a state or action that has not yet been completed. On the other hand, if we take a sentence like 我不喜欢看电影, we can see that 不, another negation word, indicates that one does not want to do something.

More examples:

我 们 还 没 有 吃 午 饭。

Wǒmen hái méiyǒu chī wǔfàn.

We have not eaten lunch yet.

我 不 吃 饭。

Wǒ bù chīfàn.

I don't (want to) eat.

王 老 师：你 交 作 业 (jiāo zuòyè, hand in homework) 了 没 有？

Wáng Lǎoshī: Nǐ jiāo zuòyè le méi yǒu?

格 林：我 不 交 作 业。

Gélín: Wǒ bù jiāo zuòyè.

王 老 师：你 是 说 你 没 交 作 业，对 (duì, right) 吧？

Wáng Lǎoshī: Nǐ shì shuō nǐ méi jiāo zuòyè, duì ba?

格 林：对，我 没 交。

Gélín: Duì, wǒ méi jiāo.

Professor Wang: Have you handed in your homework?

Green: I do not want to hand in my homework.

Professor Wang: You mean you have not handed it in yet, right?

Green: Yes, I have not handed it in yet.

5. 那算了

算了 means "forget it." It is used when you are ready to give up on something or do not want to continue with it.

For example:

你 不 想 去 跳 舞，那 算 了。

Nǐ bù xiǎng qù tiàowǔ, nà suàn le.

You don't want to go dancing, so let's forget it.

算 了，别 说 了。

Suàn le, bié shuō le.

Forget it. Stop talking.

6. Refusal Strategies

Refusing someone is not always a simple matter of saying "no." As in most cultures, Chinese people use a variety of strategies, ranging from extremely polite and indirect to blunt and straightforward, to say "no." In Dialogue 2, we see Susan employing a number of these strategies. She starts out being very polite, using a "regret + explanation" strategy (1), but later drops the "regret" and adopts an "explanation" alone strategy (2). Ultimately, however, neither of these indirect strategies works, and she turns to more direct refusals, simply turning down the request with a "no" (3) and (4). This time the refusal is clearly understood and John gives up.

xù   shù

叙   述

▶ **Narration**

∙∙

shēng   cí

生   词

🔘 **New Words**

	Chinese	Pinyin	Part of Speech	English
1.	一起	yìqǐ	Ad	together; in company
2.	拒绝	jùjué	V	refuse; reject; turn down; decline
3.	原来	yuánlái	Adj	original; former

pīn   yīn   kè   wén

拼   音   课   文

🔘 **Text with Pinyin**

▶▶▶

wáng jiā shēng qǐng zhāng xiǎo mèi qù dà huá diàn
王   家   生   请   张   小   妹   去   大   华   电

yǐng yuàn kàn měi guó dà piānr. zhāng xiǎo mèi hěn
影   院   看   美   国   大   片   儿。张   小   妹   很

xǐ huān měi guó diàn yǐng. tā men shuō hǎo míng tiān
喜   欢   美   国   电   影。他   们   说   好   明   天

xià wǔ sì diǎn zài shí sì lù qì chē zhàn jiàn,
下   午   四   点   在   十   四   路   汽   车   站   见,

yī qǐ qù kàn diàn yǐng, bù jiàn bù sàn.
一   起   去   看   电   影,不   见   不   散。

yuē hàn (John) qǐng sū shān (Susan) kàn diàn yǐng, kě
约   翰 (John)   请   苏   珊 (Susan)   看   电   影,可

shì sū shān bù xǐ huān kàn diàn yǐng, tā yě bù
是   苏   珊   不   喜   欢   看   电   影,她   也   不

xǐ huān dǎ qiú. yuē hàn yào qǐng tā yī qǐ qù
喜   欢   打   球。约   翰   要   请   她   一   起   去

shēng rì wǎn huì hé qù jiǔ bā, dàn shì sū shān
生   日   晚   会   和   去   酒   吧,但   是   苏   珊

<table>
<tr><td>dōu</td><td>jù</td><td>jué</td><td>le.</td><td>yuán</td><td>lái</td><td>tā</td><td>yào</td><td>gēn</td><td>nán</td><td>péng</td><td>yǒu</td></tr>
<tr><td>都</td><td>拒</td><td>绝</td><td>了。</td><td>原</td><td>来</td><td>她</td><td>要</td><td>跟</td><td>男</td><td>朋</td><td>友</td></tr>
</table>

<table>
<tr><td>qù</td><td>tiào</td><td>wǔ.</td></tr>
<tr><td>去</td><td>跳</td><td>舞。</td></tr>
</table>

◀◀◀

hàn zì kè wén
汉   字   课   文
Text in Chinese Characters

▶▶▶

　　王家生请张小妹去大华电影院看美国大片。张小妹很喜欢美国电影。他们说好明天下午四点在十四路汽车站见，一起去看电影，不见不散。

　　约翰 (John) 请苏珊 (Susan) 看电影，可是苏珊不喜欢看电影，她也不喜欢打球。约翰要请她一起去生日晚会和去酒吧，但是苏珊都拒绝了。原来她要跟男朋友去跳舞。

◀◀◀

yǔ yán yīng yòng zhù shì
语   言   应   用   注   释
Notes on Language Usage

*1. 说好

好 is used after a verb to indicate completion. 说好 indicates that "we talked and decided," or "it is settled that...." This type of sentence is called a "complement of result" in grammar terminology.

For example:

说 好 晚 上 见， 我 们 不 见 不 散。
Shuō hǎo wǎnshang jiàn, wǒmen bùjiàn bùsàn.
We decided to meet tonight. We will not leave without seeing each other.

我 跟 苏 珊 说 好 去 吃 中 国 饭。
Wǒ gēn Sūshān shuō hǎo qù chī Zhōngguófàn.
Susan and I decided to go eat Chinese food.

打 球—打 好 球
dǎqiú—dǎ hǎo qiú
finish playing ball

跳 舞—跳 好 舞
tiàowǔ—tiào hǎo wǔ
finish dancing

看 电 影—看 好 电 影

kàn diànyǐng—kàn hǎo diànyǐng

finish watching a movie

(For details, please see Grammar Book I, Lesson 8.)

*2. 约翰要请她一起去生日晚会和去酒吧

This type of sentence is called a "pivotal sentence" in grammar. In this type of sentence, the object (receiver) of the first verb is at the same time the subject (actor) of the second verb. In this sentence, 她 (she) functions as the object (receiver) of the action 请 (invite), but also as the subject (actor) of the action 去 (go), indicating that she has been invited to go.

More examples:

我 请 王 家 生 吃 饭。

Wǒ qǐng Wáng Jiāshēng chīfàn.

I am treating Jiasheng Wang to dinner.

约 翰 请 苏 珊 跳 舞。

Yuēhàn qǐng Sūshān tiàowǔ.

John is inviting Susan to dance.

(For details, please see Grammar Book I, Lesson 4.)

▶ English Translations of the Texts

Dialogue 1

(Two freshmen at a Chinese college)

Jiasheng Wang: Xiaomei, let's go see a movie tomorrow.

Xiaomei Zhang: What movie?

Jiasheng Wang: The newly released American blockbuster movie.

Xiaomei Zhang: Hey, that's awesome! Where is it (playing)?

Jiasheng Wang: Dahua Movie Theater. Take the Route 14 bus and get off at Da Xin Road.

Xiaomei Zhang: Where is the Route 14 bus stop?

Jiasheng Wang: Go out of the school's northern gate and turn left. It is next to the traffic light at the second intersection.

Xiaomei Zhang: When shall we go?

Jiasheng Wang: How about 4:00 p.m.?

Xiaomei Zhang: Good. Tomorrow afternoon at the Route 14 bus stop. Don't leave without me.

Jiasheng Wang: See you.

Dialogue 2

(Two freshmen at an American college)

John: Susan, let's go see a movie tomorrow night.

Susan: I'm sorry, I don't like movies.

John: Then how about playing ball at the gym?

Susan: Playing ball is too tiring.

John: In that case, how about going to Xiaonian Wang's birthday party?

Susan: That's so boring.

John: How about going to a bar (to have fun)?

Susan: No, we are not yet of drinking age.

John: OK, OK. Why don't you just stay home and sleep.

Susan: No. I'm going out dancing with my boyfriend.

Narration

Wang Jiasheng asks Zhang Xiaomei to go to the Dahua Movie Theater to see an American blockbuster movie. Zhang Xiaomei likes American movies very much. They decide to meet at the Route 14 bus stop at 4:00 tomorrow afternoon. They will not leave without seeing each other, and will go to the movie together.

John asks Susan to go to a movie with him, but Susan does not like movies. She does not like playing ball either. John asks her to go to a birthday party or to a bar with him. But Susan refuses. It turns out that she will go out dancing with her boyfriend.

xué   pīn   yīn

学   拼   音

Learning Pinyin

▶ A public performance in Central Park, Manhattan.

Syllable Separation Marks

One of the distinctive characteristics of modern Chinese is that all characters are one-syllable speech units. While most characters can be words by themselves and have grammatical functions within a sentence, the majority of Chinese words are composed of two or more characters or syllables. As we learned in the previous section, finals such as [a], [o] and [e] can stand alone as syllables without a preceding initial, and all the syllables end with either a final (vowel) or one of the two nasal sounds [n] or [ng]. As a result, in two-syllable words, if the second syllable begins with a vowel, confusion may occur when reading the pinyin. So it is necessary to use an apostrophe to separate the two syllables. For example, pí'ǎo with an apostrophe between the two syllables means 皮袄 "leather coat", but without the apostrophe, it is read as "piao," a different word.

Here are more examples:

nǚ'ér (daughter)

Tiān'ānmén (Tiananmen Square, or The Gate of Heavenly Peace, in Beijing)

Xī'ān (name of the place where the terracotta soldiers were unearthed)

Spelling Rules

Spelling refers to the process of linking an initial with a final in order to form a syllable. For example, when you see the syllable [fou], you should know that it is the initial [f] combined with the final [ou] and not the initial [fo] plus the final [u]. The following are the rules for spelling. Use these rules as your guidelines when you write in pinyin. Please refer to the introduction for an overview of initials and finals.

Rule 1. Final [o] only combines with the initials in Group 1: [b, p, m, f]. Final [e] does not combine with [b, p, m, f] except in the interrogative particle [me].

bó (thin)   pò (broken)

mō (touch)   fó (Buddha)

Rule 2. Final [u] cannot combine with the initials in Group 3: [j, q, x].

As a result, the [u] after [j, q, x] is actually [ü] with the two umlaut marks omitted.

jū (originally jǖ) → to live

qū (originally qǖ) → district

xū (originally xǖ) → need

Rule 3. Besides [j, q, x], the final [ü] and all the compound finals that begin with [ü] can only be combined with two other initials [l and n] and the umlaut marks are retained in these syllables.

lǜ –(green)   nǚ (female)

Rule 4. When the compound finals beginning with [i] stand alone as syllables without an initial, the letter [i] is changed into [y].

ia	ie	iang
↓	↓	↓
yā (press)	yě (also)	yáng (sheep)

However, there are exceptions to this rule. When the simple final [i] and compound finals [in] and [ing] stand alone without preceding initials, the semi vowel [y] is added to the front of the syllable and the [i] remains.

i	in	ing
↓	↓	↓
yī (one)	yīn (sound)	yìng (hard)

Rule 5. When the compound finals beginning with [u] stand alone as syllables without an initial, the letter [u] is changed to [w].

uo	uai	uang
↓	↓	↓
wǒ (I or me)	wài (outside)	wáng (king, or a surname)

The simple final [u] is an exception to this rule. When it occurs without an initial, the special initial [w] is added.

u	u
↓	↓
wū (house)	wǔ (the number five)

Rule 6. There are two different ways of forming a syllable for the three compound finals [iou, uei, uen]. When they are preceded by initials other than [y] and [w], the [o] in [iou] drops and the spelling of the final changes to [iu], while the [e] in [uei] and [uen] drops and the spelling changes to [ui] and [un], respectively. But when they stand alone as syllables, rules 4 and 5 apply to their spelling and the vowels [o] and [e] remain in the syllables.

For example:

a. [iou], [uei] and [uen] combine with initials other than [y] and [w]:

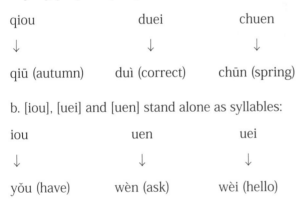

qiou	duei	chuen
↓	↓	↓
qiū (autumn)	duì (correct)	chūn (spring)

b. [iou], [uei] and [uen] stand alone as syllables:

iou	uen	uei
↓	↓	↓
yǒu (have)	wèn (ask)	wèi (hello)

Rule 7. When the finals beginning with [ü] occur without a preceding initial, the umlaut mark drops and the semi vowel [y] is added in front of the syllable.

For instance:

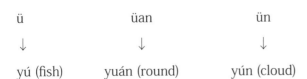

ü	üan	ün
↓	↓	↓
yú (fish)	yuán (round)	yún (cloud)

PINYIN

xué   hàn   zì

学　汉　字

Learning Chinese Characters

Basic Character Strokes

Writing Chinese characters is one of the basic skills required for learning the language. Chinese learners must first recognize the shape of a character, know its pronunciation and meaning, and know how to reproduce the character in order to be fully literate. Even in the computerized Chinese classroom, in which characters are typed rather than written by hand, it is still important to understand character structures, as they provides important clues for understanding and memorizing characters. Let's begin by acquainting ourselves with the basics of Chinese character strokes.

Types of Strokes

Chinese characters are not written in alphabetic or syllabic symbols but by combining strokes called bǐhuà. A Chinese word can consist of as few as one stroke, such as 一, or as many as 17–20 strokes, such as 赢. There are about 23–27 different strokes that are used to form characters, with six being the most basic and fundamental. The following are lists of (1) the six basic strokes, (2) the most frequently used combination strokes and (3) rules of stroke order.

[1]　hàn   zì   jī   běn   bǐ   huà

　　　　汉　字　基　本　笔　画

Basic Strokes of Chinese Characters

笔画 Stroke	笔画的名称 Name of the Stroke	笔画的书写 Direction in Which the Stroke is Written	范例 Example Characters Formed with the Stroke
丶	点 diǎn (the dot)	↘	今　太
一	横 héng (the horizontal stroke)	→	二　下
丨	竖 shù (the vertical stroke)	↓	上　十
丿	撇 piě (the sweep to the left)	↙	八　人
丶	捺 nà (the sweep to the right)	↘	大　人
／	提 tí (the upward stroke)	↗	抄　我

(2) hàn   zì   cháng yòng fù   hé   bǐ   huà
汉   字   常   用   复   合   笔   画

Combination Strokes of Chinese Characters

笔画 Stroke	笔画的名称 Name of the Stroke	笔画的书写 Direction in Which the Stroke is Written	范例 Example Characters Formed with the Stroke
ㄱ	横折 héngzhé (the horizontal turn)	ㄱ	口 日
ㄴ	竖折 shùzhé (the vertical turn)	ㄴ	亡 忙
⅃	竖钩 shùōu (the vertical hook)	⅃	小 丁
⌐	横钩 hénggōu (the horizontal hook)	⌐	字 民
ㄴ	竖弯钩 shùwāngōu (the vertical turn-hook)	ㄴ	乱 龙

(3) bǐ   shùn guī   zé
笔   顺   规   则

Rules of Stroke Order

When writing Chinese characters, it is important to write the strokes in the correct order. This is necessary for writing the character clearly and accurately, and for knowing the number of strokes in a given character, if you need to look it up in a dictionary. The table below shows the order in which strokes are written.

bǐ shùn guī zé 筆 順 規 則 (Rules for Stroke Order in Chinese)	Rules for Stroke Order in English	Examples Lì zì 例 字
xiān héng hòu shù 先 橫 後 豎	First horizontal, then vertical	十 一 丨
xiān piě hòu nà 先 撇 後 捺	First left falling, then right falling	人 丿 丶
cóng shàng dào xià 從 上 到 下	From top to bottom	您 你 心
cóng zuǒ dào yòu 從 左 到 右	From left to right	好 女 子
cóng wài dào nèi 從 外 到 內	From outside to inside	月 几 二
xiān lǐ biān hòu fēng kǒu 先 裏 邊 後 封 口	First inside, then seal at the bottom	國 门 一
xiān zhōng jiān hòu liǎng biān 先 中 間 後 兩 邊	First middle, then both sides	小 亅 八

tīng shuō liàn xí

听 说 练 习

▶ **Exercises for Listening and Speaking**

· ·

🎧 一、完成对话。**(1. Work in pairs to complete the dialogue.)**

(An American student meets his new Chinese friend on campus.)

A: Xiǎo Wén, dào Dà Huá Diànyǐngyuàn zěnme qù?

B: _____

A: 14 lù gōnggòng qìchē zhàn zài nǎr?

B: _____

A: Kěshì běi xiàomén zài nǎr?

B: Guò le tǐyùguǎn jiù shì. Nǐ qù diànyǐngyuàn kàn shénme diànyǐng?

A: _____

B: Wǒ yě xiǎng qù, wǒmen kěyǐ yìqǐ qù.

A: _____

B: Wǒmen shénme shíhòu qù?

A: _____

🎧 二、听对话，回答问题。**(2. Listen to the conversation and answer the questions.)**

1. What did A invite B to do?

_____

2. Why didn't B want to play ball?

_____

3. Did B want to go to the party?

_____

4. What did B want to do?

_____

5. What did they finally agree to do?

_____

三、先听对话，然后两人一组朗读。**(3. Listen to the following conversation without looking at the book, and then read it aloud in pairs, first by following the pinyin, then by following the characters.)**

Jiǎ:	Wǒmen xiàwǔ chūqù wánr ba.
Yǐ:	Duìbuqǐ, wǒ sān diǎn zài jiā xué Yīngwén.
Jiǎ:	Nà yìqǐ qù wǎnhuì.
Yǐ:	Wǎnhuì duō méi yìsi.
Jiǎ:	Qù kàn Měiguó dàpiān zěnmeyàng?
Yǐ:	Qù kàn Měiguó dàpiān? Zhēn bàng! Wǒ yào gēn wǒ nánpéngyou yìqǐ qù.
Jiǎ:	Nǐ yǒu nánpéngyou le?
Yǐ:	Wáng Jiāshēng shì wǒ nánpéngyou.
jiǎ:	Nà wǒ zuò shénme ne?
Yǐ:	Nǐ gēn wǒmen yìqǐ qù ba.
jiǎ:	Nà hǎo ba, yīhuìr jiàn.

甲：	我们下午出去玩儿吧。
乙：	对不起，我三点在家学英文。
甲：	那一起去晚会。
乙：	晚会多没意思。
甲：	去看美国大片怎么样？
乙：	去看美国大片？真棒！我要跟我男朋友一起去。
甲：	你有男朋友了？
乙：	王家生是我男朋友。
甲：	那我做什么呢？
乙：	你跟我们一起去吧。
甲：	那好吧，一会儿见。

四、角色表演 **(4. Role Play)**

1. A: Invite your friend out on Saturday night.

   B: You have been invited to go out, but you don't want to go. Find some excuses to refuse the invitation.

2. A: You are a new student. You want to go to the library but do not know where it is. You ask an older student that you meet on campus where it is.

B: You are an older student on the way to see a movie. A freshman asks you how to get to the library. You tell him/her how to get to the library, but at the same time, invite him/her to see the movie with you.

dián năo yŭ hàn zì liàn xí
电 脑 与 汉 字 练 习

▶ **Exercises for Computing and Learning Characters**

· ·

一、打出下面段落。 *(1. Type the following passage.)*

　　王小年请他的中国朋友去看电影，可是他的中国朋友不喜欢看电影。他问王小年去不去打球，王小年说没意思。他们说好坐三路公共汽车去酒吧玩儿。

二、把下面拼音句子打成汉字。*(2. Type the following pinyin sentences and select the appropriate characters from the list that appears on your computer screen.)*

1. Míngtiān wǎnshang wǒmen qù kàn diànyǐng ba.

2. Chū xiàomén, yī guǎi, zài dì èr ge shízì lùkǒu yǒu yī ge tǐyùguǎn.

3. 14 lù chēzhàn zài hónglǜdēng pángbiān.

4. Tāmen dào hē jiǔ de niánlíng le ma?

5. Suàn le, wǒ yào gēn wǒ de nánpéngyǒu qù tiàowǔ, nǐ zài jiā shuìjiào ba.

三、圈出正确的汉字。 *(3. Circle the correct character to fill in the blanks.)*

1. 你每＿＿（开、毛、兀、天、大）去酒吧喝酒吗？

2. ＿＿（不、吓、下、丁、才）课以后我们去吃中国饭。

3. 老师是在美国＿＿（千、仨、牲、生、仁）的吗？

4. 你喜欢看 ___（曰、目、旦、日、闩）报还是晚报？

5. 我们去学校的舞 ___（仓、荟、会、令、全），好吗？

四、读生字，找出偏旁部首。*(4. The characters in each of the following groups share a radical. Read the characters and write the shared radicals).*

Example: 这 迎 shared radical：辶

1. 红 绿 shared radical:_____

2. 酒 汽 shared radical:_____

3. 看 睡 shared radical:_____

4. 拐 打 shared radical:_____

5. 意 思 shared radical:_____

五、把汉字分成部件。*(5. Test your understanding of character structure by dividing the following characters into their component parts.)*

Example: 吗—>口 马

1. 明—>_____

2. 男—>_____

3. 意—>_____

4. 思—>_____

5. 原—>_____

六、学生字。*(6. Learning New Characters)*

独体词组复合词。(Form compound words based on single-character words.)

注释 (Note): Most Chinese characters are words themselves, called 独 (dú, single) 体 (tǐ, body) 词. In this exercise you will be asked to find compound words that contain some common single-character words you have already learned.

Study the following characters selected from the New Words lists: 大* 二 不 好* 的

1. Copy each character by hand using the character writing demonstration sheet.

2. For each character marked with an asterisk, find the compounds in which the characters are used in the text, and write the compound words next to the characters.

3. With the assistance of a dictionary or an online dictionary, write down three more compounds in which these single-character words appear.

4. For each character marked with an asterisk, make a sentence with one of the three new compounds.

Character Writing Demonstration Sheet 第三课　　姓名＿＿＿＿＿＿

Pinyin	Strokes	Structure	English	Radical	Traditional Form
dà	3	single-body	big	大	大

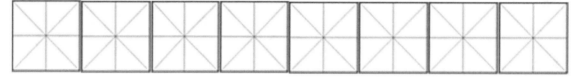

Pinyin	Strokes	Structure	English	Radical	Traditional Form
èr	2	single-body	two	一	二

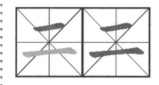
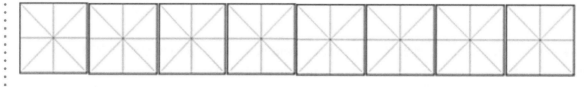

Pinyin	Strokes	Structure	English	Radical	Traditional Form
bù	4	single-body	not	一	不

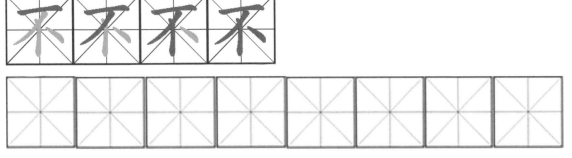

Pinyin	Strokes	Structure	English	Radical	Traditional Form
hǎo	6	left-right	good	女	好

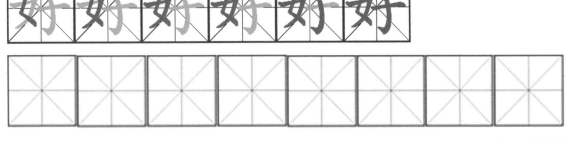

Pinyin	Strokes	Structure	English	Radical	Traditional Form
de	8	left-right	(a particle)	白	的

kè wén liàn xí

课 文 练 习

▶ **Exercises for Understanding the Texts**

· ·

一、根据课文回答问题。*(1. Answer the questions orally based on the text.)*

对话（1）

1. 王家生和张小妹明天要去做什么？

   What are Jiasheng Wang and Xiaomei Zhang going to do tomorrow?

2. 美国大片是什么意思？

   What is the meaning of 美国大片？

3. 他们到哪儿去看电影？

   Where are they going to see the movie?

4. 他们怎么去看电影？

   How will they go?

5. "不见不散" 是什么意思？

   What is the meaning of 不见不散？

对话（2）

1. 约翰请苏珊做什么？

   What did John invite Susan to do?

2. 苏珊为什么不去？

   Why didn't Susan want to go?

3. 苏珊喜欢打球吗？为什么？

   Does Susan like playing ball?

4. 为什么苏珊不想去王小年的生日晚会？

   Why didn't Susan want to go to Xiaonian Wang's birthday party?

5. 为什么苏珊不去酒吧？

   Why didn't Susan go to the bar?

6. 苏珊明天晚上要去做什么？

   What was Susan going to do the next night?

二、完成对话。*(2. Complete the dialogue orally.)*

A: 王小年，去打球吧。

B: _____。

A: 下午两点，怎么样？

B: _____。

A: 那，晚上六点，好吗？

B: _____？

A: 在学校体育馆。

B: _____。

三、先填空，再朗读句子。*(3. Fill in the blanks by choosing the correct negation word 沒 or 不, and then read the sentences aloud.)*

1. 我姐姐跟我哥哥都_____是大学生。

2. 王小年有一个哥哥和一个妹妹，他_____有弟弟。

3. 苏珊去餐厅吃饭了，因为她_____吃饭。

4. Green 说他_____叫格林了，小文给他起了一个中文名字。

5. 你妹妹有_____有中文名字？

四、作文 *(4. Composition)*

Type a few sentences (5-6) expressing what you like to do in your spare time and what you dislike.

五、翻译 *(5. Translation)*

Translate the following sentences orally in class. Then type your translations in Chinese using the words and phrases provided.

1. Xiaonian Wang, let's go play ball. （吧）Play ball? Oh, no, it's too tiring. （太．．．）

3. How about going to a party tomorrow? （那，怎么样）

4. You don't like my calling you by your English name, so I'll call you by your Chinese name.

5. It's not 10 o'clock yet. Let's go see a movie. （没到，吧）

6. You don't like movies? OK, forget it. （算了吧）

7. Let's meet at the gate of our school. Don't leave without me. （不见不散）

8. Professor Wang will treat his students to Chinese food tomorrow. （请）Oh, super! Where are they going to eat? （哪儿）

bǔ　chōng yuè　dú　liàn　xí
补　充　阅　读　练　习
▶ Supplementary Reading Exercises

(1) Controlled Vocabulary

Read the following two passages and answer the questions.

A:　大华电影院，你好！
B:　请问，明天有什么电影？
A:　新到的美国大片。
B:　太好了，还有票(piào, ticket) 吗？
A:　有，你要几张(zhāng, measure word) ？

Questions

1. Where did this conversation take place?

2. What did the woman want?

3. What kind of movie was playing at the theater?

4. Were tickets available?

A: 请问，到大华电影院怎么走？
B: 在学校门口坐十四路汽车到大新路下车。
A: 车站是在北校门的左边吗？
B: 是，在那个路口的红绿灯旁边。
A: 谢谢，谢谢！
B: 不客气。

Questions

1. Where did this conversation take place?

2. Where is the movie theater?

3. How does one get to the movie theater?

4. Where is the bus stop?

(2) Open Vocabulary

This exercise is called "Open Vocabulary" because it contains some vocabulary words that have not been introduced in this book. In this exercise, you should first look for words you already recognize, and then try to guess the meaning of an entire phrase or sentence based on the words you already know. When you get stuck, use a dictionary to look up words whose meanings are crucial to your understanding of the passage. You can also retrieve an electronic version of this text from the accompanying online materials, and use an online dictionary or translation program to help you read it.

After answering the questions, try to tell the story to a classmate in your own words without looking at the original text.

只用一只眼睛看

A: 电影票多少钱一张？
B: 一块钱，孩子。
A: 我只带了五毛钱。能不能让我进去？我只用一只眼睛看。

Questions

1. Where did this conversation take place?

2. What did the child want?

3. How much was the ticket?

4. Why did the child want to see the movie with just one eye?

Chinese Customs and Culture

....

zhōng guó de shǎo shù mín zú

中　国　的　少　数　民　族

▶ **China's Ethnic Minorities**

In contrast to its neighbors Japan and Korea, China is not a homogeneous country in ethnic or cultural terms. In fact, in addition to strong regional divisions, the People's Republic of China contains more than fifty minority groups within its borders. The Chinese government officially recognizes fifty-six ethnic groups, with the largest being the Han 汉 or "ethnic Chinese" nationality. According to most estimates, the Han comprise about 92-93 percent of the population of the People's Republic of China. With a total population of 1.3 billion people, this means that China has more than 90 million non-Han citizens, a number comparable to a large independent nation; by way of comparison, Germany has about 80 million people, while France, Italy, and the United Kingdom have about 60 million each.

Many of the minority groups of China are the descendants of people the Chinese once considered "barbarians." Like the peoples of ancient Greece and Rome, the Chinese had a strong sense of the superiority of their civilization and regarded other ethnicities with suspicion and contempt. Traditionally, this feeling of superiority was strongest with regard to the nomadic and pastoral people who lacked agriculture, writing, and other key features that the Chinese had developed much earlier. This negative attitude was somewhat reversed after the establishment of the People's Republic, when the Chinese government embarked on a propaganda campaign to show their good will to their ethnic minority citizens, perhaps in order to contrast their position with the imperialism and colonialism of Western capitalist countries. The Constitution of the People's Republic specifically guarantees equal rights for minority groups.

The ethnic diversity of China is often not evident to the casual observer or short-term visitor, as a major portion of the minority nationalities live outside the major urban centers of coastal China. Minority groups in China are referred to as 少数民族 (shǎoshù mínzú). Shǎoshù means "minority" and mínzú means "ethnicity." The single character 族 (zú) is usually attached to the name of an ethnic group; for example, 汉族 refers to the ethnic Han Chinese. It is important to remember that the English word "Chinese" can also refer more broadly to 中国人, or any people of Chinese heritage, regardless of ethnicity.

The most populous ethnic groups in China live in their own autonomous regions or provinces. The largest group numbers over 18 million and is called the 壮族 (Zhuàngzú). They live primarily in the far south of China in Guangxi province, where they have their own autonomous region called the 广西壮族自治区 (Guǎngxī Zhuàngzú Zìzhìqū). The Zhuang are ethnically related to the people of Thailand and Laos, and their language belongs to the Tai linguistic family. The Zhuang are one of five minority nationalities that, in addition to their own autonomous regions, also have publishing and broadcasting in their native languages. The other groups in this category are the Koreans 朝鲜族 (Cháoxiǎnzú), Tibetans 藏族 (Zàngzú), Mongolians 蒙古族 (Měnggǔzú), and Uighurs 维吾尔族 (Wéiwú'ěrzú).

The Koreans occupy many areas in the northeast of China, centering around the Yanbian Korean Autonomous Prefecture[1] 延边朝鲜族自治州 (Yánbiān Cháoxiǎnzú Zìzhìzhōu) in Jilin 吉林 (Jílín) Province. They number over two million people, and many have close contacts with their fellow Koreans in North and South Korea. In recent years, China has experienced a "Korean Wave," 韩流 (Hánliú) a surge of interest in South Korean popular culture, including music, TV shows, and fashion that has increased trade and cultural exchange with South Korea and opened new opportunities for ethnic Koreans in China.

The Tibetans in China number more than six million. Most live in the far southwest of China, the 西藏自治区 (Xīzàng Zìzhìqū, Tibet Autonomous Region), and are followers of Buddhism and a native religion called Bon. The Tibetans have been the focus of an internationally prominent separatist movement led by the Dalai Lama, whose Tibetan government in exile is located in India. The capital of the province of Tibet is Lhasa.

The Mongolians in China's Inner Mongolia 内蒙古 (Nèiménggǔ) province actually outnumber the Mongolians living in the independent nation of Mongolia. The Mongolians retain many of their traditions, including the Buddhist religion and a nomadic lifestyle. While the Mongolians of the independent nation of Mongolia write in a Russian-derived Cyrillic script, those in China's Inner Mongolia continue to use the traditional script (adapted from an old Uighur script) for writing their language.

The Uighurs number more than eight million people. They live primarily in Xinjiang province 新疆维吾尔自治区 (Xīnjiāng Wéiwú'ěr Zìzhìqū) in China's far northwest. They are a Turkic group and are Muslims. The Uighurs once ruled a vast empire in Central Asia and have a strong sense of ethnic and national identity. Like the Tibetans, the Uighurs have had a strong separatist movement. The Uighurs write their language (which is related to Turkish and other Central Asian Turkic languages) in the Arabic script.

The other prominent Muslim group in China is known as the Hui 回族 (Huízú). The classification of the Hui in China is a matter of controversy as many of them are ethnic Chinese whose descendants converted to Islam, while others are descendants of Muslim traders who settled in China and intermarried with local women. The Hui are the main inhabitants of Ningxia province 宁夏回族自治区 (Níngxià Huízú Zìzhìqū).

▶ Test Your Knowledge

Identify these regions and ethnic minorities in China.

Do some Internet research to answer the questions below. Then discuss your findings with your teacher.

1. How many provinces are there in the People's Republic of China? Which do you think are the richest and which are poorest?
2. Where are the largest concentrations of minority peoples in China?
3. What are the two largest Muslim groups in China? Where are they located? Identify their autonomous regions on the map.
4. Which two minority groups in China are strong practitioners of Buddhism? Where are they located? Identify their autonomous regions on the map.
5. Guangxi province has the most minority groups of any Chinese province. Compile a list of as many Guangxi minority groups as you can.

---

[1] 自治区 (Zìzhìqū, autonomous region) is equivalent to a province in China, while 自治州 (Zìzhìzhōu, autonomous prefecture) is an administrative level directly under a province.

xué zhōng wén
学　中　文
Learning Chinese

▶ **Objectives:**

1. To talk about Chinese language studies
2. To ask questions about language study

duì   huà   yī

对   话   （一）

DIALOGUE 1

zěn   me   xué   zhōng wén

怎   么   学   中   文

▶ **How to Study Chinese**

··

shēng cí

生   词

 **New Words**

	Chinese	Pinyin	Part of Speech	English
1.	会	huì	AV	be able to; can; know (how to)
2.	一点儿	yīdiǎnr	CE	a bit; a little
3.	现在	xiànzài	N	now; at present
4.	觉得	juéde	V	feel; think
5.	难	nán	Adj	difficult; hard
6.	语音	yǔyīn	N	speech sounds; pronunciation
7.	语法	yǔfǎ	N	grammar
8.	汉字	Hànzì	N	Chinese character
9.	最	zuì	Ad	most; -est
10.	用	yòng	V	use; employ; apply
11.	就	jiù	Ad	right away; already; as soon as; only; merely; exactly; precisely
12.	容易	róngyì	Adj	easy; likely; liable

126   **LESSON 4** ▶ Learning Chinese

13.	多	duō	Adj	many; much
14.	声调	shēngdiào	N	tone; the tone of a Chinese character
15.	比较	bǐjiào	Ad	fairly; comparatively; quite
16.	特别	tèbié	Adj/Ad	special; particular; especially; particularly
17.	时候	shíhou	N	time; moment
18.	开始	kāishǐ	V/N	begin; start; initial stage; beginning
19.	发	fā	V	send out; issue; deliver; distribute; express
20.	音	yīn	N	sound
21.	准	zhǔn	V/Adj	allow; permit; standard; accurate; exact
22.	哪里	nǎli	QW	where; (a polite response to decline a compliment)
23.	每	měi	Adj	every; each; per; often
24.	还	hái	Ad	still; yet; too; as well; in addition
25.	练	liàn	V	practice; train; drill
26.	难怪	nánguài	Ad	no wonder; understandable; pardonable
27.	老外	lǎowài	CE	(used in Mainland China to refer to foreigners)
	外	wài	Adj	outside; foreign; external
28.	这么	zhème	Pron	so
29.	拼音	pīnyīn	N	pinyin, the combination of sounds into syllables; spelling
30.	输入	shūrù	V	input; import
31.	省下	shěngxià	V	save up
	省	shěng	V	save; omit

32.	时间	shíjiān	N		time
33.	练习	liànxí	V		practice; exercise
34.	会话	huìhuà	N		conversation
35.	阅读	yuèdú	N		reading
36.	写作	xiězuò	N		writing
37.	写	xiě	V		write; compose
38.	抄写	chāoxiě	V		copy; transcribe
39.	等	děng	V		wait; await; when; till
40.	高	gāo	Adj		tall; high; of a high level or degree
41.	年级	niánjí	N		grade; year
42.	认识	rènshi	V		know; understand; recognize
43.	千	qiān	Num		thousand
44.	手	shǒu	N		hand
45.	方法	fāngfǎ	N		method; way; means
46.	听起来	tīngqǐlái	V		sound like
	听	tīng	V		listen
47.	试	shì	V		try

pīn yīn kè wén

拼 音 课 文

Text with Pinyin

▶▶▶

As you read, underline the compound words and phrases, as below:

kuài qù cān tīng chī fàn ba, zài jiàn.
快 去 餐 厅 吃 饭 吧，再 见。

gé lín: nǐ hǎo! qǐng wèn nǐ huì shuō zhōng wén ma?
格 林： 你 好！请 问 你 会 说 中 文 吗？

wáng xiǎo nián: wǒ huì shuō yī diǎnr. nǐ zěn me huì
王 小 年：我 会 说 一 点 儿。你 怎 么 会
shuō zhōng wén?
说 中 文 ？

gé lín: wǒ zài zhōng guó xué le yī nián zhōng wén.
格 林： 我 在 中 国 学 了 一 年 中 文。
xiàn zài hái zài shàng zhōng wén kè.
现 在 还 在 上 中 文 课。

wáng xiǎo nián: nǐ jué de zhōng wén nán ma?
王 小 年：你 觉 得 中 文 难 吗？

gé lín: yǔ yīn hé yǔ fǎ bù tài nán, hàn zì
格 林： 语 音 和 语 法 不 太 难，汉 字
zuì nán. kě shì wǒ yòng diàn nǎo xué, jiù
最 难。可 是 我 用 电 脑 学，就
róng yì duō le.
容 易 多 了。

wáng xiǎo nián: zhōng wén de shēng diào yě bǐ jiào nán, wǒ
王 小 年：中 文 的 声 调 也 比 较 难，我
dōu shuō bù hǎo.
都 说 不 好。

格 林： gé lín:
在 中 国 的 时 候，老 师 告 诉
zài zhōng guó de shí hòu, lǎo shī gào su
我 们，从 开 始 就 发 准 每 一
wǒ men, cóng kāi shǐ jiù fā zhǔn měi yī
个 音 和 声 调，下 课 以 后 还
gè yīn hé shēng diào, xià kè yǐ hòu hái
要 多 练。
yào duō liàn.

王 小 年： wáng xiǎo nián:
难 怪 你 这 个 老 外 说 得 这
nán guài nǐ zhè ge lǎo wài shuō de zhè
么 准。
me zhǔn.

格 林： gé lín:
哪 里，哪 里。我 说 得 还 不 好，
nǎ lǐ, nǎ lǐ. wǒ shuō de hái bù hǎo,
不 太 流 利。
bù tài liú lì.

王 小 年： wáng xiǎo nián:
请 告 诉 我 怎 么 用 电 脑 学
qǐng gào sù wǒ zěn me yòng diàn nǎo xué
汉 字，好 吗？
hàn zì, hǎo ma?

格 林： gé lín:
好。我 从 开 始 就 用 拼 音 输
hǎo. wǒ cóng kāi shǐ jiù yòng pīn yīn shū
入 汉 字，省 下 了 很 多 时 间
rù hàn zì, shěng xià le hěn duō shí jiān
练 习 发 音、会 话、阅 读 和 写
liàn xí fā yīn, huì huà, yuè dú hé xiě
作。
zuò.

王 小 年： wáng xiǎo nián:
那 你 会 不 会 写 汉 字？
nà nǐ huì bù huì xiě hàn zì?

格林: gé lín

我 wǒ 也 yě 练 liàn 习 xí 抄 chāo 写 xiě 汉 hàn 字 zì，但 dàn 是 shì 会 huì 写 xiě 的 de 不 bù 太 tài 多 duō。老 lǎo 师 shī 说 shuō 等 děng 我 wǒ 们 men 到 dào 了 le 高 gāo 年 nián 级 jí，认 rèn 识 shi 了 le 几 jǐ 千 qiān 个 ge 汉 hàn 字 zì 了 le，那 nà 时 shí 再 zài 学 xué 手 shǒu 写 xiě 汉 hàn 字 zì 就 jiù 不 bù 那 nà 么 me 难 nán 了 le。

王 小 年: wáng xiǎo nián

这 zhè 个 ge 方 fāng 法 fǎ 听 tīng 起 qǐ 来 lai 不 bù 错 cuò，我 wǒ 以 yǐ 后 hòu 也 yě 要 yào 试 shì 试 shì。

汉 字 课 文
hàn zì kè wén

Text in Chinese Characters

格林:　你好！请问你会说中文吗？

王小年：我会说一点儿。你怎么会说中文？

格林:　我在中国学了一年中文。现在还在上中文课。

王小年：你觉得中文难吗？

格林:　语音和语法不太难，汉字最难。可是我用电脑学，就容易多了。

王小年：中文的声调也比较难，我都说不好。

格林:　在中国的时候，老师告诉我们，从开始就发准每一个音和声调，下课以后还要多练。

王小年：难怪你这个老外说得这么准。

格林：　哪里，哪里。我说得还不好，不太流利。

王小年：请告诉我怎么用电脑学汉字，好吗？

格林：　好。我从开始就用拼音输入汉字，省下了很多时间练习发音、会话、阅读和写作。

王小年：那你会不会写汉字？

格林：　我也练习抄写汉字，但是会写的不太多。老师说等我们到了高年级，认识了几千个汉字了，那时再学手写汉字就不那么难了。

王小年：这个方法听起来不错，我以后也要试试。

yǔ　yán　yīng　yòng　zhù　shì
语　言　应　用　注　释
Notes on Language Usage

*1. 一点儿

一点儿 means "a little."

For example:

王 小 年 会 说 一 点 儿 中 文。

Wáng Xiǎonián huì shuō yīdiǎnr Zhōngwén.

Xiaonian Wang can speak a little Chinese.

A: 你 跟 我 们 一 起 吃 一 点 儿 吧。

Nǐ gēn wǒmen yīqǐ chī yīdiǎnr ba.

Eat a little something with us.

B: 我 十 二 点 才 吃 饭，不 吃 啦。

Wǒ shí'èr diǎn cái chīfàn, bù chī la.

I just ate at 12:00. I can't eat.

*2. 我在中国学了一年中文。I've studied Chinese in China for a year.

在中国 is a prepositional phrase. In Chinese, a prepositional phrase is placed before the verb, unlike English, where it comes after a verb. Compare the following Chinese sentences and their English equivalents.

他 妈 妈 在 大 学 教 书。

Tā māma zài dàxué jiàoshū.

His mother teaches at a university.

王 小 年 在 家 说 广 东 话。

Wáng Xiǎonián zài jiā shuō Guǎngdōnghuà.

Xiaonian Wang speaks Cantonese at home.

(For details, please see Grammar Book I, Lesson 2.)

*3. 现在还在上中文课。I am still taking Chinese.

在 is used here to indicate an action in progress. It can be replaced by 正在.

For example:

A: 王 小 年 呢？

　　Wáng Xiǎonián ne?

B: 他 （正） 在 打 电 话 呢。

　　Tā zhèngzài dǎ diànhuà ne.

A: Where is Xiaonian Wang?

B: He is making a phone call.

妹 妹 正 在 看 书。

Mèimei zhèngzài kànshū.

My little sister is reading a book.

(For details, please see Grammar Book I, Lesson 7.)

*4. 可是我用电脑学，就容易多了。But it became much easier when I used a computer to learn (Chinese characters).

There are many different uses of the word 就. Here it means that the second clause follows directly after the first. In this way, it is close to the English "then" or "and so." 就 is pronounced in the neutral tone here.

For example:

那 个 中 国 学 生 一 说 中 文 就 想 家。

Nàge Zhōngguó xuéshēng yī shuō Zhōngwén jiu xiǎng jiā.

When that Chinese student speaks Chinese, he misses home.

认 识 了 几 千 个 汉 字 再 学 手 写 就 不 那 么 难 了。

Rènshi le jǐ qiān ge Hànzì zài xué shǒuxiě jiu bù nàme nán le.

If one knows a few thousand characters, then handwriting Chinese is not that difficult.

(For details, please see Grammar Book I, Lesson 9.)

5. 我都说不好。 **Even I can't say it well.**

都 means "even" here. It is sometimes used in conjunction with 连 (lián, even). 都 is pronounced in the neutral tone.

For example:

王 小 年 都 不 喜 欢 广 东 菜。

Wáng Xiǎonián dou bù xǐhuān Guǎngdōng cài.

Even Xiaonian Wang does not like Cantonese food.

(连)王 老 师 都 不 知 道 格 林 有 中 文 名 字。

Lián Wáng lǎoshī dou bù zhīdào Gélín yǒu Zhōngwén míngzi.

Even Professor Wang did not know that Green has a Chinese name.

(For details on the use of 连 (lián, even), please see Grammar Book I, Lesson 10.)

6. 难怪你这个老外说得这么准。 **No wonder you, a foreigner, speak so accurately.**

难怪 means "no wonder," introducing a realization or deduction one has made.

For example:

难 怪 王 小 年 和 他 的 中 国 朋 友 去 吃 广 东 饭，

Nánguài Wáng Xiǎonián hé tā de Zhōngguó péngyǒu qù chī Guǎngdōngfàn,

他 们 是 广 东 老 乡。

tāmen shì Guǎngdōng lǎoxiāng.

No wonder Xiaonian Wang and his Chinese friend went to eat Cantonese food; they are both from Guangdong.

难 怪 王 小 年 中 文 说 得 不 流 利，他 是 在 美 国 生 的。

Nánguài Wáng Xiǎonián Zhōngwén shuō de bù liúlì, tā shì zài Měiguó shēng de.

No wonder Xiaonian Wang cannot speak Chinese fluently. He was born in America.

7. 说得这么准

得 + adjective is called a "complement of degree" in grammar. The complement indicates the degree or nature of the action. Another example can be found in Lesson 2:

你 的 中 文 怎 么 说 得 不 流 利？

Nǐ de Zhōngwén zěnme shuō de bù liúlì?

How come your Chinese is not fluent?

(For details, please see Grammar Book I, Lesson 5.)

8. 老外，老中

老外 is used in Mainland China to refer to foreigners. It is used colloquially. The Chinese have also created the expression 老中 to refer to themselves, as a corresponding term for 老外. 老外＝ 老＋外（国人）and 老中＝老＋中（国人）.

9. 哪里，哪里

This phrase means "where, where?" and is used to respond to a compliment in Chinese. Its pragmatic function is to reject the praise being given. Responding to a compliment in Chinese is very different from doing so in English. In English, when one is praised, he or she should respond with "thank you." However, in China, accepting someone's praise is considered highly inappropriate. The proper way of responding to praise is to show modesty by rejecting it.

For example:

A: 你 的 中 文 说 得 很 流 利。

Nǐ de Zhōngwén shuō de hěn liúlì.

You speak Chinese fluently.

B: 哪 里，哪 里，不 好，不 好。

Nǎlǐ, nǎlǐ, bù hǎo, bù hǎo.

No, no, it's not good at all.

A: 你 的 中 文 发 音 很 准。

Nǐ de Zhōngwén fāyīn hěn zhǔn.

Your Chinese pronunciation is very accurate.

B: 哪 里，哪 里。

Nǎlǐ, nǎlǐ.

No, no.

It is not right to say 谢谢, because if you say so it means that you agree with the compliment, and you will be considered arrogant. However, many young, educated people have now adopted influences from Western languages and will sometimes use 谢谢 to respond to a compliment, particularly if they are speaking to a foreigner.

*10. 你会不会写汉字？ Do you know how to write characters?

a) 会

会 is an auxiliary verb, here meaning "to know how to do" something, especially a learned skill.

For example:

格 林 会 说 中 文，王 小 年 呢？

Gélín huì shuō Zhōngwén, Wáng Xiǎonián ne?

Green can speak Chinese, how about Xiaonian Wang?

你 会 做 今 天 的 作 业 吗 ？

Nǐ huì zuò jīntiān de zuòyè ma?

Do you know how to do today's homework?

(For details, please see Grammar Book I, Lesson 5.)

b) 会不会

This is an "A-not-A" type of question. The format of this type of question is to combine the affirmative form of the verb or adjective and the negative form of the same verb or adjective together to ask a question. The speaker expects either an affirmative or negative answer. When you use "A-not-A" questions, you cannot use other question particles such as 吗 and 吧.

For example:

你 是 不 是 中 国 人 ？

Nǐ shì bù shì Zhōngguó rén?

Are you Chinese?

中 文 难 不 难 ？

Zhōngwén nán bù nán?

Is Chinese difficult?

格 林 有 没 有 中 国 朋 友 ？

Gélín yǒu méiyǒu Zhōngguó péngyou?

Does Green have any Chinese friends?

(For details, please see Grammar Book I, Lesson 2.)

11. 听起来

This phrase means "sounds like..."

For example:

那 个 电 影 听 起 来 很 有 意 思 。

Nàge diànyǐng tīng qǐlái hěn yǒu yìsi.

The movie sounds very interesting.

(For details, please see Grammar Book I, Lesson 9.)

duì huà èr
对 话 （二）

DIALOGUE 2

wèn wèn tí
问 问 题

▶ Asking Questions

··

shēng cí
生 词

◉ New Words

	Chinese	Pinyin	Part of Speech	English
1.	问题	wèntí	N	question; problem
2.	作业	zuòyè	N	school assignment; homework
3.	里	lǐ	N	inside
4.	单数	dānshù	N	single number
5.	组	zǔ	N	group; set; series
6.	以前	yǐqián	TW	before; formerly; previously
7.	意思	yìsi	N	meaning
8.	句	jù	N	sentence
9.	刚才	gāngcái	Ad	just now; a moment ago
10.	书	shū	N	book
11.	好像	hǎoxiàng	V/Ad	seem; be like
12.	对	duì	Adj	right
13.	介词	jiècí	N	preposition
14.	同	tóng	Prep/Adj	with; same

15.	向	xiàng	Prep	face; turn towards
16.	懂	dǒng	N	understand; know
17.	走	zǒu	V	walk; go, leave
18.	谢谢	xièxie	V	thanks; thank you
19.	客气	kèqi	Adj	polite; courteous; modest

pīn yīn kè wén
拼 音 课 文

Text with Pinyin

▶▶▶

gé lín:	lǎo shī, wǒ kě yǐ wèn nín liǎng gè wèn
格 林:	老 师，我 可 以 问 您 两 个 问
	tí ma?
	题 吗？

| gāo lǎo shī: | shén me wèn tí? |
| 高 老 师: | 什 么 问 题？ |

gé lín:	zuò yè lǐ yǒu yī jù huà shuō: "xiǎo wáng
格 林:	作 业 里 有 一 句 话 说 "小 王
	tā men shàng kè qù le." xiǎo wáng shì dān
	他 们 上 课 去 了。" 小 王 是 单
	shù, wéi shén me yòng "tā men?"
	数，为 什 么 用 "他 们？"

gāo lǎo shī:	zhè lǐ shuō de shì xiǎo wáng hé tā de
高 老 师:	这 里 说 的 是 小 王 和 他 的
	péng yǒu men, yě jiù shì gēn tā yī qǐ
	朋 友 们，也 就 是 跟 他 一 起
	de nà zǔ rén.
	的 那 组 人。

格林: gé lín:
我们以前在书里学的"跟"是"和"的意思。可是在"跟他一起的那组人"这句话里，"跟"好像不是"和"的意思。

wǒ men yǐ qián zài shū lǐ xué de "gēn" shì "hé" de yì sī. kě shì zài "gēn tā yī qǐ de nà zǔ rén" zhè jù huà lǐ, "gēn" hǎo xiàng bú shì "hé" de yì sī.

高老师: gāo lǎo shī:
对，"跟"也可以作介词，意思是"同"(with)、"向"、"对"(to)。

duì, "gēn" yě kě yǐ zuò jiè cí, yì si shì "tóng"(with)、"xiàng"、"duì"(to).

格林: gé lín:
懂了，谢谢老师，我走了。

dǒng le, xiè xie lǎo shī, wǒ zǒu le.

高老师: gāo lǎo shī:
不客气，再见。

bù kè qi, zài jiàn.

hàn zì kè wén
汉 字 课 文
🔘 **Text in Chinese Characters**

▶▶▶

格林： 老师，我可以问您两个问题吗？

高老师：什么问题？

格林： 作业里有一句话说：<u>小王他们</u>上课<u>去</u>了。"小王"是
单数，为什么用 "他们"？

高老师：这里说的是小王和他的朋友们，也就是跟他一起的
那组人。

格林： 我们以前在书里学的"跟"是"和"的意思。可是在
"跟他一起的那组人"这句话里"跟"好像不是"和"
的意思。

高老师：对，"跟"也可以作介词，意思是"同"(with)、
"向"、"对"(to)。

格林： 懂了，谢谢老师，<u>我走了</u>。

高老师：不客气，再见。

◀◀◀

yǔ yán yīng yòng zhù shì
语 言 应 用 注 释
Notes on Language Usage

1. 小王他们上课去了。**Xiao Wang and his group went to class.**

a) 小王他们 means "Xiao Wang and his group."

For example:

小 王 他 们 明 天 不 去 看 电 影，他 们 去 打 球。

Xiǎo Wáng tāmen míngtiān bù qù kàn diànyǐng, tāmen qù dǎ qiú.

Xiao Wang and his friends are not going to see the movie tomorrow. They are going to play ball.

老 张 他 们 去 看 电 影。

Lǎo Zhāng tāmen qù kàn diànyǐng.

Lao Zhang and his friends are going to see the movie.

b) 上课去了

去 is used after the verb and object to indicate direction of the action. Here it indicates that 小王他们 (Xiao Wang and his group) move away from where the speaker is to class. This type of sentence is called a simple directional complement.

For example:

王 家 生 和 张 小 妹 看 电 影 去 了 。

Wáng Jiāshēng hé Zhāng Xiǎomèi kàn diànyǐng qù le.

Jiasheng Wang and Xiaomei Zhang went (out) to see the movie.

(For details, please see Grammar Book I, Lesson 8.)

2. 我走了

我走了 means "I am leaving." The word 走 has two meanings; one is "to walk," and the other is "to leave."

For example:

我 们 走 到 电 影 院 去 。

Wǒmen zǒu dào diànyǐngyuàn qù.

We will walk to the movie theater.

飞 机 场 很 远 ，不 能 走 去 。

Fēijīcháng hěn yuǎn, bù néng zǒu qù.

The airport is very far. We can't walk there.

▶ University students learning Chinese in Shanghai.

老师 很 忙，我们 走 吧。

Lǎoshī hěn máng, wǒmen zǒu ba.

The teacher is very busy, so let's go.

小 王，我 走 了。我 要 去 上 课。

Xiǎo Wáng, wǒ zǒu le. Wǒ yào qù shàng kè.

Xiao Wang, I've got to go. I am going to class.

NARRATION

xù   shù

叙 述

▶ **Narration**

....

shēng cí

生 词

New Words

	Chinese	Pinyin	Part of Speech	English
1.	讨论	tǎolùn	V	discuss
2.	四声	sìshēng	N	the four tones

pīn yīn kè wén

拼 音 课 文

Text with Pinyin

▶▶▶

wáng	xiǎo	nián	hé	gé	lín	tǎo	lùn	xué	xí	zhōng	wén
王	小	年	和	格	林	讨	论	学	习	中	文

de	wèn	tí.	gé	lín	shuō	zhōng	wén	yǔ	yīn	hé	yǔ	fǎ
的	问	题。	格	林	说	中	文	语	音	和	语	法

bù	tài	nán,	kě	shì	hàn	zì	bǐ	jiào	nán.	wáng	xiǎo	nián
不	太	难，	可	是	汉	字	比	较	难。	王	小	年

jué	de	zhōng	wén	de	shēng	diào	yě	bǐ	jiào	nán,	tè	bié
觉	得	中	文	的	声	调	也	比	较	难，	特	别

是四声，因为他在家说广东话。王小年说格林中文发音很好，可是格林说他说得不好，不流利。他还告诉王小年怎么用电脑学习中文。他从开始就用拼音输入汉字，省下来了很多时间练习发音、会话、阅读和写作。他也练习抄写汉字，可是会写的汉字不太多。老师说等他们到了高年级，认识了几千个汉字了，那时再学手写汉字就不那么难了。格林说他现在觉得学中文不太难了。王小年说这个方法听起来不错，他以后也要试试。

Text in Chinese Characters

▶▶▶

　　王小年和格林讨论学习中文的问题。格林说中文语音和语法不太难，可是汉字比较难。王小年觉得中文的声调也比较难，特别是四声，因为他在家说广东话。王小年说格林中文发音很好，可是格林说他说得不好，不流利。他还告诉王小年怎么用电脑学习中文。他从开始就用拼音输入汉字，省下来了很多时间练习发音、会话、阅读和写作。他也练习抄写汉字，可是会写的汉字不太多。老师说等他们到了高年级，认识了几千个汉字了，那时再学手写汉字就不那么难了。格林说他现在觉得学中文不太难了。王小年说这个方法听起来不错，他以后也要试试。　◀◀◀

▶ English Translations of the Texts

Dialogue 1

Green:	Hello. May I ask you if you can speak Chinese?
Xiaonian Wang:	I can speak a little. How did you learn to speak Chinese?
Green:	I studied Chinese in China for a year, and I'm still taking Chinese now.
Xiaonian Wang:	Do you think Chinese is difficult?
Green:	The pronunciation and grammar are not too difficult. Chinese characters are the most difficult, but it became much easier when I used a computer to learn (Chinese characters).
Xiaonian Wang:	The intonation of Chinese is also quite hard. Even I can't say it well.
Green:	When I was in China, the teacher told us to pronounce every sound and tone accurately from the very beginning. We also practiced a lot after class.
Xiaonian Wang:	No wonder you, a foreigner, speak so accurately.
Green:	No, no. I still do not speak well and I am not very fluent.
Xiaonian Wang:	Could you tell me how to use the computer to learn Chinese?
Green:	Sure. I input Chinese characters with pinyin from the very beginning. So I saved a lot of time for practicing pronunciation, conversation, and reading and writing compositions.
Xiaonian Wang:	Then do you know how to write characters?
Green:	I also practice copying characters, but can write very little. The teacher said that when we get to the advanced level, we will have learned a few thousand characters. By that time, learning how to write characters by hand will not be that difficult.
Xiaonian Wang:	This method sounds good. I will also try it.

NARRATION

Dialogue 2

Green:	Professor, can I ask you a couple of questions?
Professor Gao:	What questions?
Green:	In the homework, there is a sentence, "Xiao Wang, they, are going to class." Xiao Wang is a singular noun. Why is "they" used here?
Professor Gao:	Here, it refers to "Xiao Wang and his friends," that is, the group with him.
Green:	The word 跟 we learned before means "and." But in this sentence, "the group with him," 跟 does not seem to mean "and."
Professor Gao:	Yes, 跟 can also be used as a preposition. The meaning is "with" or "to."
Green:	Got it, thank you, Professor. I have to go.
Professor Gao:	You're welcome. Bye.

Narration

Xiaonian Wang and Green are discussing the difficulties of learning Chinese. Green says that pronunciation and grammar in Chinese are not too difficult, but that Chinese characters are more difficult. Xiaonian Wang also thinks that the intonation of Chinese is quite hard, especially the four tones, because he speaks Cantonese at home. Wang says that Green's Chinese pronunciation is very good. But Green says that he does not speak well. He does not speak fluently. He also tells Xiaonian Wang how to study Chinese with a computer. He input Chinese characters with pinyin from the very beginning, so he saved a lot of time for practicing pronunciation, conversation, and reading and writing compositions. He also practices copying characters, but he can write very few characters. The teacher says that when they get to the advanced level, they will have learned a few thousand

▶ Learning Chinese calligraphy.

characters. By that time, learning how to write characters by hand will not be that difficult. Green says he feels that learning Chinese is not too difficult now. Xiaonian Wang says that this method sounds good. He would like to try it.

tīng shuō liàn xí
听 说 练 习
▶ Exercises for Listening and Speaking

....

🔘 一、完成对话。*(1. Work in pairs to complete the dialogue.)*

A: Nǐ zěnme huì shuō Zhōngwén?

B: _____

A: Nǐ juéde Zhōngwén nán xué ma?

B: _____

A: Duì nǐmen lǎowài shì Hànzì nán, kěshì duì wǒ zhège lǎozhōng fāyīn gèng nán.

B: _____

A: Yīnwéi wǒ zài jiā shuō Guǎngdōng huà, shuō pǔtōnghuà yīn fā bù zhǔn, shēngdiào gèng nán.

B: _____

A: Yǐhòu wǒ gēn nǐ yìqǐ liàn fāyīn.

B: _____

🔘 二、听对话，回答问题。*(2. Listen to the conversation and answer the questions.)*

1. How does one study Chinese with the computer?

_____

2. Does B write Chinese characters by hand?

_____

3. What can B do with the time saved by typing characters rather than handwriting them?

_____

4. Will B learn how to write by hand later?

_____

5. Does A agree with B's method?

_____

三、先听对话，然后两人一组朗读。*(3. Listen to the following conversation without looking at the book, and then read it aloud in pairs, first by following the pinyin, then by following the characters.)*

Jiǎ: Lǎoshī hǎo.

Yǐ: Nǐ hǎo, yǒu shénme wèntí ma?

Jiǎ: Xiǎo Wáng shì dānshù, wèi shénme yào yòng "tāmen?"

Yǐ: Wèn de hěn hǎo. Zhèlǐ "Xiǎo Wáng tāmen" shì yī ge cízǔ, shuō de shì Xiǎo Wáng hé tā de péngyoumen.

Jiǎ: Nà wǒ yě kěyǐ shuō "Wáng Xiǎonián tāmen" ma?

Yǐ: Duì, nǐ yě kěyǐ shuō "Wáng Xiǎonián tāmen, Gé Lín tāmen, Gāo Lǎoshī tāmen." Háiyǒu shénme wèntí?

Jiǎ: Méiyǒu le.

Yǐ: Yǒu wèntí jiù lái wèn wǒ.

Jiǎ: Hǎo, xiè xie lǎoshī.

甲：老师好。

乙：你好，有什么问题吗？

甲：小王是单数，为什么要用"他们"？

乙：问得很好。这里"小王他们"是一个词组，说的是小王和他的朋友们。

甲：那我也可以说"王小年他们"吗？

乙：对，你也可以说王小年他们，格林他们，高老师他们。还有什么问题？

甲：没有了。

乙：有问题就来问我。

甲：好，谢谢老师。

四、角色表演 *(4. Role Play)*

1. A: You are in China studying Chinese. This is the first day of your job as an English tutor. Please explain to your student in Chinese how to study English well.

   B: You live in China and you have a new English tutor from the United States. You try to find out how difficult it will be for you to study English.

2. You are classmates in a Chinese class. Discuss how best to study Chinese and how to use a computer for studying Chinese.

diàn nǎo yǔ   hàn zì   liàn xí
电　脑　与　汉　字　练　习
▶ **Exercises for Computing and Learning Characters**

· ·

一、打下面段落。*(1. Type the following passage.)*

　　格林说中文语音不太难，可是汉字比较难。格林告诉王小年怎么用电脑学习中文。他从开始就用拼音输入汉字，省了很多时间练习发音、会话、阅读和写作。王小年说他以后也要试试这个方法。

二、把下面拼音句子打成汉字。*(2. Type the following pinyin sentences and select the appropriate characters from the list that appears on your computer screen.)*

1. Huānyíng, huānyíng. Nǐ chīfàn le ma? Kuài qù cāntīng chīfàn ba, zàijiàn.

2. Wǒ shì dì-sān dài yímín, shì zài Měiguó zhǎngdà de.

3. Lǎoshī, wǒ kěyǐ wèn nín liǎng ge wèntí ma?

4. Zài Zhōngguó de shíhou, lǎoshī gàosu wǒmen cóng kāishǐ jiù fā zhǔn měi yī ge yīn hé shēngdiào. Xiàkè yǐhòu háiyào duō liàn.

5. Wǒ cóng kāishǐ jiù yòng pīnyīn shūrù Hànzì, shěng le hěn duō shíjiān liànxí fāyīn, huìhuà, yuèdú hé xiězuò.

三、圈出正确的汉字。*(3. Circle the correct character to fill in the blanks.)*

1. 王朋的女朋友是 ＿＿＿＿（汐、补、处、外、补）国人吗？

2. 他的女朋友不是大学生，是 ＿＿＿＿（膏、亨、享、高、篙）中学生。

3. 他 ＿＿＿ (卜、土、工、上、仕)大学以后就不写作了。

4. 你 ＿＿＿ (用、甬、佣、勿、甩)电脑写作文还是笔？

5. 我的手表是 ＿＿＿ (刁、刀、方、房、七)的不是圆的。

四、读生字，找出偏旁部首。*(4. The characters in each of the following groups share a radical. Read the characters and write the shared radicals.)*

Example: 这 迎　shared radical: 辶

1. 谢 认 语 识 读 试　shared radical:＿＿＿＿＿＿

2. 间 阅　shared radical:＿＿＿＿＿＿

3. 意 思　shared radical:＿＿＿＿＿＿

4. 法 汉 汽　shared radical:＿＿＿＿＿＿

5. 写 客　shared radical:＿＿＿＿＿＿

6. 练 组　shared radical:＿＿＿＿＿＿

▶ International Studies Institute at Nanjing University.

五、把汉字分成部件。*(5. Test your understanding of character structure by dividing the following characters into their component parts.)*

Example: 吗—>口　马

1. 时—>_____

2. 音—>_____

3. 拼—>_____

4. 始—>_____

5. 懂—>_____

六、学生字 *(6. Learning New Characters)*

独体词组复合词。(Form compound words based on single-character words.)

注释 (Note): Most Chinese characters are words themselves, called 独 (dú, single) 体 (tǐ, body) 词. In this exercise you will be asked to find compound words that contain some common single-character words you have already learned.

Study the following characters selected from the New Words lists: 我　小*　就　是　作*

1. Copy each character by hand using the character writing demonstration sheet.

2. For each character marked with an asterisk, find the compounds in which the characters are used in the text, and write the compound words next to the characters.

3. With the assistance of a dictionary or an online dictionary, write down three more compounds in which these single-character words appear.

4. For each character marked with an asterisk, make a sentence with one of the three new compounds.

Character Writing Demonstration Sheet 第四课 　　　姓名＿＿＿＿＿＿

Pinyin	Strokes	Structure	English	Radical	Traditional Form
wǒ	7	single-body	I, me	丿	我

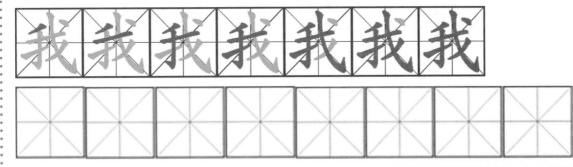

Pinyin	Strokes	Structure	English	Radical	Traditional Form
xiǎo	3	single-body	small, little	小	小

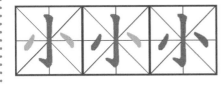

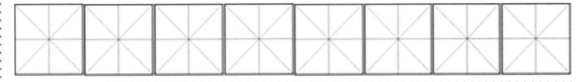

Pinyin	Strokes	Structure	English	Radical	Traditional Form
jiù	12	left-right	then, only, as soon as	亠	就

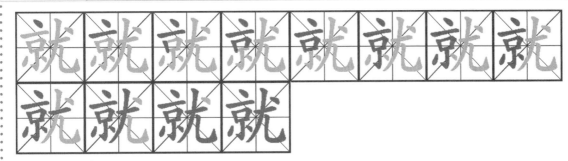

EXERCISES

Pinyin	Strokes	Structure	English	Radical	Traditional Form
shì	9	top-bottom	be	日	是

是 是 是 是 是 是 是 是
是

Pinyin	Strokes	Structure	English	Radical	Traditional Form
zuò	7	left-right	do	亻	作

作 作 作 作 作 作 作

kè   wén liàn xí
课　文　练　习
▶ **Exercises for Understanding the Texts**

．．

一、根据课文回答问题。*(1. Answer the questions orally based on the text.)*

对话(1)

1. 王小年会说中文吗？

   Does Xiaonian Wang know how to speak Chinese?

2. 格林为什么会说中文？

   Why does Green know how to speak Chinese?

3. 格林觉得学中文什么比较难？

   According to Green, what is difficult about learning Chinese?

4. 王小年觉得什么比较难？

   What does Xiaonian Wang think is difficult?

5. 为什么格林的中文说得那么准？

   Why is Green's Chinese pronunciation so good?

6. 用电脑学中文有什么好处 (hǎochù, advantage)？

   What is the advantage of learning Chinese on a computer?

7. 格林会写很多汉字吗？

   Can Green write many Chinese characters?

8. 课文中的"老外"和"老中"是什么意思？

   What do 老外 and 老中 mean in the text?

对话（2）

1. 格林为什么去见老师？

   Why did Green go to see the teacher?

2. 格林问了老师几个问题？

   How many questions did Green ask the teacher?

3. 他的第一个问题是什么？

   What was his first question?

4. 你知道怎么回答那个问题吗？
   Do you know how to answer that question?

5. "跟" and "和" 是什么意思？
   What do 跟 and 和 mean?

二、完成对话。*(2. Complete the dialogues orally.)*

学生：请问，王老师在吗？
老师：_____ 。

学生：我想问您两个问题。
老师：_____ 。

学生：为什么我常听我的中国朋友们说"哪里，哪里"？
老师：_____ 。

学生：那，为了客气我们用英语也可以说 "where, where" 吗？
老师：_____ 。

学生：老师，我懂了，谢谢您。
老师：_____ 。

三、先完成下列句子，再朗读句子。*(3. Complete the following sentences by using (会 and/or 一点), then read the sentences aloud).*

1. 王小年的父母是广东人，他 _____
   (knows how to speak a little Cantonese) 。

2. 在中国，很多人都 _____ (can "play" a little 乒乓, ping pong) 。

3. 约翰想请苏珊去跳舞，可是苏珊说她 _____ (doesn't know how) 。

4. A: 你会用电脑写中文吗？

   B: _____ (yes, a little) 。

5. 格林想请王小年帮他练习说中文，可是王小年 _____
   (doesn't know much) 。

四、作文 (4. Composition)

Type a few sentences (6-7) talking about the difficulties and joys of learning Chinese.

五、翻译 (5. Translation)

Translate the following sentences orally in class. Then type your translations in Chinese using the words and phrases provided:

1. Xiaonian Wang can speak a little Mandarin Chinese. (普通话, pǔtōnghuà) (一点儿+N)

2. Green felt a little tired playing ball. (一点儿 + Adjective)

3. As long as you keep practicing, writing Chinese characters is not very difficult. (就)

4. If you don't like me calling you by your English name, then I'll use your Chinese name. (那，就)

5. No wonder you are so happy. You and your girlfriend saw the new American blockbuster movie. (难怪)

6. What's the problem with your eyes? (眼睛 yǎnjing) Let me have a look! (reduplication of verb)

7. Xiaonian Wang can speak a little Cantonese because his grandparents speak Cantonese. (会)

8. Your method sounds not bad. (V+起来)

9. Do you know how to write the character "difficult"? (会)

10. Did you understand what the teacher said? (说+的)

bǔ   chōng   yuè   dú   liàn   xí
补   充   阅   读   练   习

▶ Supplementary Reading Exercises

. . . .

(1) Controlled Vocabulary

Read the following two passages and answer the questions.

格林学中文

格林是一个美国学生，他在中国学过一年中文，现在还在上中文课。他觉得中文的语法很容易，语音也不太难。因为他在中国学中文的时候，一开始老师就让他们发准每一个音和声调，所以他的发音很好，比一些会说广东话的 ABC 还准，可是他中文说得还不流利。他很想找一个中国学生帮他练习说中国话。

格林觉得学写汉字比学语音和语法都难，练习写字要用很长时间。但是他用电脑学中文以后，就容易多了，还可以用省下来的时间多练习发音，会话，阅读和写作。

Questions

1. 格林是在哪儿学的中文？

2. 他是怎么学发音的？

3. "ABC"在这儿是什么意思？

4. 格林觉得写中文字好学吗？

5. 用电脑学中文有什么好处？ (hǎochù, advantage)

(2) Open Vocabulary

This exercise is called "Open Vocabulary" because it contains some vocabulary words that have not been introduced in this book. In this exercise, you should first look for words you already recognize, and then try to guess the meaning of an entire phrase or sentence based on the words you already know. When you get stuck, use a dictionary to look up words whose meanings are crucial to your understanding of the passage. You can also retrieve an electronic version of this text from the accompanying online materials, and use an online dictionary or translation program to help you read it.

After answering the questions, try to tell the story to a classmate in your own words without looking at the original text.

	Chinese	Pinyin	Part of Speech	English
1.	客气话	kèqihuà	CE	an expression of modesty or politeness
2.	婚礼	hūnlǐ	N	wedding ceremony; wedding
3.	漂亮	piàoliang	Adj	pretty; beautiful
4.	新郎	xīnláng	N	bridegroom
5.	不够	bú gòu	CE	not enough; insufficient

6. 眉毛	méimáo	N	eyebrow; brow
7. 鼻子	bízi	N	Nose
8. 笑	xiào	V	smile; laugh
9. 参加	cānjiā	V	join; attend; take part in; give
10. 有礼貌	yǒu lǐmào	CE	to be courteous or polite; to have manners
11. 新娘	xīnniáng	N	bride
12. 只	zhǐ	Adv	only; merely
13. 头发	tóufa	N	hair (on the human head)
14. 眼睛	yǎnjīng	N	eye
15. 嘴	zuǐ	N	mouth

处处都漂亮

一位刚学中文的外国朋友不知道"哪里，哪里，"是客气话。一次他去参加中国朋友的婚礼，很有礼貌地说新娘非常漂亮，新郎客气地说"哪里，哪里！"这位外国朋友就回答说："眼睛漂亮。"可是新郎还是说"哪里，哪里！"这位朋友想"哦，中国人觉得只说眼睛漂亮还不够。"就用刚学的中国话说："头发，眉毛，眼睛，鼻子，嘴都漂亮！"大家听了都笑了起来。

Questions

1. What does 哪里 mean?

2. Why did the bridegroom say 哪里?

3. What did the "foreign friend" think about what the bridegroom said?

4. What did the "foreign friend" say then?

5. Why did everybody start laughing at what he said?

zhōng guó   wén   huà   xí   sú
中   国   文   化   习   俗

Chinese Customs and Culture

. . . .

dú shū yǔ kē jǔ kǎo shì zhì dù
读   书   与   科   举   考   试   制   度

▶ Education and the Legacy of the Imperial Examination System

读书 (reading a book) also means "to study" or "learn" in Chinese. From ancient times, education was considered to be a ladder of social ascendancy in China, and positions in the government bureaucracy (considered the best and most important jobs) were parceled out on the basis of performance on an imperial examination that was theoretically open to anyone in society.

One of the most famous sayings about "studying" in China is from a Song dynasty (960-1279) poem written by Wang Zhu:

天   子   重   英   豪 ， 文   章   教   尔   曹 。
tiān zǐ   zhòng yīng háo   wén zhāng jiāo ěr   cáo

万   般   皆   下   品 ， 唯   有   读   书   高 。
wàn bān   jiē   xià pǐn   wéi yǒu   dú   shū gāo

It can be literally translated as: "The emperor values heroes; books can teach you (how to be one). Everything else is low-grade; only study is above all."

Here is another Song dynasty poem that encourages study:

书   中   自   有   千   盅   粟 ，
shū zhōng zì   yǒu qiān zhōng sù

书   中   自   有   黄   金   屋 ，
shū zhōng zì   yǒu huáng jīn   wū

书   中   自   有   颜   如   玉 。
shū zhōng zì   yǒu yán   rú   yù

"In books, there is ample food; in books, there are houses made of gold; in books, there are beautiful women." The poem speaks of the rewards of a good life to be gained by performing well on the exam.

The Imperial Civil Service Examination began in 605 AD under the Sui dynasty, developed and matured under the Tang (618–907) and Song dynasties (960–1279) and continued through the Qing dynasty (1616–1911), lasting continuously for 1300 years. The Imperial Civil Service Examination had huge influence on the Chinese society, and China's neighbors Japan, Korea and Vietnam also imported this system. In modern times, the Civil Service Personnel Examination, as well as the college entrance examination, evolved from this system.

The Imperial Civil Service Examination was held in order to select officials for the government. If a person studied well, he could pass the examination and would have the chance to be appointed to an official position. If someone became an official, he would receive respect from others and obtain both power and fortune. Many poor scholars studied for years and years in the hope of passing the examination and getting an official position.

Classical Chinese literature is filled with stories of virtuous scholars working feverishly to pass the exams. The higher the level of the examination one passed, the higher the official position one got. The person coming in first among all those taking the exams was awarded the rank of 状元 (zhuàngyuan). During the Tang Dynasty, 80 percent of the prime ministers were chosen from among the Jinshi, those who attained the highest level of achievement on the examination. In the space of 320 years, the government of the Song dynasty held a total of 118 Imperial Civil Service Examinations with more than 20,000 people passing the highest level and becoming Jinshi. In the 277 years of the Ming Dynasty, 89 examinations were held with 17,000 people attaining the rank of Jinshi. In the 265 years of the Qing Dynasty, 120 examinations were held with 26,000 people becoming Jinshi.

Although the Imperial Civil Service Examination has not been in existence for over a century, its profound influence on Chinese culture and educational system, as well as people's behavior and thinking, persists. The college entrance examination in China today can be seen as an extension of this imperial examination system. Every summer, over a period of two days, all prospective college students across China take the same examination. Each student must test in seven subjects. If a student fails to pass the examination, he or she has to wait for one year to take the examination again. The test load has become a little less heavy since 1999. Still, all of the examinees are tested on three subjects: math, Chinese, and foreign language. In addition, there is a comprehensive test of biology, chemistry, and physics for those who apply to science and engineering schools, and a test of history, geography, and politics for those who pursue study in the humanities.

In China, as in many other East Asian countries, going to a prestigious university is a prerequisite to entering the social and cultural elite, and the path to a good job and a profitable future. Failing the exam, they have to do some less prestigious work such as service work, factory work, or do business. Although business may make money, it is still less respectfully treated than a prestigious university graduate, because traditionally businessmen are low on social status. But the situation began to change since China's economic reform.

▶ Test Your Knowledge Who is the "Number One Scholar"?

With a partner, alternate questions, moving from the bottom through the top. The student answering the most questions correctly will attain the degree of Jinshi.

> What is the title conferred on the one who comes in first in the highest imperial examination?
> (Answer in Chinese.)

Why did so many young people study so hard in ancient China?	How long is the college entrance examination in China? How many subjects are tested?

How many prime ministers were of the Jinshi rank in the Tang dynasty?	How long did the Qing dynasty last and how many exams were given?	How long did the Imperial Civil Service Examination last in Chinese history?

When did the Imperial Civil Service Examination begin?	When did the Imperial Civil Service Examination reach maturity?	Which dynasty was the last to offer the test?	List two countries that imported the Imperial Civil Service Examination from China.

Answers:

> What is the title conferred on the one who comes in first in the highest imperial examination?
> (Answer in Chinese.)
>
> 状元 zhuàngyuan

Why did so many young people study so hard in ancient China? (to get an official position)	How long is the college entrance examination in China? How many subjects are tested? (3 days, 7 subjects)

How many prime ministers were of the Jinshi rank in the Tang dynasty? (80 percent)	How long did the Qing dynasty last and how many exams were given? (267 years, 120 exams)	How long did the Imperial Civil Service Examination last in Chinese history? (1,300 years)

When did the Imperial Civil Service Examination begin? (in 605 AD in the Sui dynasty)	When did the Imperial Civil Service Examination reach maturity? [during the Tang (618-907) and Song dynasties (960-1279)]	Which dynasty was the last to offer the test? (Qing dynasty)	List two countries that imported the Imperial Civil Service Examination from China. (Japan, Korea, or Vietnam)

qù mǎi dōng xī
去 买 东 西
Going Shopping

▶ **Objectives:**

1. To ask for prices, bargain, and purchase items
2. To return and exchange items

duì   huà   yī
对   话   （一）

DIALOGUE 1

qù   chāo   shì
去   超   市

▶ **Going to the Supermarket**

....

shēng   cí
生   词

🔘 **New Words**

	Chinese	Pinyin	Part of Speech	English
1.	超(级)市(场)	chāo(jí) shì(chǎng)	N	supermarket
2.	买	mǎi	V	buy; purchase
3.	一些	yīxiē	M	(a measure word used for some, a few, a little)
4.	东西	dōngxi	N	thing; creature
5.	牛奶	niúnǎi	N	milk
6.	面包	miànbāo	N	bread
7.	奶酪	nǎilào	N	cheese
8.	可乐	kělè	N	cola
9.	除了…以外	chúle…yǐwài	Conj	except; besides; in addition to
10.	别的	biéde	Adj	other; another
11.	洗衣粉	xǐyīfěn	N	detergent
12.	肥皂	féizào	N	soap

13.	洗发液	xǐfàyè	N	shampoo
14.	纸巾	zhǐjīn	N	tissue
15.	先	xiān	Ad	first; earlier; before
16.	拿	ná	V	hold; take; seize
17.	块	kuài	M	(a measure word used for a piece, a lump, a chunk, and money, or yuan)
18.	毛	máo	M	(a measure word used for a fractional unit of money)
19.	分	fēn	M	(a measure word used for a unit of money); point; mark
20.	多少	duōshǎo	QW	how much, how many
21.	钱	qián	N	cash; money
22.	半	bàn	Adj	half; semi-
23.	加仑	jiālún	M	(a measure word used for gallon)
24.	袋	dài	N	bag; sack; pocket
25.	哎	āi	Int	hey!; look out!
26.	比	bǐ	V/Prep	compare; contrast; than
27.	上	shàng	Adj	upper; up; upward; superior; the previous (week)
28.	星期	xīngqī	N	week
29.	贵	guì	Adj	expensive; costly; noble
30.	只	zhǐ	Ad	only; merely
31.	减价	jiǎnjià	V	mark down; reduce the price
32.	所以	suǒyǐ	Conj	so; therefore; as a result

33.	便宜	piányí	Adj	cheap
34.	刀	dāo	N	knife; sword
35.	叉	chā	N	fork
36.	杯子	bēizi	N	cup; glass
37.	餐巾纸	cānjīnzhǐ	N	napkin
38.	哇	wā	Int	wow
39.	车	chē	N	vehicle; car
40.	付	fù	V	pay
41.	带	dài	V	take; bring; carry; belt; ribbon; tape
42.	现金	xiànjīn	N	cash
43.	够	gòu	Ad	enough; sufficient; adequate
44.	信用卡	xìnyòngkǎ	N	credit card
45.	售货员	shòuhuòyuán	N	cashier, shop assistant; sales clerk
	售	shòu	V	sell
	货	huò	N	goods; commodity
	员	yuán	N	a person engaged in some field of activity
46.	找	zhǎo	V	look for; try to find; seek; want to see; give change

▶▶▶

gé lín:
格 林： wǒ men qù chāo shì, hǎo ma?
我 们 去 超 市，好 吗？

wáng xiǎo nián:
王 小 年： hǎo a, wǒ xiǎng mǎi yī xiē chī de dōng
好 啊，我 想 买 一 些 吃 的 东
xi hé yòng de dōng xi.
西 和 用 的 东 西。

zài chāo jí shì chǎng
（在 超 级 市 场）

gé lín:
格 林： wǒ yào mǎi niú nǎi, miàn bāo, nǎi lào hé
我 要 买 牛 奶、面 包、奶 酪 和
kě lè. nǐ ne?
可 乐。你 呢？

wáng xiǎo nián:
王 小 年： chú le chī de yǐ wài, wǒ hái yào mǎi
除 了 吃 的 以 外，我 还 要 买
xǐ yī fěn, féi zào, xǐ fā yè hé zhǐ
洗 衣 粉、肥 皂、洗 发 液 和 纸
jīn.
巾。

gé lín:
格 林： wǒ men xiān qù ná chī de ba. niú nǎi
我 们 先 去 拿 吃 的 吧。牛 奶
duō shǎo qián bàn jiā lún?
多 少 钱 半 加 仑？

wáng xiǎo nián:
王 小 年： niú nǎi yī kuài qī máo qián bàn jiā lún,
牛 奶 一 块 七 毛 钱 半 加 仑、
miàn bāo yī kuài bā máo jiǔ yī dài. āi,
面 包 一 块 八 毛 九 一 袋。哎，
zěn me kě lè bǐ shàng xīng qī guì le?
怎 么 可 乐 比 上 星 期 贵 了？

shàng xīng qī zhǐ yào liǎng kuài qián, jīn tiān
上 星 期 只 要 两 块 钱，今 天
yào sān kuài qī máo wǔ fēn.
要 三 块 七 毛 五 分。

gé lín: shàng xīng qī jiǎn jià, suǒ yǐ pián yí. zhè
格 林： 上 星 期 减 价，所 以 便 宜。这
xīng qī niú nǎi jiǎn jià, hái shì ná niú
星 期 牛 奶 减 价，还 是 拿 牛
nǎi ba.
奶 吧。

wáng xiǎo nián: nǐ ná hǎo le ma? wǒ men qù nà biān
王 小 年：你 拿 好 了 吗？我 们 去 那 边
zhǎo yòng de dōng xi ba.
找 用 的 东 西 吧。

gé lín: hǎo. wǒ yào mǎi yī xiē dāo, chā, bēi zi
格 林： 好，我 要 买 一 些 刀、叉、杯 子
hé cān jīn zhǐ shén me de.
和 餐 巾 纸 什 么 的。

wáng xiǎo nián: wā, wǒ jīn tiān mǎi le yī chē dōng xi.
王 小 年：哇，我 今 天 买 了 一 车 东 西。
wǒ men qù fù qián ba.
我 们 去 付 钱 吧。

（付钱以后）

格　林：　我今天买的东西太多了，带的现金不够，用信用卡付的钱。

王小年：　我也买了不少，我给售货员八十块，她只找了我三块两毛二分钱。

汉字课文

🔘 **Text in Chinese Characters**

▶▶▶

格林：　　我们去超市，好吗？

王小年：　好啊，我想买一些吃的东西和用的东西。

（在超级市场）

格林：　　我要买牛奶、面包、奶酪和可乐。你呢？

王小年：　除了吃的以外，我还要买洗衣粉、肥皂、洗发液和纸巾。

格林：　　我们先去拿吃的吧。牛奶多少钱半加仑？

王小年：　牛奶一块七毛钱半加仑、面包一块八毛九一袋。哎，怎么可乐比上星期贵了？上星期只要两块钱，今天要三块七毛五分。

格林：　　上星期减价，所以便宜。这星期牛奶减价，还是拿牛奶吧。

王小年： 你拿好了吗？我们去那边找用的东西吧。

格林： 好，我要买一些刀、叉、杯子和餐巾纸什么的。

王小年： 哇，我今天买了一车东西。我们去付钱吧。

（付钱以后）

格林： 我今天买的东西太多了，带的现金不够，用信用卡付的钱。

王小年： 我也买了不少，我给售货员八十块，她只找了我三块两毛二分钱。

yǔ   yán   yīng   yòng   zhù   shì
语   言   应   用   注   释
Notes on Language Usage

1. 超市

超市 is a shortened form of 超级市场. Modern Chinese contains many short forms like this and it is important to know both the long and short versions of the words.

More examples are:

北京大学 (Běijīng Dàxué) = 北大 (Beijing University)

南京大学 (Nánjīng Dàxué) = 南大 (Nanjing University)

地下铁路 (dìxià tiělù) = 地铁 (subway)

家庭教师 (jiātíng jiàoshī) = 家教 (private teacher, tutor)

*2. 除了……以外，还……

This phrase meaning "in addition to" or "besides" (除了……以外) is usually followed by 还 or 也. The sentence in this lesson 除了吃的以外，我还要买……" means "In addition to food, I also need to buy..."

More examples:

除 了 格 林 以 外， 苏 珊 也 去 过 中 国。

Chúle Gé Lín yǐwài, Sū Shān yě qù guò Zhōngguó.

Susan, in addition to Green, has also been to China.

格 林 除 了 学 习 中 文 以 外， 还 学 习 日 文。

Gé Lín chúle xuéxí Zhōngwén yǐwài, hái xuéxí Rìwén.

In addition to Chinese, Green also studies Japanese.

*3. 吃的

After 的, 东西 is omitted. 的 is used to refer to "those kinds of things," or things in the same category.

For example: 吃的，穿的，用的 *(things to eat, to wear, to use).*

A: 你 要 买 什 么 样 的 运 动 衣？

Nǐ yào mǎi shénmeyàng de yùndòngyī?

B: 我 要 买 好 看 的。

Wǒ yào mǎi hǎokàn de.

A: What kind of sportswear do you want to buy?

B: I want to buy good-looking (sportswear).

(For details, please see Grammar Book I, Lesson 4.)

4. 牛奶多少钱？牛奶一块七毛钱半加仑。

How much is the milk? Milk is $1.70 for a half-gallon.

When asking about price, the sentence pattern is: thing you want to buy + 多少钱 + number + measure word. 毛衣多少钱一件？ (How much is a sweater?) When answering, 多少钱 is changed to an amount of money.

For example:

毛 衣 二 十 八 块 五 毛 钱 一 件。

Máoyī èrshí bā kuài wǔ máo qián yī jiàn.

The sweater is $28.50.

面 包 多 少 钱 一 个？ 面 包 一 块 三 毛 五 一 个。

Miànbāo duōshǎo qián yī ge? Miànbāo yī kuài sān máo wǔ yī ge.

How much is the bread? A dollar and 35 cents per loaf.

(For more about expressions with money, please see Grammar Book I, Lesson 3.)

*5. 比

比 functions the same way as "than" in English and is used for making comparisons. The sentence pattern is: A + 比 + B + adjective. The sentence 可乐比上星期贵了 is a short form. The full sentence is 可乐，这个星期比上星期贵了。(Cola is more expensive this week than last week.)

More examples:

中 文 语 法 比 英 文 (语 法) 容 易。

Zhōngwén yǔfǎ bǐ Yīngwén yǔfǎ róngyì.

Chinese grammar is easier than English (grammar).

奶 酪 比 牛 奶 贵。

Nǎilào bǐ niúnǎi guì.

Cheese is more expensive than milk.

(For details, please see Grammar Book I, Lesson 8.)

6. 还是

还是 is an adverb. It is used to express the most satisfactory solution from among a number of options that have already been introduced. It can be translated as "had better."

Examples:

看 电 视 没 意 思，还 是 去 看 美 国 大 片 吧。

Kàn diànshì méi yìsi, hái shì qù kàn Měiguó dà piān ba.

Watching TV is boring. We'd better see the American blockbuster movie.

打 的 太 贵，还 是 坐 地 铁 吧。

Dǎdī tài guì, hái shì zuò dì tiě ba.

It's too expensive to take a cab. (You'd) better take the subway.

*7. 什么的 and 等

Both mean "etc., so on and so forth," and are used at the end of a list.

For example:

我 今 天 买 了 很 多 吃 的，奶 酪、 牛 奶、可 乐、面 包 什 么 的。

Wǒ jīntiān mǎi le hěn duō chī de, nǎi lào, niú nǎi, kě lè, miàn bāo shénme de.

Today I bought a lot of tasty food—cheese, milk, cola, bread and so on.

格 林 会 很 多 外 语，日 文、法 文、中 文 等。

Gé Lín huì hěn duō wàiyǔ, Rìwén, Fǎwén, Zhōngwén děng.

Green can speak many foreign languages—Japanese, French, Chinese etc.

Note that 什么的 is used in spoken Chinese, while 等 is more formal. 等 can also be written 等等; the meaning is the same.

duì huà èr
对 话 （二）

DIALOGUE 2

tuì yī fu
退 衣 服

▶Returning Clothes

••

shēng cí
生 词

🔘 New Words

	Chinese	Pinyin	Part of Speech	English
1.	小姐	xiǎojiě	N	miss; young lady
2.	退	tuì	V	return; move back
3.	颜色	yánsè	N	color; countenance; facial expression
4.	件	jiàn	M	(a measure word used for clothing)
5.	蓝	lán	Adj	blue
6.	换	huàn	V	exchange; return; trade; change
7.	种	zhǒng	M	(a measure word used for kind, sort, type)
8.	衣服	yīfu	N	clothing; clothes
9.	黄	huáng	Adj	yellow
10.	毛衣	máoyī	N	woollen sweater; sweater
11.	运动衣	yùndòngyī	N	sportswear
	运动	yùndòng	V	sports
	衣	yī	N	clothes; clothing

12.	黑	hēi	Adj	black; dark
13.	西装	xīzhuāng	N	Western-style suit
14.	打折	dǎzhé	V	sell at a discount; give a discount
15.	合适	héshì	Adj	suitable; appropriate

pīn yīn kè wén
拼 音 课 文
Text with Pinyin
▶▶▶

gé lín:		xiǎo	jiě,	wǒ	xiǎng	tuì	zhè	jiàn	yī	fú.	
格 林：		小	姐，	我	想	退	这	件	衣	服。	

shòu huò yuán:	qǐng	wèn	nín	wéi	shén	me	yào	tuì	zhè	jiàn
售 货 员：	请	问	您	为	什	么	要	退	这	件
	yī	fu	ne?							
	衣	服	呢？							

gé lín:	wǒ	bù	xǐ	huān	zhè	jiàn	de	yán	sè,
格 林：	我	不	喜	欢	这	件	的	颜	色。
	nǐ	men	yào	shì	yǒu	lán	yán	sè	de,
	你	们	要	是	有	蓝	颜	色	的，
	wǒ	jiù	huàn	yī	jiàn.				
	我	就	换	一	件。				

shòu huò yuán:	zhè	zhòng	yī	fú	zhǐ	yǒu	hóng	de,	huáng	de,
售 货 员：	这	种	衣	服	只	有	红	的、	黄	的、
	lǜ	de,	méi	yǒu	lán	de.	nín	kě	yǐ	shì
	绿	的，	没	有	蓝	的。	您	可	以	试
	shì	lán	máo	yī.						
	试	蓝	毛	衣。						

格林: wǒ bù xiǎng mǎi máo yī, yǒu lán yùn dòng yī ma?
我 不 想 买 毛 衣，有 蓝 运 动 衣 吗？

售货员: yùn dòng yī zhǐ yǒu hēi de.
运 动 衣 只 有 黑 的。

格林: nà wǒ mǎi jiàn lán xī zhuāng ba. xiǎo jiě, pián yí diǎnr hǎo ma?
那 我 买 件 蓝 西 装 吧。小 姐，便 宜 点 儿 好 吗？

售货员: hǎo, gěi nín dǎ jiǔ zhé.
好，给 您 打 九 折。

格林: zài pián yí diǎnr ba.
再 便 宜 点 儿 吧。

售货员: nà gěi nín dǎ bā zhé. qǐng shì shì zhè jiàn.
那 给 您 打 八 折。请 试 试 这 件。

格林: zhè jiàn hěn hé shì, xiè xiè.
这 件 很 合 适，谢 谢。

hàn zì kè wén

汉 字 课 文

🔘 Text in Chinese Characters

▶▶▶

格林： 小姐，我想退这件衣服。

售货员： 请问您为什么要退这件衣服呢？

格林： 我不喜欢这件的颜色。你们<u>要是</u>有蓝颜色的，我就换一件。

售货员： 这种衣服只有红的、黄的、绿的，没有蓝的。您可以试试蓝毛衣。

格林： 我不想买毛衣，有蓝运动衣吗？

售货员： 运动衣只有黑的。

格林： 那我买件蓝西装吧。小姐，便宜点儿好吗？

售货员： 好，给您<u>打九折</u>。

格林： 再便宜点儿吧。

售货员： 那给您打八折。请试试这件。

格林： 这件很合适，谢谢。

◀◀◀

yǔ yán yīng yòng zhù shì

语 言 应 用 注 释

Notes on Language Usage

*1. 要是

要是 means "if." It is often used in spoken Chinese.

For example:

要 是 用 电 脑 学 习 中 文 就 容 易 多 了。

Yàoshì yòng diànnǎo xuéxí Zhōngwén jiù róngyì duō le.

Using a computer to study Chinese would be much easier.

要 是 你 有 时 间，我 们 去 超 市。

Yàoshì nǐ yǒu shíjiān, wǒmen qù chāoshì.

If you have time, let's go to the bar.

2. 打九折

打折 means "to give a discount." 打九折 means 10 percent off (so you pay 9/10 or 90 percent of the price, hence the use of 九). Please note the differences in expression between Chinese and English here. 五折 means 50 percent off, and 八五折 is 15 percent off. Other useful phrases for talking about prices are: 减价—(jiǎnjià, on sale), 半价—(bànjià, half price), 买一送一—(mǎiyī sòngyī, buy one get one free), and 优惠价—(yōuhuìjià, discount price).

3. Bargaining in Chinese

It is quite common to bargain when shopping in China. Phrases usually used for bargaining are:

太 贵 了。

Tài guì le.

Too expensive.

便 宜 点 儿 嘛。

Piányí diǎnr ma.

Can you make it a little cheaper?

优 惠 一 点 吧。

Yōuhuì yī diǎn ba.

Can you give a small discount?

打 折 吗？

Dǎ zhé ma?

Will you give a discount?

打 几 折？

Dǎ jǐ zhé?

What's the discount?

你 要 是 便 宜 点 儿，我 就 在 这 儿 买。

Nǐ yàoshì piányí diǎnr, wǒ jiù zài zhèr mǎi.

If your price is a little cheaper, I will buy it here.

那 家 才 卖 三 块，你 怎 么 卖 五 块？

Nà jiā cái mài sān kuài, nǐ zěnme mài wǔ kuài?

The other store sells it for only $3.00; how come you are asking $5.00?

For example:

A: 减 价 啦，快 来 买。On sale now, hurry up and buy.

  Jiǎnjià la, kuài lái mǎi.

B: 这 件 衣 服 多 少 钱 一 件？ How much are these clothes?

Zhè jiàn yīfú duōshǎo qián yī jiàn?

A: 二 十 块。 Twenty dollars.

Èrshí kuài.

B: 太 贵 了，十 块。 Too expensive. (How about) $10.00?

Tài guì le, shí kuài.

A: 十 块 不 卖。 I won't sell for $10.00.

Shí kuài bù mài.

B: 那 十 二 块。 Then, $12.00.

Nà shí'èr kuài.

A: 十 五 块，少 一 分 不 卖。 Fifteen dollars, not a penny less.

Shíwǔ kuài, shǎo yī fēn bù mài.

B: 十 三 块，不 卖 我 走 了。 Thirteen dollars. If you don't sell, I'll go.

Shísān kuài, bù mài wǒ zǒu le.

A: 好，十 三 就 十 三 吧，给 钱。 OK, $13. 00. Give me the money.

Hǎo, shísān jiù shísān ba, gěi qián.

xù   shù

敍   述

▶ **Narration**

● ●

shēng cí

生   词

New Words

	Chinese	Pinyin	Part of Speech	English
1.	日用品	rìyòngpǐn	N	daily necessities
2.	瓶	píng	N	bottle

pīn yīn kè wén
拼　音　课　文

Text with Pinyin

wáng xiǎo nián gēn gé lín qù chāo jí shì chǎng mǎi
王小年跟格林去超级市场买

dōng xī, tā men yào mǎi yī xiē chī de dōng xi hé
东西，他们要买一些吃的东西和

rì yòng pǐn. tā men ná le niú nǎi, miàn bāo, nǎi lào
日用品。他们拿了牛奶、面包、奶酪

hé kě lè, tā men hái mǎi le xǐ yī fěn, féi zào,
和可乐，他们还买了洗衣粉、肥皂、

xǐ fà yè hé zhǐ jīn. gé lín hái mǎi le yī xiē
洗发液和纸巾。格林还买了一些

dāo, chā, bēi zi hé cān jīn zhǐ děng. mǎi kě lè de
刀、叉、杯子和餐巾纸等。买可乐的

shí hòu, wáng xiǎo nián jué dé kě lè bǐ shàng xīng qī
时候，王小年觉得可乐比上星期

guì le. shàng xīng qī zhǐ yào liǎng kuài qián yī píng, jīn
贵了。上星期只要两块钱一瓶，今

tiān yào sān kuài qī máo wǔ fēn qián. gé lín gào su
天要三块七毛五分钱。格林告诉

tā shàng xīng qī jiǎn jià, suǒ yǐ pián yí. zhè xīng qī
他上星期减价，所以便宜。这星期

niú nǎi jiǎn jià, wáng xiǎo nián ná le niú nǎi. tā men
牛奶减价，王小年拿了牛奶。他们

mǎi le yī chē dōng xi. gé lín dài de xiàn jīn bù le
买了一车东西。格林带的现金不了

gòu, yòng xìn yòng kǎ fù de qián. wáng xiǎo nián huā le
够，用信用卡付的钱。王小年花了

qī shí liù kuài qī máo bā fēn qián.
七十六块七毛八分钱。

NARRATION

hàn   zì   kè   wén
汉   字   课   文
Text in Chinese Characters
▶▶▶

王小年跟格林去超级市场买东西，他们要买一些吃的东西和日用品。他们拿了牛奶、面包、奶酪和可乐，他们还买了洗衣粉、肥皂、洗发液和纸巾。格林还买了一些刀、叉、杯子和餐巾纸等*。买可乐的时候，王小年觉得可乐比上星期贵了。上星期只要两块钱一瓶，今天要三块七毛五分钱。格林告诉他上星期减价，所以便宜。这星期牛奶减价，王小年拿了牛奶。他们买了一车东西。格林带的现金不够，用信用卡付的钱。王小年花了七十六块七毛八分钱。

* For more on the use of 等, please see Notes on Language Usage 7 in Dialogue 1.   ◀◀◀

▶ English Translations of the Texts

· ·

Dialogue 1

Green:	Let's go to the supermarket, OK?
Xiaonian Wang:	OK. I want to buy some food and things for daily use.

(In the supermarket)

Green:	I want to buy milk, bread, cheese and cola. How about you?
Xiaonian Wang:	Besides food, I also need to buy detergent, soap, shampoo and tissues.
Green:	Let's get food first. How much is a half-gallon of milk?
Xiaonian Wang:	Milk is $1.70 for a half-gallon. Bread is $1.89 for a bag. What? Cola is more expensive than last week. It was only $2.00 last week. It costs $3.75 today.
Green:	It was on sale last week, so it was cheaper then. Milk is on sale this week. You should get milk.
Xiaonian Wang:	Did you get what you need? Let's go over there to get stuff for daily use.
Green:	OK. I want to buy some knives, forks, cups and napkins, etc.
Xiaonian Wang:	Wow, I bought a whole cart of stuff today. Let's go check out.

(After paying)

Green:	I bought too much today. I did not bring enough cash. I had to pay with my credit card.
Xiaonian Wang:	I also bought a lot. I gave the cashier $80.00. She only gave me $3.22 in change.

Dialogue 2

Green:	Miss, I want to return this jacket.
Sales clerk:	May I ask why you want to return this jacket?
Green:	I don't like the color. If you have a blue one, I will exchange it.
Sales clerk:	We only have red, yellow, and green for this kind of jacket. No blue ones. You can try a blue sweater.
Green:	I don't want to buy a sweater. Do you have blue sportswear?
Sales clerk:	We only have black sportswear.
Green:	Then I want to buy a blue suit. Miss, could you make it a little cheaper?
Sales clerk:	Alright, I'll give you 10 percent off.
Green:	Could you make it even cheaper?
Sales clerk:	Then, 20 percent off. Please try this one.
Green:	It fits well. Thank you.

Narration

Xiaonian Wang and Green went shopping at the supermarket. They wanted to buy some food and things for daily use. They got milk, bread, cheese and cola. They also bought detergent, soap, shampoo and tissues. Green also bought some knives, forks, cups and napkins, etc. When they got the cola, Xiaonian Wang felt that it was more expensive than last week. It was only $2.00 last week, but it cost $3.75 today. Green told him that it was on sale last week, so it was cheap. This week milk is on sale. Xiaonian Wang got milk. They each bought a whole cart full of stuff. Green did not bring enough cash. He paid with a credit card. Xiaonian Wang spent $76.78.

▶ Chinese shops in Flushing, New York.

▶ Exercises for Listening and Speaking

∙∙∙

🔊 一、完成对话。*(1. Work in pairs to complete the dialogue.)*

A: Nǐ qù nǎr le?

B: _____

A: Nǐ mǎi le shénme hǎochī de?

B: _____

A: Nǐ hái mǎi le shénme?

B: _____

A: Miànbāo duōshǎo qián?

B: _____

A: Nà kělè ne?

B: _____

A: Wǒ yě yào mǎi kělè.

B: _____

🔊 二、听对话，回答问题。*(2. Listen to the conversation and answer the questions.)*

1. How much is a bag of bread?

_____

2. What item costs $3.22?

_____

3. How much does B spend altogether?

_____

4. What is his change?

三、先听对话，然后两人一组朗读。*(3. Listen to the following conversation without looking at the book, and then read it aloud in pairs, first by following the pinyin, then by following the characters.)*

Jiǎ: Xiǎojiě, wǒ xiǎng tuì zhè jiàn yīfu.

Yǐ: Qǐng wèn nín wèishénme yào tuì zhè jiàn yīfu ne?

Jiǎ: Wǒ bù xǐhuān zhè jiàn yīfu de yánsè.

Yǐ: Duìbuqǐ, wǒmen zhèr bù kěyǐ tuì yīfu, zhǐ kěyǐ huàn.

Jiǎ: Nà jiù huàn yí jiàn ba, hái yǒu shénme yánsè de?

Yǐ: Zhè jiàn yīfu shì hóng de, kěyǐ ma?

Jiǎ: Wǒ bù xǐhuān.

Yǐ: Nín yàoshi bù xǐhuān zài shìshì zhè jiàn.

Jiǎ: Zhè jiàn kěyǐ, jiù shì tài guì le. Piányi diǎnr hǎo ma?

Yǐ: Gěi nín dǎ jiǔ zhé.

Jiǎ: Dǎ jiǔ zhé tài shǎo le, zài piányi diǎnr.

Yǐ: Hǎo, bā zhé ba. Zhè jiàn yīfu shì yī bǎi líng jiǔ kuài qī máo sì, nín zài fù sì kuài liù máo sān.

Jiǎ: Hǎo, zhè shì wǔ kuài qián.

Yǐ: Zhǎo nín qián, huānyíng zài lái.

甲：小姐，我想退这件衣服。

乙：请问您为什么要退这件衣服呢？

甲：我不喜欢这件衣服的颜色。

乙：对不起，我们这儿不可以退衣服，只可以换。

甲：那就换一件吧，还有什么颜色的？

乙：这件衣服是红的，可以吗？

甲：我不喜欢。

乙：您要是不喜欢再试试这件。

甲：这件可以，就是太贵了。便宜点儿好吗？

乙：给您打九折。

甲：打九折太少了，再便宜点儿。

乙：好，八折吧。这件衣服是一百零九块七毛四，您再付四块六毛三。

甲：好，这是五块钱。

乙：找您钱，欢迎再来。

四、角色表演 *(4. Role Play)*

1. A: You are a supermarket cashier and are helping a customer to check out.

   B: You are a customer at a supermarket. You are checking out and asking the different prices of the things you buy.

2. A: You are working at a small clothing store. A customer is returning a shirt. You are trying to persuade her/him not to return it, but instead to exchange it for something else.

   B: You are returning a shirt you bought yesterday. You are trying to exchange it for another one. You bargain the price of the new shirt down from the original price.

diàn nǎo yǔ   hàn zì   liàn xí
电 脑 与 汉 字 练 习

▶ Exercises for Computing and Learning Characters

· ·

一、打出下面段落。*(1. Type the following passage.)*

A: 小姐，便宜点儿好吗？

B: 那要看你买多少。

A: 我买一台 (tái, measure word for TV set)

B: 五台打九折，十台打八折。

A: 可是我不需要那么多电视机(diànshìjī, TV set)啊！你就便宜一点儿吧。那我不买了。

B: 好，给你九五折。一台一千七百四十三块六毛二，打折后是一千六百五十六块四毛四。你给一千六百五十块吧。

二、把下面拼音句子打成汉字。*(2. Type the following pinyin sentences and select the appropriate characters from the list that appears on your computer screen.)*

1. Wǒ yào mǎi niúnǎi, miànbāo, nǎilào hé kělè. Nǐ ne?

2. Zhè zhǒng yīfu zhǐ yǒu hóng de, huáng de, lǜ de, lán de, hé kāfēisè de.

3. Zài Zhōngguó de shíhòu, lǎoshī ràng wǒmen yī kāishǐ jiù fā zhǔn měi yí gè yīn hé shēngdiào. Xiàkè hái yào duō liàn.

4. Wǒ cóng kāishǐ jiù yòng pīnyīn shūrù Hànzì, shěng xià le hěn duō shíjiān liànxí fāyīn, huìhuà, yuèdú hé xiězuò.

三、圈出正确的汉字。 *(3. Circle the correct character to fill in the blanks.)*

1. 学校的 ___（牛、车、东、革、冻）边是电影院吗？

2. 我昨天没买牛奶，买了五 ___（抱、色、名、句、包）饼干。

3. 我没有带毛 ___（币、内、布、市、巾），你有多的吗？

4. 我们应该去练习 ___（和、合、会、今、仓）唱。

5. 你从 ___（洒、血、牺、西、四）校门出去，往左转就到了。

四、读生字，找出偏旁部首。 *(4. The characters in each of the following groups share a radical. Read the characters, and write the shared radicals).*

   Example: 这 迎 shared radical: 辶

1. 级 纸 shared radical:_____

2. 退 运 适 shared radical:_____

3. 货 贵 shared radical:_____

4. 付 便 shared radical:_____

5. 场 块 shared radical:_____

6. 洗 液 shared radical:_____

7. 衣 袋 装 shared radical:_____

8. 换 打 找 shared radical:_____

9. 钱 金 shared radical:_____

五、把汉字分成部件。 *(5. Test your understanding of character structure by dividing the following characters into their component parts.)*

   Example: 吗—>口 马

1. 奶 —>_____   4. 合 —>_____

2. 肥 —>_____   5. 动 —>_____

3. 装 —>_____   6. 期 —>_____

六、学生字 (6. Learning New Characters)

独体词组复合词。(Form compound words based on single-character words.)

注释 (Note): Most Chinese characters are words themselves, called 独 (dú, single) 体 (tǐ, body) 词. In this exercise you will be asked to find compound words that contain some common single-character words you have already learned.

Study the following characters selected from the New Words lists: 加　分*　所　子　毛*

1. Copy each character by hand using the character writing demonstration sheet.

2. For each character marked with an asterisk, find the compounds in which the characters are used in the text, and write the compound words next to the characters.

3. With the assistance of a dictionary or an online dictionary, write down three more compounds in which these single-character words appear.

4. For each character marked with an asterisk, make a sentence with one of the three new compounds.

Character Writing Demonstration Sheet 第五课　　姓名＿＿＿＿＿＿＿

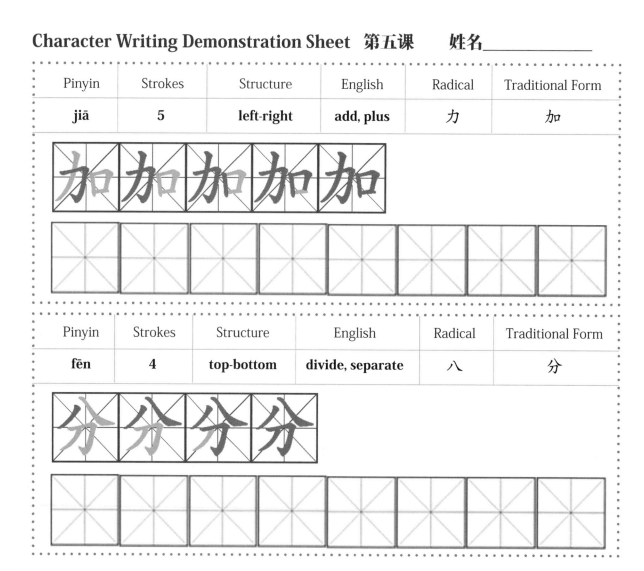

Pinyin	Strokes	Structure	English	Radical	Traditional Form
jiā	5	left-right	add, plus	力	加

Pinyin	Strokes	Structure	English	Radical	Traditional Form
fēn	4	top-bottom	divide, separate	八	分

Pinyin	Strokes	Structure	English	Radical	Traditional Form
suǒ	8	left-right	place	户	所

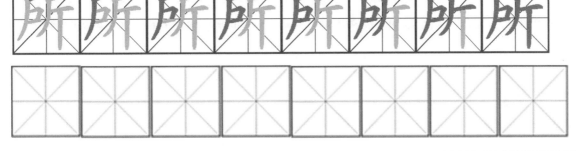

Pinyin	Strokes	Structure	English	Radical	Traditional Form
zǐ	3	single-body	son	子	子

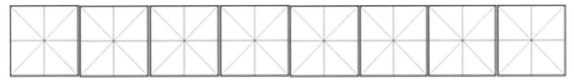

Pinyin	Strokes	Structure	English	Radical	Traditional Form
máo	4	single-body	hair, a fractional unit of money in China	毛	毛

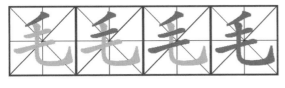

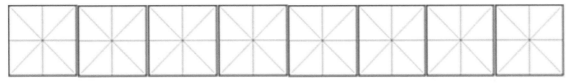

kè   wén liàn xí

课　文　练　习

▶ **Exercises for Understanding the Texts**

· ·

一、根据课文回答问题。**(1. Answer the questions orally based on the text.)**

对话（1）

1. 格林要找王小年去哪儿？
   Where did Green ask Xiaonian Wang to go?

2. 格林想买什么？
   What did Green want to buy?

3. 王小年要买什么？
   What did Xiaonian Wang want to buy?

4. 牛奶半加仑多少钱？
   How much was a half-gallon of milk?

5. 可乐的钱为什么跟上星期不一样？
   Why was the price of cola different from last week?

6. 格林是怎么付的钱？
   How did Green pay for his groceries?

7. 王小年买东西一共花(spend)了多少钱？
   How much did Xiaonian Wang spend on his groceries?

对话（2）

1. 格林到商店做什么？
   Why was Green in the store?

2. 他为什么要换那件外衣？
   What was wrong with that jacket?

3. 格林喜欢什么颜色？
   What color did Green want?

4. 格林最后买了一件什么衣服？
   What kind of clothes did Green finally buy?

5.格林买衣服便宜了多少钱？

How much of a discount did Green get?

二、完成句子。*(2. Complete the sentences orally).*

1.上星期可乐减价，_____ (therefore it was cheap)。

2.这星期牛奶减价，_____ (we'd better buy some milk)。

3._____ ，(In addition to milk and bread) 格林还买了奶酪。

4.你们要是有蓝色的运动衣，_____ (I'll buy one then)。

5.这种毛衣今天减价，_____ (It is 25 percent off)。

三、先完成下列句子，再朗读句子。*(3. Complete the following sentences by choosing* 太，真，很 *or* 比较，*and then read the sentences aloud.)*

1.今天的作业_____多了。

2.这家饭馆_____忙！

3.这个工作_____有意思。

4.格林觉得中文的语法不太难，可是汉字_____难。

5.老师告诉我们第五课的生词_____多。

6.王小年觉得中文的四声_____难了。

7.我妈妈_____喜欢吃美国饭。

8.你_____客气！还是我自己来吧。

四、改寫。*(4. Rewrite the following sentences using* 除了……以外，还……*)*

Example: 王小年学习中文，王小年也学习日文。

→王小年除了学习中文以外，也学习日文。

1.王小年买了一些吃的东西。王小年还买了一些用的东西。

2.苏珊不想跟约翰去看电影。苏珊也不喜欢跟约翰去打球。

3. 格林的中文语法很好。格林的发音也很好。

4. 王家生明天不能请张小妹看美国大片。他没有时间，也没有钱。

5. 我妈妈喜欢吃中国饭。我妈妈也喜欢吃美国饭。

五、作文。 *(5. Composition)*

Write a few sentences (6-7) talking about a shopping experience.

六、翻译。 *(6. Translation)*

Translate the following sentences orally in class. Then type your translations in Chinese using the words and phrases provided.

1. In addition to some daily necessities, my mother also bought sportswear for me. (除了……以外，还……)

2. Besides Chinese, Green can also speak a little Japanese (日文, Rìwén). (除了……以外，还……)

3. I feel that Chinese grammar is easier than English. (比)

4. The price of milk is higher than last week. (比)

5. No, the price of milk is not higher than last week. The price of cola is. (不比)

6. How much is this blue sweater? It is $30.99. (多少钱)

7. It is so boring to watch TV at home. We'd better go to a party instead. (还是)

8. If you don't feel like going to a party, how about a blockbuster movie? (要是)

9. I'll buy the black suit, if you give me a 20 percent discount. (打折)

10. I still need to buy some things for daily use such as shampoo, detergent, napkins, tissues, etc. (等等)

bǔ   chōng yuè   dú   liàn   xí
补   充   阅   读   练   习

▶ **Supplementary Reading Exercises**

···

(1) Controlled Vocabulary

Read the following passage and answer the questions either in Chinese or English:

	Chinese	Pinyin	Part of Speech	English
1.	打	dá	M	(a measure word used for a dozen)
2.	选	xuǎn	V	choose; pick
3.	糟糕	zāogāo	Adj	how terrible; too bad
4.	钱包	qiánbāo	N	wallet; purse
5.	昨天	zuótiān	TW	yesterday
6.	穿	chuān	V	wear
7.	只好	zhǐhǎo	Ad	have to; be forced to
8.	扫兴地	sǎoxìngdi	Ad	disappointedly

王小年买东西

　　王小年的朋友明天要到王小年那儿开晚会。王小年到超市买东西。他拿了一些刀叉、杯子和餐巾纸什么的，又去找吃的东西。他拿了牛奶、面包、奶酪，看到可乐减价，上星期要三块七毛五分钱，今天只要两块钱。他想他的朋友都喜欢喝可乐，就拿了两打。他选了一车东西，就去付钱。"糟糕。钱包怎么没有了？"原来钱包在他昨天穿的蓝西装里，可是他今天换了一件红运动衣。没有钱包怎么买东西？他只好扫兴地回家了。

Questions

1. 王小年为什么买东西？Why did Xiaonian Wang go shopping?

2. 他买了什么吃的东西？What food did he buy?

3. 他为什么买可乐？Why did he buy cola?

4. 王小年的钱包呢？Where is Xiaonian Wang's wallet?

5. 他买到东西了吗？为什么？Did he buy what he wanted? Why?

(2) Open Vocabulary

This exercise is called "Open Vocabulary" because it contains some vocabulary words that have not been introduced in this book. In this exercise, you should first look for words you already recognize, and then try to guess the meaning of an entire phrase or sentence based on the words you already know. When you get stuck, use a dictionary to look up words whose meanings are crucial to your understanding of the passage. You can also retrieve an electronic version of this text from the accompanying online materials, and use an online dictionary or translation program to help you read it. After answering the questions, try to tell the story to a classmate in your own words without looking at the original text.

只有一根不好使

A. 冬冬，火柴买回来了吗？

B. 爸爸，买回来了。

A. 火柴好使吗？

B. 我已经一根一根试过了，只有一根不好使。

Questions

1. 孩子刚才去做什么了？Where did the son just come back from?

2. 他买到了吗？Did the boy get what he wanted?

3. 火柴怎么了？What do you think happened to the matches?

4. "好使"是什么意思？What does the word "好使" mean?

买苹果

母亲：我让孩子来买一斤苹果，可是你只给了半斤。

店主：我的秤没有问题，太太，你应该称一称你的孩子。

Questions

1. 为什么妈妈去找卖东西的人？

   Why does the mother come back to see the shopkeeper?

2. 卖东西的人的秤有问题吗？

   Is there any problem with the vendor's scale?

3. 为什么卖东西的人说妈妈应该称一称孩子？

   Why does the shopkeeper suggest that she should weigh her child?

zhōng guó wén huà xí sú
中　国　文　化　习　俗

Chinese Customs and Culture

···

zhōng guó de huò bì yǔ gòu wù
中　国　的　货　币　与　购　物

▶ **Chinese Money and Shopping**

As the new millennium dawned, China's economy reached dizzying rates of growth and leaped past many venerable economic powers. In 2005, it was the fourth largest economy on earth, trailing only the United States, Japan, and Germany. In 2006, China's economy looked certain to overtake Germany's within three to five years. These economic changes have brought fundamental shifts in the social life of the nation, and an increasingly materialistic and brand-conscious mentality, especially among younger people.

Along the famous shopping streets of Shanghai, for example, top international brand-name designers are feverishly opening new stores, even though the number of Chinese consumers who can actually afford their products is still miniscule. But these international retailers have an eye on the future, when they anticipate tremendous personal wealth among urban Chinese. Although many face this new capitalist future with skepticism and trepidation, many others embrace it as a return to China's past glory as a commercial and economic center.

A well-developed system of commerce seems to have been part of Chinese life from the very beginning, and archaeologists are continuing to uncover the origins of the Chinese economy. Many Chinese characters with reference to trade or commercial activities include the radical 贝 (bèi, shell). As you might guess, this is because shells were one of the earliest forms of currency used in China. Metal currency came into use in the late Zhou dynasty (770–249 BC). In the Qin dynasty (221–206 BC), we see the emergence of round copper coins with square holes in the center. In 970 AD, the first paper money was issued. China was the first country in the world to use paper currency. Paper money was officially legalized during the Ming dynasty in 1375 AD. Along with copper currency, silver currency was also used in the Qing dynasty (1644–1911 AD). In 1935, the Nationalist government issued an order to prohibit the use of silver and copper coins.

China's currency now is called the Renminbi, meaning "the people's money." There are a total of nine denominations: 100 *yuan*, 50 *yuan*, 20 *yuan*, 10 *yuan*, 5 *yuan*, 2 *yuan* and 1 *yuan*. Smaller bills include 5 *jiao*, 2 *jiao*, 1 *jiao*, 5 *fen*, 2 *fen* and 1 *fen*. Coins come in 1 *yuan*, 5 *jiao*, 1 *jiao*, 5 *fen* and 1 *fen* denominations, but the Chinese government has recently declared that the paper bills for 1, 2, and 5 *fen* are no longer in circulation. From 1980 through 1995, Bank of China issued another kind of money called "Foreign Exchange Certificates (FECs)." FECs were used by foreigners traveling in China to buy commodities that were in short supply or imported items at the Friendship Stores. The use of FECs was discontinued on January 1, 1995. From the establishment of the People's Republic in 1949, China had a planned socialist economy. All businesses were controlled by the state. In addition to money, the state issued coupons for grain and other commodities that were in short supply. Food coupons were circulated between 1955 and 1993. Since that time, China has undergone far-reaching economic reforms that have utterly reshaped standards of living. While some state-owned stores continue to operate, there has been a growing trend toward privatization, and foreign companies and joint ventures have proliferated throughout the country. At the time this was being written, Wal-Mart (沃尔玛, Wòěrmǎ) had 57 stores operating in 23 Chinese cities. Carrefour (家乐福, jiālèfú), the European

▶ Denominations of *Renminbi* from five *jiao* to 50 *yuan* from the People's Republic of China.

retail giant opened its 60th store in Chongqing, China in 2005. Chinese supermarket chains have spread rapidly across China. In addition, neighborhood convenience stores, free markets, night markets and street peddlers have added to the retail mix for Chinese consumers.

Usually the big department stores and supermarkets sell all kinds of goods, from food and daily necessities to clothing and jewelry. But fresh foods are only sold in the supermarkets and outdoor markets. Prices in these stores are higher, and the quality of the goods is comparatively better. Some big department stores also have supermarkets inside them. If you just need some small items for daily use, the neighborhood convenience store is a good choice. However, if you want to have the fun of bargaining, enjoying food stands, buying cheap and fresh vegetables and fruits, or selecting handicrafts, night markets and free markets are better choices. These different types of stores and markets mesh together into a convenient shopping network for Chinese consumers. If you travel to China, remember that bargaining is a common practice in most of the outdoor stores and markets in China, but not in the large department stores and chain stores, where items have fixed prices.

▶ Foreign Exchange Certificates.

▶ What items were purchased on this receipt?

▶ Test Your Knowledge Where to go shopping?

You are traveling in China and want to buy the items listed below. Please tell (a) where you can get the most items; (b) where you can get as many of the following items as possible at the cheapest prices; (c) where you can get each individual item on sale (list as many store types as you can) and; (d) where you can bargain and where you cannot.

1. | milk and bread for breakfast |

2. | a silk scarf for your grandmother |

A. big department store

3. | an MP3 player for your brother |

4. | a suitcase to bring your gifts home |

B. convenience store

5. | a dress for your girlfriend |

C. free market

6. | fresh fruit for a party |

7. | a handbag for your mom |

D. gift shop

8. | hair pins for your sister |

E. night market

9. | a tie of silk embroidery for your dad |

F. supermarket

10. | a pair of leather shoes for yourself |

Answer Sheet:

(a) Store type and item numbers:

(b) Store type and item numbers:

(c) Item 1: Store type_____   Item 2: Store type_____

   Item 3: Store type_____   Item 4: Store type_____

   Item 5: Store type_____   Item 6: Store type_____

   Item 7: Store type_____   Item 8: Store type_____

   Item 9: Store type_____   Item 10: Store type_____

(d) Store type (Check the ones where you can bargain):

   ( ) big department store   ( ) convenience store

   ( ) free market   ( ) gift store

   ( ) night market   ( ) supermarket

Answers:

(a) Store type and item numbers: Big department store, all 10 items (items 1 and 6 may not be sold at some department stores, but many now have supermarkets within them.)

(b) Store type and item numbers: Night market, items 2, 4, 5, 6, 7, 8 10

   (Free markets are more focused on certain types of goods, such as clothing, vegetables and fruit, birds, fish and flowers, etc. Night markets are usually more comprehensive.)

(c) Item 1: Store type F, A, B   Item 2: Store type E, A, C, D

   Item 3: Store type A   Item 4: Store type E, A, C

   Item 5: Store type E, A, C   Item 6: Store type F, A, B, C, E

   Item 7: Store type A, C, D, E   Item 8: Store type A, B, C, D, E, F

   Item 9: Store type A, C, D, E   Item 10: Store type A, C, E

(d) Store types (check the ones where you can bargain):

   ( ) big department store   ( ) convenience store

   (X) free market   (X) gift shop

   (X) night market   ( ) supermarket

dì liù kè
第 六 课
LESSON 6

....

chéng chē
乘　车
Transportation

▶ **Objectives:**

1. To talk about public transportation
2. To tell how to get to a destination by public transportation

duì huà yī
对　话　(一)

DIALOGUE 1

zěn me qù jī chǎng
怎　么　去　机　场

▶ **How to Get to the Airport**

shēng cí
生　词
New Words

	Chinese	Pinyin	Part of Speech	English
1.	知道	zhīdào	V	know; realize; be aware of
2.	肯尼迪机场	Kěnnídí Jīcháng	PN	John F. Kennedy (JFK) Airport (in New York)
3.	机场	jīchǎng	N	airport; airfield
4.	当然	dāngrán	Ad	certainly; of course; to be sure
5.	方便	fāngbiàn	Adj	convenient
6.	地铁	dìtiě	N	subway = 地下铁路
	地	dì	N	ground, land
7.	大中央车站	Dàzhōngyāng Chēzhàn	PN	Grand Central Station (in New York)
8.	号	hào	N	sign; number; size; date
9.	然后	ránhòu	Ad	then; after that; afterwards

10.	时代广场	Shídài Guǎngchǎng	PN	Times Square (in New York)
11.	再	zài	Ad	another time; again; once more
12.	终点	zhōngdiǎn	N	terminal point; destination; finish
13.	线	xiàn	N	route; line; thread; string; wire; clue
14.	又……又	yòu…yòu	Conj	both...and...
15.	数字	shùzì	N	numeral; figure; digit
16.	字母	zìmǔ	N	letters of an alphabet; alphabet
17.	波士顿	Bōshìdùn	PN	Boston
18.	线路	xiànlù	N	route; line
19.	乘	chéng	V	ride; multiply
20.	大巴	dàbā	N	bus
21.	麻烦	máfan	Adj/V	troublesome; inconvenient; to trouble somebody; bother
22.	听说	tīngshuō	V	be told; it is said that...
23.	乱	luàn	Adj/N	in disorder; a mess; in confusion; disorder
24.	还是	háishì	Ad	still; nevertheless; all the same; had better; or
25.	只是	zhǐshì	Ad	merely; only; just; simply; however; but then
26.	办法	bànfǎ	N	way; means; measure
27.	长途	chángtú	Adj	long-distance
	长	cháng	Adj	long
28.	不错	bùcuò	Adj	not bad; pretty good; correct; right

pīn yīn kè wén
拼 音 课 文
🔘 **Text with Pinyin**

▶▶▶

sū shān: yuē hàn, nǐ zhī dào zěn me qù kěn ní dí jī chǎng ma?
苏 珊：约 翰，你 知 道 怎 么 去 肯 尼 迪 机 场 吗？

yuē hàn: dāng rán zhī dào.
约 翰：当 然 知 道。

sū shān: zěn me qù zuì hǎo?
苏 珊：怎 么 去 最 好？

yuē hàn: nà yào kàn nǐ shì yào shěng qián hái shì yào fāng biàn.
约 翰：那 要 看 你 是 要 省 钱 还 是 要 方 便。

sū shān: xiān shuō zěn me shěng qián ba.
苏 珊：先 说 怎 么 省 钱 吧。

yuē hàn: nà nǐ kě yǐ zuò dì tiě. xiān zuò liù hào chē dào dà zhōng yāng chē zhàn, rán hòu huàn qī hào chē, zuò liǎng zhàn dào shí dài guǎng chǎng, zài zuò A chē dào zhōng diǎn.
约 翰：那 你 可 以 坐 地 钱。先 坐 6 号 车 到 大 中 央 车 站，然 后 换 7 号 车，坐 两 站 到 时 代 广 场，再 坐 A 车 到 终 点。

sū shān: dì tiě bú shì hóng xiàn, lán xiàn ma? zěn me yòu shì shù zì yòu shì zì mǔ?
苏 珊：地 钱 不 是 红 线、蓝 线 吗？怎 么 又 是 数 字 又 是 字 母？

约翰：你说的是波士顿的地铁，那儿的地铁用颜色。纽约地铁线路多，所以又有数字又有字母。你下了地铁还要换乘去机场的大巴。

苏珊：太麻烦了，听说纽约的地铁也很乱。你还是说说怎么去方便吧。

约翰：那当然是坐出租汽车了，又快又方便，只是贵了点儿，要五十块钱左右。

苏珊：那也太贵了，就没有别的办法了吗？

约翰：你还可以坐地铁到时代广场的长途汽车站，那里有到机场的大巴，只要十几块钱。

sū shān: zhè gè bàn fǎ bú cuò, wǒ jiù qù cháng tú
苏 珊：这 个 办 法 不 错，我 就 去 长 途
qì chē zhàn ba.
汽 车 站 吧。

hàn zì kè wén
汉 字 课 文
Text in Chinese Characters

苏珊：　约翰，你知道怎么去肯尼迪机场吗？

约翰：　当然知道。

苏珊：　怎么去最好？

约翰：　那要看你是要省钱还是要方便。

苏珊：　先说怎么省钱吧。

约翰：　那你可以坐地铁。先坐6号车到大中央车站，然后换
　　　　7号车，坐两站到时代广场，再坐A车到终点。

苏珊：　地铁不是红线、蓝线吗？怎么又是数字又是字母？

约翰：　你说的是波士顿的地铁，那儿的地铁用颜色。纽约地
　　　　铁线路多，所以又有数字又有字母。你下了地铁还要
　　　　换乘去机场的大巴。

▶ 纽约的地铁怎么又有数字又有字母？
(The subway entrance at 42nd Street, Manhattan).

苏珊： 太麻烦了，听说纽约的地铁也很乱。你还是<u>说说</u>怎么去方便吧。

约翰： 那当然是坐出租汽车了，又快又方便，<u>只是贵了点儿</u>，要五十块钱<u>左右</u>。

苏珊： 那<u>也太贵了</u>，就没有别的办法了吗？

约翰： 你还可以坐地铁到时代广场的长途汽车站，那里有到机场的大巴，只要十几块钱。

苏珊： 这个办法不错，我就去长途汽车站吧。

yǔ   yán   yīng   yòng   zhù   shì
语   言   应   用   注   释

Notes on Language Usage

*1. 要看你是要省钱还是要方便。 **It depends on which is more important to you: saving money or convenience.**

a) 要看

要看 means "depends on [whether or not]…"

> *For example:*
>
> A: 你 跟 我 去 看 电 影 吗？
>
> Nǐ gēn wǒ qù kàn diànyǐng ma?
>
> Are you going to the movies with me?
>
> B: 要 看 你 请 不 请 我 吃 饭。
>
> Yào kàn nǐ qǐng bù qǐng wǒ chīfàn.
>
> That depends on whether or not you treat me to dinner.

今 天 晚 上 能 不 能 看 电 影 要 看 我 有 没 有 作 业。

Jīntiān wǎnshang néng bù néng kàn diànyǐng yào kàn wǒ yǒu méiyǒu zuòyè.

Whether I can go to the movie tonight depends on whether or not I have homework.

b) 是……还是……

是……还是…… means "either A or B," and it is used in making choices. The first 是 can sometimes be omitted.

> *For example:*
>
> 你 今 天 晚 上 (是) 吃 中 国 饭 还 是 吃 美 国 饭？
>
> Nǐ jīntiān wǎnshang (shì) chī Zhōngguófàn háishì chī Měiguófàn?
>
> Will you have Chinese or American food tonight?

你 周 末 是 打 球 还 是 跳 舞？

Nǐ zhōumò shì dǎqiú háishì tiàowǔ?

Are you going to play ball or dance on the weekend?

(For details, please see Grammar Book I, Lesson 4.)

*2. 又是数字又是字母

The phrase 又...又 indicates simultaneous actions or the coexistence of two qualities or states.

For example:

我 的 同 屋 一 个 又 高 又 大，一 个 又 矮 (ǎi, short) 又 瘦 (shòu, thin)。

Wǒ de tóngwū yī gè yòu gāo yòu dà, yī gè yòu ǎi yòu shòu.

One of my roommates is big and tall. The other is short and thin.

王 小 年 他 们 又 唱 歌 (chànggē, sing) 又 跳 舞，玩 儿 得 很 高 兴 (gāoxìng, glad; happy)。

Wáng Xiǎonián tāmen yòu chànggē yòu tiàowǔ, wánr de hěn gāoxìng.

Xiaonian Wang and his friends were singing and dancing. They were having a good time.

3. 大巴

大巴 means "bus." In China, buses used to be called 公共汽车. This term is still used, as can be seen in this lesson. However, the term 公共汽车 is used exclusively for public buses. Now people like to call other buses 大巴, 中巴, or 小巴 depending on the size of the bus. This term is only used in informal spoken Chinese.

4. 说说

We refer to the repeating of a verb twice as "reduplication." The reduplication of a verb indicates a short, quick action, or is used to soften one's tone, especially when asking someone to do something.

For example:

你 坐 坐，她 一 会 儿 就 来。

Nǐ zuòzuò, tā yīhuìr jiù lái.

Take a seat. She'll be back in a moment. (indicating "it won't take long")

A: 我 昨 天 买 的 奶 酪 怎 么 没 了？

Wǒ zuótiān mǎi de nǎilào zěnme méi le?

B: 你 在 冰 箱 (bīngxiāng, refrigerator) 里 找 找，不 会 没 有 的。

Nǐ zài bīngxiāng lǐ zhǎozhǎo, bù huì méiyǒu de.

A: How come the cheese that I bought yesterday disappeared?

B: Look for it in the refrigerator. It can't be gone.

(For details, please see Grammar Book I, Lesson 10.)

5. 只是贵了点儿，要五十块钱左右。 **But it's a little too expensive. It's about $50.00.**

a) 只是

只是 is a conjunction meaning "only." It is used in the second clause of a sentence to convey contrast, as in "it's only that..." or "except that..." in English. It introduces a revision to the first clause. In the text, it indicates the speaker's reservation about the idea of taking a taxi.

For example:

这件衣服不错，只是颜色不好看。

Zhè jiàn yīfú bú cuò, zhǐshì yánsè bù hǎokàn.

These clothes are not bad, except that the color is not good.

他写得不错，只是发音不太准。

Tā xiě de bùcuò zhǐshì fāyīn bù tài zhǔn.

He writes well, it's only that his pronunciation is not very accurate.

b) 贵了

了 indicates excess, and is usually used after an adjective. It has the meaning of 太. Here it refers to the fact that the taxi fare is too high. Other examples are:

这件衣服，你穿 (chuān, wear)，长了。

Zhè jiàn yīfú, nǐ chuān cháng le.

If you wear these clothes, they will be too long.

今天玩儿晚 (wǎn, late) 了。

Jīntiān wánr wǎn le。

We played till very late today.

c) 点儿

点儿=一点儿

*d) 左右

左右 means "about, around" and is used after a number + measure phrase.

For example:

那本有意思的书要五十块钱左右。

Nà běn yǒuyìsi de shū yào wǔshí kuài qián zuǒyòu.

That interesting book costs about $50.00.

A: 我们几点见？

Wǒmen jǐ diǎn jiàn?

B: 七点左右。

Qī diǎn zuǒyòu.

A: When do we meet?

B: At about 7:00.

6. 那也太贵了 That's too expensive.

Here, 也 is used for emphasis and can sometimes be translated as "even."

For example:

今 天 的 晚 会 连 老 师 也 来 了。

Jīntiān de wǎnhuì lián lǎoshī yě lái le.

Even the teachers came to today's party.

那 样 做 也 太 差 了。

Nàyàng zuò yě tài chà le.

Doing it that way is very bad.

duì   huà   èr

对   话   (二)

DIALOGUE 2

zài   zhōng guó   chéng chē

在   中   国   乘   车

▶ **Taking Public Transportation in China**

shēng cí

生   词

🔘 **New Words**

	Chinese	Pinyin	Part of Speech	English
1.	广州	Guǎngzhōu	PN	Guangzhou
2.	上海	Shànghǎi	PN	Shanghai
3.	但	dàn	Conj	but; yet; still; nevertheless
4.	扩建	kuòjiàn	V	to expand; extend (a factory, mine, or other large infastructure)

5.	另外	lìngwài	Ad	in addition to; moreover; besides
6.	南京	Nánjīng	PN	Nanjing
7.	城市	chéngshì	N	city; town
8.	正在	zhèngzài	Ad	(used to indicate an action in progress) in the process of; be doing
9.	修建	xiūjiàn	V	build; construct; erect
10.	常	cháng	Ad	frequently; often; usually
11.	通	tōng	V	open; through; get through
12.	上班	shàngbān	VO	to go to work; start work
13.	下班	xiàbān	VO	to finish work; to get off work
14.	平时	píngshí	Ad	at ordinary times; in normal times; usually
15.	一样	yīyàng	Adj	the same; equally; alike; as...as....
16.	差不多	chàbuduō	Adj	almost; nearly; about the same; similar
17.	前	qián	Adj	front; forward; ahead; before; preceding; former
18.	后	hòu	Adj	back; behind; rear; after; afterwards
19.	投币箱	tóubìxiāng	N	cash box; cash register
	投	tóu	V	throw; cast; send
	币	bì	N	money; currency
	箱	xiāng	N	box; case; trunk; anything in the shape of a box
20.	硬	yìng	Adj	hard; stiff; tough; firm
21.	空调	kōngtiáo	N	air-conditioning
22.	次	cì	M	(a measure word used for action, time[s])

23.	打的	dǎdī	V	take a taxi; take a cab
	出租汽车	chūzū qìchē	N	taxi
24.	出租	chūzū	V	rent; lease (out)

▶▶▶

wáng	xiǎo	nián:	zhōng	guó	yǒu	dì	tiě	ma?			
王	小	年:	中	国	有	地	铁	吗?			

gé	lín:	běi	jīng,	guǎng	zhōu	hé	shàng	hǎi	yǒu,	bǐ	niǔ
格	林:	北	京、	广	州	和	上	海	有,	比	纽
		yuē	de	dì	tiě	piāo	liàng	duō	le,	dàn	xiàn
		约	的	地	铁	漂	亮	多	了,	但	线
		lù	hěn	shǎo,	hái	zài	kuò	jiàn.	lìng	wài	nán
		路	很	少,	还	在	扩	建。	另	外,	南
		jīng	děng	chéng	shì	zhèng	zài	xiū	jiàn	dì	tiě.
		京	等	城	市	正	在	修	建	地	铁。

wáng	xiǎo	nián:	nǐ	zài	zhōng	guó	de	shí	hòu	cháng	zuò	shén
王	小	年:	你	在	中	国	的	时	候	常	坐	什
		me	chē?								
		么	车?								

gé	lín:	wǒ	cháng	cháng	zuò	gōng	gòng	qì	chē.	wǒ	men
格	林:	我	常	常	坐	公	共	汽	车。	我	们
		xué	xiào	bù	tōng	dì	tiě.				
		学	校	不	通	地	铁。				

wáng	xiǎo	nián:	gōng	gòng	qì	chē	shàng	rén	duō	ma?
王	小	年:	公	共	汽	车	上	人	多	吗?

gé   lín:
格　林：

shàng xià bān de shí hòu rén bǐ jiào duō,
上　下　班　的　时　候　人　比　较　多，

píng shí hái hǎo.
平　时　还　好。

wáng xiǎo nián:
王　小　年：

zài zhōng guó zuò gōng gòng qì chē gēn měi
在　中　国　坐　公　共　汽　车　跟　美

guó yī yàng ma?
国　一　样　吗？

gé   lín:
格　林：

chà bù duō. cóng qián mén shàng chē, hòu mén
差　不　多。从　前　门　上　车，后　门

xià chē, shàng le chē xiān fù qián, shì wǎng
下　车，上　了　车　先　付　钱，是　往

tóu bì xiāng tóu qián. kě yǐ shì yìng bì,
投　币　箱　投　钱。可　以　是　硬　币，

yě kě yǐ shì zhǐ bì, dàn bù zhǎo qián.
也　可　以　是　纸　币，但　不　找　钱。

wáng xiǎo nián:
王　小　年：

chē shàng yǒu kōng tiáo ma?
车　上　有　空　调　吗？

gé   lín:
格　林：

yǒu de yǒu, yǒu de méi yǒu. yǒu kōng tiáo
有　的　有，有　的　没　有。有　空　调

de chē bǐ méi yǒu kōng tiáo de chē guì
的　车　比　没　有　空　调　的　车　贵

yí kuài qián.
一　块　钱。

wáng xiǎo nián:
王　小　年：

nǐ měi cì qù chéng lǐ dōu zuò gōng gòng
你　每　次　去　城　里　都　坐　公　共

qì chē ma?
汽　车　吗？

gé   lín:
格　林：

bù, wǒ yǒu de shí hòu dǎ dī.
不，我　有　的　时　候　打　的。

王 小 年：什 么 是 "打 的？"
wáng xiǎo nián: shén me shì "dǎ dī"?

格 林： 就 是 坐 出 租 汽 车，现 在 在
gé lín: jiù shì zuò chū zū qì chē, xiàn zài zài
中 国 都 叫 "打 的。"
zhōng guó dōu jiào dǎ dī.

王 小 年：真 有 意 思。我 下 次 去 中 国
wáng xiǎo nián: zhēn yǒu yì sī. wǒ xià cì qù zhōng guó
也 打 的。
yě dǎ dī.

◀◀◀

▶ Chinatown subway entrance in New York City.

hàn zì kè wén
汉 字 课 文
Text in Chinese Characters

▶▶▶

王小年： 中国有地铁吗？

格林： 北京、广州和上海有，比纽约的地铁漂亮多了，但线
路很少，还在扩建。另外，南京等城市正在修建地铁。

王小年： 你在中国的时候常坐什么车？

格林： 我常常坐公共汽车。我们学校不通地铁。

王小年： 公共汽车上人多吗？

格林： 上下班的时候人比较多，平时还好。

王小年： 在中国坐公共汽车跟美国一样吗？

格林： 差不多。从前门上车，后门下车，上了车先付钱，是往投币箱投钱。可以是硬币，也可以是纸币，但不找钱。

王小年： 车上有空调吗？

格林： 有的有，有的没有。有空调的车比没有空调的车贵一块钱。

王小年： 你每次去城里都坐公共汽车吗？

格林： 不，我有的时候打的。

王小年： 什么是"打的"？

格林： 就是坐出租汽车，现在在中国都叫"打的"。

王小年： 真有意思。我下次去中国也打的。

DIALOGUE 2

▶ A taxi in New York city.

yǔ　yán　yīng　yòng　zhù　shì
语　言　应　用　注　释
Notes on Language Usage

1. 北京、广州和上海有，比纽约的地铁漂亮多了。 **Beijing, Guangzhou and Shanghai have subway systems that are much more beautiful than the New York (subway).**

In this sentence, 多了 means "much more" and it is used as a complement to supplement 漂亮.

> ### For example:
>
> 哥　哥　比　我　大　多　了。
>
> Gēge bǐ wǒ dà duō le.
>
> My big brother is much older than me.
>
> 这　个　电　影　比　那　个　电　影　有　意　思　多　了。
>
> Zhège diànyǐng bǐ nàge diànyǐng yǒuyìsi duō le.
>
> This movie is much more interesting than that one.
>
> (For more on comparisons, please see Grammar Book I, Lesson 8.)

2. 另外

另外 is a conjunction here, meaning "besides" or "in addition to." What follows 另外 expands on what has been said before.

> ### For example:
>
> 我　夏　天　去　了　北　京、上　海。另　外　我　还　去　西　安　看　了　我　的　老　同　学。
>
> Wǒ xiàtiān qù le Běijīng, Shànghǎi. Lìngwài wǒ hái qù Xī'ān kàn le wǒ de lǎo tóngxué.
>
> I went to Beijing and Shanghai during the summer. In addition, I also went to Xi'an to see my old classmate.
>
> 格　林　在　超　市　买　了　很　多　好　吃　的　东　西，另　外　还　买　了　餐　巾　纸、和　刀　叉　等。
>
> Gélín zài chāoshì mǎi le hěn duō hǎochī de dōngxi, lìngwài hái mǎi le cānjīnzhǐ, hé dāo chā děng.
>
> Green bought a lot of tasty food in the supermarket, in addition, he bought some napkins, knives and forks, etc.

3. 我们学校不通地铁。 **The subway is not connected to our school.**

通 here means "leads to" or "open."

> ### For example:
>
> 在　中　国　还　有　很　多　山　区 (shānqū) 不　通　汽　车。
>
> Zài Zhōngguó hái yǒu hěn duō shānqū bù tōng qìchē.
>
> In China, there are still many mountainous regions that cannot be reached by motor vehicle.

4. 公共汽车上

公共汽车上 means "on the bus." 上 can also be used to indicate being on board other types of vehicles, such as trains, cars, airplanes, boats, etc.: 火车上 huǒchēshàng (on the train)、汽车上 (in the car)、飞机上 (on the airplane)、船上 chuánshàng (on the boat).

5. 平时还好 It's OK at normal times.

还 is used to modify an adjective to imply that the speaker finds something comparatively satisfactory.

For example:

纽约的地铁还好。

Niǔyuē de dìtiě hái hǎo.

The subway in New York is OK.

那个电影还不难看。

Nàge diànyǐng hái bù nánkàn.

That movie is not bad.

*6. 差不多

差不多 appears in the dialogue as an adjective, meaning "similar" or "about the same."

For example:

这两个字差不多。

Zhè liǎng gè zì chàbuduō.

The two characters look similar.

差不多的公共汽车都有空调。

Chàbuduō de gōnggòng qìchē dōu yǒu kōngtiáo.

Almost all the buses have air-conditioning. (差不多 modifies the noun.)

差不多 can be also used as an adverb, meaning "almost" or "nearly." It indicates nearness in degree, quantity or state.

For example:

我妹妹和我姐姐差不多高。

Wǒ mèimei hé wǒ jiějie chàbuduō gāo.

My little sister is about the same height as my big sister.

我的朋友差不多都喜欢吃中国饭。

Wǒ de péngyǒu chàbuduō dōu xǐhuān chī Zhōngguófàn.

Almost all of my friends like to eat Chinese food. (差不多 modifies the verb.)

*7. 有的有，有的没有。" **Some (buses) have (air conditioning), and some do not (have it)."**

有的……有的 means "some...some." A noun is implied after 有的, but if it is understood in context, the noun can be omitted.

For example:

我 们 班 的 女 生 有 的 好 看，有 的 聪 明(cōngmíng)。

Wǒmen bān de nǚshēng yǒu de hǎokàn, yǒu de cōngmíng.

Among the female students in our class, some are pretty, and some are smart. (女生 is mentioned in the first part of the sentence, so it is omitted after 的.)

有 的 男 生 很 帅(shuài)，有 的(男生)很 有 才。

Yǒu de nánshēng hěn shuài, yǒu de nánshēng hěn yǒu cái.

Some male students are handsome, and some are very talented.

8. 有空调的车比没有空调的车贵一块钱。**The fare of the buses with air-conditioning is one dollar more than those without.**

This is a comparative sentence telling the exact difference between two things. The sentence pattern is: A 比 B + Adj. + number + measure + N.

For example:

牛 奶 比 可 乐 贵 一 块 钱。

Niúnǎi bǐ kělè guì yī kuài qián.

Milk is one dollar more than cola.

弟 弟 比 我 小 三 岁。

Dìdi bǐ wǒ xiǎo sān suì.

My younger brother is three years younger than me.

(For details, please see Grammar Book I, Lesson 8.)

9. 打的 **(pronounced dǎdī) to take a taxi**

This phrase has been used in Mainland China since the 1990s and means "to take a taxi." Originally a Cantonese phrase from Hong Kong, it found its way into the Mainland through movies and other media. Now a group of words using 的 have been created, such as: 的士 (taxi), 的哥 (male taxi driver), 的姐 (female taxi driver), 的票 (taxi receipt), 面的 (minivan taxi). This kind of car was first called 面包车, or "bread car," because the shape of the car looks like a loaf of bread. 打的 has now developed into the more popular phrase 打车 for taking a taxi.

xù shù

敘 述

▶ **Narration**

· ·

shēng cí

生 词

New Words

	Chinese	Pinyin	Part of Speech	English
1.	决定	juédìng	V/N	decide; make up one's mind; decision; resolution
2.	总	zǒng	Adj	general; overall; total; chief
3.	零钱	língqián	N	small change; pocket money
4.	无人	wúrén	Adj	unmanned; self service
5.	票	piào	N	ticket; ballot

pīn yīn kè wén

拼 音 课 文

Text with Pinyin

▶▶▶

sū shān wèn yuē hàn zěn me qù kěn ní dí jī
苏 珊 问 约 翰 怎 么 去 肯 尼 迪 机

Chǎng, yuē hàn gào su tā kě yǐ chéng dì tiě, xiān chéng
场 ，约 翰 告 诉 她 可 以 乘 地 铁 ，先 乘

liù hào chē dào dà zhōng yāng chē zhàn, rán hòu huàn qī
6 号 车 到 大 中 央 车 站 ，然 后 换 7

hào chē zuò liǎng zhàn dào shí dài guǎng cháng, zài chéng A
号 车 坐 两 站 到 时 代 广 场 ，再 乘 A

chē dào zhōng diǎn. zuì hòu hái yào huàn qù jī chǎng de
车 到 终 点 。最 后 还 要 换 去 机 场 的

dà bā. kě shì sū shān shuō tài má fan. yuē hàn shuō
大 巴 。可 是 苏 珊 说 太 麻 烦 。约 翰 说

可以坐出租汽车，可是苏珊说太
贵。最后苏珊决定到时代广场的
长途汽车总站去乘到飞机场的
大巴。

在中国乘公共汽车和美国一
样，前门上车，后门下车。上车先买
票，车上不找零，所以又叫无人售
票车。格林在北京的时候，常常乘
公共汽车去城里。可是有的时候
他也打的，也就是叫出租汽车。现
在中国的城市出租汽车很多，也
很方便。

hàn zì kè wén
汉 字 课 文

🔊 **Text in Chinese Characters**

▶▶▶

　　苏珊问约翰怎么去肯尼迪机场，约翰告诉她可以乘地铁，先
乘6号车到大中央车站，然后换7号车坐两站到时代广场，再乘
A车到终点。最后还要换去机场的大巴。可是苏珊说太麻烦。约
翰说可以坐出租汽车，可是苏珊说太贵。最后苏珊决定到时代
广场的长途汽车总站去乘到飞机场的大巴。
　　在中国乘公共汽车和美国一样，前门上车，后门下车。上
车先买票，车上<u>不找零</u>，所以又叫<u>无人售票车</u>。格林在北京的

时候，常常乘公共汽车去城里。可是有的时候他也打的，也就是叫出租汽车。现在中国的城市出租汽车很多，也很方便。 ◀◀◀

yǔ   yán   yīng   yòng   zhù   shì
语   言   应   用   注   释
Notes on Language Usage

1. 不找零

In this phrase 钱 is omitted. The phrase is actually 不找零钱, meaning no change is given on the bus.

2. 无人售票车

In China, many buses have conductors on them that sell tickets. Buses without conductors who sell tickets are known as 无人售票车.

▶ English Translations of the Texts

. . . .

Dialogue 1

Susan:	John, do you know how to get to JFK Airport?
John:	Of course I know. It depends on which is more important to you: saving money or convenience.
Susan:	First tell me the money-saving way.
John:	In that case, you can take the subway. You can take the #6 train to Grand Central Station, then change to the #7 train. You'll get to Times Square after two stops. Then you can take the A train to the end.
Susan:	Aren't the subway lines called the Red Line or Blue Line? How come there are both numbers and letters?
John:	You're thinking of the subway in Boston. The subway there uses color for routes. In the New York subway, there are many routes, so both numbers and letters are used. After you get off the subway, you still need to change to the airport bus.
Susan:	That's too much trouble. I heard that the subway in New York is also messy and chaotic. You'd better tell me the (more) convenient way.
John:	Of course. Take a taxi. It's both quick and convenient, but it's a little more expensive. It's about 50 dollars.
Susan:	That's too expensive. Is there any other way?
John:	You can take the subway to the long-distance bus station at Times Square. You will find the bus that goes to the airport. It costs only a little more than 10 dollars.
Susan:	That's not bad. I'll go to the long-distance bus station.

Dialogue 2

Xiaonian Wang:	Are there subways in China?
Green:	Yes, Beijing, Guangzhou and Shanghai have subway systems that are much more beautiful than the New York (subway). But the routes are very few. They're still expanding. In addition, Nanjing and other cities are building subway systems.
Xiaonian Wang:	What transportation did you usually take in China?
Green:	I often took the bus. The subway didn't go to our school.
Xiaonian Wang:	Are there many people on the bus?
Green:	There are quite a lot of people during rush hour. It's OK at normal times.
Xiaonian Wang:	Is riding a bus in China the same as in America?
Green:	About the same. Passengers get on board at the front door, and get off at the back door. When you get on board, you should pay first by putting money into the cash box. You may pay with coins or bills. But no change is given.
Xiaonian Wang:	Do the buses have air-conditioning?
Green:	Some do, some don't. The fare of the buses with air-conditioning is one dollar more than those without.
Xiaonian Wang:	Did you take the bus every time you went downtown?
Green:	No, sometimes I would "dadi."
Xiaonian Wang:	What is dadi?
Green:	Taking a taxi. It is now called dadi in China.
Xiaonian Wang:	That's funny. I will dadi the next time I go to China.

Narration

Susan asks John how to get to JFK Airport. John tells her that she could take the subway. She could take the #6 train to Grand Central Station first, then change to the #7 train and take it two stops to Times Square. She could then take the A train to her destination. In the end, she would also need to take the airport bus to get to the airport. But Susan says it is too much trouble, so John says that she could take a taxi. But Susan says it is too expensive. Finally, Susan decides to go to the long-distance bus station at Times Square and take the airport bus.

Riding a bus in China is the same as in America. One gets on board at the front door and gets off at the back door. When one gets on board, one needs to buy a ticket first. No change is given on the bus. So, it is also called an "unmanned bus." When Green was in Beijing, he often took city buses downtown. But sometimes he also would "dadi," or "take a taxi." There are many taxi cabs in Chinese cities, and they are very convenient.

tīng shuō liàn xí

听 说 练 习

▶ **Exercises for Listening and Speaking**

. . . .

🔘 一、完成对话。*(1. Work with a partner to complete the dialogues.)*

A: Qǐng wèn dào fēijīchǎng zěnme zǒu?

B: _____

A: Niǔyuē de dìtiě zěnme yòu shì shùzì yòu shì zìmǔ?

B: _____

A: Chúle zuò dìtiě hái kěyǐ zěnme qù jīchǎng?

B: _____

A: Kěshì chūzūchē tài guì le, jiù méiyǒu bié de fāngfǎ le ma?

B: _____

A: Zhège fāngfǎ bù tài máfan, yě bù tài guì, wǒ jiù qù chángtú qìchēzhàn ba.

B: _____

🔘 二、听对话，回答问题。*(2. Listen to the conversation on the audio recording and answer the questions.)*

1. Why does B know how to get to the airport?

_____

2. What is the problem associated with taking a taxi?

_____

3. What is the inexpensive way to get to the airport?

_____

4. Where can A take the airport bus?

_____

三、先听对话，然后两人一组朗读。*(3. Listen to the following conversation without looking at the book, and then read it aloud in pairs, first by following the pinyin, then by following the characters.)*

Jiǎ: Nǐ zài Zhōngguó de shíhòu cháng zuò gōnggòng qìchē ma?

Yǐ: Cháng zuò.

Jiǎ: Gōnggòng qìchē shàng rén duō ma?

Yǐ: Shàngxiàbān de shíhòu rén bǐjiào duō, píngshí hái hǎo.

Jiǎ: Tīng shuō Zhōngguó de gōnggòng qìchē shàng dōu yǒu rén mài piào?

Yǐ: Bù, yě yǒu wúrén shòupiào chē.

Jiǎ: Wúrén shòupiào chē gēn Měiguó de gōnggòng qìchē yīyàng ma?

Yǐ: Chàbuduō. Cóng qiánmén shàng chē, hòumén xià chē, shàng le chē xiān fù qián, shì wǎng tóubìxiāng tóu qián.

Jiǎ: Yàoshi gōnggòngqìchē rén duō nǐ zěnme bàn?

Yǐ: Wǒ jiù dǎdī.

Jiǎ: Shénme shì "dǎdī"?

Yǐ: Jiùshì zuò chūzū qìchē.

Jiǎ: Bù jiào zuò chūzū qìchē le? Yǒuyìsi. Hǎo, xiàcì wǒ yě dǎdī.

甲：你在中国的时候常坐公共汽车吗？

乙：常坐。

甲：公共汽车上人多吗？

乙：上下班的时候人比较多，平时还好。

甲：听说中国的公共汽车上都有人卖票？

乙：不，也有无人售票车。

甲：无人售票车跟美国的公共汽车一样吗？

乙：差不多。从前门上车，后门下车，上了车先付钱，是往投币箱投钱。

甲：要是公共汽车人多你怎么办？

乙：我就打的。

甲：什么是"打的"？

乙：就是坐出租汽车。

甲：不叫坐出租汽车了？有意思。好，下次我也打的。

四、角色表演。*(4. Role Play.)*

1. A: Suppose you are a stranger traveling in this city and don't know how the transportation system works. Try to find out information by asking a passerby.

   B: A visitor from another city asks you for help. Please explain how the public transportation system works, including the city buses and subways.

2. A: You are an attendant working at a gas station. Someone approaches you and asks how to get to the airport. Try to give detailed directions.

B: You got lost on the way to the airport. Ask the gas station attendant for help.

diàn nǎo yǔ   hàn zì   liàn xí
电 脑 与 汉 字 练 习

▶ **Exercises for Computing and Learning Characters**

. . . .

一、打出下面段落。*(1. Type the following passage.)*

A: 先生 (xiānsheng, mister; sir)，打的。

B: 你们到哪儿？

A: 我们到南京路 (Nánjīnglù, Nanjing Road) 买东西。

B: 你们走去就可以了。

A: 怎么走？

B: 出门往左，过三个红绿灯，往右拐再过五个十字路口，再往右拐，过三个红绿灯，然后再往右拐一直 (yìzhí, straight) 走，过五个十字路口。

A: 我们就到南京路了？

B: 不，又回来了。

二、把下面拼音句子打成汉字。*(2. Type the following pinyin sentences and select the appropriate characters from the list that appears on your computer screen.)*

1. Xiǎojiě, dào Shídài Guǎngchǎng duōshǎo qián?

2. Chéng yī zhàn hé dào zhōngdiǎnzhàn yīyàng, dōu shì liǎng kuài qián.

3. Nà yào kàn nǐ shì yào shěng qián háishì yào fāngbiàn.

4. Tài máfan le, tīng shuō Niǔyuē de dìtiě yě hěn luàn.

5. Běijīng hé Shànghǎi de dìtiě bǐ Niǔyuē de piàoliang duō le, dàn xiànlù hěn shǎo, hái zài kuòjiàn.

三、圈出正确的汉字。*(3. Circle the correct character to fill in the blanks.)*

1. 肯尼迪飞 ___（几、机、鸡、饥、讥）场在曼哈顿的东南边。

2. 我想去体育 ___（汤、杨、扬、场、肠），可是不知道在哪儿？

3. 请问，去时代广场的 ___（他、她、池、地、圳）铁在哪儿？

4. 中国城市的交 ___（桶、迪、退、逋、通）已经好多了。

5. 王友的 ___（敷、敕、数、偻、耧）学和英文都很好。

四、读生字，找出偏旁部首。*(4. The characters in each of the following groups share a radical. Read the characters and write the shared radicals.)*

   Example: 这 迎 shared radical: 辶

1. 场 地 城 shared radical: _____

2. 终 线 shared radical: _____

3. 投 打 扩 shared radical: _____

4. 途 道 通 shared radical: _____

5. 样 机 shared radical: _____

6. 钱 铁 错 shared radical: _____

7. 海 波 汽 shared radical: _____

8. 说 调 shared radical: _____

五、把汉字分成部件。*(5. Test your understanding of character structure by dividing the following characters into their component parts.)*

   Example: 吗—>口 马

1. 站 —>_____

2. 终 —>_____

3. 知 —>_____

4. 城 —>_____

5. 听 —>_____

六、学生字 *(6. Learning New Characters)*

独体词组复合词。(Form compound words based on single-character words.)

注释 (Note): Most Chinese characters are words themselves, called 独 (dú, single) 体 (tǐ, body) 词. In this exercise you will be asked to find compound words that contain some common single-character words you have already learned.

Study the following characters selected from the New Words lists: 地*　正　有　中*　上

1. Copy each character by hand using the character writing demonstration sheet at the end of this lesson.

2. For each character marked with an asterisk, find the compounds in which the characters are used in the text, and write the compound words next to the characters.

3. With the assistance of a dictionary or an online dictionary, write down three more compounds in which these single-character words appear.

4. For each character marked with an asterisk, make a sentence with one of the three new compounds.

Character Writing Demonstration Sheet 第六课　　　姓名＿＿＿＿＿＿

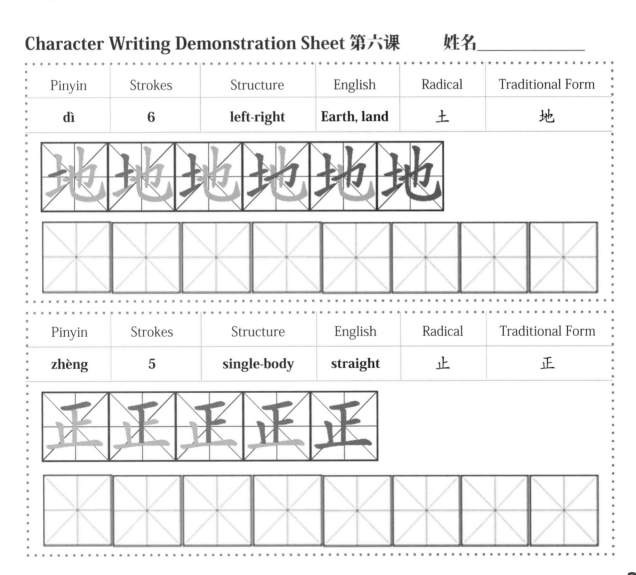

Pinyin	Strokes	Structure	English	Radical	Traditional Form
dì	6	left-right	Earth, land	土	地

Pinyin	Strokes	Structure	English	Radical	Traditional Form
zhèng	5	single-body	straight	止	正

Pinyin	Strokes	Structure	English	Radical	Traditional Form
yǒu	6	single-body	have	月	有

有 有 有 有 有 有

Pinyin	Strokes	Structure	English	Radical	Traditional Form
zhōng	4	single-body	middle, center	丨	中

中 中 中 中

Pinyin	Strokes	Structure	English	Radical	Traditional Form
shàng	3	single-body	up, upper	卜	上

上 上 上

kè   wén liàn xí
课   文   练   习

▶ **Exercises for Understanding the Texts**

··

一、根据课文回答问题。*(1. Answer the questions orally based on the text.)*

对话(1)

1. 苏珊要到哪儿去？
   Where is Susan going?

2. 要是苏珊想省钱，她怎么去机场？
   What is the best way to go to the airport if Susan wants to save money?

3. 为什么苏珊不想省钱？
   Why doesn't Susan want to save money?

4. 去机场方便的方法要花多少钱？
   How much does it cost to use the convenient way to go to the airport?

5. 要是苏珊坐大巴去机场，她要到哪儿上车？
   If Susan takes the shuttle to go to the airport, where does she catch the bus?

对话(2)

1. 格林认为中国的地铁怎么样？
   What does Green think about the subways in China?

2. 格林在中国的时候常坐什么车？
   What kind of transportation did Green often take when he was in China?

3. 为什么格林不坐地铁？
   Why didn't Green take the subway?

4. 说一说在中国怎么坐汽车？
   Please tell how to take a bus in China.

5. 带空调的汽车车票一张多少钱？不带的呢？
   How much does it cost for a bus with air-conditioning?
   How much is the ticket for a bus without air-conditioning?

6. "打的" 是什么意思？

What does 打的 mean?

二、完成对话。*(2. Complete the dialogue orally using* 就是,那就要看*.)*

1. 那本书很有意思,_____。

(It is just a little too long.)

2. 我们今天到哪儿去吃晚饭？_____。

(It depends on what kind of food you like.)

3. 你认识小王吗？_____。

(It depends on which Xiao Wang you are talking about.)

4. 这件毛衣很便宜，_____。

(It is just that it's a little too big for me.)

5. 你知道去中国城怎么走吗？_____。

(It depends on whether you are taking the subway or the bus.)

三、先用 "比" 和 "Num+M" 改写下面的句子，再朗读。*(3. Rewrite the following-ing sentences using* 比 *and a number + measure, then read the sentences aloud.)*

Example:

坐地铁两块钱，出租汽车五十块钱。

（坐地铁比出租汽车便宜四十八块钱。）

1. 这件黑上衣五十九块九毛九，那件蓝的二十四块九毛九。

2. 哥哥今年买运动衣用了九十块，我今年用了六十块。

3. 从学校坐地铁到JFK 机场要一个半小时，坐出租车一个小时。

4. 上个星期可乐两块钱，这个星期三块七毛五。

5. 我今天写作业用了四个小时，昨天只用了一半的时间。

四、用"有的……有的"或"只是"回答下列问题。*(4. Use 有的……有的 or 只是 to answer the following questions orally.)*

1. A: 你们班的学生都是美国人吗？

   B: _____ 。

2. A: 你家的人都喜欢吃什么饭？

   B: _____ 。

3. A: 北京的公共汽车都有空调吗？

   B: _____ 。

4. A: 坐出租到你家又快又方便，是吧？

   B: _____ 。

5. A: 你的朋友都喜欢听音乐 (yīnyuè, music) 吗？

   B: _____ 。

6. A: 这件衣服你穿真好看，买一件吧？

   B: _____ 。

五、作文 *(5. Composition)*

Write a paragraph (7-10 sentences) to describe the public transportation system in your city. Make sure to use the given words and phrases.

1. 又是……又是   2. 只是   3. 另外   4. 有的……有的   5. 差不多
6. 除了以外，还

六、翻译 *(6. Translation)*

Translate the following sentences orally in class. Then type your translations in Chinese using the words and phrases provided.

1. Are you going to a dance party this weekend?

2. It depends on whether or not I can finish my homework. (要看)

3. Do you like dancing or playing ball? (是……还是)

4. At Xiaonian Wang's birthday party, some of his friends were dancing, some were drinking cola and some were playing on the computer. (有的，有的)

5. It is easy to learn to speak Chinese, but pronouncing the four tones accurately is a little tough. (只是)

6. This sportswear fits me very well, but it's just a bit too expensive for me. (只是，点儿)

7. When is Xiaonian Wang's birthday party going to start? About eight o'clock. (左右)

8. My younger sister has a lot more money than I do. (比，多了)

9. This black jacket is better than the blue one, but the price is almost the same. (差不多)

10. At the supermarket, Xiaonian Wang bought some soap, detergent and shampoo. In addition, he also bought something to eat. (另外)

bǔ　chōng　yuè　dú　liàn　xí
补　充　阅　读　练　习
▶ Supplementary Reading Exercises

Controlled Vocabulary

Read the following passage and answer the questions either in Chinese or in English.

	Chinese	Pinyin	Part of Speech	English
1.	中心	zhōngxīn	N	center; heart; core
2.	干净	gānjìng	Adj	clean; neat and tidy
3.	石景山	Shíjǐngshān	N	name of a place in Beijing

(1) 中国的地铁

　　在中国的城市里，乘车都很方便，可是有地铁的时间没有美国长。很多年只有北京、上海，和广州三个大城市有地铁。

　　北京的地铁是六十年代开始修建的。那时只有从北京市中心到石景山一条线路，七二年试通车，七八年修好现在的线路以后，全线开始通车。

　　中国的地铁站都很漂亮，每个车站看上去都不一样，也比较干净。北京的地铁刚通车的時候，坐一次车一毛钱，后来要付两毛，五毛。现在的地铁票比以前贵多了，坐一条线，车票三块钱，换线就要付四块钱，五块钱。

Questions

1. 在中国有哪几个城市有地铁？

   Which cities in China have subway systems?

2. 北京有地铁大约多长时间了？

   Approximately how long has the city of Beijing had its subway system?

3. 北京的地铁是什么时候开始通车的？

   When did the subway in Bejing begin operating?

4. 北京地铁开运时的车票多少钱一张？

   How much was the fare at the beginning?

5. 现在车票多少钱一张？

   How much is the fare now?

6. 现在旅客要是需要换车要付多少钱？

   How much does a passenger have to pay if he/she needs to change to another line?

(2) Open Vocabulary

This exercise is called "Open Vocabulary" because it contains some vocabulary words that have not been introduced in this book. In this exercise, you should first look for words you already recognize, and then try to guess the meaning of an entire phrase or sentence based on the words you already know. When you get stuck, use a dictionary to look up words whose meanings are crucial to your understanding of the passage. You can also retrieve an electronic version of this text from the accompanying online materials, and use an online dictionary or translation program to help you read it.

After answering the questions, try to tell the story to a classmate in your own words without looking at the original text.

	Chinese	Pinyin	Part of Speech	English
1.	驾照	jiàzhào	N	driver's license; permit
2.	主考(官)	zhǔkǎo(guān)	N	chief examiner; proctor
3.	离开	líkāi	V	leave; depart from
4.	昏迷	hūnmí	V	stupor; coma

(2) 不知道

汤姆考汽车驾照回到家,太太问他:"怎么样,考过了吗?"

"不知道。"汤姆说。"怎么不知道呢?在你离开考场的时候,主考官是怎么对你说的呢?""他什么也没说。当我离开的时候,他还在昏迷着。"

Questions

1. 汤姆回家以前去做什么了？What did Tom do before he went back home?

2. 他考过了吗？Did he pass the test?

3. 他为什么不知道结果？Why didn't he know the results?

4. 你觉得主考官怎么了？What do you think happened to the proctor?

zhōng guó   wén   huà   xí   sú
中　国　文　化　习　俗
Chinese Customs and Culture

···

zhōng guó　de　jiāo　tōng
中　国　的　交　通
▶ Transportation in China

Like most sectors of Chinese society, the transportation system has changed radically since the start of economic reform in the 1970s. While owning a car is still an unattainable dream for most Chinese, the rush hour gridlock in major urban centers like Beijing and Shanghai is a clear indication of the growth of car ownership in China. In 2003, official statistics indicated that more than 10 million people in China owned personal autos. China is poised to become the world's second largest market for cars, as personal incomes soar and the government pumps billions of dollars into building the highway infrastructure. And although foreign auto makers have seized the opportunity to develop their Chinese sales, the vast majority of Chinese people continue to use mass transit as their sole means of transportation.

Air Travel

China's airline industry has witnessed steady growth since the late 1970s. By the end of 2003, a total of 1,176 domestic and international airlines were operating in China. According to a landmark pact signed between China and the United States on June 18, 2004, the number of weekly flights between the two countries would increase nearly five times from a limit of 54 weekly round trip flights to 249 flights within a period of six years. At the end of 2004, China had 133 airports for commercial flights, and a total of 1,279 commercial flight routes, 1,035 of them domestic routes reaching all large and medium-sized cities, and 244 of them international routes, connecting China with more than 70 cities overseas.

Airline tickets can be booked through travel agencies, local offices of the Civil Aviation Administration of China (CAAC) or at large hotels. Some ticket agents often give big discounts to attract customers. As in the United States, the check-in times for all domestic flights are one hour before departure and two hours before departure for international flights.

▶ Traditional transport in modern times—Yunnan, China.

Train Travel

China has one of the busiest rail networks in the world. At present, the train is still the primary means of transportation in China. The comprehensive rail network goes to every part of the country, including the "Roof of the World," Tibet. On a global basis, China's rail transport volume is one of the world's largest, having six percent of the world's operating railways, and carrying 25 percent of the world's total railway workload. Travel by rail can be an enjoyable, relaxing, and inexpensive way to see China's countryside. There are five kinds of long distance trains in China. Fast (K trains), Faster (T trains, with limited stops), Tourist (N trains) and Express (Z trains, no stops). In 2007, a new type of train began to offer express service between major cities. They are called D trains (动车组), and they are currently the fastest and most expensive trains in China. It only takes 3 hours and 39 minutes from Beijing to Shenyang (709 kilometers) on a D train.

There are four classes on Chinese trains:

1. Hard seat (硬座, yìngzuò, YZ): This is the cheapest way to travel.
2. Soft seat (软座, ruǎnzuò, RZ): This class is not always available, but when it is available, it offers more comfortable, cushioned seats than the hard seat class.
3. Hard sleeper (硬卧 yìngwò, YW): This is a sleeper car containing six beds per section. The berths are open to the passageway.
4. Soft sleeper (软卧 ruǎnwò, RW): There are four beds per private compartment in the soft sleeper cars.

▶ What type of seat is this?

Long Distance Buses

China's comprehensive highway network reaches every part of the country. China is currently investing significant funds in creating and improving its 1.76 million kilometers of highways. All China's tourist cities have good transportation and communication facilities.

Almost all major cities and towns have long-distance bus stations. Tickets are sold at the bus

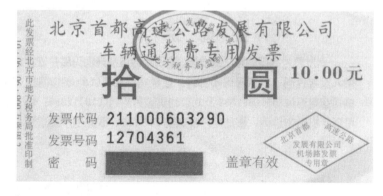

▶ Highway fee receipt in Beijing.

station itself and need not be booked in advance. Ticket prices may vary according to the condition of the buses, but there is no class difference within the same bus. Bus travel is often cheaper than train travel of the same distance.

City Buses

All major Chinese cities have their own local public transportation networks. Most buses run from 6 am to 11 pm, with some providing 24-hour service. Fares typically range from one to three *yuan*, depending on the length of the route, the condition of the bus itself, and whether or not the bus has air-conditioning. In major tourist cities, the destinations are reported in both Chinese and English.

▶ **A bus ticket.**

Tourist Buses

In some tourist cities, special tourist bus lines are designed for visitors to tour the main sights in and around the city. Almost all of these tourist buses are air-conditioned and fares differ according to the length of the route.

▶ **A tourist bus ticket.**

▶ **Bus stop signs in Shanghai.**

▶ Bus stop signs in Beijing.

Taxis

Taking a taxi in both large and small cities is very convenient. Cabs can be hailed as anywhere in the world by simply waving one's hand. When taking taxis, meters should always be used. Remember that there is no custom of tipping, and your driver will not expect one.

Bicycles

China has been dubbed the "Kingdom of Bicycles." Although private ownership of cars has grown in recent years, bicycle is still the primary means of transportation for most people in China. During rush hours in big cities, you can see commuters riding in a stream of bicycles, in lanes specially designed for bicycle traffic. The cheapest (new) 1-speed adult bikes start at around US $40.00. Chinese cities are generally flat, and so gearing has never been a particularly important aspect of cycling in China. While bicycles in China have no lights, all of them have bicycle bells for alerting others.

The Subway

Currently in China, the cities of Beijing, Shanghai, Guangzhou and Nanjing have subway systems. Many of these systems are brand new, and so traveling by subway is generally quick, comfortable, and clean. Announcements are usually made in both Chinese and English, but are not always easy to hear. In Hong Kong, the announcements are in Mandarin, Cantonese, and English. Traveling via the subway is quick and clean. If it goes where you want to go, you should definitely try it.

▶ Test Your Knowledge How will you get there?

1. I am traveling from Shanghai to Beijing. I can take (choose as many as you can):

   ( ) A. subway ( ) B. train ( ) C. long-distance bus ( ) D. plane ( ) E. bicycle ( ) F. taxi

2. I am traveling from Shanghai to Beijing, but I have only 30 *yuan*. I can possibly take (choose as many as you can):

   ( ) A. subway ( ) B. train ( ) C. long-distance bus ( ) D. plane ( ) E. bicycle ( ) F. taxi

3. I am touring Beijing. I want to go to the Great Wall. I can take (choose as many as you can):

   ( ) A. subway ( ) B. train ( ) C. long-distance bus ( ) D. plane ( ) E. city bus ( ) F. taxi ( ) G. bicycle

4. I am touring Beijing. I want to go to Tian'anmen Square. I can take (choose as many as you can):

   ( ) A. subway ( ) B. train ( ) C. long-distance bus ( ) D. plane ( ) E. city bus ( ) F. taxi ( ) G. bicycle

Answers:

1. I am traveling from Shanghai to Beijing. I can take (choose as many as you can):

   B, C, D

2. I am traveling from Shanghai to Beijing., but I have only 30 yuan, I can possibly take (choose as many as you can):

   B, C

3. I am touring Beijing. I want to go to the Great Wall. I can take (choose as many as you can):

   B, C, E, F, G

4. I am touring Beijing. I want to go to Tian'anmen Square. I can take (choose as many as you can):

   A, E, F, G

▶ A subway entrance at Gulou, Nanjing.

dì qī kè
第 七 课
LESSON 7

lǔ   xíng
旅   行
Travel

▶ **Objectives:**

1. To make travel plans
2. To book and purchase airline tickets
3. To change airline tickets

duì   huà   yī
对　　话　　(一)

DIALOGUE 1

qù   xià   wēi   yí   guò   shèng dàn   jié
去　夏　威　夷　过　圣　诞　节
▶ **Going to Hawaii for Christmas**

shēng   cí
生　　词
New Words

	Chinese	Pinyin	Part of Speech	English
1.	圣诞节	Shèngdàn Jié	N	Christmas
2.	彼德	Bǐdé	PN	Peter (a name)
3.	回	huí	V	return; go back; turn around; answer; reply
4.	小时	xiǎoshí	N	hour
5.	飞机	fēijī	N	aircraft; airplane; plane
6.	洛杉矶	Luòshānjī	PN	Los Angeles
7.	转	zhuǎn	V	turn; transfer
8.	再说	zàishuō	Conj	what's more; besides
9.	感恩节	Gǎn'ēn Jié	N	Thanksgiving
10.	那么	nàme	Conj	then; in that case; such being the case
11.	远	yuǎn	Adj	far; distant; remote
12.	夏威夷	Xiàwēiyí	PN	Hawaii

13.	过	guò	V/Par	spend (time); celebrate a special occasion; (an aspectual particle)
14.	多	duō	Adj/Ad	many; much; more; far more
15.	真的	zhēnde	Ad	really
16.	马上	mǎshàng	Ad	at once; immediately; right away
17.	旅行社	lǚxíngshè	N	travel agency
	旅行	lǚxíng	N	travel; journey; tour
18.	电话	diànhuà	N	telephone; phone; phone call
19.	订	dìng	V	subscribe to (a newspaper, etc.); book (seats, tickets, etc.); order (merchandise, etc.)
20.	航空	hángkōng	N	aviation
21.	公司	gōngsī	N	company; corporation
22.	西北航空公司	Xīběi Hángkōng Gōngsī	PN	Northwest Airlines
23.	空中	kōngzhōng	N	in the sky; in the air
24.	俱乐部	jùlèbù	N	club
25.	会员证	huìyuánzhèng	N	membership card
	会员	huìyuán	N	member
	证	zhèng	N	(ID) card; certificate
26.	行	xíng	V	go; travel; all right; OK
27.	记得	jìde	V	remember
28.	没关系	méiguānxì	CE	it doesn't matter; it's nothing; that's all right; never mind

pīn yīn kè wén
拼 音 课 文

🔊 **Text with Pinyin**

▶▶▶

sū shān: nǐ shèng dàn jié huí jiā ma?
苏 珊： 你 圣 诞 节 回 家 吗？

bǐ dé: bù zhī dào. huí jiā yào xiān zuò wǔ liù gè
彼 德： 不 知 道。 回 家 要 先 坐 五、 六 个
xiǎo shí de fēi jī dào luò shān jī, zài zhuǎn
小 时 的 飞 机 到 洛 杉 矶， 再 转
fēi jī, tài lèi le. zài shuō, wǒ gǎn ēn jié
飞 机， 太 累 了。 再 说， 我 感 恩 节
cái huí qù guò.
才 回 去 过。

sū shān: nǐ jiā zěn me nà me yuǎn? zài nǎr?
苏 珊： 你 家 怎 么 那 么 远？ 在 哪 儿？

bǐ dé: zài xià wēi yí.
彼 德： 在 夏 威 夷。

sū shān: zài xià wēi yí guò shèng dàn jié, nà duō yǒu
苏 珊： 在 夏 威 夷 过 圣 诞 节， 那 多 有
yì si. wǒ gēn nǐ yì qǐ qù, zěn me yàng?
意 思。 我 跟 你 一 起 去， 怎 么 样？

bǐ dé: zhēn de? nà tài hǎo le. wǒ men mǎ shàng gěi
彼 德： 真 的？ 那 太 好 了。 我 们 马 上 给
lǚ xíng shè dǎ diàn huà dìng fēi jī piào.
旅 行 社 打 电 话 订 飞 机 票。

sū shān: nǐ zuò nǎ jiā háng kōng gōng sī de fēi jī?
苏 珊： 你 坐 哪 家 航 空 公 司 的 飞 机？

bǐ dé: nǐ zuò nǎ jiā de, wǒ jiù zuò nǎ jiā de.
彼 德： 你 坐 哪 家 的， 我 就 坐 哪 家 的。

苏珊： sū shān: nà hǎo, jiù zuò xī běi ba. wǒ yǒu xī běi
那 好，就 坐 西 北 吧。我 有 西 北
háng kōng gōng sī de kōng zhōng jù lè bù huì
航 空 公 司 的 空 中 俱 乐 部 会
yuán zhèng.
员 证。

彼德： bǐ dé: xíng. kě shì wǒ jì de nǐ bà ba, mā ma
行。可 是 我 记 得 你 爸 爸、妈 妈
gěi nǐ mǎi le huí jiā de fēi jī piào, nǐ
给 你 买 了 回 家 的 飞 机 票，你
bù huí qù kàn tā men ma?
不 回 去 看 他 们 吗？

苏珊： sū shān: méi guān xi. wǒ qǐng tā men gěi wǒ gǎi piào,
沒 关 系。我 请 他 们 给 我 改 票，
wǎn jǐ tiān huí qù.
晚 几 天 回 去。

彼德： bǐ dé: hǎo, wǒ men qù dìng piào.
好，我 们 去 订 票。

hàn zì kè wén
汉 字 课 文
🔘 **Text in Chinese Characters**

▶▶▶

苏珊：你圣诞节回家吗？

彼德：不知道。回家要先坐五、六个小时的飞机到洛杉矶，再
转（飞）机，太累了。再说我感恩节才回去过。

苏珊：你家怎么那么远？在哪儿？

彼德：在夏威夷。

苏珊：在夏威夷过圣诞节，那多有意思。我跟你一起去，怎么
样？

彼德：<u>真的</u>？那太好了。我们马上给旅行社打电话订飞机票。

苏珊：你坐哪家航空公司的飞机？

彼德：你坐<u>哪家</u>的，我就坐<u>哪家</u>的。

苏珊：那好，就坐西北吧。我有西北航空公司的空中俱乐部会员证。

彼德：<u>行</u>。可是我记得你爸爸、妈妈给你买了回家的飞机票，你不回去看他们吗？

苏珊：没关系。我叫他们给我改票，<u>晚几天回去</u>。

彼德：好，我们去订票。

yǔ yán yīng yòng zhù shì
语   言   应   用   注   释
Notes on Language Usage

1. 先坐五、六个小时的飞机到洛杉矶，再转(飞)机。**First take a five or six hour flight to Los Angeles, and then change planes.**

*a) 先……再……

先 means "first," and 再 means "then." Both are adverbs used before verbs to indicate a sequence of actions.

For example:

先坐 6 号车到大中央车站，然后换 7 号车，

Xiān zuò liù hào chē dào Dàzhōngyāng Chēzhàn, ránhòu huàn qī hào chē,

► Christmas in Hawaii.

坐 两 站 到 时 代 广 场 ， 再 坐 A 车 到 终 点 。（第六课）

zuò liǎng zhàn dào Shídài Guǎngchǎng, zài zuò A chē dào zhōngdiǎn.

First you can take the #6 train to Grand Central Station, then change to the #7 train. You will get to Times Square after two stops. Then you can take the A train to the end. (Lesson 6)

他 每 天 都 是 先 刷 牙 (shuāyá, to brush one's teeth) 再 洗 脸 (xǐliǎn, to wash one's face) 。

Tā měitiān dōu shì xiān shuāyá zài xǐliǎn.

Every day he first brushes his teeth, then washes his face.

b) 五 、六个

In Chinese, two adjacent numbers followed by a measure word can be used together to indicate a rough quantity around these two numbers. This is limited to the numbers one to nine.

For example:

三 、四 本 ；七 、八 张 ；八 、九 天 。

Sānsì běn; qībā zhāng; bājiǔ tiān.

Three or four books; seven or eight pieces of paper; eight or nine days.

我 每 天 都 要 学 六 、七 个 生 词 。

Wǒ měitiān dōu yào xué liù, qī gè shēngcí.

Every day I learn about six or seven new words.

The same usage can be applied to ten and above in the following way:

十 一 、二 个 ；十 四 、五 岁 ；三 十 二 、三 岁 ；五、六 十 个 人 等 等 。

Shíyī, èr ge; shísì, wǔ suì; sānshí'èr; sān suì; wǔ, liùshí ge rén děngděng.

Eleven or twelve (pieces), fourteen or fifteen years old, thirty-two or thirty-three years old, fifty or sixty people, etc.

2. 我感恩节才回去过。 **I've just been home for Thanksgiving.**

过 is an aspectual particle, and it is placed after a verb to indicate past experience.

For example:

我 去 过 中 国 。

Wǒ qù guò Zhōngguó.

I have been to China.

(For details, please see Grammar Book I, Lesson 7.)

*3. 你家怎么那么远？ **How come your home is so far away?**

N + 怎么 + 这么/那么 + Adj/Verb "How come...so...?; Why...so...?"

> **For example:**
>
> 你 的 电 脑 怎 么 这 么 小 ？
>
> Nǐ de diànnǎo zěnme zhème xiǎo?
>
> How come your computer is so small?
>
> 超 市 怎 么 那 么 远 ？
>
> Chāoshì zěnme nàme yuǎn?
>
> How come the supermarket is so far?
>
> 你 怎 么 这 么 说 ？
>
> Nǐ zěnme zhème shuō?
>
> How can you talk like that?

4. 在夏威夷过圣诞节，那多有意思。 **It would be a lot of fun to spend Christmas in Hawaii.**

*a) 过

过 is a verb here, used to mean "to celebrate a special occasion," such as 过生日 (celebrate a birthday), 过年 (celebrate the New Year), 过春节 (Chūnjié, celebrate Spring Festival), 过中秋节 (Zhōngqiūjié, celebrate Mid-Autumn Festival), 过感恩节 (celebrate Thanksgiving), 过圣诞节 (celebrate Christmas) 等。

> **For example:**
>
> 你 在 哪 儿 过 春 节 ？
>
> Nǐ zài nǎr guò Chūnjié?
>
> Where are you going to spend the Spring Festival?

*b) 多

多 is an adverb, and it is often used to add emphasis or in exclamatory sentences. It is the same as 多么 "how..." or "so..."

> **For example:**
>
> 那 个 小 孩 长 得 多 好 玩 。
>
> Nàge xiǎohái zhǎng de duō hàowán.
>
> That child is so cute!
>
> 你 妈 妈 做 的 菜 多 好 吃 ， 我 吃 得 太 饱 了 。
>
> Nǐ māma zuò de cài duō hǎochī, wǒ chī de tài bǎo le.
>
> Your mother's food is so delicious. I ate until I was full.

5. 真的？

真的 means "really?" This phrase is used for situations in which the speaker can hardly believe what is being said, or believes that something is too good to be true.

For example:

A: 明 天 校 长 给 我 们 班 上 课。

Míngtiān xiàozhǎng gěi wǒmen bān shàngkè.

The school president will teach our class tomorrow.

B: 真 的？谁 告 诉 你 的？

Zhēnde? Shéi gàosù nǐ de?

Really? Who told you?

A: 要 是 你 会 做 这 道 题，我 给 你 十 块 钱。

Yàoshì nǐ huì zuò zhè dào tí, wǒ gěi nǐ shíkuài qián.

If you can solve this problem, I will give you 10 bucks.

B: 真 的？

Zhēnde?

Really?

6. 你坐哪家的，我就坐哪家的。 I will take whichever you take.

Chinese speakers sometimes use the same question word twice in one sentence, in this case meaning, "Whichever one you take, I will take." Here the question words are not used to ask questions, but rather to state "whoever," whatever," "whichever," "however," etc. Both question words refer to the same person, object, matter, time, place, etc. The first clause sets up a condition or range for the second clause, and the second clause follows up by referring back to the same noun.

More examples:

1. 谁 知 道 谁 回 答 这 个 问 题。

Shéi zhīdào, shéi huídá zhège wèntí.

Whoever knows how to answer this question, please answer it.

2. 谁 有 车，我 就 跟 谁 去。

Shéi yǒu chē, wǒ jiù gēn shéi qù.

I will go with whomever has a car.

3. 你 买 什 么，我 就 买 什 么。

Nǐ mǎi shénme, wǒ jiù mǎi shénme.

I will buy whatever you buy.

4. 你 喜 欢 哪 个，我 就 送 你 哪 个。

Nǐ xǐhuān nǎge, wǒ jiù sòng nǐ nǎge.

Whichever one you like, I will give you that one.

5. 你 想 怎 么 说，就 怎 么 说。

Nǐ xiǎng zěnme shuō, jiù zěnme shuō.

Say whatever you want.

6. 哪 儿 有 好 玩 儿 的，他 就 去 哪 儿 玩 儿。

Nǎr yǒu hǎo wánr de, tā jiù qù nǎr wánr.

He will go wherever it is fun.

The choice of question word depends on what the speaker is talking about. If he/she is talking about a person, he/she should use 谁 as in examples (1) and (2). For an object or matter, use 什么 as in (3); for a place use 哪儿 as in (6); for manner, use 怎么 as in (5); for "which one," use 哪 + a measure word as in (4).

7. 行

Here 行 means "all right" or "OK." It is used to reply to a suggestion or request.

For example:

A: 你 去 超 市 的 时 候 给 我 买 点 儿 面 包。

Nǐ qù chāoshì de shíhòu gěi wǒ mǎi diǎnr miànbāo.

When you go to the supermarket, get some bread for me.

B: 行。

Xíng.

OK.

行 了，行 了，你 吃 得 太 多 了。

Xíng le, xíng le, nǐ chī de tài duō le.

OK, OK. You ate too much.

8. 记得

记得 means "to remember" or "recall". For example,

我 记 得 你 今 天 过 生 日。

Wǒ jìde nǐ jīntiān guò shēngrì.

I remember today is your birthday.

那 个 人 我 记 得，上 星 期 他 来 看 王 老 师 了。

Nàge rén wǒ jìde, shàng xīngqī tā lái kàn Wáng lǎoshī le.

I remember that person. He came to see Professor Wang last week.

9. 晚几天回去

晚 means "late" or "later on."

For example:

A: 你 怎 么 又 晚 了，都 上 课 半 个 小 时 了。

Nǐ zěnme yòu wǎn le, dōu shàngkè bàn gè xiǎoshí le.

How come you are late again? Class started half an hour ago.

B: 昨 天 我 睡 得 很 晚，今 天 起 晚 了。

Zuótiān wǒ shuì de hěn wǎn, jīntiān qǐ wǎn le.

I went to bed late last night, so I got up late today.

我 先 去 开 门，你 可 以 晚 点 去。

Wǒ xiān qù kāimén, nǐ kěyǐ wǎn diǎn qù.

I'll first go open the door. You can go a little later.

▶ The Shanghai Museum.

▶ The Pearl Tower, Shanghai.

▶ The Pudong area of Shanghai.

duì   huà   èr
对   话   (二)

Dialogue 2

gǎi   fēi   jī   piào
改   飞   机   票

▶ **Changing an Airplane Ticket**

shēng cí
生   词

🔘 **New Words**

	Chinese	Pinyin	Part of Speech	English
1.	改	gǎi	V	change; transform; alter; revise; correct
2.	晚	wǎn	Adj/N	evening; night; late; later
3.	喂	wèi/wéi	Int	hello; hey
4.	国际	guójì	N	international
5.	先生	xiānsheng	N	mister (Mr.); gentleman; sir
6.	噢	ō	Int	Oh!
7.	航班	hángbān	N	scheduled flight; flight number
8.	起飞	qǐfēi	V	(of an aircraft) take off
9.	职员	zhíyuán	N	office worker; staff member
10.	查	chá	V	check; examine; look into; investigate
11.	因为	yīnwèi	Conj	because; for
12.	罚金	fájīn	N	fine; forfeit
13.	美元	měiyuán	N	American dollar; US dollar

14.	只好	zhǐhǎo	Ad	have to
15.	成	chéng	V	accomplish; succeed; become
16.	芝加哥	Zhījiāgē	PN	Chicago
17.	早上	zǎoshang	N	(early) morning
18.	需要	xūyào	V/N	need; want; require; needs
19.	另	lìng	Adj	other; another
20.	一共	yīgòng	Ad	altogether; in all
21.	如果	rúguǒ	Conj	if; in case; in the event of
22.	旧金山	Jiùjīnshān	PN	San Fransisco
23.	美东(时间)	Měidōng (shíjiān)	PN	American Eastern (time zone)
24.	当天	dāngtiān	N	the same day; that very day
25.	款	kuǎn	N	a sum of money; fund
26.	号码	hàomǎ	N	number
27.	到期	dàoqī	V	become due; mature; expire

pīn　yīn　kè　wén
拼　音　课　文
🔘 **Text with Pinyin**

▶▶▶

sū　shān　bà　ba: wèi, qǐng wèn shì guó jì lǚ xíng shè
苏　珊　爸　爸：喂，请　问　是　国　际　旅　行　社
　　　　　　　　ma?
　　　　　　　吗？

旅行社: 是。我可以帮助您吗，先生？
lǚ xíng shè: shì. wǒ kě yǐ bāng zhù nín ma, xiān sheng?

苏珊爸爸：噢，我要改机票。
sū shān bà ba: ō, wǒ yào gǎi jī piào.

旅行社: 没问题。请您告诉我名字，航空公司，日期和航班号。
lǚ xíng shè: méi wèn tí. qǐng nín gào su wǒ míng zi, háng kōng gōng sī, rì qī hé háng bān hào.

苏珊爸爸：是我女儿的，她叫 Susan White，12月18日坐西北航空公司，251航班从夏威夷到纽约肯尼迪机场。
sū shān bà ba: shì wǒ nǚ ér de, tā jiào Susan White, shí'èr yuè shíbā rì zuò xī běi háng kōng gōng sī, èr wǔ yī háng bān cóng xià wēi yí dào niǔ yuē kěn ní dí jī chǎng.

（旅行社职员查电脑）
(lǚ xíng shè zhí yuán chá diàn nǎo)

旅行社: 找到了。因为您买的是便宜票，改票要付罚金100美元。请问您要怎么改？
lǚ xíng shè: zhǎo dào le. yīn wéi nín mǎi de shì pián yí piào, gǎi piào yào fù fá jīn yībǎi měi yuán. qǐng wèn nín yào zěn me gǎi?

苏珊爸爸: 那也只好付了。请改成 12 月 24 号，从夏威夷到波士顿。

旅行社: 好。12 月 24 号上午 8 点离开夏威夷，到洛杉矶转机去芝加哥，再从芝加哥到纽约，再转到波士顿，25 号早上 6 点到。需要另付 80 美元，再加 100 美元罚金，一共 180 美元。

苏珊爸爸: 可是要转那么多次，太麻烦了。有没有快一点儿的？

旅行社: 如果 25 号早上 6 点走，到旧金山转机，美东时

间 当 天 晚 10 点 可 以 到
jiān dāng tiān wǎn shí diǎn kě yǐ dào

波 士 顿。
bō shì dùn.

苏珊爸爸 (sū shān bà ba): 那 好。
nà hǎo.

旅行社 (lǚ xíng shè): 请 问 您 怎 么 付 款？
qǐng wèn nín zěn me fù kuǎn?

苏珊爸爸 (sū shān bà ba): 信 用 卡。
xìn yòng kǎ.

旅行社 (lǚ xíng shè): 好，请 告 诉 我 信 用 卡 号
hǎo, qǐng gào su wǒ xìn yòng kǎ hào

码 和 到 期 时 间。
mǎ hé dào qī shí jiān.

苏珊爸爸 (sū shān bà ba): 5 2 3 4 - 5 6 7 8 - 9
wǔ èr sān sì wǔ liù qī bā jiǔ

8 7 6 - 5 4 3 2，2 0
bā qī liù wǔ sì sān èr, èr líng

0 9 年 11 月 5 日。
líng jiǔ nián shíyī yuè wǔ rì.

旅行社 (lǚ xíng shè): 谢 谢。
xiè xiè.

hàn zì kè wén
汉 字 课 文

🔊 **Text in Chinese Characters**

▶▶▶

苏珊爸爸： 喂，请问是国际旅行社吗？

旅行社： 是。我可以帮助您吗，先生？

苏珊爸爸： 噢，我要改机票。

旅行社：	没问题。请您告诉我名字，航空公司，日期和航班号。
苏珊爸爸：	是我女儿的，她叫 Susan White，12月18日坐西北航空公司，<u>251航班</u>从夏威夷到纽约肯尼迪机场。

（旅行社职员查电脑）

旅行社：	<u>找到了</u>。因为您买的是便宜票，改票要付罚金100美元。请问您要怎么改？
苏珊爸爸：	那也<u>只好</u>付了。请改成12月24号，从夏威夷到波士顿。
旅行社：	好。12月24号上午8点离开夏威夷，到洛杉矶转机去芝加哥，再从芝加哥到纽约，再转到波士顿，25点早上6点到。需要另付80美元，再加100美元罚金，一共180美元。
苏珊爸爸：	可是要转那么多次，太麻烦了。有没有快一点儿的？
旅行社：	如果25点早上6点走，到旧金山转机，美东时间当天晚10点可以到波士顿。
苏珊爸爸：	那好。
旅行社：	请问您怎么付款？
苏珊爸爸：	信用卡。
旅行社：	好，请告诉我信用卡号码和到期时间。
苏珊爸爸：	5234-5678-9876-5432，2009年11月5日。
旅行社：	谢谢。

yǔ   yán   yīng   yòng   zhù   shì
语   言   应   用   注   释
Notes on Language Usage

1. 喂

喂 is used to begin a phone call in Chinese. It is the same as "hello" in English.

2. 我可以帮助您吗，先生？ **Sir, may I help you?**

This sentence is translated directly from English, and is now used often in large stores, hotels and airports in China.

3. 噢

噢 is an interjection, used to answer someone who calls you or to show your understanding of what someone has said. It has no specific meaning.

For example:

A: 李 苏， 快 走， 要 上 课 了。

   Lǐ Sū, kuài zǒu, yào shàngkè le.

B: 噢， 来 了。

   Ò, lái le.

A: Su Li, hurry up, it's time for class.

B: OK, I'm coming.

A: 王 天， 电 话。

   Wáng Tiān, diànhuà.

B: 噢， 知 道 了。 谢 谢！

   Ò, zhīdào le. Xièxiè.

A: Tian Wang, phone call.

B: Got it, thank you.

4. 251 航班

The number is read "èrwǔyāo." In speech, the number 1 often reads as yāo when saying numbers one at a time. For example: phone number 718-251-1679 (qīyāobā-èrwǔyāo-yāoliùqījiǔ); flight number 891 (bājiǔyāo) 航班; train 2717 (èrqīyāoqī) 次 (cì).

A: 王 老 师 的 办 公 室 在 哪 儿？

   Wáng Lǎoshī de bàngōngshì zài nǎr?

   Where is Professor Wang's office?

B: 在 三 楼 315。

   zài sān lóu sānyāowǔ。

   Number 315 on the third floor.

5. 找到了 I found it / I got it.

找到 is a verb + complement of result structure. 找 means "look for," 找到 means "find," and 到 indicates the result of the action 找.

For example:

A: 你 刚 才 找 谁？

Nǐ gāngcái zhǎo shéi?

Whom were you looking for just now?

B: 我 找 王 老 师。

Wǒ zhǎo Wáng Lǎoshī.

I was looking for Professor Wang.

A: 你 找 到 了 吗？

Nǐ zhǎo dào le ma?

Did you find him?

B: 没 找 到，他 上 课 去 了。

Méi zhǎo dào, tā shàngkè qù le.

No, he went to teach.

我 找 到 那 本 书 了，在 王 小 年 那 儿。

Wǒ zhǎo dào nà běn shū le, zài Wáng Xiǎonián nàr.

I found the book. Xiaonian Wang has it.

(For details, please see Grammar Book I, Lesson 8.)

*6. 那也只好付了。 I guess I have to pay the penalty.

只好 is an adverb, and it is used before the verb to show that one is doing something unwillingly.

For example:

你 已 经 买 了，我 不 喜 欢 吃，也 只 好 吃 了。

Nǐ yǐjīng mǎi le, wǒ bù xǐhuān chī, yě zhǐhǎo chī le.

You already bought it. Even if I don't like it, I still have to eat it.

地 铁 虽 然 麻 烦，为 了 省 钱 我 只 好 坐 了。

Dìtiě suīrán máfán, wéile shěngqián wǒ zhǐhǎo zuò le.

Although taking the subway is inconvenient, I have to take it in order to save money.

xù   shù

叙   述

▶ **Narration**

··

shēng cí

生   词

🔘 **New Words**

	Chinese	Pinyin	Part of Speech	English
1.	寒假	hánjià	N	winter vacation
2.	已经	yǐjīng	Ad	already
3.	给	gěi	Prep/V	to; for; give; grant
4.	积累	jīlěi	V	accumulate
5.	飞行	fēixíng	V	flight; flying
6.	里程	lǐchéng	N	mileage
7.	这样	zhèyàng	Pron	so; such; like this; this way

pīn   yīn   kè   wén

拼   音   课   文

🔘 **Text with Pinyin**

▶▶▶

hán	jià	sū	shān	yuán	lái	yào	huí	jiā,	bà	ba	mā
寒	假	苏	珊	原	来	要	回	家，	爸	爸	妈

ma	yǐ	jīng	gěi	tā	mǎi	le	shí'èr	yuè	shíbā	rì	de	fēi
妈	已	经	给	她	买	了	12	月	18	日	的	飞

jī	piào.	kě	shì	tā	yào	gēn	tā	de	tóng	xué	bǐ	dé
机	票。	可	是	她	要	跟	她	的	同	学	彼	德

qù	xià	wēi	yí	wánr.		tā	men	zuò	xī	běi	háng	kōng
去	夏	威	夷	玩	儿。	他	们	坐	西	北	航	空

公司的飞机，因为苏珊是西北航空公司的空中俱乐部会员，可以积累飞行里程。

因为苏珊要去夏威夷，她爸爸只好给她改飞机票。他得把12月18日的票改到25日，这样苏珊圣诞节就可以回家。从夏威夷回波士顿很麻烦，要先飞到旧金山，再转机到波士顿，还要再付80美元的差价和100美元的罚金。可是苏珊的爸爸只好这样改。◀◀◀

hàn zì kè wén
汉 字 课 文

Text in Chinese Characters

▶▶▶

　　寒假苏珊原来要回家，爸爸妈妈已经给她买了12月18日的飞机票。可是她要跟她的同学彼德去夏威夷玩儿。他们坐西北航空公司的飞机，因为苏珊是西北航空公司的空中俱乐部会员，可以积累飞行里程。

　　因为苏珊要去夏威夷，她爸爸只好给她改飞机票。他得把12月18日的票改到25日，这样苏珊圣诞节就可以回家。从夏威夷回波士顿很麻烦，要先飞到旧金山，再转机到波士顿，还要再付80美元的差价和100美元的罚金。可是苏珊的爸爸只好这样改。◀◀◀

yǔ　　yán　　yīng　yòng　zhù　　shì
语　　言　　应　　用　　注　　释
Notes on Language Usage

1. 可以积累飞行里程。**(She) can accumulate mileage.**

This refers to the airline's frequent flier program, in which travelers can earn free tickets for the air mileage they accumulate.

2. 他得把12月18日的票改到25日。 **He has to change the ticket from December 18 to 25.**

*a) 得 **(děi)**

Here 得 is an auxiliary verb meaning "have to, must."

For example:

如　果　去　夏　威　夷，我　们　得　先　订　飞　机　票。

Rúguǒ qù Xiàwēiyí, wǒmen děi xiān dìng fēijīpiào.

If we go to Hawaii, we must book airline tickets first.

我　带　的　现　金　不　够，得　用　信　用　卡　付　钱。

Wǒ dài de xiànjīn bú gòu, děi yòng xìnyòngkǎ fùqián.

I did not bring enough cash. I have to pay with a credit card.

(For details, please see Grammar Book I, Lesson 5.)

b) 把 **(bǎ)**

把 is a preposition. The 把 construction is a special sentence structure in Chinese, indicating how somebody or something is used, influenced, or acted upon. The object of 把 is the object acted upon or influenced. 把 must precede the main verb. The sentence pattern is:

Subject + 把 + object + V + other element.

For example:

我　把　鸡　蛋　(jīdàn, egg)　吃　了。

Wǒ bǎ jīdàn chī le.

I ate the egg.

爸　爸　把　苏　珊　的　票　改　好　了。

Bàba bǎ Sūshān de piào gǎi hǎo le.

Dad has changed Susan's ticket.

(For details, please see Grammar Book I, Lesson 10.)

▶ English Translations of the Texts

Dialogue 1

Susan:	Are you going home for Christmas (vacation)?
Peter:	I don't know yet. If I go home, I need to first take a five or six hour flight to Los Angeles, and then change planes. It's too tiring. And also, I've just been home for Thanksgiving.
Susan:	How come your home is so far away? Where is it?
Peter:	In Hawaii.
Susan:	It would be a lot of fun to spend Christmas in Hawaii. I'll go with you, is that OK?
Peter:	Really? That's wonderful. Let's call a travel agency to reserve the airline tickets right now.
Susan:	Which airline will you take?
Peter:	I will take whichever you take.
Susan:	That's good. Let's take Northwest. I am a member of Northwest Airlines' frequent flier program.
Peter:	OK. But I remember that your parents bought a plane ticket for you to go home. Won't you go back to visit them?
Susan:	It's OK. I can ask them to change the ticket for me. I will go back home a few days later [than originally scheduled].
Peter:	Good. Let's go reserve the tickets.

Dialogue 2

Susan's Dad:	Hello, (may I ask) is this International Travel Agency?
Travel Agent:	Yes. May I help you, sir?
Susan's Dad:	Yes, I want to change a ticket.
Travel Agent:	No problem. Please tell me the name, airline, and the date and flight number.
Susan's Dad:	It is for my daughter, her name is Susan White. She is on Northwest Airlines Flight 251 from Hawaii to JFK Airport, New York on December 18.
	(The travel agent checks her computer.)
Travel Agent:	Got it. Because you purchased a discount ticket, you need to pay a $100 penalty. May I ask how you want to change?
Susan's Dad:	I guess I have to pay the penalty. Please change the flight from Hawaii to Boston on December 24.
Travel Agent:	OK. (She will be) leaving Hawaii at 8 a.m. on Dec. 24, changing planes in Los Angeles and going to Chicago, then going from Chicago to New York. Then (she will) transfer to Boston and arrive at 6 a.m. on the 25th. You need to pay $80 extra for the ticket, plus a $100 penalty. $180 altogether.
Susan's Dad:	But she needs to change planes so many times. It's very inconvenient. Is there anything quicker?

Travel Agent:	If she leaves at 6:00 a.m. on the 25th and changes flights in San Francisco, she can arrive in Boston at 10:00 p.m. Eastern time, the same day.
Susan's Dad:	That's good.
Travel Agent:	May I ask how you will pay?
Susan's Dad:	Credit card.
Travel Agent:	All right, please tell me the card number and expiration date.
Susan's Dad:	5234-5678-9876-5432, 11/5/2009.
Travel Agent:	Thank you.

Narration

Susan originally planned to go directly home for winter break. Her parents had already bought her an airline ticket for December 18. But she wants to go to Hawaii with her classmate Peter for fun. They will take Northwest Airlines because Susan is a member of Northwest's frequent flier program. She can accumulate mileage.

Because Susan wants to go to Hawaii, her father has to change her plane ticket from December 18 to 25 for her. This way Susan can arrive home on Christmas. It is very inconvenient to fly from Hawaii back to Boston. She needs to fly to San Francisco first, then transfer to Boston. Moreover, Susan's father needs to pay an extra $80 and a $100 penalty. He has no choice but to make the change this way.

tīng shuō liàn xí

听　说　练　习

▶ **Exercises for Listening and Speaking**

· ·

🔘 一、完成对话。*(1. Work in pairs to complete the dialogue.)*

A: Nǐ jiā zài nǎr?

B: _____

A: Zài Xiàwēiyí? Nàme yuǎn. Nà nǐ shénme shíhòu huíjiā?

B: _____

A: Nà nǐ zài Xiàwēiyí guò Shèngdàn Jié yídìng hěn yǒuyìsi le?

B: _____

A: Wǒ kěyǐ gēn nǐ qù ma?

B: _____

A: Nà tài hǎo le.

B: _____

A: Méi guānxì, wǒ jiào bàba gěi wǒ gǎi piào.

B: _____

A: Hǎo, wǒmen qù dìng qù Xiàwēiyí de jīpiào.

🔊 二、听对话，回答问题。 **(2. Listen to the conversation and answer the questions.)**

1. How did A go home?

_____

2. Why does B want to take Northwest Airlines?

_____

3. Why can't A book a ticket now?

_____

4. How do they book their tickets?

_____

🔊 三、先听对话，然后两人一组朗读。 **(3. Listen to the following conversation without looking at the book, and then read it aloud in pairs, first by following the pinyin, then by following the characters.)**

Jiǎ: Guójì Lǚxíngshè ma?

Yǐ: Shì.

Jiǎ: Wǒ dìng le yī zhāng qù Běijīng de fēijīpiào, xiǎng gǎi shíjiān.

Yǐ: Qǐng nín gàosu wǒ nín de míngzi, hángkōng gōngsī, rìqī hé hángbān hào.

Jiǎ: Wǒ jiào Zhāng Dàzhōng, 12 yuè 18 rì zuò Zhōngguó Hángkōnggōngsī, 251 hángbān cóng Kěnnídí Jīchǎng qǐfēi.

Yǐ: Nín yào zěnme gǎi?

Jiǎ: Wǒ yào gǎi chéng 12 yuè 5 rì de piào.

Yǐ: Kěyǐ.

Jiǎ: Qǐng wèn gǎi piào yào fù fájīn ma?

Yǐ: Yīnwèi shì piányi piào, yào fù 100 měiyuán de fájīn.

Jiǎ: Yào fù 100 měiyuán? Shǎo yīdiǎn hǎo ma?

Yǐ: Duìbuqǐ, bù xíng.

Jiǎ: Hǎo ba, nà yě zhǐhǎo fù le.

Yǐ: Gǎi hǎo le.

Jiǎ: Hǎo, zàijiàn.

甲： 国际旅行社吗？

乙： 是。

甲： 我订了一张去北京的飞机票，想改时间。

乙： 请您告诉我您的名字，航空公司，日期和航班号。

甲： 我叫张大中，12月18日坐中国航空公司，251航班从肯尼迪机场起飞。

乙： 您要怎么改？

甲： 我要改成12月5日的票。

乙： 可以。

甲： 请问改票要付罚金吗？

乙： 因为是便宜票，要付100美元的罚金。

甲： 要付100美元？少一点好吗？

乙： 对不起，不行。

甲： 好吧，那也只好付了。

乙： 改好了。

甲： 好，再见。

四、角色表演。*(4. Role Play)*

1. A: You are a college student talking about your plans for winter vacation with a friend of yours. Tell him/her where you plan to go, what transportation you want to take, and how much money you want to spend.

   B: You are discussing your travel plans for winter vacation with your friend. You happen to have been where your friend wants to go. You make suggestions about what to see, how to get there and a possible budget.

2. A: You are a student trying to book an airline ticket home for Christmas by calling a travel agency.

   B: You are a travel agent who is helping the student to get a good deal.

dià n nǎo yǔ   hàn zì   liàn xí
电　脑　与　汉　字　练　习
▶ Exercises for Computing and Learning Characters
. . . .

一、打出下面段落。*(1. Type the following passage.)*

A:　小姐，买一张飞机票多少钱？

B:　你到哪儿？

A:　到哪儿都行。我就想乘飞机玩玩。

B:　那去中国吧，可以坐15个小时。

A:　时间太长了，最好上去(shàngqù, go up)就下来(xiàlai, come down)。

B:　那你乘游览(yóulǎn, tour)直升飞机(zhíshēng fēijī, helicopter)。

A:　好啊，可是我怕(pà, fear)坐飞机。

B:　你还是在家睡觉吧。

二、把下面拼音句子打成汉字。*(2. Type the following pinyin sentences and select the appropriate characters from the list that appears on your computer screen.)*

1. Zài Xiàwēiyí guò Shèngdàn Jié, nà duō yǒuyìsi. Wǒ gēn nǐ yīqǐ qù, zěnmeyàng?

2. Tā jiào Susan White, 12 yuè 18 rì zuò Xīběi Hangkōng Gōngsī, 251 hángbān cóng Kěnnídí Jīchǎng qǐfēi.

3. Wǒ yào mǎi niúnǎi, miànbāo, nǎilào, shuǐguǒ hé kělè.

4. Nǐ hái kěyǐ zuò dìtiě dào Shídài Guǎngchǎng de chángtú qìchēzhàn, nàlǐ yǒu dào fēijīchǎng de dàbā.

5. Yīnwéi Sū Shān yào qù Xiàwēiyí, tā bàba zhǐhǎo gěi tā gǎi fēijīpiào.

三、圈出正确的汉字。*(3. Circle the correct character to fill in the blanks.)*

1. 你暑假 ＿＿ (会、回、四、固、洄)家还是旅游？

2. 我想去体育场玩美式足球，＿＿ (往、彷、珩、性、行)吗？

3. 从洛杉矶到夏威夷 ＿＿ (进、运、芫、元、远)吗？

4. 请问你是中国文化俱乐部的会 ＿＿（负、愿、员、源、贡)吗？

5. 我忘了带借书 ＿＿（怔、政、征、正、证）了，可以用你的吗？

四、读生字，找出偏旁部首。*(4. The characters in each of the following groups share a radical. Read the characters and write the shared radicals.)*

Example: 这 迎   shared radical: 辶

1. 远 过 这   shared radical:＿＿＿＿＿＿＿＿

2. 样 机 查 果   shared radical:＿＿＿＿＿＿＿＿

3. 订 证 说 记   shared radical:＿＿＿＿＿＿＿＿

4. 假 俱   shared radical:＿＿＿＿＿＿＿＿

5. 积 程   shared radical:＿＿＿＿＿＿＿＿

6. 经 给   shared radical:＿＿＿＿＿＿＿＿

7. 时 晚 早   shared radical:＿＿＿＿＿＿＿＿

8. 如 好   shared radical:＿＿＿＿＿＿＿＿

五、把汉字分成部件。*(5. Test your understanding of character structure by dividing the following characters into their component parts.)*

Example: 吗 —> 口 马

1. 转 —>＿＿＿＿＿＿＿＿＿   4. 到 —>＿＿＿＿＿＿＿＿＿

2. 需 —>＿＿＿＿＿＿＿＿＿   5. 证 —>＿＿＿＿＿＿＿＿＿

3. 空 —>＿＿＿＿＿＿＿＿＿

六、学生字 *(6. Learning New Characters)*

独体词组复合词。(Form compound words based on single-character words.)

注释 (Note): Most Chinese characters are words themselves, called 独 (dú, single) 体 (tǐ, body) 词. In this exercise you will be asked to find compound words that contain some common single-character words you have already learned.

Study the following characters selected from the New Words lists: 成* 把 如* 了 要 他 人* 在

1. Copy each character by hand using the character writing demonstration sheet.

2. For each character marked with an asterisk, find the compounds in which the characters are used in the text, and write the compound words next to the characters.

3. With the assistance of an online dictionary or a dictionary, write down three more compounds in which these single-character words appear.

4. For each character marked with an asterisk, make a sentence with one of the three new compounds.

Character Writing Demonstration Sheet 第七课   姓名＿＿＿＿＿＿＿

Pinyin	Strokes	Structure	English	Radical	Traditional Form
chéng	6	single-body	succeed	戈	成

成 成 成 成 成 成

Pinyin	Strokes	Structure	English	Radical	Traditional Form
bǎ	7	left-right	hold	扌	把

把 把 把 把 把 把 把

Pinyin	Strokes	Structure	English	Radical	Traditional Form
rú	6	left-right	like, as	女	如

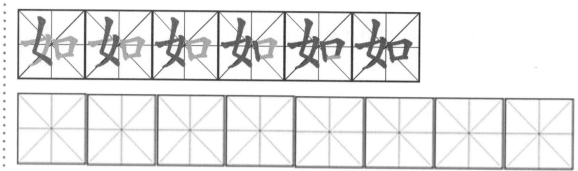

Pinyin	Strokes	Structure	English	Radical	Traditional Form
le	2	single-body	(a particle)	亅	了

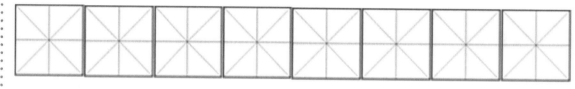

Pinyin	Strokes	Structure	English	Radical	Traditional Form
yào	9	top-bottom	want	西	要

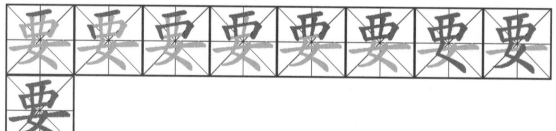

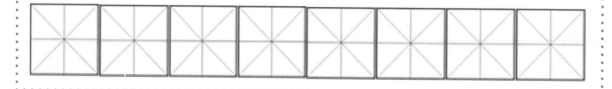

Pinyin	Strokes	Structure	English	Radical	Traditional Form
tā	5	left-right	he	亻	他

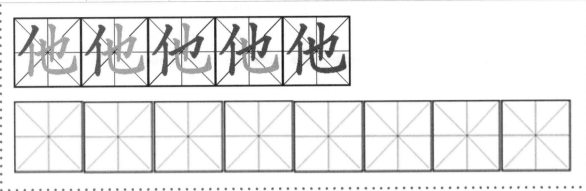

Pinyin	Strokes	Structure	English	Radical	Traditional Form
rén	2	single-body	human being, people	人	人

Pinyin	Strokes	Structure	English	Radical	Traditional Form
zài	6	half encloser	exist, at	土	在

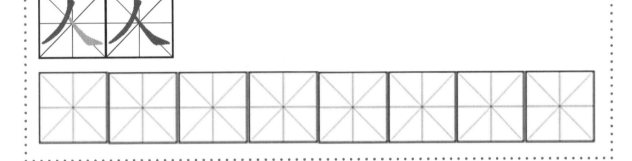

EXERCISES

kè wén liàn xí

课 文 练 习

▶ **Exercises for Understanding the Texts**

· ·

一、根据课文回答问题。*(1. Answer the questions orally based on the text.)*

对话（1）

1. 这个对话发生在什么时候？

   When did the conversation take place?

2. 彼得回家要在哪儿转机？他六个小时就能到家吗？

   Where does Peter make a connection when he goes home?
   Can he arrive home in six hours?

3. 苏珊为什么要跟彼得回夏威夷？

   Why does Susan want to go to Hawaii with Peter?

4. 苏珊为什么要坐西北航空公司的飞机？

   Why does Susan decide to take Northwest Airlines?

5. 苏珊是不是已经买好回家的机票了？是谁给她买的？

   Has Susan purchased her ticket home? Who did it for her?

对话（2）

1. 为什么苏珊爸爸给旅行社打电话？

   Why did Susan's father call the travel agency?

2. 苏珊的机票原来是从哪儿飞到哪儿的？"航班号"是多少？

   What was the route of Susan's original flight? What was her flight number?

3. 改票要付多少罚金？

   How much is the penalty for changing her ticket?

4. 要是苏珊坐二十四号的飞机回家，需要转几次飞机？

   If Susan takes the flight home on the 24th, how many times does she have to change planes?

5. 苏珊的爸爸是怎么付的机票？

   How did Susan's father pay for the ticket?

二、完成对话。**(2. Complete the dialogue orally using 过.)**

1. A: 你知道去中国城怎么走吗？

    B: 不知道，因为_____。

2. A: 你妈妈喜欢吃中国饭吗？

    B: 我不知道，因为她 _____。

3. A: 今天学校演美国大片，你想跟我去看吗？

    B: 对不起，我_____，是昨天跟约翰看的。

4. A: 格林的中文发音真好！

    B: 他在中国_____。

5. A: 你是中国人，为什么不会说中文？

    B: 因为我出生在美国，没_____，所以不会说中文。

三、先翻译，然后根据先后顺序组句成段。**(3. Translate the following sentences into Chinese, and then make them into a narrative using the adverbs 先, 再, 然后再, and 最后 [at last].)**

1. Peter left school at 7:00 early in the morning on December 18.

   _____

2. He walked to the subway station.

   _____

3. He rode on the train for an hour.

   _____

4. He changed to the bus going to JFK Airport.

   _____

5. He had to make a connection in LA after a six-hour flight.

   _____

6. He arrived in Hawaii five hours later.

_____

7. He took a taxi home.

_____

四、用由疑问词组成的短语回答下列问题，然后朗读。*(4. Use question words to answer the following questions. Then read the dialogues aloud.)*

Example: A: 你中午吃什么？

B: 你吃什么我就吃什么。

1.　A: 圣诞节你要上哪儿去？

B: _____。

2.　A: 你要跟谁一起去？

B: _____。

3.　A: 你想买哪家的飞机票？

B: _____。

4.　A: 你坐哪个线路地铁去机场？

B: _____。

5.　A: 你什么时候回学校？

B: _____。

五、作文 *(5. Composition)*

Write a paragraph (8-10 sentences minimum) that tells about your plans for Thanksgiving break. Make sure to use the given words and phrases.

1. 因为……所以　2. 再说　3. 马上　4. 只好　5. 除了……以外　6. 还/也

六、翻译 *(6. Translation)*

Translate the following sentences orally in class. Then type your translations in Chinese using the words and phrases provided.

1. To study Chinese, one has to learn pronunciation and the four tones first before learning grammar and how to write characters. (先，（然后）再)

2. At yesterday's party, first we ate some Chinese food, then we watched a movie, and after that, we danced. (先，再，然后)

3. How come you wrote this character this way? (怎么这么)

4. How come this sweater is so expensive? (怎么那么)

5. I have read this book. It is very interesting. (verb + 过)

6. Have you ever taken the subway to JFK airport? Yes, I have. (verb + 过)

7. Xiaonian Wang celebrated his birthday last weekend. (过 as a verb)

8. Every day, Green studies Chinese for about two or three hours. (adjacent numbers)

9. Which sweater do you want to buy? I'll buy whichever one is cheaper. (QW)

10. She says whatever she wants to say. (QW)

11. Have you found your airplane ticket? Yes, I have. (找到)

12. Taking a taxi from the airport is very expensive, but I have to do it because there is no bus or subway that goes to my school. (只好)

bǔ　chōng yuè　dú　liàn　xí
补　充　阅　读　练　习

▶ Supplementary Reading Exercises

. . . .

(1) Controlled Vocabulary

Read the following passage and answer the following questions either in Chinese or in English.

放假去哪儿？

　　彼德的家住在夏威夷。寒假要到了，彼德还没有想好是不是要回家去过圣诞节。因为他感恩节刚回过家，而回家路上要用十几个小时，他觉得太累了，所以想留在学校。彼德的同学苏珊没去过夏威夷，想跟彼德一起到夏威夷去过圣诞节，彼德听了很高兴 (gāoxìng, happy)。可是苏珊的父母已经给她订好了回波士顿的机票，所以她得告诉她的父母帮她改机票，晚几天再回家。

Questions

1. 彼德的老家在哪儿？
   Where is Peter's hometown?

2. 他为什么还没有决定是不是回家？
   Why hasn't he decided whether or not he will go home yet?

3. 苏珊是谁？
   Who is Susan?

4. 苏珊的家在哪儿？
   Where is Susan's hometown?

5. 苏珊原来的计划是什么？
   What was Susan's original plan?

(2) Open Vocabulary

This exercise is called "Open Vocabulary" because it contains some vocabulary words that have not been introduced in this book. In this exercise, you should first look for words you already recognize, and then try to guess the meaning of an entire phrase or sentence based on the words you already know. When you get stuck, use a dictionary to look up words whose meanings are crucial to your understanding of the passage. You can also retrieve an electronic version of this text from the accompanying online materials, and use an online dictionary or translation program to help you read it. After answering the questions, try to tell the story to a classmate in your own words without looking at the original text.

	Chinese	Pinyin	Part of Speech	English
1.	岁	suì	M	(a measure word used for year of age)
2.	外婆	wàipó	N	(maternal) grandmother
3.	卖	mài	V	sell
4.	叔叔	shūshu	N	uncle
5.	久	jiǔ	Adj	long, for a long time
6.	只要	zhǐyào	Conj	as long as
7.	回答	huídá	V	answer; reply

下火车六岁

　　珊珊跟妈妈坐火车去看外婆。上火车以前，妈妈跟珊珊说："要是卖票的叔叔问你几岁，你就说是五岁了。"在火车上卖票的叔叔真的问珊珊今年几岁了，珊珊听了妈妈的话，告诉叔叔她五岁了。"五岁就这么高了。"

　　卖票的叔叔问，"还有多久你就六岁了？"

　　"一下火车。"珊珊回答说。

Questions

1. 珊珊和妈妈坐火车上哪儿去？

   Where are Shanshan and her mother going by train?

2. 妈妈告诉珊珊什么了？

   What did the mother tell Shanshan to say?

3. 妈妈为什么告诉他要那么说？

   Why did her mother want her to say that?

4. 珊珊现在几岁？

   How old do you think Shanshan is now?

zhōng guó   wén   huà   xí   sú

中   国   文   化   习   俗

Chinese Customs and Culture

· ·

xīn   shǎng jīng   jù

欣   赏   京   剧

▶ **Enjoying and Appreciating Beijing Opera**

The Chinese Theater Tradition

On first hearing Beijing Opera 京剧 (Jīngjù), the reaction of most visitors to China is "what's that cacophony?!" While it must be noted that most young Chinese—brought up on Mandarin and Cantonese pop music and karaoke—have the same reaction as outsiders to China do, the art form known as Beijing Opera is truly one of China's great cultural treasures, and a repository of Chinese traditional narrative and song. In a city with such fantastic sights as the Great Wall 万里长城 (Wànlǐ Chángchéng), the Forbidden City 故宫 (Gùgōng), Tian'anmen Square 天安门广场 (Tiān'ānmén Guǎngchǎng), the Temple of Heaven 天坛 (Tiāntán), the Ming Dynasty Tombs 明朝十三陵(Míng Cháo Shísānlíng), and the Summer Palace 颐和园(Yíhéyuán), a trip to the Beijing Opera is usually high on most tourists' lists.

▶ Beijing Opera

The Beijing Opera style emerged in the middle of the nineteenth century as a synthesis of a multitude of existing theatrical forms. It thus represents a summation of Chinese drama as a tradition. The origins of Chinese theater itself, however, are shrouded in mystery, and drama as an art form was not well-respected in ancient China. The Confucian tradition that came to dominate Chinese thought privileged poetry 诗(shī), philosophy 经 (jīng) and history 史 (shǐ). Confucian scholars therefore looked down on the writing of fictional stories, referring to them as 小说 (xiǎo shuō), literally "small talk," the term used even today in China (and also Japan and Korea) for "novels" and "stories."

As a form that presented fictional narratives, the theater was also held in low regard among the social and cultural elites in ancient times. Chinese theater was not given a great boost of energy until the rule of the Mongols under the Yuan 元 (1279–1368) dynasty. The Mongols themselves held performers and entertainers in high esteem, and the drama rose rapidly in terms of its social respectability and status. Similarly, Chinese government officials, no longer able to take the civil service examinations, had less need to use poetic forms to express themselves, and many turned to theater and story as their media of literary expression. The drama achieved great popularity during the Ming 明 (1368–1644) dynasty with what is perhaps the most famous Chinese play, Tang Xianzu's 汤显祖 (Tāng Xiǎnzǔ) Peony Pavilion 牡丹亭 (Mǔ Dāntíng).

The Beijing Opera inherited this illustrious tradition and synthesized it to create an art form that is both popular and literary. It is based on four different role types: (1) male roles 生 (shēng); (2) female roles 旦 (dàn); (3) painted faces 净 (jìng); and (4) clowns 丑 chǒu. The jing or "painted face" roles are often the most impressive. These roles tend to portray great generals or brave heroes, and the actors who portray them command the stage with their strong singing and striking presence. Their costumes and makeup include long beards, large platform shoes, and heavy shoulder pads.

Famous Characters on the Beijing Opera Stage

The Monkey King 孙悟空 (Sūn Wùkōng)

One of the most famous characters on the Beijing Opera stage is the fabulous Monkey King. Sun Wukong, as he is known in Chinese, is one of the best known literary figures throughout East Asia. The story of the Monkey King finds its most canonical treatment in the classical novel known as the *Journey to the West* 西游记 (Xī Yóu Jì), attributed to the scholar Wu Cheng En 吴承恩 (Wú Chéng'ēn). The story follows the monk Xuanzang 玄奘 (Xuánzàng), a real historical personage, and his journey across Central Asia to India to obtain Buddhist scriptures. In the narrative, Xuanzang is accompanied by three fantastic companions, the strongest of which is Sun Wukong, the king of the monkeys. Sun Wukong is armed with a magical staff whose size he can change at will. Among his many abilities and magic powers is the ability to blow hairs off his body and transform them into little monkeys that become an instant army, fighting with him against his enemies. Xuanzang's other two companions are the pig monster Zhu Bajie 猪八戒 (Zhū Bājiè) and the river monster 沙悟净 (Shā Wùjìng). Sun Wukong is most famous for wreaking havoc in heaven in the opera known as 大闹天宫 (Dànào Tiāngōng). Today, the Monkey King appears in comic books, live action and animated television series, and video games across the Chinese speaking world, Japan and Korea. The best known English translation of the *Journey to the West* is by Anthony Yu.

The Romance of the Three Kingdoms 三国演义 (Sānguó Yǎnyì)

Another important literary work for the Beijing Opera is the classical novel called *Romance of the Three Kingdoms* 三国演义 (Sānguó Yǎnyì), which tells the tale of the wars that engulfed China after the fall of the Han 汉 dynasty. The novel is attributed to Luo Guanzhong 罗贯中 (Luó Guànzhōng). It most famously recounts the brotherhood alliance of the great heroes Liu Bei 刘备 (Liú Bèi), Zhang Fei 张飞 (Zhāng Fēi), and Guan Yu 关羽 (Guān Yǔ), their partnership with the brilliant strategist and Daoist scholar Zhuge Liang 诸葛亮 (Zhūgé Liàng), and their struggles against the warlord Cao Cao 曹操 (Cáo Cāo). The Beijing Opera known as "The Changban Slopes" 长阪坡 (Chángbàn Pō) recounts one of the most famous battles between Liu Bei and Cao Cao, in which one of Liu Bei's generals rescues his wife and son just as Cao Cao is crushing Liu Bei's military forces. The

Romance of the Three Kingdoms is arguably even more famous and influential in China, Japan, and Korea than the Monkey King. It has been made into an incredibly popular video game series, endless comic books, contemporary novels, and live action and animated television series. The strategies employed by Zhuge Liang and Cao Cao have even been used by business leaders as models for emulation in the business world. The best known English translation of The Romance of the Three Kingdoms is by Moss Roberts.

Outlaws of the Marsh 水浒传 (Shuǐhǔ Zhuàn)

One more important source for Beijing Opera performances is the Robin Hood-like story of the *Outlaws of the Marsh*, based on the novel edited by Luo Guanzhong, supposed author of the *Romance of the Three Kingdoms*. This is the novel translated into English by Pearl Buck as *All Men Are Brothers*. The story recounts the exploits of the outlaw Song Jiang 宋江 (Sōng Jiāng) and his followers, including such famous heroes as Lu Zhishen 鲁智深 (Lǔ Zhìshēn), Lin Chong 林冲 (Lín Chōng), Wu Song 武松 (Wǔ Sōng), and Li Kui 李逵 (Lǐ Kuí). One well-known opera called "Li Kui Visits His Mother" 李逵探母 (Lǐ Kuí Tàn Mǔ) recounts Li Kui's discovery of his mother's blindness when he returns to visit her after a long absence. He decides to bring his mother back to the outlaw stronghold he calls home, but on the way leaves her to go and fetch some water. When he comes back, he discovers that four tigers have killed his mother and he launches into a merciless onslaught that results in the death of the ferocious animals. The hero Wu Song is also famous for his battle with a tiger.

The best-known English translation of the *Outlaws of the Marsh* is by John Dent-Young.

The Four Masterworks of the Chinese Novel 四大名著 (Sì Dà Míng Zhù)

Romance of the Three Kingdoms, *Journey to the West*, and *Outlaws of the Marsh* are considered, along with the great eighteenth century work *Dream of the Red Chamber* 红楼梦 (Hóng Lóu Mèng) as the "four masterworks of the Chinese novel." They have been incredibly important sources of cultural reflection and reinvention throughout Chinese history, and continue to be popular even today.

The best known English translation of the *Dream of the Red Chamber* (also known as the *Story of the Stone* 石头记 Shítóu Jì) is by David Hawkes.

▶ Test Your Knowledge How well do you know these famous Chinese novels?

宋江	曹操	林冲
武松	孙悟空	关羽
鲁智深	三国演义	李逵
张飞	沙悟净	水浒传
玄奘	诸葛亮	大闹天宫
刘备	李逵探母	西游记
长阪坡	吴承恩	猪八戒
罗贯中 (use twice)		

Romance of the Three Kingdoms	Pinyin	Chinese Characters
Chinese title		
Author's name		
Title of an opera based on the story		
Main character name		
Main character name		
Main character name		
Main character name		
Main character name		
Journey to the West	Pinyin	Chinese Characters
Chinese title		
Author's name		
Title of an opera based on the story		
Main character name		
Main character name		
Main character name		
Main character name		
Outlaws of the Marsh	Pinyin	Chinese Characters
Chinese title		
Author's name		
Title of an opera based on the story		
Main character name		
Main character name		
Main character name		
Main character name		
Main character name		

dì bā kè
第 八 课

LESSON 8

yóu jú hé yín háng
邮 局 和 银 行

At the Post Office and Bank

▶ **Objectives:**

1. To send mail at the post office
2. To deposit and withdraw money at the bank

duì   huà   yī

对　话　(一)

DIALOGUE 1

jì   dōng xī

寄　东　西

▶ **Sending Mail**

．．．

shēng cí

生　　词

● **New Words**

	Chinese	Pinyin	Part of Speech	English
1.	邮局	yóujú	N	post office
2.	办	bàn	V	do; handle; manage; attend to
3.	护照	hùzhào	N	passport
4.	事	shì	N	matter; affair; thing
5.	寄	jì	V	send; post; mail
6.	包裹	bāoguǒ	N/V	package; bundle; wrap up; bind up
	包	bāo	V/N	wrap; bundle; bag
7.	纸盒	zhǐhé	N	cardboard box
	纸	zhǐ	N	paper
	盒	hé	N	box; case
8.	怕	pà	N/V	fear; dread; be afraid of; afraid
9.	压	yā	V	press; push down; hold down; weigh down

10.	对方	duìfāng	N	the other (or opposite) side; the other party
11.	收到	shōudào	V	receive; get; achieve; obtain
12.	信封	xìnfēng	N	envelope
13.	泡沫塑料	pàomò sùliào	N	foam plastics
	泡沫	pàomò	N	foam
	塑料	sùliào	N	plastics
14.	保护	bǎohù	V	protect; safeguard
15.	邮件	yóujiàn	N	postal matter; post; mail
16.	特快专递	tèkuài zhuāndì	CE	express mail
17.	安全	ānquán	Adj	safe; secure
18.	慢	màn	Adj	slow
19.	急	jí	Adj	impatient; anxious; worry; urgent; pressing
20.	挂号	guàhào	V	register (at a hospital, etc.); send by registered mail
21.	回执	huízhí	N	a short note acknowledging receipt of something; receipt
22.	签字	qiānzì	VO	sign
23.	花	huā	V	spend; expend
24.	填	tián	V	fill; stuff; write; fill in
25.	表	biǎo	N	table; form; list; meter; watch

pīn yīn kè wén
拼 音 课 文

Text with Pinyin

▶▶▶

gé lín:
格 林：
wǒ yào qù yóu jú bàn hù zhào, nǐ yǒu
我 要 去 邮 局 办 护 照，你 有
shì ma?
事 吗？

wáng xiǎo nián:
王 小 年：
wǒ xiǎng qù jì (yī) gè bāo guǒ, kě shì
我 想 去 寄 （一） 个 包 裹，可 是
méi yǒu dōng xi bāo.
没 有 东 西 包。

gé lín:
格 林：
méi guān xì, dào nàr mǎi gè zhǐ hé
没 关 系，到 那 儿 买 个 纸 盒
jiù kě yǐ le.
就 可 以 了。

wáng xiǎo nián:
王 小 年：
nà hǎo, wǒ men yī qǐ qù ba.
那 好，我 们 一 起 去 吧。

zài yóu jú
（在 邮 局）

zhí yuán:
职 员：
kě yǐ bāng zhù nín ma?
可 以 帮 助 您 吗？

wáng xiǎo nián:
王 小 年：
wǒ xiǎng mǎi gè zhǐ hé jì dōng xi.
我 想 买 个 纸 盒 寄 东 西。

zhí yuán:
职 员：
pà yā ma?
怕 压 吗？

wáng xiǎo nián:
王 小 年：
bù pà, dàn wǒ xiǎng zhī dào duì fāng shōu
不 怕，但 我 想 知 道 对 方 收
dào méi yǒu.
到 没 有。

職　員：
zhí yuán:

那好，你可以用这种信封，里面有泡沫塑料，可以保护邮件。要是你寄特快专递，你就可以查到对方什么时候收到，又快又安全，只要十三块九毛五。

王　小　年：
wáng xiǎo nián:

特快专递好是好，就是太贵了。还可以寄什么样的邮件？慢一点没关系。

職　员：
zhí yuán:

如果不急，你可以寄这种挂号，对方收到后要在回执上签字，然后回执会寄回给你，只要花差不多一半的钱。

王　小　年：
wáng xiǎo nián:

好，我就寄这种。

职　员：　请　填　写　这　份　表，一　共　是　五
zhí　yuán:　qǐng　tián　xiě　zhè　fèn　biǎo, yī　gòng　shì　wǔ

块　四　毛　五　分　钱。
kuài　sì　máo　wǔ　fēn　qián.

◀◀◀

hàn　zì　kè　wén
汉　字　课　文

Text in Chinese Characters

▶▶▶

格林：　　我要去邮局办护照，你有事吗？

王小年：　我想去寄(一)个包裹，可是没有东西包。

格林：　　没关系，到那儿买个纸盒就可以了。

王小年：　那好，我们一起去吧。

（在邮局）

职员：　　可以帮助您吗？

王小年：　我想买个纸盒寄东西。

职员：　　怕压吗？

王小年：　不怕，但我想知道对方收到没有。

职员：　　那好，你可以用这种信封，里面有泡沫塑料，可以保护邮件。要是你寄特快专递，你就可以查到对方什么时候收到，又快又安全，只要十三块九毛五。

王小年：　特快专递好是好，就是太贵了。还可以寄什么样的邮件？慢一点没关系。

职员：　　如果不急，你可以寄这种挂号，对方收到后要在回执上签字，然后回执会寄回给你，只要花差不多一半的钱。

王小年：　好，我就寄这种。

职员：　　请填写这份表，一共是五块四毛五分钱。

◀◀◀

yǔ   yán yīng yòng zhù   shì
语   言   应   用   注   释
Notes on Language Usage

1. 你有事吗？ Is there anything I can do for you?

There are two meanings for the phrase 有事吗？ Here it means "Is there anything that I can do (take/get) for you (while I'm there)?" When used as a statement, 有事 indicates that "I have something to attend to" and it is often used when you want to excuse yourself in order to take care of some other business. The phrase 有事吗？ can also be used to ask whether someone has "anything planned" or "anything to do," and this is used when you want to invite someone somewhere.

Examples:

明 天 我 进 城，你 有 事 吗？

Míngtiān wǒ jìnchéng, nǐ yǒu shì ma?

I am going downtown tomorrow. Is there anything that I can do for you?

你 进 城 有 什 么 事？

Nǐ jìnchéng yǒu shénme shì?

What are you going to do downtown?

A: 今 天 晚 上 你 有 事 吗？我 们 看 电 影 去 吧。

   Jīntiān wǎnshàng nǐ yǒu shì ma? Wǒmen kàn diànyǐng qù ba.

   Are you free tonight? Let's go to see a movie.

B: 周 末 我 没 事，我 们 星 期 六 去 吧。

   Zhōumò wǒ méi shì, wǒmen xīngqīliù qù ba.

   I am free on the weekend. Let's go on Saturday.

2. 我想去寄个包裹。 I want to send a parcel.

The number 一 is omitted before the measure word 个. If there is no number before the measure word, it is understood to be 一. Other numbers cannot be omitted.

For example:

我 要 去 邮 局 寄(一)本 书。

Wǒ yào qù yóujú jì (yī) běn shū.

I am going to the post office to send a book.

妹 妹 买 了 件 新 衣 服。

Mèimèi mǎi le jiàn xīn yīfú.

(My) little sister bought a new dress.

姐 姐 买 了 四 件 新 衣 服。

Jiějiě mǎi le sì jiàn xīn yīfú.

(My) older sister bought four new dresses.

3. 那好

This phrase is used to show agreement.

For example,

A: 晚 上 再 做 作 业 吧，咱 们 去 打 球。

　　Wǎnshàng zài zuò zuòyè ba, zánmen qù dǎqiú.

B: 那 好，等 我 写 完 这 句 话 就 走。

　　Nà hǎo, děng wǒ xiěwán zhè jù huà jiù zǒu.

A:　Do your homework in the evening. Let's go play ball.

B:　OK. Let's go right after I finish this sentence.

*4. 特快专递好是好，就是太贵了。 Although Express Mail is good, it is too expensive.

This sentence pattern consists of two parts. The first part explains a fact, and the second part indicates some doubt or reservations about that fact. The sentence pattern is: Adj + 是 + Adj, 就是/可是…… In this sentence, the first clause 特快专递好是好 admits the fact that 特快专递 is good, and the 就是 introduces the idea that "even though it is good" there is something that the speaker does not like about it, in this case that it is too expensive, 太贵了.

More examples:

去 夏 威 夷 好 玩 儿 是 好 玩 儿，就 是 太 贵 了。

Qù Xiàwēiyí hàowánr shì hàowánr, jiù shì tài guì le.

It's fun to spend Christmas in Hawaii, but it's too expensive.

这 件 衣 服 好 看 是 好 看，就 是 太 大 了。

Zhè jiàn yīfú hǎokàn shì hǎokàn, jiùshì tài dà le.

This dress is nice looking, but it is too big.

5. 还可以寄什么样的邮件？ **What other ways can I send this?**

a) 还

还 here means "as well, in addition." It is often used in conjunction with "除了……（以外）.

For example:

除 了 邮 局(以 外)，人 们 还 常 常 使 用 中 外 私 营 邮 递 公 司

Chúle yóujú yǐwài, rénmen hái chángcháng shǐyòng zhōng wài sīyíng yóudì gōngsī

寄 快 件 和 包 裹。

jì kuàijiàn hé bāoguǒ.

In addition to the post office, people often use domestic and foreign privately owned delivery companies to send express mail or parcels. (Lesson 8)

学 习 中 文，除 了 多 看 （以 外），还 要 多 说，多 写。

Xuéxí Zhōngwén, chúle duō kàn (yǐwài), hái yào duō shuō, duō xiě.

In addition to reading a lot, one also needs to speak and write more when learning Chinese.

(See Lesson 5 in this textbook for more examples.)

b) 什么样的 (what kind of)

For example:

A: 你 喜 欢 什 么 样 的 运 动 衣？

　　Nǐ xǐhuān shénmeyàng de yùndòngyī?

B: 什 么 样 的 都 可 以。

　　Shénmeyàng de dōu kěyǐ.

A: What kind of sportswear do you like?

B: Any kind is fine.

*6. 只要花差不多一半的钱。 **You only need to spend about half of the money.**

只要 indicates a necessary condition and is used in the first clause in conjunction with 就 or 都. In this sentence, we can say: 只要花差不多一半的钱(就可以寄了.)

More examples:

只 要 周 末 没 事，他 就 去 图 书 馆 看 书。

Zhǐ yào zhōumò méi shì, tā jiù qù túshūguǎn kànshū.

Whenever he is free on weekends, he goes to the library to read.

我 只 要 给 他 打 个 电 话 ， 他 就 来 。

Wǒ zhǐ yào gěi tā dǎ gè diànhuà, tā jiù lái.

As long as I call him, he will come.

7. 好 ， 我 就 寄 这 种 。 **Great, I'll go with this kind of mail.**

就 is used here for emphasis.

For example,

我 今 天 就 不 去 ， 看 他 怎 么 办 。

Wǒ jīntiān jiù bù qù, kàn tā zěnme bàn.

I simply won't go today. See what he can do about it.

谁 说 这 个 字 错 了 ， 我 就 这 么 写 。

Shéi shuō zhège zì cuò le, wǒ jiù zhème xiě.

Who says it's wrong? This is just the way I write it.

(For details, please see Grammar Book I, Lesson 8.)

▶ A post office in Shanghai.

duì huà èr
对 话 (二)

DIALOGUE 2

nǐ huì yòng xiàn jīn jī ma
你 会 用 现 金 机 吗?

▶ **Do You Know How to Use the ATM?**

shēng cí
生 词
🔘 **New Words**

	Chinese	Pinyin	Part of Speech	English
1.	现金机	xiànjīnjī	N	cash machine; ATM
	机=机器	jī = jīqì	N	machine
2.	银行	yínháng	N	bank
3.	卡	kǎ	N	card
4.	放	fàng	V	let go; set free; put
5.	进去	jìnqù	V	go in; get in; enter
6.	密码	mìmǎ	N	secret code; password
7.	取	qǔ	V	take; get; fetch
8.	按	àn	V	press; push down
9.	咦	yí	Int	well; why
10.	机器	jīqì	N	machine; machinery; apparatus
11.	坏	huài	Adj/V	bad; go bad; spoil; ruin
12.	柜台	guìtái	N	counter

13. 存折	cúnzhé	N	deposit book; bank book
存	cún	V	deposit
折	zhé	N	booklet
14. 账号	zhànghào	N	account number
15. 单	dān	N	sheet; bill; list
16. 凭	píng	Prep	depending on; go by; base on
17. 照片	zhàopiàn	N	photograph; picture
18. 证件	zhèngjiàn	N	credentials; papers; certificate; ID
19. 办理	bànlǐ	V	handle; conduct; transact

pīn yīn kè wén
拼　音　课　文
🔘 **Text with Pinyin**

▶▶▶

huáng fāng:
黄　方：

duì bù qǐ, wǒ bú huì yòng zhè ge xiàn jīn
对 不 起，我 不 会 用 这 个 现 金

jī. nǐ néng jiāo wǒ zěn me yòng ma?
机。你 能 教 我 怎 么 用 吗？

gé lín:
格　林：

ò, hěn róng yì. zhǐ yào bǎ nǐ de yín háng
哦，很 容 易。只 要 把 你 的 银 行

kǎ cóng zhè ge kǒu fàng jìn qù, shū rù nǐ
卡 从 这 个 口 放 进 去，输 入 你

de mì mǎ, zài shū rù yào qǔ de qián shù,
的 密 码，再 输 入 要 取 的 钱 数，

àn OK jiù kě yǐ le.
按 OK 就 可 以 了。

huáng fāng: yí, zěn me qián bù chū lái ne?
黄 方：咦，怎 么 钱 不 出 来 呢？

gé lín: wǒ kàn kan. ēn, yuán lái shì jī qì huài le.
格 林：我 看 看。嗯，原 来 是 机 器 坏 了。
nà nǐ dào guì tái qù qǔ ba.
那 你 到 柜 台 去 取 吧。

huáng fāng: kě shì wǒ méi yǒu cún zhé.
黄 方：可 是 我 没 有 存 折。

gé lín: zài měi guó yín háng bù yòng cún zhé. nǐ zhī
格 林：在 美 国 银 行 不 用 存 折。你 只
yào zhī dào nǐ de zhàng hào, tián yī zhāng qǔ
要 知 道 你 的 账 号，填 一 张 取
kuǎn dān, píng dài zhào piàn de zhèng jiàn jiù kě
款 单，凭 带 照 片 的 证 件 就 可
yǐ bàn lǐ le.
以 办 理 了。

huáng fāng: zhēn de, nà cún qián ne?
黄 方：真 的，那 存 钱 呢？

gé lín: cún qián gēn qǔ qián yī yang, kě yǐ yòng xiàn
格 林：存 钱 跟 取 钱 一 样，可 以 用 现
jīn jī, yě kě yǐ zài guì tái bàn lǐ.
金 机，也 可 以 在 柜 台 办 理。

huáng fāng: yuán lái zhè me fāng biàn, nà wǒ shì shi.
黄 方：原 来 这 么 方 便，那 我 试 试。
xiè xiè.
谢 谢！

gé lín: bù kè qì, zài jiàn.
格 林：不 客 气，再 见。

hàn zì kè wén

汉 字 课 文

🔊 **Text in Chinese Characters**

▶▶▶

黄方：对不起，我不会用这个现金机。你能教我怎么用吗？

格林：哦，很容易。只要把你的银行卡从这个口放进去，输入你的密码，再输入要取的钱数，按OK就可以了。

黄方：咦，怎么钱不出来呢？

格林：我看看。嗯，原来是机器坏了。那你到柜台去取吧。

黄方：可是我没有存折。

格林：在美国银行不用存折。你只要知道你的账号，填一张取款单，凭带照片的证件就可以办理了。

黄方：真的，那存钱呢？

格林：存钱跟取钱一样，可以用现金机，也可以在柜台办理。

黄方：原来这么方便，那我试试。谢谢！

格林：不客气，再见。

◀◀◀

yǔ yán yīng yòng zhù shì

语 言 应 用 注 释

Notes on Language Usage

1. 现金机 is also called 自动柜员机 (zìdòng guìyuán jī) in China.

*2. 只要把你的银行卡从这个口放进去。**You just need to put your bank card in this slot.**

This is the "把" construction, emphasizing how somebody or something is used, influenced, or acted upon, as we learned in Lesson 7.

For example:

那 个 中 国 同 学 把 银 行 卡 丢 (diū, lose) 了。

Nàge Zhōngguó tóngxué bǎ yínháng kǎ diū le.

That Chinese student lost his bank card. (The Chinese student had his bank card lost.)

苏 珊 爸 爸 得 把 12 月 18 日 的 票 改 到 25 日。

Sūshān bàba dei bǎ shí'èr yuè shíbā rì de piào gǎi dào èrshíwǔ rì.

Susan's dad has to change the ticket from December 18 to December 25. (Susan's dad has to get the ticket changed from December 18 to December 25.)

(For details, please see Grammar Book I, Lesson 10.)

3. 咦，怎么钱不出来呢？ Hey, how come the money isn't coming out?

咦 is an interjection that indicates bewilderment. For example,

咦，我 刚 才 还 看 见 那 支 笔，怎 么 找 不 到 了？

Yí, wǒ gāngcái hái kànjiàn nà zhī bǐ, zěnme zhǎo bu dào le?

Well, I just saw that pen. How come I can't find it?

咦，他 进 纽 约 大 学 才 三 年 怎 么 就 毕 业 了？

Yí, tā jìn Niǔyuē Dàxué cái sān nián zěnme jiù bìyè le?

He entered NYU only three years [ago], so how is it that he has already graduated?

4. 嗯，原来是机器坏了。 Mm, the machine is broken.

嗯 is an interjection indicating a positive response to a question, like "mm hmm" in English.

For example:

嗯，我 懂 了。

Ēn, wǒ dǒng le.

Mm, I got it.

▶ Great Eastern Bank in Flushing, Queens, New York.

嗯，马上 就 好 了。

Ēn, mǎshàng jiù hǎo le.

Mm, I'll finish it right away.

*5. 原来这么方便····· I never realized it was so convenient.

原来 is an adverb that indicates the discovery of something previously unknown.

For example:

难 怪 他 今 天 这 么 高 兴，原 来 他 的 女 朋 友 要 来 看 他 了。

Nánguài tā jīntiān zhème gāoxìng, yuánlái tā de nǚpéngyǒu yào lái kàn tā le.

No wonder he is so happy today. It turns out his girlfriend is coming to see him.

原 来 苏 珊 有 男 朋 友 了，我 才 知 道 她 为 什 么 不 跟 约 翰
出 去 玩 儿。

Yuánlái Sūshān yǒu nánpéngyǒu le, wǒ cái zhīdào tā wèishénme bù gēn Yuēhàn chūqù wánr.

So, Susan has a boyfriend. Now I know why she didn't go out with John.

yuè   dú

阅　读

▶ Reading

....

shēng cí

生　词

🔘 New Words

	Chinese	Pinyin	Part of Speech	English
1.	种类	zhǒnglèi	N	kind; type; variety
2.	平信	píngxìn	N	ordinary mail
3.	邮票	yóupiào	N	postage stamp; stamp
4.	海运	hǎiyùn	N	sea transportation; ocean shipping; sea mail; by sea
5.	快件	kuàijiàn	N	express mail; priority mail
6.	等	děng	Par	etc.; and so on; and so forth

294 LESSON 8 ▶ At the Post Office and Bank

7.	一般	yībān	Adj	general; ordinary; common
8.	信件	xìnjiàn	N	letters; mail
9.	邮寄	yóujì	V/N	send by post; post; mail
10.	重要	zhòngyào	Adj	important; significant; major
11.	份	fèn	M	share; portion
12.	登记	dēngjì	V	register; check in; enter one's name
13.	收件人	shōujiànrén	N	addressee; consignee
14.	投递	tóudì	V	deliver
15.	优先	yōuxiān	Adj	have priority; take precedence
16.	使用	shǐyòng	V	make use of; use; employ; apply
17.	私营	sīyíng	Adj	privately owned; privately operated; private
18.	邮递	yóudì	V/N	send by post (or mail); postal (or mail) delivery

pīn yīn kè wén

拼 音 课 文

🔊 **Text with Pinyin**

▶▶▶

zài zhōng guó yóu jú yóu jiàn de zhǒng lèi hěn duō,
在 中 国 邮 局 邮 件 的 种 类 很 多,
yǒu píng xìn, guà hào, háng kōng, hǎi yùn hé kuài jiàn děng.
有 平 信、挂 号、航 空、海 运 和 快 件 等。
píng xìn jiù shì yī bān xìn jiàn, tiē le yóu piào jiù
平 信 就 是 一 般 信 件,贴 了 邮 票 就
kě yǐ jì. bǐ jiào zhòng yào de xìn jiàn yī bān jì
可 以 寄。比 较 重 要 的 信 件 一 般 寄

挂号，因为每份信件邮局都要登
记，收件人要签字。国际邮件可以
寄航空或海运。航空快，但是贵，而
海运便宜得多。快件种类很多，有
特快专递、第二日投递、三日到的
优先邮件等。除了邮局，人们还常
常使用中外私营邮递公司寄快
件和包裹。

hàn zì kè wén
汉字课文
🔘 **Text in Chinese Characters**

▶▶▶

　　在中国邮局邮件的种类很多，有平信、挂号、航空、海运
和快件等。平信就是一般信件，贴了邮票就可以寄。比较重要
的信件一般寄挂号，因为<u>每份信件邮局都要登记</u>，<u>收件人要签</u>
字。国际邮件可以寄航空或海运。航空快，但是贵，<u>而</u>海运便
宜得多。快件种类很多，有特快专递、第二日投递、三日到的
优先邮件等。除了邮局，人们还常常使用中外私营邮递公司寄
快件和包裹。

◀◀◀

yǔ yán yīng yòng zhù shì
语 言 应 用 注 释
Notes on Language Usage

*1. 每份信件邮局都要登记，收件人要签字。**Because the post office needs to register each piece of mail, the recipient needs to sign for it.**

This is a "topic-comment" sentence. In this type of sentence, the object is moved to the beginning of the sentence to serve as the topic and the rest of the sentence is a comment on that topic. This is a very popular type of sentence in Chinese. This sentence could also be rendered as: 邮局要登记每份信件。 In order to make this into a topic-comment structure, 每份信件 is moved to the beginning and 都 is added.

More examples:

我没有桌子 (zhuōzi, desk) 和椅子 (yǐzi, chair)。

Wǒ méiyǒu zhuōzi hé yǐzi.

→ 桌子和椅子我都没有。

    Zhuōzi hé yǐzi wǒ dōu méiyǒu.

    I don't have desks and chairs.

苏珊的爸爸改好了她的飞机票。

Sūshān de bàba gǎi hǎo le tā de fēijīpiào.

→ 苏珊的飞机票她爸爸都改好了。

    Sūshān de fēijī piào tā bàba dōu gǎi hǎo le.

    Susan's father has changed her airline ticket.

(For details, please see Grammar Book I, Lesson 4.)

2. 航空快，但是贵，而海运便宜得多。 **Air mail is faster, but (more) expensive. (However,) sea mail is much cheaper.**

而 is a conjunction meaning "but." The meanings of the elements connected by 而 are opposite or contrary.

For example:

他已经三十多岁了，而我还是叫他"小王"。

Tā yǐjīng sānshí duō suì le, ér wǒ háishì jiào tā "Xiǎo Wáng."

He is already over 30, but I still call him "Young Wang."

都夏天了，而他还穿着毛衣。

Dōu xiàtiān le, ér tā hái chuān zhe máoyī.

Summer is here, but he still wears a sweater.

▶ English Translations of the Texts

. . . .

Dialogue 1

Green:	I'm going to the post office to get (process) a passport. Is there anything I can do for you (while I'm there)?
Xiaonian Wang:	I want to send a parcel. But I don't have anything to wrap it with.

Green:	It doesn't matter. You can buy a cardboard box there.
Xiaonian Wang:	That's good. Let's go together.
	(At the post office)
Clerk:	May I help you?
Xiaonian Wang:	I want to buy a cardboard box to send something in.
Clerk:	Is it fragile?
Xiaonian Wang:	No. But I want to know whether the addressee receives it or not.
Clerk:	OK, you can use this envelope. It is padded inside to protect the mail. If you send it by Express Mail, you can track when the addressee receives it. It is both quick and safe. It costs only $13.95.
Xiaonian Wang:	Although Express Mail is good, it is too expensive. What other ways can I send it? It's OK if it is a little slow.
Clerk:	If you are not in a hurry, you can send it by this kind of certified mail. The recipient has to sign upon receiving it. A receipt will be sent back to you. It costs about half as much (as Express Mail).
Xiaonian Wang:	Great, I'll go with this kind of mail.
Clerk:	Please fill out this form. Altogether it'll be $5.45.

Dialogue 2

Fang Huang:	Excuse me. I don't know how to use this cash machine. Can you teach me (how to use it)?
Green:	Oh, it's easy. You just need to put your bank card in this slot, enter your password and the amount of money that you want to withdraw, then press OK. That's it.
Fang Huang:	Hey, how come the money isn't coming out?
Green:	Let me see. Mm, the machine is broken. You can go to the counter to withdraw money.
Fang Huang:	But I don't have my bank book with me.
Green:	You don't need a bank book in an American bank. You only need to know your account number. You fill out the withdrawal form and process it with a photo ID.
Fang Huang:	Really? How about depositing money?
Green:	Depositing is the same as withdrawing. You can use the cash machine, or do it at the counter.
Fang Huang:	I never realized it was so convenient. Let me try. Thanks.
Green:	You're welcome. Bye.

Reading

There are many ways to send mail at the Chinese post office, including ordinary mail, registered mail, air and sea mail, and express mail. Ordinary mail is regular post. You can send it out by simply putting stamps on it and mailing it. Important mail can be sent by registered mail, because the post office needs to register each piece of mail and the recipient needs to sign for it. International mail can be sent by air or by sea. Air mail is faster, but (more) expensive. Sea mail is much cheaper. There are many kinds of fast mail, such as express mail, second day delivery, priority mail that arrives within three days, etc. Besides the post office, people often use privately owned delivery companies, both domestic and foreign, to send mail.

tīng shuō liàn xí
听　说　练　习

▶ Exercises for Listening and Speaking

• •

一、完成对话。*(1. Work in pairs to complete the dialogue.)*

A: Kěyǐ bāngzhù nín ma?

B: _____

A: Nín yòng shénme bāo?

B: _____

A: Rúguǒ pà yā yòng zhège xìnfēng, rúguǒ bù pà yā, jiù yòng zhège xìnfēng.

B: _____

A: Méi guānxì, xìnfēng lǐ yǒu pàomò sùliào, kěyǐ bǎohù yóujiàn.

B: _____

A: Nín yào jì shénmeyàng de yóujiàn?

B: _____

A: Nà jiù jì tèkuài zhuāndì, yòu kuài yòu ānquán, zhǐyào shísān kuài jiǔ máo wǔ.

B: _____

A: Nǐ kěyǐ jì zhè zhǒng guàhào, duìfāng shōu dào hòu yào zài huízhí shàng qiānzì, ránhòu huízhí huì jì huí gěi nǐ, zhǐyào huā chàbùduō yībàn de qián.

B: _____

A: Qǐng tiánxiě zhè fèn biǎo.

B: _____

A: Yígòng shì wǔ kuài sì máo wǔ fēn qián.

二、听对话，回答问题。*(Listen to the following conversation and answer the questions.)*

1. Where are they going?

   _____

2. Why are there so many people today?

   _____

3. What do they need to do before standing in the line?

   _____

4. What did A forget to bring with him?

   _____

5. Is there a way to withdraw money without lining up?

   _____

三、先听对话，然后两人一组朗读。*(3. Listen to the following conversation without looking at the book, and then read it aloud in pairs, first by following the pinyin, then by following the characters.)*

Jiǎ:	Nǐ qù nǎr?
Yǐ:	Wǒ qù yóujú bàn hùzhào.
Jiǎ:	Zěnme yóujú yě kěyǐ bàn hùzhào?
Yǐ:	Zhōngguó de yóujú bù kěyǐ bàn hùzhào ma?
Jiǎ:	Zhōngguó de yóujú kě bù bàn hùzhào. Dàn Zhōngguó de yóujú kěyǐ cúnqián.
Yǐ:	Yóujiàn yǒu shénme zhǒnglèi?
Jiǎ:	Yóujiàn de zhǒnglèi hěn duō, yǒu píngxìn, guàhào, hángkōng, hǎiyùn hé kuàijiàn děng.
Yǐ:	Shénme shì píngxìn?
Jiǎ:	Píngxìn jiù shì yībān xìnjiàn, tiē le yóupiào jiù kěyǐ jì.
Yǐ:	Rúguǒ wǒ yào jì zhòngyào de dōngxi ne?
Jiǎ:	Bǐjiào zhòngyào de xìnjiàn yībān jì guàhào, yīnwéi měi fèn xìnjiàn yóujú dōu yào dēng jì, shōujiànrén yào qiān zì.
Yǐ:	Nà jì guójì yóujiàn ne?

Jiǎ: Guójì yóujiàn fēn hángkōng hé hǎiyùn liǎng zhǒng.

Yǐ: Nǎ zhǒng hǎo?

Jiǎ: Hǎiyùn piányi shì piányi, kěshì yǒu shíhòu tài màn.

Yǐ: Yào duōcháng shíjiān?

Jiǎ: Cóng Zhōngguó jì hǎiyùn dào Měiguó, yībān liǎng sān ge yuè, màn de sān sì ge yuè.

Yǐ: Nà yě tài màn le.

Jiǎ: Dōngxi bù duō háishì jì hángkōng hǎo.

Yǐ: Duì.

甲：你去哪儿？

乙：我去邮局办护照。

甲：怎么邮局也可以办护照？

乙：中国的邮局不可以办护照吗？

甲：中国的邮局可不办护照。但中国的邮局可以存钱。

乙：邮件有什么种类？

甲：邮件的种类很多，有平信、挂号、航空、海运和快件等。

乙：什么是平信？

甲：平信就是一般信件，贴了邮票就可以寄。

乙：如果我要寄重要的东西呢？

甲：比较重要的信件一般寄挂号，因为每份信件邮局都要登记，收件人要签字。

乙：那寄国际邮件呢？

甲：国际邮件分航空和海运两种。

乙：哪种好？

甲：海运便宜是便宜，可是有时候太慢。

乙：要多长时间？

甲：从中国寄海运到美国，一般两三个月，慢的三四个月。

乙：那也太慢了。

甲：东西不多还是寄航空好。

乙：对。

四、角色表演 *(4. Role Play)*

1. A: Suppose you are a foreign student and don't know how to use a bank in the United States. Try to get information from someone who knows.

   B: You go to a bank to deposit money. You see a foreign student who needs help, and go over to help him/her.

2. A: You are a customer who wants to send a package to a friend. You want to make sure your friend receives it safely, but do not want to spend too much money.

   B: You are a clerk in the post office trying to help a customer send his/her important package by the safest and least expensive service.

diàn nǎo yǔ   hàn zì   liàn xí
电　脑　与　汉　字　练　习
▶ Exercises for Computing and Learning Characters

. . . .

一、打出下面段落。*(Type the following passage.)*

A: 小姐，寄挂号信多少钱？

B: 你寄国内 (guónèi, domestic)；还是国际？

A: 我寄国际。

B: 不超过一磅19块9毛5。

A: 太贵了。我没有那么多钱。

B: 那你就寄航空，只要8毛钱。

A: 可是我连8毛钱也没带。

B: 你有多少钱？

A: 只有3分钱。

B: 那你回去发电子邮件 (diànzǐ yóujiàn, e-mail) 吧，不要钱。

二、把下面拼音句子打成汉字。*(2. Type the following pinyin sentences and select the appropriate characters from the list that appears on your computer screen.)*

1. Zài Měiguó yóujú yóujiàn de zhǒnglèi hěn duō, yǒu píngxìn、guàhào、hángkōng、hǎiyùn hé kuàijiàn děng. Guójì yóujiàn kěyǐ jì hángkōng huò hǎiyùn.

2. Yīnwèi Sū Shān yào qù Xiàwēiyí, tā bàba zhǐhǎo gěi tā gǎi fēijīpiào. Cóng Xiàwēiyí huí Bōshìdùn hěn máfan, yào xiān fēi dào Jiùjīnshān zhuǎn jī, hái yào zài fù 80 Měiyuán de chājià hé 100 Měiyuán de fájīn.

3. Wáng Jiāshēng: chū běi xiǎo mén, wǎng zuǒ guǎi, zài dì èr gè shí zì lùkǒu, hóng lǜ dēng pángbiān.

4. Kuàijiàn zhǒnglèi hěn duō, yǒu tèkuài zhuāndì, dì èr rì tóudì, sān rì dào de yōuxiān yóujiàn děng.

三、圈出正确的汉字。*(3. Circle the correct character to fill in the blanks.)*

1. 王家生要去 ___（由、油、郡、邮、柚）局，不去 ___（垠、钢、钥、铀、银）行。

2. 苏珊爸爸 ___（啪、怛、恒、帕、怕、）她圣诞节不能到家，给她改了 23 号的票。

3. 夏天我跟朋友去大 ___（泳、汩、海、侮、梅）玩儿。

4. 今天学的生词我 ___（痊、会、仝、全、荃）会了。

5. 昨天我 ___（近、进、运、尽、速）了俱乐部，就 ___（甜、恬、填、滇、镇）表。

四、读生字，找出偏旁部首。*(4. The characters in each of the following groups share a radical. Read the characters and write the shared radicals.)*

Example: 这 迎　shared radical: 辶

1. 泡 沫 海　shared radical:_____

2. 信 件 优 使 份　shared radical:_____

3. 投 按 挂　shared radical:_____

4. 怕 快　shared radical:_____

5. 递 运 进　shared radical:_____

6. 填 坏 压　shared radical:_____

五、把汉字分成部件。*(5. Test your understanding of character structure by dividing the following characters into their component parts.)*

Example: 吗—>口　马

1. 照 —>_____

2. 取 —>_____

3. 盒 —>_____

4. 信 —>_____

5. 安 —>_____

六、学生字 *(6. Learning New Characters)*

独体词组复合词。 (Form compound words based on single-character words.)

注释 (Note): Most Chinese characters are words themselves, called 独 (dú, single) 体 (tǐ, body) 词. In this exercise you will be asked to find compound words that contain some common single-character words you have already learned.

Study the following characters selected from the New Words lists: 事* 全 或 能 使 年* 得 家*

1. Copy each character by hand using the character writing demonstration sheet.

2. For each character marked with an asterisk, find the compounds in which the characters are used in the text, and write the compound words next to the characters.

3. With the assistance of a dictionary or an online dictionary, write down three more compounds in which these single-character words appear.

4. For each character marked with an asterisk, make a sentence with one of the three new compounds.

Character Writing Demonstration Sheet 第八课   姓名_____

Pinyin	Strokes	Structure	English	Radical	Traditional Form
shì	8	single-body	matter, thing	一	事

事 事 事 事 事 事 事 事

Pinyin	Strokes	Structure	English	Radical	Traditional Form
quán	6	top-bottom	complete, whole, entire	人	全

全 全 全 全 全 全

Pinyin	Strokes	Structure	English	Radical	Traditional Form
huò	8	half encloser	perhaps, maybe	戈	或

或 或 或 或 或 或 或 或

Pinyin	Strokes	Structure	English	Radical	Traditional Form
shǐ	8	left-right	make, cause	亻	使

使 使 使 使 使 使 使 使

Pinyin	Strokes	Structure	English	Radical	Traditional Form
néng	10	left-right	can, be able to	厶	能

能 能 能 能 能 能 能 能

能 能

Pinyin	Strokes	Structure	English	Radical	Traditional Form
nián	6	single-body	year	丿	年

年 年 年 年 年 年

Pinyin	Strokes	Structure	English	Radical	Traditional Form
dé	11	left-right	get obtain, gain	彳	得

得 得 得 得 得 得 得 得

得 得 得

Pinyin	Strokes	Structure	English	Radical	Traditional Form
jiā	10	top-bottom	family, household, home	宀	家

家 家 家 家 家 家 家 家
家 家

kè   wén   liàn   xí

课   文   练   习

▶ Exercises for Understanding the Texts

一、根据课文回答问题。 *(1. Answer the questions orally based on the text.)*

对话(1)

1. 格林要去邮局做什么？

    What did Green want to do at the post office?

2. 王小年要去邮局做什么？

    What did Xiaonian Wang want to do at the post office?

3. 王小年为什么不寄平信？

    Why didn't Xiaonian Wang want to send the letter by regular mail?

4. 王小年为什么不想寄特快专递？

    Why didn't Xiaonian Wang want to send the letter by express mail?

5. 寄挂号信比寄特快专递省多少钱？

    How much money can one save by sending by registered mail instead of express mail?

对话(2)

1. 黄方和格林在哪儿？
   Where were Huang Fang and Green?

2. 黄方是不是在美国出生的中国人？
   Is Huang Fang an American-born Chinese?

3. 为什么黄方不能从现金机里取出钱来？
   Why couldn't Huang Fang get money from the ATM machine?

4. 什么是"存折"？在美国的银行取钱用存折吗？
   What is a "存折"? Do people need a 存折 to withdraw money in an American bank?

5. 那在美国的银行怎么取钱？存钱呢？
   How do people withdraw and deposit money in the United States?

二、用"Adj is Adj, but"完成下列对话完成对话。**(2. Complete the dialogue orally using the "Adj is Adj, but..." structure.)**

> **Example:** A: 这件衣服很好看。
>
> B: 好看是好看，就是太小了。

1. A: 坐地铁去机场很省钱。

   B: _____。

2. A: 坐出租汽车去机场很方便。

   B: _____。

3. A: 格林的中文发音真好！

   B: _____。

4. A: 你看这件衣服我穿好看吗？

   B: _____。

5. A: 这种水果(shuǐguǒ, fruit)真大！

   B: _____。

三、用 "把" 改写下列句子，然后朗读。 *(3. Rewrite the sentences using the 把 structure. Then read the sentences aloud.)*

Example: 妹妹吃了我的面包。→ 妹妹把我的面包吃了。

1. 妹妹开走了我的车。

2. 苏珊买好了去夏威夷的飞机票。

3. 格林从银行取了钱。

4. 因为银行的现金机坏了，所以王小年不能取出钱来。

5. 王小年寄出了他的挂号信。

四、用 "topic-comment" structure 回答下列问题。 *(4. Use the "topic-comment" structure to answer the following questions orally.)*

Example: 王小年有邮票吗？→ 邮票王小年有很多。

1. 王小年寄出去他的信了吗？

2. 你做完今天的中文作业了吗？

3. 你妹妹找到她的银行卡了吗？

4. 苏珊去没去过夏威夷？

5. 你听懂了老师今天讲的语法吗？

五、作文 *(5. Composition)*

Write a paragraph (8–10 sentences minimum) to talk about your experience of using the post office or bank. Make sure to use the given words and phrases.

1. Adj 是 Adj，就是　　2. 只要　　3. 原来　　4. 而　　5. 把 structure
6. 除了……以外，还

六、翻译 *(6. Translation)*

Translate the following sentences orally in class. Then type your translations in Chinese using the words and phrases provided.

1. It is true that post offices in the US are convenient, but the waiting (děng, 等) times are too long. (Adj 是 Adj, 就是)

2. Taking a taxi to the airport is convenient, but it is too expensive. (Adj 是 Adj, 就是)

3. In addtion to English, do you also speak Chinese? (还⋯⋯)

4. In addition to Xiaonian Wang, who else do you know in this class (bān, 班)? (还⋯⋯)

5. Whenever he is here, he will help us. (只要⋯⋯就)

6. I feel better as long as I have friends who can help me. (只要⋯⋯就)

7. Please help me mail this registered letter to my mother. (把 structure)

8. Don't leave your passport home when you go on a business trip abroad (guówài, 国外). (把 structure)

9. No wonder his Chinese pronunciation is so good. He has lived in China for six months. (原来)

10. Taking the subway to the airport is cheap, but too troublesome, while taking the shuttle bus is both economical and convenient. (而)

bǔ	chōng	yuè	dú	liàn	xí
补	充	阅	读	练	习

▶ Supplementary Reading Exercises

· ·

(1) Controlled Vocabulary

Read the following passage and answer the following questions either in Chinese or in English.

	Chinese	Pinyin	Part of Speech	English
1.	明信片	míngxìnpiàn	N	postcard
2.	骑	qí	V	ride (an animal or bicycle)
3.	传真	chuánzhēn	N	fax; facsimile
4.	邮递员	yóudìyuán	N	letter carrier; postal worker

邮局和银行

黄方是刚从中国来美国上学的留学生，他觉得在美国虽然信箱很多，寄信很方便，可是邮局很少，要寄邮件和包裹就得走很远。但是美国的银行比邮局多多了，在纽约市，差不多每两、三个街口就有一家银行。

在美国的邮局，除了可以买邮票和寄各种各样的邮件以外，还可以办护照，买寄包裹用的各种纸盒。邮局的职员也很好，可是每次都要等很长时间。

中国的银行没有美国那么多，可是邮局很多，邮局不但可以寄邮件，寄包裹等，还卖邮票和明信片，也可以存钱，但是只可以存人民币（中国的钱）。中国的邮局工作时间很长，邮递员骑车送信，他们穿的衣服跟信箱的颜色一样，都是绿的。

Questions

1. 黄方对美国邮局和银行有什么看法？

   What did Huang Fang discover about post offices and banks in the United States?

2. 在美国的邮局都可以做什么？

   What can people do at a US post office?

3. 中国的邮局有什么别的服务？

   What other services do post offices in China offer to the public in contrast to those in the US?

4. 中国的信箱是什么颜色？

   What color are mailboxes in China?

5. 中国的邮递员怎么送信？

   How do postmen/women in Chinese post offices deliver mail to recipients?

6. 他们的衣服是什么颜色？

   What color are their uniforms?

(2) Authentic Material

请按下面的表格回答下列问题。(Below is a postal form for mailing parcels from the Chinese post office. In the spaces on the form, write the numbers that correspond to the questions below.)

Example: For Question 1: "Where do you put the sender's name on the form" you would write "1" in the large center block after 姓名.

1. Where do you put the sender's name on the form?

2. If you send this parcel to Huang Fang, where do you put his name?

3. Where do you put your address?

4. The total charge is 234 yuan RMB. Where do you put the amount?

5. Where should you sign when mailing the parcel?

6. Where should Huang Fang sign?

7. Can you guess where you should write Huang Fang's zip code?

国 内 普 通 包 裹 详 情 单　（通知单联）

收件人	□□□□□□	寄件人声明 如包裹无法投递,请 1. 退还寄件人 2. 抛弃处理 3. 改寄	包裹号码: 接收局号码:	①投递局存
	详细地址:-----------------			
	姓　名:　　　电　话:			式四份、请用力填写
寄件人	详细地址:-----------------	内 装 何 物		
	姓　名:		收寄人员签章: 检查人员签章:	
	邮政编码:　　　电　话:	保价金额:　　元	重　量:　　克	
领取人证件内容 证件名称:--------- --------- 证件号码:--------- --------- 发证机关:--------- ---------		领取人签章 收件单位公章	单　价:　　元 保价费:　　元 其　他:　　元 共　计:　　元	

填写本单前，请认真阅读背面的"使用须知"，若认可并遵守、请在此签字 --------------。

zhōng guó wén huà xí sú

中 国 文 化 习 俗

Chinese Customs and Culture

....

Zhōng guó de yóu jú diàn huà hé hù lián wǎng

中 国 的 邮 局 电 话 和 互 联 网

▶ Postal, Phone and Internet Services in China

The Internet

The first Internet café 网吧 (wǎngbā) opened in Beijing in 1995. According to the Chinese government, since that time, China has become the nation with the second largest number of Internet users. Just as in most of the developed world, the Internet is widely available in China. You will be able to find facilities with Internet access in most major cities. Business centers in four and five star hotels provide Internet services for visitors, and Internet cafes are increasingly plentiful. One of the best places to look out for Internet cafes is near a university.

Internet usage continues to grow exponentially and has been especially pronounced in the area of gaming. Reflecting the already vibrant computer cultures in neighboring South Korea, Japan, Taiwan, and Hong Kong, most urban Chinese under the age of thirty consider the Internet an absolutely essential fact of life. Chinese young people frequently "surf the Internet" 上网 (shàngwǎng), visit web sites 网站 (wǎngzhàn), peruse web pages 网页 (wǎngyè), play computer games 电脑游戏 (diànnǎo yóuxì) and download 下载 (xiàzǎi) software 软体 (ruǎnjiàn) and attempt to guard against viruses 病毒 (bìngdú).

As Chinese people continue to use the Internet more and more frequently, the Chinese government has redoubled its efforts to censor and block content they decide is inappropriate for Chinese citizens. Google, Microsoft, and Yahoo have all received vociferous criticism worldwide for their cooperation with the Chinese government in blocking content from Chinese users. Detractors point out that these companies are aiding the Chinese government in repressing its citizens, while the companies themselves defend their actions by saying that by entering the Chinese market, they are sowing the seeds of a more robust civil society.

While most young Chinese prefer to send their messages electronically, the majority of Chinese still do so the old fashioned way, with what is purported to be the world's first systematic postal network.

The Chinese Postal System

The Chinese Postal Service has clear title to the world's oldest continuously operating mail system. The origins of China's postal and communication services date as far back as the Shang dynasty (16th–11th century BC). There are records about organized courier services on unearthed bones and tortoise shells that survive from that time. Messenger and military communications by fire and smoke from beacon towers developed rapidly in the Zhou and Qin dynasties (c. 11th–2nd century BC), satisfying the needs for frontier defense and state unity, as well as transferring intelligence and political messages. The horse courier service, even during those early years, was well organized, strictly regulated, and highly efficient. This service was substantially expanded during the subsequent Han dynasty (206 BC–220 AD). The fire-smoke system began to be phased out during the Qing Dynasty (1644–1911). As an institution, however, it was not till the late Qing that the chain of courier posts and beacons was replaced by a modern equivalent.

Nowadays, if you visit China, you can see post offices with eye-catching green emblems, in cities and towns throughout the country. Post offices are usually found on main streets, at railway stations and airports, and near major scenic spots. They are open daily from 08:00–19:00. The domestic mail is very fast and the cost is quite low, normally 0.60 yuan for local delivery and 0.80 yuan for inter-city mail. Within some cities, there is often same-day delivery; between large cities, delivery is usually overnight. The international postal service is also quite efficient. Under normal circumstances, it will only take about 5–10 days for airmail letters or postcards to reach an international destination. Chinese post offices offer Express Mail Service (EMS) to most domestic and international destinations. A number of international courier companies also have offices in China, including DHL, UPS, TNT and FedEx. They are now accessible to more than 10,000 cities in 170 countries and regions.

▶ A branch of the Bank of China in Beijing.

▶ Chinese stamps

▶ A busy post office in Beijing.

▶ A mailbox on the street.

▶ A public phone in China.

Telecommunications in China

China is increasingly reliant on optical cables and is extending its use of ground satellite communication stations. At the end of 2004, China had 647.26 million telephone subscribers, 312.44 million fixed lines and 334.82 million mobiles phone subscribers, constituting the world's second-largest telephone network. China started its mobile telecommunications business in 1987 and the mobile network now covers all the large and medium-sized cities, and more than 2,800 small cities and county seats. Internal roaming service exists with over 150 countries and regions all over the world. China has been the world's largest cell phone market for a number of years.

When making a domestic call in China, you should dial the domestic prefix 0 plus the area code and phone number. When making an international call, just dial the international prefix 00, plus the country code, area code and number. In many large cities, you can now buy IP phone cards to make long distance calls at less expensive rates than regular phone service. Facilities for sending faxes are available in hotels, post offices and telecommunication centers.

▶ Test Your Knowledge Which service should you use and how?

Imagine you are traveling in China. You need to contact people or send packages. Based on the information provided above and your own common sense, decide what to do in each situation below.

1. You are in Beijing and have an urgent package that needs to be sent to an office in Shanghai. You will use: (choose the best choice)

   A. airmail

   B. regular mail

   C. Express Mail Service

2. If you need to send a letter to a friend in the same city, how much is the stamp?

   A. 0.80 yuan

   B. 0.39 yuan

   C. 0.60 yuan

3. If you want to send an e-mail in China, where can you find Internet service (choose as many as you can)?

A. a three star hotel

B. a four or five star hotel

C. an Internet Café in a shopping area

D. an Internet Café close to a university campus

4. (a) You want to make a phone call from Beijing to New York. The New York number is 212-345-6789. How do you dial? (Tell all numbers that need to be dialed.)

(b) You want to make a phone call from Shanghai to Beijing. The Beijing number is 10-2345-6789. How do you dial? (Tell all numbers that need to be dialed.)

Answers:

1. C   2. C   3. B, D   4. (a) 001-212-345-6789   (b) 010-2345-6789

shēng bìng
生 病
I Am Sick

▶ **Objectives:**

1. To communicate with a doctor
2. To be able to describe symptoms
3. To understand instructions on taking medicine

duì huà yī
对   话 (一)

DIALOGUE 1

zhāng xiǎo mèi shēng bìng le
张   小   妹   生   病   了

▶**Xiaomei Zhang Is Sick**

I'm Sick

shēng cí
生   词
💿 **New Words**

	Chinese	Pinyin	Part of Speech	English
1.	病	bìng	N	ill; sick; disease
2.	生病	shēngbìng	VO	fall ill; get sick
3.	能	néng	AV	can; be able to; be capable of
4.	得病	débìng	VO	become sick
5.	看病	kànbìng	VO	(of a doctor) see a patient; (of a patient) see (or consult) a doctor
6.	咳嗽	késòu	V	cough
7.	流	liú	V	flow; move from place to place; drift
8.	鼻涕	bítì	N	nasal mucus
9.	眼泪	yǎnlèi	N	tears
10.	发烧	fāshāo	V	have (or run) a fever; have (or run) a temperature
11.	感冒	gǎnmào	V	common cold

12.	下课	xiàkè	V	get out of class; finish class
13.	陪	péi	V	accompany; keep somebody company
14.	医院	yīyuàn	N	hospital
15.	安心	ānxīn	VO	feel at ease; be relieved; set one's mind at rest
16.	休息	xiūxi	V	have (or take) a rest; rest
17.	缺	quē	V/N	be short of; lack; be absent; vacancy; incomplete
18.	帮	bāng	V	help; assist
19.	补	bǔ	V	mend; patch; repair; make up for
20.	流感	liúgǎn	N	flu
21.	药	yào	N	medicine; drug
22.	开	kāi	V	write out (a prescription); open
23.	消炎	xiāoyán	VO	diminish inflammation; counteract inflammation
24.	退烧	tuìshāo	VO	bring down a fever
25.	水	shuǐ	N	water
26.	水果	shuǐguǒ	N	fruit
27.	清淡	qīngdàn	Adj	light; weak; delicate; not greasy or strongly flavored
28.	食物	shíwù	N	food; edible items
29.	照顾	zhàogù	V	look after; care for; attend to; show consideration for
30.	放心	fàngxīn	V	set one's mind at rest; be at ease; rest assured; feel relieved

pīn yīn kè wén
拼 音 课 文

🔘 **Text with Pinyin**

▶▶▶

---

wáng jiā shēng: gāo lǎo shī, zhāng xiǎo mèi shēng bìng le, jīn
王 家 生： 高 老 师， 张 小 妹 生 病 了， 今
tiān bù néng lái shàng kè le.
天 不 能 来 上 课 了。

---

gāo lǎo shī: tā dé shén me bìng le? qù kàn guò bìng
高 老 师： 她 得 什 么 病 了？ 去 看 过 病
ma?
吗？

---

wáng jiā shēng: tā ké sòu, liú bí tì, yǎn lèi, hǎo xiàng
王 家 生： 她 咳 嗽， 流 鼻 涕、 眼 泪， 好 像
yǒu diǎn fā shāo, kě néng gǎn mào le. děng
有 点 发 烧， 可 能 感 冒 了。 等
huìr xià le kè wǒ péi tā qù xué
会 儿 下 了 课 我 陪 她 去 学
xiào yī yuàn kàn kàn.
校 医 院 看 看。

---

gāo lǎo shī: nà hǎo, gào su tā ān xīn xiū xi, quē
高 老 师： 那 好， 告 诉 她 安 心 休 息， 缺
kè wǒ kě yǐ bāng tā bǔ.
课 我 可 以 帮 她 补。

---

wáng jiā shēng: hǎo, xiè xiè lǎo shī.
王 家 生： 好， 谢 谢 老 师。

---

dì èr tiān
（第 二 天）

---

gāo lǎo shī: zhāng xiǎo mèi zěn me yàng le?
高 老 师： 张 小 妹 怎 么 样 了？

---

wáng jiā shēng: 王家生：

tā zuó tiān qù kàn le yī shēng. yī shēng shuō shì liú gǎn.
她 昨 天 去 看 了 医 生。医 生 说 是 流 感。

gāo lǎo shī: 高老师：

chī yào le ma?
吃 药 了 吗？

wáng jiā shēng: 王家生：

yī shēng kāi le xiē gǎn mào yào, hái yǒu xiāo yán hé tuì shāo de yào. tā xiàn zài shāo yǐ jīng tuì le, jiù shì hái ké sòu, tóu téng.
医 生 开 了 些 感 冒 药，还 有 消 炎 和 退 烧 的 药。她 现 在 烧 已 经 退 了，就 是 还 咳 嗽、头 疼。

gāo lǎo shī: 高老师：

dé le liú gǎn yī bān dōu yào yī gè xīng qī cái néng hǎo. gào su tā yào duō xiū xi, duō hē shuǐ, duō chī shuǐ guǒ hé qīng dàn de shí wù.
得 了 流 感 一 般 都 要 一 个 星 期 才 能 好。告 诉 她 要 多 休 息，多 喝 水，多 吃 水 果 和 清 淡 的 食 物。

wáng jiā shēng: 王家生：

wǒ hé tóng xué men huì hǎo hāor zhào gù tā, nín fàng xīn.
我 和 同 学 们 会 好 好 儿 照 顾 她，您 放 心。

hàn   zì   kè   wén
汉   字   课   文
🔘 **Text in Chinese Characters**

▶▶▶

王家生：高老师，张小妹生病了，今天不能来上课了。

高老师：她得什么病了？去看过病吗？

王家生：她咳嗽，流鼻涕、眼泪，好像有点发烧，可能感冒了。
　　　　等会儿下了课我陪她去学校医院看看。

高老师：那好，告诉她安心休息，缺课我可以帮她补。

王家生：好，谢谢老师。

（第二天）

高老师：张小妹怎么样了？

王家生：她昨天去看了医生。医生说是流感。

高老师：吃药了吗？

王家生：医生开了些感冒药、还有消炎和退烧的药。她现在烧
　　　　已经退了，就是还咳嗽、头疼。

高老师：得了流感一般都要一个星期才能好。告诉她要好好儿
　　　　休息，多喝水，多吃水果和清淡的食物。

王家生：我和同学们好好儿照顾她，您放心。　　　　　　◀◀◀

yǔ   yán   yīng   yòng   zhù   shì
语   言   应   用   注   释
Notes on Language Usage

*1. 张小妹生病了，今天不能来上课了。**Xiaomei Zhang is sick. She can't come to class today.**

a) **Change of Status or New Situation with 了**

When 了 is placed at the end of a sentence or in the middle of a sentence at a pause, it suggests a change of status or a new situation, especially in comparison with a previous state or situation.

For example:

下 雨 了。

Xiàyǔ le.

It is raining. (It was not raining before, but now it has started raining.)

张 小 妹 的 病 好 了。

Zhāng Xiǎomèi de bìng hǎo lè.

Xiaomei Zhang has recovered. (She was sick, but now she has recovered.)

b) 能 **can**

能 is an auxiliary verb meaning "can."

For example:

我 生 病 了，不 能 跟 你 去 打 球。

Wǒ shēngbìng le, bù néng gēn nǐ qù dǎqiú.

I am sick. I can't play ball with you.

王 小 年 现 在 能 说 中 文 了。

Wáng Xiǎonián xiànzài néng shuō Zhōngwén le.

Xiaonian Wang can speak Chinese now.

(For details, please see Grammar Book I, Lesson 5.)

2. 等会儿下了课，我陪她去学校医院看看。 **(Wait for a while.) I will go with her to the school hospital after class.**

a) 会儿

会儿 is the same as 一会儿.

*b) 了

Here 了 indicates future action. When the first action (having class) is completed, I will do the second, (accompanying her to the hospital). Both actions will happen in the future.

For example:

明 天 我 吃 了 午 饭 就 去 看 张 小 妹。

Míngtiān wǒ chī le wǔfàn jiù qù kàn Zhāng Xiǎomèi.

Tommorrow I will go to see Xiaomei Zhang after I finish lunch. (Both "eating lunch" and "go to see Xiaomei Zhang" will happen in the future.)

So far, we have learned three uses of 了: 了 to indicate action completed in the past, 了 to indicate action completed in the future, and 了 to indicate change of status or new situation.

For example:

Action completed in the past:

A: 吃 饭 了 吗 ?

Chīfàn le ma?

Have you eaten?

B: 吃 了 。

Chī le.

Yes, I have.

我 去 医 院 了 。

Wǒ qù yīyuàn le.

I have been to the hospital.

(See Lesson 1 Language Usage Note 4.)

Action completed in the future:

明 天 下 午 我 学 了 中 文 就 去 打 球 。

Míngtiān xiàwǔ wǒ xué le Zhōngwén jiù qù dǎqiú.

Tomorrow afternoon I will play ball after I study Chinese.

Change of situation or new status:

我 现 在 会 说 中 文 了 。

Wǒ xiànzài huì shuō Zhōngwén le.

I can speak Chinese now.

(See Language Usage Note 1a above.)

c) 我陪她去学校医院看看

This is a pivotal sentence, first introduced in the Lesson 3 Narration.

More examples:

今 天 晚 上 我 陪 你 看 电 影 。

Jīntiān wǎnshang wǒ péi nǐ kàn diànyǐng.

I'll accompany you to see the movie tonight.

可 是 你 得 请 我 吃 饭。

Kěshì nǐ děi qǐng wǒ chīfàn.

But you must treat me to dinner.

(For details, see Grammar Book I, Lesson 4.)

3. 她昨天去看了医生。**She went to see a doctor yesterday.**

In English, we say "to see a doctor" when one is sick. But in Chinese we can either say 看医生 or 看病. However, 看病 is the more standard use for consulting a doctor, and 看医生 is used colloquially.

4. 医生开了些感冒药，还有消炎和退烧的药。**The doctor prescribed some pills for treating the flu, diminishing inflammation and bringing down her fever.**

开 is the verb used for prescribing a medicine. In Chinese it is called 开处方 (chǔfāng, prescription). Here the sentence means the doctor prescribed the medicines, not actually gave the medicines.

*5. 她现在烧已经退了，就是还咳嗽、头疼。**Her fever is gone. But she's still coughing and has a headache.**

就是 is an adverb meaning "only." It is essentially the same as 只是.

For example:

他 汉 语 说 得 很 流 利， 就 是 不 会 写。

Tā Hànyǔ shuō de hěn liúlì, jiù shì bù huì xiě.

He speaks Chinese fluently, but he cannot write.

她 买 的 衣 服 很 好 看，就 是 短 (duǎn, short) 了 点 儿。

Tā mǎi de yīfú hěn hǎokàn, jiù shì duǎn le diǎnr.

The dress that she bought is pretty. It's just a little short.

(Also see Lesson 6 in this textbook).

duì huà èr

对 话 (二)

DIALOGUE 2

wǒ dù zi téng

我 肚 子 疼

▶ **My Stomach Hurts**

· ·

shēng cí

生 词

New Words

	Chinese	Pinyin	Part of Speech	English
1.	舒服	shūfu	Adj	comfortable; well
2.	疼	téng	Adj/V	ache; pain; sore; love dearly
3.	大夫	dàifu	N	doctor
4.	肚子	dùzi	N	belly; abdomen; stomach
5.	厉害	lìhai	Adj	severe; sharp; terrible
6.	拉肚子	lādùzi	VO	suffer from diarrhea; have loose bowels
7.	上吐下泻	shàngtù xiàxiè	CE	vomit and diarrhea; suffer from vomiting and diarrhea
8.	哎哟	āiyō	Int	hey; ouch; ow
9.	让	ràng	V	let; allow; make
10.	检查	jiǎnchá	V	check up; inspect; examine
11.	夜里	yèlǐ	TW	at night
12.	饿	è	Adj	hungry; starve
13.	冰箱	bīngxiāng	N	refrigerator; freezer

14.	剩菜	shèngcài	N	leftover food; leftovers
	剩	shèng	V	surplus; remnant; leave (over)
	菜	cài	N	vegetable; food; dish
15.	一定	yīdìng	Ad	definitely; certainly; surely; necessarily
16.	化验	huàyàn	V	laboratory test
17.	血	xiě	N	blood; related by blood
18.	大便	dàbiàn	N	defecate; have a bowel movement; stool
19.	大约	dàyuē	Ad	approximately; about; probably
20.	结果	jiéguǒ	N	result; outcome
21.	急性	jíxìng	Adj	acute
22.	肠炎	chángyán	N	enteritis; intestinal inflammation

pīn   yīn   kè   wén
拼   音   课   文

Text with Pinyin

▶▶▶

| yī | shēng: | nǎr | | bù | shū | fu? |
| 医 | 生： | 哪 | 儿 | 不 | 舒 | 服？ |

gé	lín:	dài	fu,	wǒ	dù	zi	téng	de	lì	hai,	lā	dù
格	林：	大	夫，	我	肚	子	疼	得	厉	害，	拉	肚
		zi,	jīn	tiān	zǎo	shang	shàng	tù	xià	xiè.	āi	yō,
		子，	今	天	早	上	上	吐	下	泻。	哎	哟，
		āi	yō.									
		哎	哟									

| yī | shēng: | ràng | wǒ | lái | jiǎn | chá | yī | xià. | zhè | lǐ | téng | ma? |
| 医 | 生： | 让 | 我 | 来 | 检 | 查 | 一 | 下。 | 这 | 里 | 疼 | 吗？ |

（yī shēng jiǎn chá gé lín de dù zi）
（医 生 检 查 格 林 的 肚 子）

gé lín: bù téng.
格 林：不 疼。

yī shēng: zhèr ne? nǐ zuó tiān yǒu méi yǒu chī shén
医 生：这 儿 呢？你 昨 天 有 没 有 吃 什
me bù hǎo de shí wù?
么 不 好 的 食 物？

gé lín: zuó tiān yè lǐ shuì jiào qián wǒ è le, chī
格 林：昨 天 夜 里 睡 觉 前 我 饿 了，吃
le xiē bīng xiāng lǐ de shèng cài.
了 些 冰 箱 里 的 剩 菜。

yī shēng: nà yī dìng shì cài huài le. nǐ hái yào qù
医 生：那 一 定 是 菜 坏 了。你 还 要 去
huà yàn xiě hé dà biàn.
化 验 血 和 大 便。

guò le dà yuē bàn gè xiǎo shí
（过 了 大 约 半 个 小 时）

yī shēng: huà yàn jié guǒ lái le, nǐ dé le jí xìng
医 生：化 验 结 果 来 了，你 得 了 急 性
cháng yán. wǒ gěi nǐ kāi diǎnr yào. zhè zhǒng
肠 炎。我 给 你 开 点 儿 药。这 种
yào yī tiān chī sān cì, yī cì yī piàn. yào
药 一 天 吃 三 次，一 次 一 片。要
shi guò sān tiān bù hǎo, nǐ zài lái.
是 过 三 天 不 好，你 再 来。

gé lín: xiè xie dài fu, zài jiàn.
格 林：谢 谢 大 夫，再 见。

hàn zì kè wén
汉 字 课 文
🔘 **Text in Chinese Characters**

▶▶▶

医生：哪儿不舒服？

格林：大夫，我肚子疼得厉害，拉肚子，今天早上上吐下泻。
　　　哎哟，哎哟……

医生：让我来检查一下。这里疼吗？

（医生检查格林的肚子。）

格林：不疼。

医生：这儿呢？你昨天有没有吃什么不好的食物？

格林：昨天夜里睡觉前我饿了，吃了些冰箱里的剩菜。

医生：那一定是菜坏了。你还要去化验血和大便。

（过了大约半个小时。）

医生：化验结果来了，你得了急性肠炎。我给你开点儿药。
　　　这种药一天吃三次，一次一片。要是过三天不好，
　　　你再来。

格林：谢谢大夫，再见。

yǔ yán yīng yòng zhù shì
语 言 应 用 注 释
Notes on Language Usage

1. 让我来检查一下。**Let me check it for you.**

*a) 来

来 means "do" here. It is used colloquially in place of a more specific verb, or to indicate "to come to do something."

For example:

我 自 己 (zìjǐ, oneself) 来 吧。

Wǒ zìjǐ lái ba.

Let me do it myself. (The speaker sees another person doing something for him and offers to do it instead.)

我 们 来 想 想 办 法。

Wǒmen lái xiǎngxiǎng bànfǎ.

Let's come up with some ideas and see what we can do.

*b) 一下

一下 is a "complement of frequency," which is used to indicate how many times something is done. 下 is used to count short and quick actions.

For example:

他 打 了 我 一 下。

Tā dǎ le wǒ yīxià.

He hit me once.

王 老 师 敲 (qiāo, knock) 了 三 下 门。

Wáng lǎoshī qiāo le sān xià mén.

Professor Wang knocked on the door three times.

(For details, please see Grammar Book I, Lesson 9.)

2. 你昨天有没有吃什么不好的食物？Did you have any bad food yesterday?
*a) 有没有

有沒有 is an "A-not-A" type question, which was introduced in Dialogue 1 of Lesson 4 in this text-book. 有沒有 is only used to ask about completed actions.

For example:

你 有 沒 有 看 见 王 老 师？

Nǐ yǒu méiyǒu kànjiàn Wáng lǎoshī?

Did you see Professor Wang?

昨 天 你 有 沒 有 去 肯 尼 迪 机 场？

Zuótiān nǐ yǒu méiyǒu qù Kěnnídí Jīchǎng?

Did you go to JFK Airport yesterday?

(For details, please see Grammar Book I, Lesson 2.)

*b) 什么

Here 什么 refers to something generally, and is used when you are uncertain about a specific amount or specific details. Here it is not a question but it means "something" or "some."

For example:

你 有 什么 好 吃 的 东 西 给 我 一 点 儿。

Nǐ yǒu shénme hǎochī de dōngxi gěi wǒ yī diǎnr.

If you have some good food, give me some.

好 像 (hǎoxiàng, seem) 出 了 什 么 事。

Hǎoxiàng chū le shénme shì.

It seems that something is amiss.

*3. 这种药一天吃三次，一次一片。 For this type of medicine, take one tablet by mouth three times daily.

Just as in 1b above, this is a complement of frequency sentence, and here it is used to give instructions for taking medicine.

Examples:

一 天 两 次，一 次 三 片，或 遵 医 嘱 (zūn yīzhǔ, as instructed by a doctor)。

Yī tiān liǎng cì, yī cì sān piàn, huò zūn yī zhǔ.

Take three tablets by mouth twice daily or as instructed by a doctor.

饭 后 温 开 水 服 用 (wēnkāishuǐ fú yòng, with warm boiled water)。

Fàn hòu wēn kāishuǐ fú yòng.

Take after meals with warm boiled water.

不 要 和 茶、果 汁 等 一 起 服 用。

Bú yào hé chá, guǒzhī děng yìqǐ fú yòng.

Do not take with tea or juice.

和 牛 奶 一 起 吃。

Hé niúnǎi yīqǐ chī.

Take with milk.

这 些 中 药 要 用 文 火 煎 服 (wénhuǒ jiānfú, to be boiled on a low fire)。

Zhè xiē Zhōngyào yào yòng wén huǒ jiānfú.

These Chinese medicines need to be boiled on a low fire.

这 是 外 用 药 (wàiyòngyào, medicine for external use)，不 可 内 服 (nèifú, take orally)。擦 于 患 处 (cā yú huànchù, apply to the affected part of the body)。

Zhè shì wài yòng yào, bù kě nèi fú. Cā yú huànchù.

This medicine is for external use. Do not take orally. Apply it to the affected part of the body.

(For details, please see Grammar Book I, Lesson 9.)

yuè dú

阅 读

▶ **Reading**

••

shēng cí

生 词

🔘 **New Words**

	Chinese	Pinyin	Part of Speech	English
1.	教师	jiàoshī	N	teacher
2.	直接	zhíjiē	Adj	direct; immediate
3.	预约	yùyuē	V	make an appointment
4.	候诊区	hòuzhěnqū	N	waiting area
	候诊	hòuzhěn	V	wait to see the doctor
	区	qū	N	area; district
5.	着	zhe	Par	(a particle indicating an action in progress)
6.	轮	lún	V	take turns
7.	诊室	zhěnshì	N	(doctor's) consulting room
8.	完	wán	v	finish; complete
9.	药房	yàofáng	N	drugstore; pharmacy
10.	门诊	ménzhěn	N	outpatient service
11.	或者	huòzhě	Ad/Conj	or; either...or....
12.	住院	zhùyuàn	VO	be hospitalized
	住	zhù	V	live
13.	急病	jíbìng	N	acute disease

| 14. | 急诊 | jízhěn | N | emergency; emergency treatment |
| 15. | 急诊室 | jízhěnshì | N | emergency room |

pīn yīn kè wén
拼 音 课 文

Text with Pinyin

zài zhōng guó, hěn duō dà xué dōu yǒu yī yuàn. yào
在 中 国， 很 多 大 学 都 有 医 院。要

shi xué shēng hé jiào shī shēng le bìng, kě yǐ zhí jiē
是 学 生 和 教 师 生 了 病， 可 以 直 接

qù kàn, bù yòng yù yuē. kàn bìng bǐ jiào fāng biàn, xiān
去 看， 不 用 预 约。 看 病 比 较 方 便， 先

guà hào, rán hòu zài hòu zhěn qū děng zhe jiào hào. lún
挂 号， 然 后 在 候 诊 区 等 着 叫 号。 轮

dào le nǐ, jiù kě yǐ jìn yī shēng zhěn shì kàn bìng,
到 了 你， 就 可 以 进 医 生 诊 室 看 病，

kàn wán bìng qù yào fáng qǔ yào. xué xiào yī yuàn dōu
看 完 病 去 药 房 取 药。 学 校 医 院 都

shì mén zhěn, zhǐ kàn yī bān de bìng, dé le dà bìng
是 门 诊， 只 看 一 般 的 病， 得 了 大 病

huò zhě yào zhù yuàn děi qù xiào wài de dà yī yuàn.
或 者 要 住 院 得 去 校 外 的 大 医 院。

dé le jí bìng yào qù yī yuàn de jí zhěn shì kàn
得 了 急 病 要 去 医 院 的 急 诊 室 看

bìng.
病。

▶ The emergency center at a Nanjing Hospital.

hàn zì kè wén
汉 字 课 文
🔘 **Text in Chinese Characters**

▶▶▶

　　在中国，很多大学都有医院。要是学生和教师生了病，可以直接去看，不用预约。看病比较方便，先挂号，然后在候诊区等着叫号。轮到了你，就可以进医生诊室看病，看完病去药房取药。学校医院都是门诊，只看一般的病，得了大病或者要住院得去校外的大医院。得了急病要去医院的急诊室看病。　◀◀◀

yǔ yán yīng yòng zhù shì
语 言 应 用 注 释
Notes on Language Usage

*1. 不用 **need not, not necessary**

This phrase means "need not" or "not necessary."

For example:

明 天 没 有 课，你 不 用 去 学 校。

Míngtiān méiyǒu kè, nǐ bù yòng qù xuéxiào.

There is no class tomorrow. You don't need to go to school.

A: 我 得 买 新 书 吗？

    Wǒ děi mǎi xīn shū ma?

B: 不 用，旧 的 也 可 以。

    Bù yòng, jiù de yě kěyǐ.

A: Do I have to buy a new book?

B: No, a used book is fine.

(For details, please see Grammar Book I, Lesson 5.)

2. 着 (indicates action in progress)

着 here indicates an action in progress.

More examples:

他 们 正 谈 着 话 呢。

Tāmen zhèng tán zhe huà ne.

They are talking.

王 老 师 上 着 课 呢。

Wáng lǎoshī shàng zhe kè ne.

Professor Wang is teaching a class.

(For details, please see Grammar Book I, Lesson 7.)

*3. 或者

或者 means "or."

For example:

发 烧 或 者 拉 肚 子 都 应 该 去 医 院 看 病。

Fāshāo huòzhě lā dùzi dōu yīnggāi qù yīyuàn kànbìng.

One must go to the hospital to see a doctor if one has a fever or diarrhea.

在 中 国 看 病 或 者 取 药 都 很 方 便。

Zài Zhōngguó kànbìng huòzhě qǔ yào dōu hěn fāngbiàn.

In China it is very convenient to see a doctor or to get medicine.

Another word meaning "or" is 还是 (háishì). It occurred in text-based exercises and reading exercises in previous lessons. The difference between 或者 and 还是 is that 还是 is used in questions, while 或者 is used in statements.

For example:

你 喜 欢 吃 中 国 饭 还 是 美 国 饭？

Nǐ xǐhuān chī Zhōngguó fàn háishì Měiguófàn?

Do you like Chinese or American food?

你 还 是 你 妹 妹 上 个 星 期 生 病 了？

Nǐ háishì nǐ mèimei shàng ge xīngqī shēngbìng le?

Were you or your sister sick last week?

我 圣 诞 节 去 夏 威 夷 或 者 纽 约。

Wǒ Shèngdànjié qù Xiàwēiyí huòzhě Niǔyuē.

I will go to either Hawaii or New York for Christmas.

▶ English Translations of the Texts

Dialogue 1

Jiasheng Wang:	Professor Gao, Xiaomei Zhang is sick. She can't come to class today.
Professor Gao:	What's wrong with her? Did she go to see a doctor?
Jiasheng Wang:	She was coughing with a runny nose and tears. She looked like she had a fever. Perhaps she's caught a cold. I will go with her to the school hospital after class.
Professor Gao:	All right. Tell her not to worry about the school work and to rest. I can help her make up the work for the missed classes.
Jiasheng Wang:	OK. Thanks, professor.
	(The next day.)
Professor Gao:	How is Xiaomei Zhang?
Jiasheng Wang:	She went to see a doctor yesterday. The doctor said it was the flu.
Professor Gao:	Did she take medicine?
Jiasheng Wang:	The doctor prescribed some pills for treating the flu, diminishing inflammation and bringing down her fever. Her fever is gone. But she's still coughing and has a headache.
Professor Gao:	It usually takes a week to recover from the flu. Tell her to rest, drink a lot of water, and eat a lot of fruit and bland food.
Jiasheng Wang:	Don't worry. My classmates and I will take good care of her.

Dialogue 2

Doctor:	What's wrong?
Green:	Doctor, I have a severe stomachache and diarrhea. I was vomiting and had diarrhea this morning. Oh, oh, it hurts...
Doctor:	Let me check it for you. Does it hurt here?
	(The doctor checks Green's belly.)
Green:	No.
Doctor:	How about here? Did you have any bad food yesterday?
Green:	I was hungry before going to bed last night. I ate some leftovers that were in the refrigerator.
Doctor:	The food must have spoiled. You need to have a blood test and stool sample.
	(After about half an hour.)
Doctor:	The test results have arrived. You have acute enteritis. Let me prescribe some medicine for you. For this medicine, take one tablet by mouth three times daily. If you don't feel well after three days, come to see me again.
Green:	Thank you, doctor. Bye.

Reading

In China, many universities have their own clinics (school hospitals). If students and staff are sick, they can go there directly; no appointment is needed. It is quite convenient to see a doctor. You register first, then you wait for your number to be called in the waiting area. When it is your turn, you can go into the doctor's consulting room to see him or her. Then you can have your prescription filled at the clinic's pharmacy. Generally speaking, school clinics only provide outpatient services, and they only treat ordinary ailments. If someone gets a severe disease, or needs to be hospitalized, he or she should go to a large hospital outside the school. For emergencies, you should go to the emergency room.

tīng shuō liàn xí

听　说　练　习

▶ **Exercises for Listening and Speaking**

· ·

一、完成对话。*(1. Work in pairs to complete the dialogue.)*

A: Năr bù shūfu?

B: _____

A: Fāshāo ma?

B: _____

A: Ràng wǒ lái jiǎnchá yīxià. Zhèlǐ téng ma?

B: _____

A: Zhèr ne?

B: _____

A: Zhè jǐ tiān hěn duō rén dé liúgǎn, gēn nǐ yīyàng, késou, liú bítì. Nǐ jiā yǒu rén dé liúgǎn ma?

B: _____

A: En, hái yǒu diǎnr fāshāo, nǐ dé le liúgǎn, wǒ gěi nǐ kāi yīdiǎnr yào.

B: _____

A : Gǎnmào yào, háiyǒu xiāoyán hé tuìshāo de yào. Yǒu wèntí ma?

B: _____

A : Yào hǎohaor xiūxi, duō hē shuǐ, duō chī shuǐguǒ hé qīngdàn de shíwù.

B : _____

🔘 二、听对话，回答问题。*(Listen to the conversation and answer the questions).*

1. What happened to Jiasheng Wang?

   _____

2. What did he eat last night?

   _____

3. Did he go to see the doctor?

   _____

4. Why didn't he go to see the doctor?

   _____

5. When will he go to see the doctor?

   _____

Jiǎ: Lǎoshī, wǒ de péngyou shēngbìng le, tā shì yī ge Měiguó liúxuéshēng.

Yǐ: Qù xiào yīyuàn kàn le ma?

Jiǎ: Xuéxiào yīyuàn zài nǎr?

Yǐ: Zài běi xiàomén nàr.

Jiǎ: Kànbìng yào yùyuē ma?

Yǐ: Bù yòng.

Jiǎ: Nà wǒmen zěnme zhǎo yīshēng kànbìng ne?

Yǐ: Dào nàr guàhào.

Jiǎ: Nà ná yào ne?

Yǐ: Yě zài nàr ná.

Jiǎ: Yīyuàn yǒu yàofáng ma?

Yǐ: Yǒu.

Jiǎ: Yīyuàn néng kàn jízhěn ma?

Yǐ: Néng kàn.

Jiǎ: Yàoshi dé le dà bìng huòzhě yào zhùyuàn zěnme bàn?

Yǐ: Nà yào dào xiàowài de dà yīyuàn qù.

Jiǎ: Dà yīyuàn zài nǎr?

Yǐ: Rúguǒ xūyào qù, yīshēng huì gàosu nǐ de.

Jiǎ: Hǎo, wǒ xiān péi tā qù xiào yīyuàn kànkàn.

Yǐ: Hǎo, kuài qù ba.

甲：老师，我的朋友生病了，她是一个美国留学生。

乙：去校医院看了吗？

甲：学校医院在哪儿？

乙：在北校门那儿。

甲：看病要预约吗？

乙：不用。

甲：那我们怎么找医生看病呢？

乙：到那儿挂号。

甲：那拿药呢？

乙：也在那儿拿。

甲：医院有药房吗？

乙：有。

甲：医院能看急诊吗？

乙：能看。

甲：要是得了大病或者要住院怎么办？

乙：那要到校外的大医院去。

甲：大医院在哪儿？

乙：如果需要去，医生会告诉你的。

甲：好，我先陪她去校医院看看。

乙：好，快去吧。

四、角色表演 *(4. Role Play)*

1. A: It's time to go to school, but you are too sick to go. Tell a friend about your illness and ask him/her to notify your teacher of your absence.

   B: When you are going to class, your friend tells you that he/she is sick. You ask about his/her illness and promise to tell the teacher about it.

2. A: You are a doctor examining a patient.
   B: You are a patient seeing the doctor for a stomachache.

diàn nǎo yǔ   hàn zì   liàn xí
电   脑   与   汉   字   练   习
▶ **Exercises for Computing and Learning Characters**

· ·

一、打出下面段落。*(Type the following passage.)*

1.　我肚子疼得厉害，拉肚子，今天早上上吐下泻。

2.　她咳嗽，流鼻涕、眼泪，好像有点发烧，可能感冒了。

3.　小宝(bǎo, name): 爸爸，星期六我们去公园(gōngyuán, park)吧。

　　爸爸：可是我要去医院看一个生病的老师。

　　小宝：那今天我们去看电影。

　　爸爸：可是我今天头疼，发烧。我感冒了。我们改天(gǎitiān, change the date)再去吧。

　　小宝：不，你改天再生病，今天看电影。

二、把下面拼音句子打成汉字。(2. Type the following pinyin sentences and select the appropriate characters from the list that appears on your computer screen.)

1. Yīshēng kāi le xiē gǎnmào yào, háiyǒu xiāoyán hé tuìshāo de yào.

2. Nǐ hái yào qù huàyàn xiě hé dàbiàn.

3. Huàyàn jiéguǒ lái le, nǐ dé le jíxìng chángyán.

4. Yǒu jíbìng hái kěyǐ qù yīyuàn de jízhěnshì kàn jízhěn.

5. Qǐng nín gàosu wǒ nín nǚ'ér de míngzi, hángkōng gōngsī, rìqī hé hángbān hào.

三、圈出正确的汉字。(3. Circle the correct character to fill in the blanks.)

1. 我要去医院看___(疣、疖、疾、病、炳)，不是去烧___(蔡、采、菜、茶、苯)。

2. ___(登、簦、茄、芘、等)我回家给她拿___(约、要、药、茎、茳)。

3. 多喝牛奶比喝汽___(冰、永、求、水、泳)好。

4. 我___(哦、俄、娥、饿、蛾)了，咱们去吃饭吧。

5. 我累了，需要___(体、休、修、仆、仔)___(西、喜、息、夏、思)。

四、读生字，找出偏旁部首。(4. The characters in each of the following groups share a radical. Read the characters and write the shared radicals.)

Example: 这 迎   shared radical: 辶

1. 病 疼   shared radical:_____

2. 药 菜   shared radical:_____

3. 室 定 害   shared radical:_____

4. 看 眼   shared radical:_____

5. 肚 肠   shared radical:_____

6. 流 泪 消 清 淡 泻   shared radical:_____

7. 便 化 休   shared radical:_____

五、把汉字分成部件。 *(5. Test your understanding of character structure by dividing the following characters into their component parts.)*

Example: 吗—> 口 马

1. 药—>_____   4. 息—>_____

2. 菜—>_____   5. 果—>_____

3. 饿—>_____

六、学生字 *(6. Learning New Characters)*

独体词组复合词。(Form compound words based on single-character words.)

注释 (Note): Most Chinese characters are words themselves, called 独 (dú, single) 体 (tǐ, body) 词. In this exercise you will be asked to find compound words that contain some common single-character words you have already learned.

Study the following characters selected from the New Words lists: 心* 生 出* 起 三 民* 性 和

1. Copy each character by hand using the character writing demonstration sheet.

2. For each character marked with an asterisk, find the compounds in which the characters are used in the text, and write the compound words next to the characters.

3. With the assistance of a dictionary, write down three more compounds in which these single-character words appear.

4. For each character marked with an asterisk, make a sentence with one of the three new compounds.

Character Writing Demonstration Sheet 第九课   姓名_____

Pinyin	Strokes	Structure	English	Radical	Traditional Form
xīn	**4**	**single-body**	**heart, mind**	心	心

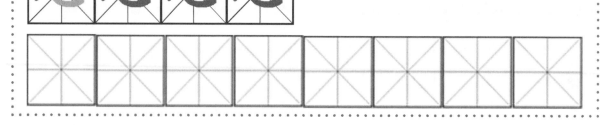

Pinyin	Strokes	Structure	English	Radical	Traditional Form
shēng	5	single-body	give birth to, grow	生	生

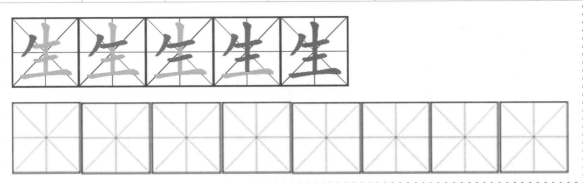

Pinyin	Strokes	Structure	English	Radical	Traditional Form
chū	5	single-body	go or come out	屮	出

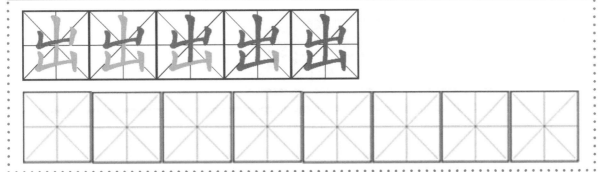

Pinyin	Strokes	Structure	English	Radical	Traditional Form
qǐ	10	half encloser	rise, get up	走	起

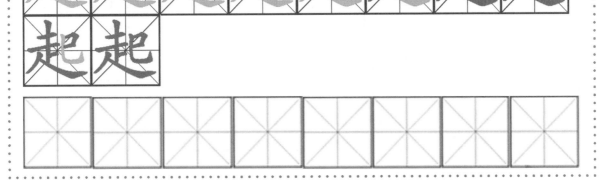

EXERCISES

Pinyin	Strokes	Structure	English	Radical	Traditional Form
sān	3	single-body	three	一	三

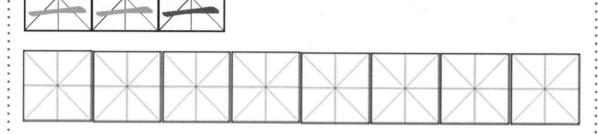

Pinyin	Strokes	Structure	English	Radical	Traditional Form
mín	5	single-body	the people	乙（乛）	民

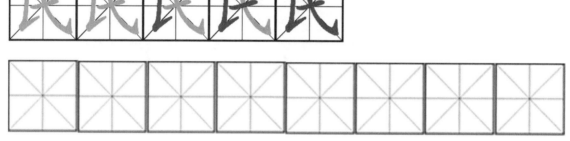

Pinyin	Strokes	Structure	English	Radical	Traditional Form
xìng	8	left-right	nature, sex	忄	性

Pinyin	Strokes	Structure	English	Radical	Traditional Form
hé	8	left-right	and	禾	和

和 和 和 和 和 和 和 和

kè   wén liàn xí

课   文   练   习

▶ Exercises for Understanding the Texts

一、根据课文回答问题。*(1. Answer the questions orally based on the text.)*

对话（1）

1. 张小妹为什么不能到学校上课？
   Why couldn't Xiaomei Zhang go to school?

2. 她去看过医生了吗？
   Did she see a doctor?

3. 谁要给张小妹补课？
   Who will make up the missed lessons for Xiaomei Zhang?

4. 张小妹得的是什么病？
   What is the problem with Xiaomei Zhang?

5. 医生给张小妹开了什么药？
   What medicine did the doctor prescribe?

6. 高老师让王家生告诉张小妹什么？
   What did Professor Gao ask Jiasheng Wang to tell Xiaomei Zhang?

对话（2）

1. 格林为什么去看医生？
   Why did Ge Lin go to see the doctor?

2. 医生检查了格林的肚子以后问了他什么？
   What did the doctor ask Ge Lin after examining his abdomen?

3. 格林昨天吃什么了？
   What did Ge Lin eat the day before?

4. 医生要格林先去做什么？
   What did the doctor tell Ge Lin to do first?

5. 医生说格林得的是什么病？
   What was the disease that Ge Lin was suffering from, according to the doctor?

6. 医生告诉格林什么？
   What instructions did the doctor give to Ge Lin?

二、翻译句子前半部分，然后用"一下，一会儿，"完成下列句子。
(2.Translate the first half of the sentences below, and then complete them with 一下 or 一会儿.)

1. I'll finish my homework in five minutes, _____ (could you wait a moment)?

2. Doctor Gao, Xiaomei Zhang is sick. _____ (Could you give her a check-up?)

3. Please wait for me here, _____ (I'll be back soon).

4. Professor Wang is at a meeting, _____ (he will be back soon).

5. Your sportswear looks so good. _____ (May I try it on?)

三、用"还是，或者"填空，然后朗读。**(3. Fill in the blanks with 还是 or 或者, and then read the sentences aloud).**

1. 苏珊_____彼德要到夏威夷过圣诞节？

2. 高老师今天怎么没来，生病了_____出差了？

3. 格林常帮我在超市买日用品_____吃的东西。

4. 张小妹喜欢看美国电影_____去酒吧。

5. 你去打球_____去看电影？

四、用 "A-not-A" 结构改写下列句子。*(4. Rewrite the following questions in the "A-not-A" question pattern and then answer each one.)*

1. 你去过夏威夷吗？

2. 格林的发音准吗？

3. 苏珊想跟约翰出去玩吗？

4. 张小妹吃了医生给她开的药以后头还疼吗？

5. 王家生能帮我们买到电影票吧？

五、作文 *(5. Composition)*

Write an article (200 characters, 10 sentences minimum) describing an experience seeing a doctor. Make sure to use the given words and phrases.

1. 一下   2. 一会儿   3. 想   4. A-not-A question   5. 能   6. 要

六、翻译 *(6. Translation)*

Translate the following sentences orally in class. Then type your translations in Chinese using the words and phrases provided.

1. May I have a look at the book you bought yesterday? (一下)

2. He said he would come to see me after a while. (一会儿)

3. The teacher told her students that she would go in a minute. (一会儿)

4. I have eaten all the food I had, do you have anything to eat? (什么 used for general reference)

5. The doctor prescribed some antibiotics for Xiaomei Zhang. (开)

6. Have you taken the medicine that the doctor prescribed for your cold? (A-not-A question)

7. I want to go to China. I practice Chinese twice a day.
   (complement of frequency—次)

8. You caught the flu. Take two tablets by mouth twice daily. (了，次，片)

9. Have you ever been to China? (A-not-A question, 过)

10. How come you are still running a fever? Have you taken the medicine the doctor prescribed for you yesterday? (A-not-A question)

11. A: Have you eaten?
    B: I will go to eat after I get out of Chinese class. (了 for completed and future actions)

bǔ   chōng yuè   dú   liàn   xí
补   充   阅   读   练   习
▶ Supplementary Reading Exercises

(1) Controlled Vocabulary

Read the following passage and answer the following questions either in Chinese or in English.

	Chinese	Pinyin	Part of Speech	English
1.	医务室	yīwùshì	N	clinic
2.	制度	zhìdù	N	system; institution
3.	医疗保险	yīliáo bǎoxiǎn	CE	medical insurance
4.	校医	xiàoyī	N	school doctor
5.	费用	fèiyòng	N	cost; expenses
6.	少	shǎo	Adj	few, less

生病怎么办？

在中国，小学、中学和大学校园里都有自己的医务室。学生多的大学还有自己的医院。九十年代以前，没有医疗保险制度，学生生了病，要是一般的感冒，头疼，拉肚子，到学校的医务室去看校医就行了，拿药也很方便。要是病得很重，校医就会帮助转到校外的医院去，学生不用花钱，连挂号费都不用付。

现在，中国的学校也像中国其它地方一样开始了医疗保险制度。各个学校的学生保险和办法也不同。可是有一点是一样的，就是学生去学校的医务室和医院去看病都要付挂号费了。以前学生拿药不用付钱，现在虽然学生生病还是先去学校的医务室，但是可以不付钱拿的药少了。有的学校还要学生付一些看病的费用。

Questions

1. 九十年代以前中国学生到哪儿去看病？

   Where did students usually go when they got sick before the 1990s?

2. 那时候学生看病用付钱吗？

   Did they have to pay at that time?

3. 如果学生的病很重怎么办？

   What happened if a student was very sick?

4. 现在学生生病了要到哪儿去看？

   Where do students go now when they are sick?

5. 去看校医要付钱吗？

   Do they have to pay to see a doctor at school clinics now?

(2) Open Vocabulary

This exercise is called "Open Vocabulary" because it contains some vocabulary words that have not been introduced in this book. In this exercise, you should first look for words you already recognize, and then try to guess the meaning of an entire phrase or sentence based on the words you already know. When you get stuck, use a dictionary to look up words whose meanings are crucial to your understanding of the passage. You can also retrieve an electronic version of this text from the accompanying online materials, and use an online dictionary or translation program to help you read it.

After answering the questions, try to tell the story to a classmate in your own words without looking at the original text.

止疼药

放学后年年急忙跑到医务室对医生说："大夫，请您给我一点儿止痛药，好吗？"

医生问："你哪里疼？"

年年说："我哪儿都不疼。不过，当我把考试试卷给我妈妈看时，她一定会头疼。"

Questions

1. 年年是做什么的？ Who is Niannian?

2. 他到医务室去做什么？ What was he doing at the school clinic?

3. 年年感冒了吗？ Did Niannian catch a cold?

4. 他为什么跟医生要止痛药？ Why did he want some painkillers?

出院

珊珊病好要出院了，高兴地与医生告别。
"再见，医生。"
珊珊的姐姐："什么？再见？你还要住医院？"
珊珊："那…… 医生……，永别了！"

Questions

1. 珊珊在什么地方？
   Where was Shanshan?

2. 珊珊在做什么？
   What was she doing?

3. 为什么她的姐姐说"你还要住医院？"
   Why did her sister say "你还要住医院?"

4. "永别了"是什么意思？
   What does "永别了" mean?

zhōng guó   wén   huà   xí   sú

中　国　文　化　习　俗

Chinese Customs and Culture

. . . .

zhōng   yī   hé   zhōng yào

中　医　和　中　药

▶ Traditional Chinese Medicine

Chinese medicine is a complete medical system that has diagnosed, treated, and prevented illness for over 23 centuries. While it can remedy ailments and alter states of mind, Chinese medicine can also enhance recuperative power, immunity, and the capacity for pleasure, work and creativity. In the West, traditional Chinese medicine is often considered alternative medicine; however, in mainland China and Taiwan, it is widely considered to be an integral part of the health care system. Traditional Chinese Medicine (中医学，中医学，Zhōngyīxué) is based on the idea that the processes of the human body are interrelated and constantly interact with the external environment. Therefore the theory looks for signs of disharmony in the external and internal environments of a person in order to understand, treat and prevent illness and disease. Traditional Chinese medical theory is based on a number of philosophical frameworks including the theory of Yin-yang, the Five Elements, the human body Meridian system, Zang Fu theory, and others.

▶ Eat healthy and live a long life—A woman celebrates her 80th birthday.

To diagnosis a patient, practitioners assess a person's health by feeling the pulse at each wrist and by observing the color and form of the face, tongue and body. This information is interpreted in the context of a patient's present and past complaints, work and living habits, physical environment, family health history, and emotional life. The major treatment techniques include massage therapy (推拿, tuīná), acupuncture (针灸, zhēnjiǔ), Chinese herbal medicine (中药, zhōngyào), Chinese food therapy (食疗, shíliáo), Qigong (气功, qìgōng) and related breathing and meditation exercises, Taijiquan (太极拳, tàijíquán), and other Chinese martial arts.

▶ The Traditional Chinese Medicine practitioner diagnoses a patient by feeling his pulse.

▶ Practicing *tai ji*.

▶ Inside a Chinese herbal medicine shop.

Within China, there has been a great deal of interaction between Traditional Chinese Medicine and Western medicine. Chinese herbal medicine includes many compounds not used in Western medicine. For their part, advanced practitioners of Traditional Chinese Medicine in China are interested in statistical and experimental techniques that can better distinguish medicines that work from those that do not. One result of this collaboration has been the creation of peer reviewed scientific journals and medical databases on Traditional Chinese Medicine. Most people in China do not see Traditional Chinese Medicine and Western medicine as being in conflict. In emergency or crisis situations, there is generally no reluctance in using conventional Western medicine. At the same time, belief in Chinese medicine remains strong in the area of maintaining and preserving health.

▶ Test Your Knowledge How would you treat these patients?

Imagine you are a Traditional Chinese Medicine practitioner. A couple of patients are visiting you now. Use the Treatment Theory below as a basis for suggesting treatment for these two patients.

Patient 1 has red eyes, a yellow coating on his tongue, and a fast pulse. You know this indicates Heat and congested Qi. He complains of stomach pains, nausea and fever.

Patient 2 has pale lips, brittle hair, a thin pulse, and a dry tongue. You know this suggests deficiency of Blood and Moisture, which undermines the function of the Liver, Heart, and Spleen. She complains that she feels tense, anxious, and irritable, has been unable to conceive, and has trouble with chronic fatigue and depression.

Treatment Theory of Traditional Chinese Medicine: The goal of treatment is to adjust and harmonize Yin and Yang—wet and dry, cold and heat, inner and outer, body and mind. This is achieved by regulating the Qi, Moisture, and Blood in the Organ Networks: weak organs need tonic, congested channels are opened, excess is dispersed, tightness is softened, agitation is calmed, heat is cooled, cold is warmed, dryness is moistened, and dampness is drained.

Now what kind of treatment for the two patients would you suggest?

For Patient 1:

For Patient 2:

▶ A Chinese herbal medicine shop in New York's Chinatown.

Answers:

For Patient 1: Prescribe herbal medicines to cool down heat and to regulate the congested Qi. Take acupuncture treatment, eat food with a cool nature and practice Taijiquan.

For Patient 2: Prescribe herbal medicines to open up channels for blood circulation and to regulate moisture, and take tonic for the liver, heart, and spleen to help restore their functions. Drink more water and eat food that is tonic for building up internal organs and blood. Doing Taijiquan is a must.

Note: This is just a game to help you understand Traditional Chinese Medicine. The answers suggested above are in no way prescriptions. Good introductions to the theory and practice of Chinese medicine include The Essential Book of Chinese Medicine published by Columbia University Press, and Nigel Wiseman's Fundamentals of Chinese Medicine. Wiseman's Practical Dictionary of Chinese Medicine is one of the standard reference works in English.

dì shí kè
第 十 课
LESSON 10

tiān qì
天 气
The Weather

▶ **Objectives:**

1. To talk about the weather
2. To read and understand the weather forecast
3. To describe the climate of a particular place

duì   huà   yī
对   话   (一)

DIALOGUE 1

tiān   qì   yù   bào   zhǔn ma
天   气   预   报   准   吗?

▶ **Is the Weather Forecast Accurate?**

shēng   cí
生   词

🔘 **New Words**

	Chinese	Pinyin	Part of Speech	English
1.	天气	tiānqì	N	weather
2.	啊	a	Int	ah, oh
3.	太阳	tàiyáng	N	the sun; sunshine; sunlight
4.	预报	yùbào	N	forecast
5.	晴天	qíngtiān	N	fine day; sunny day
6.	晴	qíng	Adj	fine; clear
7.	呀	yā	Par	(a particle indicating surprise, admiration or query)
8.	前天	qiántiān	TW	the day before yesterday
9.	踢	tī	V	kick; play (football)
10.	足球	zúqiú	N	soccer; football
11.	变	biàn	V	change; become different; become

12.	阴	yīn	Adj	overcast; shade
13.	刮	guā	V	blow; scrape
14.	风	fēng	N	wind
15.	雨	yǔ	N	rain
16.	(打)雷	(dǎ)léi	V	thunder
17.	闪电	shǎndiàn	V	lightning
18.	害得	hàide	V	cause; make (something unwelcome happen)
19.	淋	lín	V	pour; drench
20.	落汤鸡	luòtāngjī	CE	like a drenched chicken; soaked through; soaking wet
21.	阵雨	zhènyǔ	N	rain shower
22.	乌云	wūyún	N	black clouds; dark clouds
23.	过	guò	V	pass; beyond the limit
24.	反正	fǎnzhèng	Ad	anyway; anyhow; in any case
25.	湿	shī	Adj	wet; damp; humid
26.	周末	zhōumò	N	weekend
27.	雾	wù	N	fog; mist; fine spray
28.	上午	shàngwǔ	TW	morning
29.	颐和园	Yíhéyuán	PN	the Summer Palace (in Beijing)
30.	把	bǎ	M	measure word for an umbrella
31.	伞	sǎn	N	umbrella; something shaped like an umbrella

32.	宿舍楼	sùshèlóu	N	dormitory building
	宿舍	sùshè	N	dorm
	楼	lóu	N	building

pīn yīn kè wén
拼 音 课 文
Text with Pinyin
▶▶▶

wáng jiā shēng:	à, chū tài yáng le, tài hǎo le.	
王 家 生：	啊，出 太 阳 了，太 好 了。	

zhāng xiǎo mèi:	tiān qì yù bào shuō jīn tiān qíng, zhēn de
张 小 妹：	天 气 预 报 说 今 天 晴，真 的
	chū tài yáng le, zhēn zhǔn.
	出 太 阳 了，真 准。

wáng jiā shēng:	zhǔn shén me yā? qián tiān tiān qì yù bào
王 家 生：	准 什 么 呀？前 天 天 气 预 报
	yě shuō shì qíng tiān, kě shì wǒ tī zú
	也 说 是 晴 天，可 是 我 踢 足
	qiú de shí hòu tiān biàn yīn le, yòu shì
	球 的 时 候 天 变 阴 了，又 是
	guā fēng, yòu shì xià yǔ, hái dǎ léi shǎn
	刮 风，又 是 下 雨，还 打 雷 闪
	diàn, hài de wǒ lín chéng le luò tāng jī.
	电，害 得 我 淋 成 了 落 汤 鸡。

zhāng xiǎo mèi:	nà shì zhèn yǔ. yī piàn wū yún guò le,
张 小 妹：	那 是 阵 雨。一 片 乌 云 过 了，
	tiān jiù hǎo le.
	天 就 好 了。

王家生: 反正天气预报没说有阵雨，我被淋湿了。

张小妹: 好了。这个周末天气怎么样？

王家生: 星期六早上有雾，上午会转晴。

张小妹: 那我们去颐和园玩儿，怎么样？

王家生: 太好了，我给你带把太阳伞。

张小妹: 我们9点半在宿舍楼前面见。

王家生: 好，不见不散。

hàn   zì   kè   wén
汉   字   课   文

🎵 **Text in Chinese Characters**

▶▶▶

王家生：　啊，出太阳了，太好了。

张小妹：　天气预报说今天晴，真的出太阳了，真准。

王家生：　准什么呀？前天天气预报也说是晴天，可是我踢足球
　　　　　的时候天变阴了，又是刮风，又是下雨，还打雷闪电，
　　　　　害得我淋成了落汤鸡。

张小妹：　那是阵雨。一片乌云过了，天就好了。

王家生：　反正天气预报没说有阵雨，我被淋湿了。

张小妹：　好了。这个周末天气怎么样？

王家生：　星期六早上有雾，上午会转晴。

张小妹：　那我们去颐和园玩儿，怎么样？

王家生：　太好了，我给你带把太阳伞。

张小妹：　我们9点半在宿舍楼前面见。

王家生：　好，不见不散。

◀◀◀

yǔ   yán   yīng yòng zhù   shì
语   言   应   用   注   释

Notes on Language Usage

1. 啊，出太阳了，太好了。 **Hey, the sun's come out. This is great.**

啊 is an interjection. It can be pronounced with the four different tones to indicate the different feelings of the speaker. Below are examples of 啊 pronounced with the four tones. 啊 (ā) indicates an earnest request or exhortation.

For example:

作 业 你 一 定 要 给 老 师，啊！别 忘 (wàng, forget) 了。

Zuòyè nǐ yīdìng yào gěi lǎoshī, ā, bié wàng le.

You must hand in your homework to the professor—don't forget!

晚 上 早 (zǎo, early) 点 儿 回 来，啊！

Wǎnshang zǎo diǎnr huílái, ā!

Come back early!

啊 (á) Indicates an inquiry and is used after a question.

For example:

怎 么 去 机 场，你 听 懂 了 吗，啊？

Zěnme qù jīcháng, nǐ tīng dǒng le ma, á?

Did you understand how to get to the airport? Did you?

有 雨 吗？怎 么 带 着 伞？啊？

Yǒu yǔ ma? Zěnme dài zhe sǎn? Á?

Is it going to rain? Why do you have an umbrella? Huh?

啊 (ǎ) Indicates surprise.

For example:

啊？你 圣 诞 节 都 不 回 家？

Ǎ? Nǐ Shèngdàn Jié dōu bù huíjiā?

How come you're not going home for Christmas?

啊？下 大 雨 了？

Ǎ? Xià dà yǔ le?

What? Is it pouring out?

啊 (à) When pronounced with a fourth tone, 啊 can mean different things:

(1) Indicates a realization when spoken with a prolonged and heavy tone.

For example:

啊！苏 珊 原 来 是 彼 德 的 女 朋 友！

À! Sū Shān yuánlái shì Bǐdé de nǚpéngyǒu!

I see! Susan turns out to be Peter's girlfriend!

啊！他 想 看 的 是 这 个 电 影 呀！

À! Tā xiǎng kàn de shì zhège diànyǐng yā!

Oh, this is the movie that he wants to see!

(2) 啊 can also indicate agreement when pronounced with a short and light tone.

For example:

啊！就 九 点 半 见 吧！

A! Jiù jiǔ diǎn bàn jiàn ba!

OK! Let's meet at 9:30.

啊 ， 好 吧 ！

A, hǎo ba!

OK!

(3) 啊 can indicate surprise or admiration when it is pronounced with a fairly long tone. This is how it is used in this lesson.

For example:

啊 ！ 多 好 看 的 风 景 (fēngjǐng, scenery) 呀 ！

A! Duō hǎokàn de fēngjǐng yā!

Wow, how beautiful the scenery is!

啊 ！ 今 天 的 天 气 真 好 ！

A! Jīntiān de tiānqì zhēn hǎo!

Wow! Today's weather is so nice!

2. 出太阳了 **The sun has come out.**

You can also say 太阳出來了.

***3.** 准什么呀 ？ **What? I don't think it's accurate.**

This is a rhetorical question created by combining a question word (in this case, 什么) with the particle 呀 or 啊. A rhetorical question employs the question form to show disagreement. The underlying meaning of this sentence is "It is not accurate."

More examples:

A: 听 说 王 小 年 的 中 文 很 好 。

Tīngshuō Wáng Xiǎonián de Zhōngwén hěn hǎo.

I heard that Xiaonian Wang's Chinese is very good.

B: 好 什 么 呀 ？ 他 连 "四" 和 "十" 都 分 (fēn, distinguish) 不 清 (qīng, clear) (不好) 。

Hǎo shénme yā? Tā lián "sì" hé "shí" dōu fēn bù qīng (bùhǎo).

Good? He can't even tell the difference between "four" and "ten."

你 还 想 去 酒 吧 呀 ？ 你 到 二 十 一 岁 了 吗 ？(你 沒 到 二 十 一 岁)

Nǐ hái xiǎng qù jiǔbā ya? Nǐ dào èrshíyī suì le ma? (nǐ méi dào èrshíyī suì)

You want to go to the bar, too? You're not even 21.

这 样 的 好 事 为 什 么 不 做 呀 ？(应 该 做)

Zhèyàng de hǎo shì wèishénme bù zuò ya? (yīnggāi zuò.)

Why wouldn't you do such a good deed? (You should do it.)

这 课 语 法 哪 儿 难 啊？谁 都 能 看 得 懂。(不 难)

Zhè kè yǔfǎ nǎr nán a? Shéi dōu néng kàn de dǒng. (bù nán)

How is the grammar in this lesson difficult? Anybody can understand it.

谁 说 今 天 会 下 雨 呀？我 看 一 定 是 个 大 晴 天。(不 会 下 雨)

Shéi shuō jīntiān huì xiàyǔ ya? Wǒ kàn yīdìng shì ge dà qíngtiān. (bù huì xiàyǔ)

Who says it's going to rain today? I'm sure it will be a sunny day.

(For details, please see Grammar Book I, Lesson 6.)

4. 害得我淋成了落汤鸡。 I got soaked (like a drenched chicken).

*a) 害得

害得 means to cause something bad and unwelcome to happen.

For example:

今 天 我 的 闹 钟 (nàozhōng, alarm clock) 沒 响 (xiǎng)，害 得 我 上 课 晚 了。

Jīntiān wǒ de nàozhōng méi xiǎng, hài de wǒ shàng kè wǎn le.

My alarm clock didn't go off today, so I was late for class.

我 的 同 屋 (tóngwū, roommate) 每 天 晚 上 看 电 视，害 得 我 不 能 看 书。

Wǒ de tóngwū měitiān wǎnshang kàn diàn shì, hài de wǒ bù néng kàn shū.

My roommate watches TV every night, so I am unable to read.

b) 淋成了落汤鸡

This is a verb + complement of result structure, which was introduced in Lesson 7, Dialogue 2. The verbal phrase 成了落汤鸡 indicates result of the main verb 淋.

More examples:

你 找 到 王 老 师 了 吗？

Nǐ zhǎo dào Wáng lǎoshī le ma?

Have you found Professor Wang?

我 把 他 看 成 高 老 师 了。

Wǒ bǎ tā kàn chéng Gāo lǎoshī le.

I took him as Professor Gao.

(For details, please see Grammar Book I, Lesson 8.)

5. 反正天气预报没说有阵雨，我被淋湿了。 **Anyway, the weather forecast didn't say it would rain, but I got soaked.**

a) 反正

反正 is an adverb that means "anyway" or "in any case."

For example:

我 不 怕 (pà, be afraid of) 下 雨， 反 正 我 要 去。

Wǒ bù pà xiàyǔ, fǎnzhèng wǒ yào qù.

I'm not afraid of rain. In any case, (whether it rains or not), I will go.

你 要 多 少 钱 都 行， 反 正 我 没 钱。

Nǐ yào duōshǎo qián dōu xíng, fǎnzhèng wǒ méi qián.

You can charge any price. Anyway, I don't have the money.

*b) 我被淋湿了。

After 被，雨 is omitted. Here 被 is used passively. The full sentence is: 我被雨淋湿了。 (Literally, I was made wet by the rain.)

(For details on passive sentences, please see Grammar Book I, Lesson 10.)

6. 好了

好了 means "That's it" or "That's enough." It functions to interrupt or stop someone's speech or action.

好 了， 别 说 了。 烦 (fán, be vexed) 不 烦 啊？

Hǎo le, bié shuō le. Fán bù fán a?

That's it. Don't say anymore. You talk too much.

(The underlying meaning of this rhetorical question is that you talked too much and made me feel vexed.)

好 了， 就 到 这 儿。 明 天 再 说。

Hǎo le, jiù dào zhèr. Míngtiān zài shuō.

OK, let's stop here. We'll come back to it tomorrow.

duì huà èr
对 话 (二)

DIALOGUE 2

wǒ jiā xiāng de qì hòu
我 家 乡 的 气 候

▶ **The Climate in My Hometown**

....

shēng cí
生 词

🔘 **New Words**

	Chinese	Pinyin	Part of Speech	English
1.	新英格兰	Xīn Yīnggélán	PN	New England
2.	地区	dìqū	N	area; district; region
3.	季	jì	N	season
4.	分明	fēnmíng	Adj	clearly demarcated; sharply contoured; distinct; clear
5.	非常	fēicháng	Adj/Ad	extraordinary; unusual; special; very; extremely
6.	美丽	měilì	Adj	beautiful
7.	冬天	dōngtiān	N	winter
8.	冷	lěng	Adj	cold
9.	雪	xuě	N	snow
10.	温度	wēndù	N	temperature
11.	度	dù	M	degree; a unit of measurement for angles, temperature, etc.

12.	华氏	huáshì	N	the Fahrenheit (thermometer)
13.	摄氏	shèshì	N	the Centigrade (thermometer)
14.	零	líng	Num	zero; nought; -odd
15.	夏天	xiàtiān	N	summer
16.	凉快	liángkuài	Adj	nice and cool; pleasantly cool
17.	白天	báitiān	N	daytime; day
18.	热	rè	Adj	heat; hot; heat up; warm up; popular
19.	春天	chūntiān	N	spring; springtime
20.	秋天	qiūtiān	N	autumn
21.	气候	qìhòu	N	climate
22.	过去	guòqù	TW	in the past; formerly
23.	火炉	huǒlú	N	(heating) stove
24.	可怕	kěpà	Adj	fearful; frightful; terrible; terrifying
25.	其实	qíshí	Ad	actually; in fact; as a matter of fact
26.	黄梅雨季	Huángméiyǔ jì	PN	the rainy season, usually in April, May or June, in the middle and lower reaches of the Changjiang River, China
27.	潮湿	cháoshī	Adj	moist; damp

Text with Pinyin

▶▶▶

huáng fāng: 黄 方：格 林，你 是 哪 里 人？
gé lín nǐ shì nǎ lǐ rén?

gé lín: 格 林：我 是 波 士 顿 人。波 士 顿 在 新
wǒ shì bō shì dùn rén. bō shì dùn zài xīn
英 格 兰 地 区，四 季 分 明，非 常
yīng gé lán dì qū, sì jì fēn míng, fēi cháng
美 丽。
měi lì.

huáng fāng: 黄 方：听 说 波 士 顿 冬 天 很 冷，雪 很
tīng shuō bō shì dùn dōng tiān hěn lěng, xuě hěn
多。
duō

gé lín: 格 林：对，冬 天 常 常 下 雪，温 度 一 般
duì, dōng tiān cháng cháng xià xuě, wēn dù yī bān
是 二 三 十 度。
shì èr sān shí dù.

huáng fāng: 黄 方：那 也 就 是 摄 氏 零 下 了。夏 天
nà yě jiù shì shè shì líng xià le. xià tiān
呢？一 定 比 较 凉 快。
ne? yī dìng bǐ jiào liáng kuài.

gé lín: 格 林：对，夏 天 白 天 热，但 早 晚 凉。春
duì, xià tiān bái tiān rè, dàn zǎo wǎn liáng. chūn
天 和 秋 天 不 冷 不 热，非 常 舒
tiān hé qiū tiān bù lěng bú rè, fēi cháng shū
服。你 是 南 京 人 吧？你 们 那 儿
fu. nǐ shì nán jīng rén ba? nǐ men nàr
气 候 怎 么 样？
qì hòu zěn me yang?

huáng fāng:

黄 方：我 们 那 儿 冬 天 不 太 冷，但 夏
天 比 较 热。过 去 人 们 常 说 南
京 象 个 火 炉。

gé lín:

格 林：真 的 那 么 可 怕 吗？

huáng fāng:

黄 方：其 实 也 不 是，夏 天 温 度 跟 北
京 差 不 多。六 月 有 两 三 个 星
期 的 黄 梅 雨 季，差 不 多 天 天
下 雨，因 为 潮 湿，人 觉 得 很 不
舒 服。不 过 南 京 的 气 候 一 般
说 来 还 是 不 错 的。

◄◄◄

hàn zì kè wén
汉 字 课 文

Text in Chinese Characters

▶▶▶

黄方： 格林，你是哪里人？

格林： 我是波士顿人。波士顿在新英格兰地区，四季分明，
非常美丽。

黄方： 听说波士顿冬天很冷，雪很多。

格林： 对，冬天常常下雪，温度一般是二三十度。

黄方 你说的是华氏，那也就是摄氏零下了。夏天呢？
一定比较凉快。

格林： 对，夏天白天热，但早晚凉。春天和秋天不冷不热，非常舒服。你是南京人吧？你们那儿气候怎么样？

黄方： 我们那儿气冬天不太冷，但夏天比较热。过去人们常说南京象个火炉。

格林： 真的那么可怕吗？

黄方： 其实也不是，夏天温度跟北京差不多。 六月有两三个星期的黄梅雨季，差不多天天下雨，因为潮湿，人觉得很不舒服。不过南京的气候一般说来还是不错的。

yǔ yán yīng yòng zhù shì

yǔ   yán   yīng   yòng   zhù   shì
语   言   应   用   注   释

Notes on Language Usage

1. 你是哪里人？**Where are you from?**

Chinese people will frequently ask this question about another person's hometown.

2. 温度一般是二、三十度。**The temperature is usually about 20 to 30 degrees.**

One way in Chinese to express a rough number is to use two close numbers to indicate "around the number", such as 四、五个学生；七、八块钱；二、三十个孩子、五、六百个座位等。(See Textbook Lesson 7 for more examples.)

3. 那也就是摄氏零下了。**That is below zero in Celsius.**

摄氏=摄氏温度，the Centigrade temperature scale. China and most countries in the world use this system. But in America, 华氏温度，or the Fahrenheit temperature scale, is used instead. 华氏32度 is about 摄氏0度。

*4. 一定比较凉快。**It must be quite cool.**

比较 is an adverb meaning "comparatively" or "relatively" (比较好 is not as good as 好).

For example:

右边 (yòubiān, the right side) 是 一 个 比 较 大 的 房 间 (fángjiān, room)。

Yòubiān shì yī ge bǐjiào dà de fángjiān.

On the right is a relatively big room.

坐 地 铁 去 飞 机 场 时 间 比 较 长。

Zuò dìtiě qù fēijīchǎng shíjiān bǐjiào cháng.

It's quite long to take the subway to the airport.

*5. 你是南京人吧？ You're from Nanjing, right?

吧 is used in a question to indicate an assumption.

For example:

A: 张 小 妹 生 病 了 吧 ？

Zhāng Xiǎomèi shēngbìng le ba?

Xiaomei Zhang is sick, right?

B: 对 ， 她 生 病 了 。

Duì, tā shēngbìng le.

Yes, she is sick.

A: 王 老 师 是 日 本 人 吧 ？

Wáng lǎoshī shì Rìběn rén ba?

Professor Wang is Japanese, right?

B: 不 ， 他 是 中 国 人 。

Bù, tā shì Zhōngguó rén.

No, he is Chinese.

(For details on using 吧, please see Grammar Book I, Lesson 4.)

yuè dú
阅 读

▶ Reading

. . . .

shēng cí
生 词
New Words

	Chinese	Pinyin	Part of Speech	English
1.	注意	zhùyì	V	pay attention to; take note (or notice) of
2.	电视	diànshì	N	television; TV
3.	广播	guǎngbō	N	broadcast; be on the air
4.	报纸	bàozhǐ	N	newspaper; newsprint

5.	互联网	hùliánwǎng	N	Internet; (also called 因特網 yīntèwǎng)
6.	专门	zhuānmén	Adj	special; specialized
7.	频道	píndào	N	(of TV) frequency channel
8.	网站	wǎngzhàn	N	web site
9.	报	bào	V	report; announce; declare
10.	多云	duōyún	Adj	cloudy
11.	台	tái	N	broadcasting station
12.	甚至	shènzhì	Ad	even; (go) so far as to; so much so that
13.	不如	bùrú	Conj	not equal to; not as good as; inferior to; it would be better to
14.	近期	jìnqī	N	in the near future

pīn yīn kè wén
拼 音 课 文
🔊 **Text with Pinyin**

▶▶▶

xiàn zài rén men dōu hěn zhù yì tiān qì. měi tiān
现 在 人 们 都 很 注 意 天 气。 每 天

diàn shì, guǎng bō, bào zhǐ hé hù lián wǎng dōu yǒu tiān
电 视、 广 播、 报 纸 和 互 联 网 都 有 天

qì yù bào, hái yǒu zhuān mén de tiān qì yù bào diàn
气 预 报, 还 有 专 门 的 天 气 预 报 电

shì pín dào hé wǎng zhàn. nǐ kě yǐ zhī dào dāng tiān
视 频 道 和 网 站。 你 可 以 知 道 当 天

de tiān qì zěn me yang, shì yīn tiān hái shì qíng tiān,
的 天 气 怎 么 样, 是 阴 天 还 是 晴 天,

guā fēng hái shì duō yún děng. tiān qì yù bào chú le
刮 风 还 是 多 云 等。 天 气 预 报 除 了

报 当 天 的 天 气 以 外，还 预 报 两 三
bào dāng tiān de tiān qì yǐ wài, hái yù bào liǎng sān

天 的 天 气，有 的 电 视 台 还 报 五 天
tiān de tiān qì, yǒu de diàn shì tái hái bào wǔ tiān

或 者 一 个 星 期 的 天 气，甚 至 有 的
huò zhě yī gè xīng qī de tiān qì, shèn zhì yǒu de

网 站 还 报 半 个 月 的 天 气，但 一 般
wǎng zhàn hái bào bàn gè yuè de tiān qì, dàn yī bān

不 如 近 期 的 准。
bù rú jìn qī de zhǔn.

◄◄◄

hàn zì kè wén
汉 字 课 文
Text in Chinese Characters

▶▶▶

现在人们都很注意天气。每天电视、广播、报纸和互联网
都有天气预报，还有专门的天气预报电视频道和网站。你可
以知道当天的天气怎么样，是阴天还是晴天、刮风还是多云
等。天气预报除了报当天的天气以外，还预报两三天的天
气，有的电视台还报五天或者一个星期的天气，甚至有的网站
还报半个月的天气，但一般不如近期的准。

◄◄◄

yǔ yán yīng yòng zhù shì
语 言 应 用 注 释
Notes on Language Usage

*1. 你可以知道当天的天气怎么样，是阴天还是晴天、刮风还是
多云等。**You will know how the weather is on any given day, whether it is cloudy or
sunny, windy or rainy, etc.**

是……还是……

Two or more occurrences of 还是 are used to make an "alternative question," which is a question
that presents two different choices, or alternatives, to the listener. The first 还是 is expressed simply
as 是 or can be omitted. 是 and 还是 come before their respective alternatives.

For example:

你 下 个 学 期 是 学 中 文 还 是 学 日 文 ？

Nǐ xià gè xuéqī shì xué Zhōngwén hái shì xué Rìwén?

Are you going to take Chinese or Japanese next semester?

你 的 老 师 是 中 国 人 还 是 日 本 人 ？

Nǐ de lǎoshī shì Zhōngguórén háishì Rìběnrén?

Is your teacher Chinese or Japanese?

她 (是) 走 还 是 不 走 ？

Tā shì zǒu hái shì bù zǒu?

Is she leaving or not?

(For details, please see Grammar Book I, Lesson 4.)

*2. 不如 (not as...as...)

不如 can be used in two ways. One is used in a comparison to introduce the preferred choice Sometimes there is no obvious comparison and 不如 just indicates a desirable choice or preference.

吃 汉 堡 包 (hànbǎobāo, hamburger) 不 如 去 吃 中 国 饭 。

Chī hànbǎobāo bù rú qù chī Zhōngguófàn.

Eating a hamburger is not as good as eating Chinese food.

今 天 不 下 雨 ， 我 们 不 如 今 天 去 吧 。

Jīntiān bú xiàyǔ, wǒmen bù rú jīntiān qù ba.

It's not raining today. We'd better go today.

The second usage indicates that one thing is not equal to another:

姐 姐 不 如 弟 弟 高 。

Jiějie bù rú dìdi gāo.

My older sister is not as tall as my younger brother.

这 个 体 育 馆 不 如 那 个 体 育 馆 大 。

Zhège tǐyùguǎn bù rú nàge tǐyùguǎn dà.

This gym is not as big as that one.

(For details, please Grammar Book I, Lesson 8.)

▶ English Translations of the Texts

Dialogue 1

Jiasheng Wang:	Hey, the sun's come out. This is great.
Xiaomei Zhang:	The weather forecast said it would be sunny today. The sun really did come out. It's very accurate.
Jiasheng Wang:	What? I don't think it's accurate. The day before yesterday, the forecast also said it was going to be sunny. But when I was playing soccer, it turned overcast. It was windy and raining, and there was thunder and lightning. I got soaked (like a drenched chicken).
Xiaomei Zhang:	It was only a shower. When the dark clouds passed, it turned clear again.
Jiasheng Wang:	Anyway, the weather forecast didn't say it would rain, but I got soaked.
Xiaomei Zhang:	OK, OK. What will the weather be like this weekend?
Jiasheng Wang:	There will be fog early on Saturday morning. It will turn sunny later in the morning.
Xiaomei Zhang:	Then we can go to the Summer Palace, how about it?
Jiasheng Wang:	Very good. I'll bring you an umbrella to block the sunlight.
Xiaomei Zhang:	Let's meet in front of the dorm at 9:30.
Jiasheng Wang:	Good. Let's not leave until we see each other.

Dialogue 2

Fang Huang:	Green, where are you from?
Green:	I am from Boston. Boston is in New England. The four seasons are very distinct there. It is beautiful.
Fang Huang:	I hear it's very cold in winter in Boston, and it snows a lot.
Green:	That's right. It often snows in winter. The temperature is usually about 20 to 30 degrees.
Fang Huang:	That is below zero in Celsius. How about summer? It must be quite cool.
Green:	Yes. It is hot in the daytime during the summer. But early morning and night are cool. Spring and Fall are neither cold nor hot. It's very comfortable. You're from Nanjing, right? How's the climate there?
Fang Huang:	Winter is not too cold there. But summer is quite hot. In the past, people often said that Nanjing was like an oven.
Green:	Is it really that terrible?
Fang Huang:	Not really. The temperature in summer is about the same as in Beijing. There's a rainy season lasting about two or three weeks. It rains almost every day. Because of the humidity, people feel very uncomfortable. But generally speaking, the climate in Nanjing is not too bad.

Reading

Nowadays people pay close attention to the weather. Every day there are weather forecasts in the newspaper and on TV, radio, and the Internet. There are also special weather TV channels and web sites. You will know how the weather is on any given day, whether it is cloudy or sunny, windy or rainy, etc. In addition to daily weather forecasts, the weather reports also tell what the weather will be like for the next two or three days, and some TV stations even forecast the weather for the next five days or the upcoming week. There are some web sites that also forecast weather two weeks in advance. But it is often not as accurate as the short term reports.

tīng shuō liàn xí
听   说   练   习

▶ Exercises for Listening and Speaking

● 一、完成对话。 *(1. Work in pairs to complete the dialogue.)*

A: Nǐ qiántiān xiàwǔ qù nǎr le?

B: _____

A: Qiántiān xiàwǔ yòu shì guāfēng, yòu shì xiàyǔ, hái dǎléi shǎndiàn, nǐ hái qù tī zúqiú?

B: _____

A: Tiānqì yùbào yǒushíhòu yě bù zhǔn. Nǐ yīdìng gěi lín chéng le luòtāngjī.

B: _____

A: Xīngqīliù de tiānqì zěnmeyàng?

B: _____

A: Yǒu wù, huì bù huì xiàyǔ?

B: _____

A: Chū tàiyáng huì bù huì tài rè? Wǒ xiǎng qù Yíhéyuán wánr.

B: _____

A: Nà hǎo, yàoshi tiānqì yùbào bù zhǔn, xiàyǔ le yě bù pà.

B: _____

A: Wǒmen 9 diǎn bàn zài sùshèlóu qiánmian jiàn, bù jiàn bù sàn.

B: _____

🔘 二、听对话，回答问题。 *(2. Listen to the conversation and answer the questions.)*

1. How often does B see or read the weather forecast?

   _____

2. Where does he get the weather forecast?

   _____

3. What is the weather like this Saturday?

   _____

4. How did B know next Saturday's weather forecast?

   _____

5. Where did A get the weather forecast?

   _____

6. What are they going to do now?

   _____

🔘 三、先听对话，然后两人一组朗读。 *(3. Listen to the following conversation without looking at the book, and then read it aloud in pairs, first by following the pinyin, then by following the characters.)*

Jiǎ: Tīngshuō Bōshìdùn dōngtiān hěn lěng.

Yǐ: Dōngtiān chángcháng zhǐ yǒu èr-sānshí dù.

Jiǎ: Èr-sānshí dù bù shì hěn rè ma?

Yǐ: Nǐ shuō de shì Shèshì, kěshì Měiguó yòng de shì Huáshì.

Jiǎ: Yuánlái Měiguó bù yòng Shèshì, nánguài wǒ tīng bù dǒng tiānqì yùbào. Èr-sānshí dù shì Shèshì duōshǎo dù?

Yǐ: Shì língdù dào língxià shíyī-èr dù zuǒyòu.

Jiǎ: Nà shì gòu lěng de. Bōshìdùn sìjì de qìhòu zěnmeyàng?

Yǐ: Bōshìdùn sìjì fēnmíng.

Jiǎ: Xiàtiān ne? Yīdìng bǐjiào liángkuài.

Yǐ: Duì, xiàtiān zǎowǎn dōu bǐjiào liángkuài.

Jiǎ: Nà chūnqiūtiān ne?

Yǐ: Chūnqiūtiān de qìhòu kě hǎo le, bù lěng bù rè, yǔshuǐ yòu shǎo.

Jiǎ: Bōshìdùn de qìhòu gēn wǒ lǎojiā de chàbùduō, wǒ yīdìng yào qù wánr wánr.

Yǐ: Hǎo a, xià cì gēn wǒ yīqǐ qù.

甲：   听说波士顿冬天很冷。

乙：   冬天常常只有二三十度。

甲：   二三十度不是很热吗？

乙：   你说的是摄氏，可是美国用的是华氏。

甲：   原来美国不用摄氏，难怪我听不懂天气预报。二三十度是摄氏多少度？

乙：   是零度到零下十一二度左右。

甲：   那是够冷的，波士顿四季的气候怎么样？

乙：   波士顿四季分明。

甲：   夏天呢？一定比较凉快。

乙：   对，夏天早晚都比较凉快。

甲：   那春秋天呢？

乙：   春秋天的气候可好了，不冷不热，雨水又少。

甲：   波士顿的气候跟我老家的差不多，我一定要去玩玩儿。

乙：   好啊，下次跟我一起去。

四、角色表演 (4. Role Play)

1. Imagine you are a meteorologist, and give a weather report for the next five days.

2. A: You are planning an outdoor activity for the coming weekend but haven't seen the weather report. Ask a friend about this weekend's weather.

   B: Your friend asks you about this weekend's weather to plan for an outdoor activity. Tell him or her what you know about this weekend's weather.

dìàn nǎo yǔ hàn zì liàn xí

电 脑 与 汉 字 练 习

▶ **Exercises for Computing and Learning Characters**

....

一、打出下面段落。*(Type the following passage.)*

（相声 [xiàngshēng, comic dialogue]）

A: 当天广播电台 (diàntái, radio station)，现在是天气预报时间。

B: 哪儿有这个台啊？

A: 今天晴到多云。

B: 明天呢？

A: 昨天有小雨，风力 (fēnglì, wind force) 一二级 (jí, a measure of degree for wind) 转三四
级，有时四五级，但不会到七八级。

B: 那明天呢？

A: 前天下大雾，刮风，打雷，闪电，但是没有下雨。想出去玩的朋友可以
去。

B: 这是什么电台呀，我要知道的是明天。

A: 明天的天气预报明天再播。请朋友们早点儿休息，再见。

B: 啊？这就没了？

二、把下面拼音句子打成汉字。*(2. Type the following pinyin sentences and select
the appropriate characters.)*

1. Xīngqīliù zǎoshang yǒu wù, shàngwǔ huì zhuǎn qíng.

2. Bōshìdùn zài Xīnyīnggélán dìqū, sìjì fēnmíng, fēicháng měilì.

3. Yīshēng kāi le xiē gǎnmàoyào, hái yǒu xiāoyán hé tuìshāo de yào. Tā xiànzài shāo yǐjīng tuì le, jiù shì
hái késou, tóuténg.

4. Wǒ dùzi téng de lìhài, lādùzi, shàngtù xiàxiè.

5. Bǎ nǐ de yínhángkǎ cóng zhège kǒu fàng jìnqù, shūrù nǐ de mìmǎ, zài shūrù yào qǔ de qiánshù,
àn OK jiù kěyǐ le.

三、圈出正确的汉字。*(3. Circle the correct character to fill in the blanks.)*

1. 你看天阴了，还起大 ___ (疯、凤、讽、夙、风)了，要下大 ___ (雪、雷、鱼、雹、零)。

2. 我想等天 ___ (请、情、清、青、晴)了去 ___ (蹄、踢、体、堤、惕)足球。

3. 我每次去中餐馆都要喝酸辣 ___ (涌、烫、汤、佣、诵)。

4. 我就不信我的中文不 ___ (茹、汝、姑、妃、如)他。

5. 这儿的夏天怎么那么 ___ (热、煮、煎、然、熬)，象个火炉一样。

四、读生字，找出偏旁部首。*(4. The characters in each of the following groups share a radical. Read the characters and write the shared radicals.)*

Example: 这 迎 shared radical: 辶

1. 阳 阴 阵 shared radical: _____

2. 雨 雷 雪 零 雾 shared radical: _____

3. 淋 汤 湿 温 凉 潮 shared radical: _____

4. 近 道 过 shared radical: _____

5. 摄 播 把 shared radical: _____

6. 踢 足 shared radical: _____

7. 害 宿 实 shared radical: _____

8. 火 炉 shared radical: _____

9. 怕 快 shared radical: _____

五、把汉字分成部件。*(5. Test your understanding of character structure by dividing the following characters into their component parts.)*

Example: 吗—>口 马

1. 阳—>_____ 　　2. 晴—>_____ 　　3. 度—>_____

4. 频—>_____ 　　5. 踢—>_____

六、学生字 *(6. Learning New Characters)*

独体词组复合词。(Form compound words based on single-character words.)

注释 (Note): Most Chinese characters are words themselves, called 独 (dú, single) 体 (tǐ, body) 词. In this exercise you will be asked to find compound words that contain some common single-character words you have already learned.

Study the following characters selected from the New Words lists: 也　可*　工*　反　下　都　多　天*

1. Copy each character by hand using the character writing demonstration sheet.

2. For each character marked with an asterisk, find the compounds in which the characters are used in the text, and write the compound words next to the characters.

3. With the assistance of a dictionary or an online dictionary, write down three more compounds in which these single-character words appear.

4. For each character marked with an asterisk, make a sentence with one of the three new compounds.

Character Writing Demonstration Sheet 第十课　　姓名_____

Pinyin	Strokes	Structure	English	Radical	Traditional Form
yě	3	single-body	also, too	乙（乛）	也

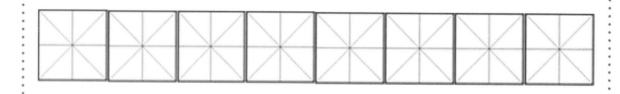

Pinyin	Strokes	Structure	English	Radical	Traditional Form
kě	5	half-encloser	but, yet	口	可

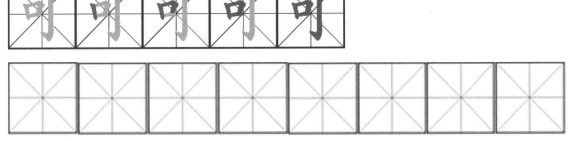

Pinyin	Strokes	Structure	English	Radical	Traditional Form
gōng	3	single-body	worker, work, labor	工	工

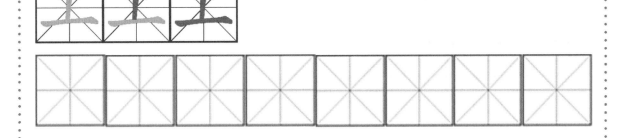

Pinyin	Strokes	Structure	English	Radical	Traditional Form
fǎn	4	half encloser	turn over, reverse	厂	反

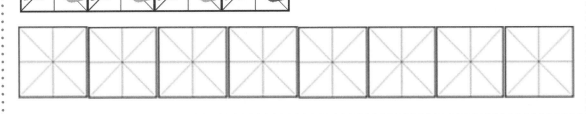

Pinyin	Strokes	Structure	English	Radical	Traditional Form
xià	3	single-body	below, down, under	卜	下

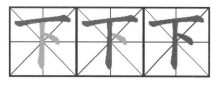

Pinyin	Strokes	Structure	English	Radical	Traditional Form
dōu	10	left-right	all, both	阝	都

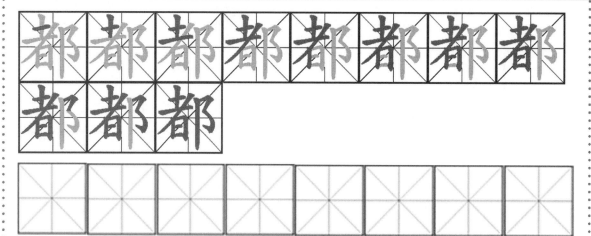

Pinyin	Strokes	Structure	English	Radical	Traditional Form
duō	6	top-bottom	many, much, more	夕	多

Pinyin	Strokes	Structure	English	Radical	Traditional Form
tiān	4	single-body	day, sky	大	天

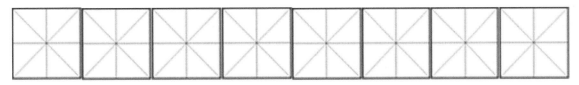

kè   wén liàn xí

课   文   练   习

▶ Exercises for Understanding the Texts

一、根据课文回答问题。*(1. Answer the questions orally based on the text.)*

对话（1）

1. 为什么张小妹说天气预报很准？

   Why did Xiaomei Zhang say that the weather forecast is very accurate?

2. 王家生前天去做什么去了？

   What did Jiasheng Wang do the day before yesterday?

3. 他为什么说天气预报不准？

   Why did he say that the weather forecast was not accurate?

4. 这个周末的天气怎么样？

   How is the weather this weekend?

5. 他们要到哪儿去玩儿？

   Where were they going for fun?

6. 他们要在哪儿见面？

   Where would they meet?

对话（2）

1. 波士顿在什么地方？

   Where is Boston?

2. 波士顿的气候怎么样？

   How is the climate in Boston?

3. 南京的气候怎么样？

   How is the climate in Nanjing?

4. 南京的夏天真的象火炉一样热吗？

   Is summer in Nanjing really as hot as an oven?

5. 波士顿有黄梅雨季吗？

   Is there a "Huangmei" rainy season in Boston?

6. 南京的黄梅雨季一般有多长？

   How long is Nanjing's "Huangmei" rainy season?

二、用感叹词"啊"不同的四听填空，然后朗读。*(For each item below, fill in the parentheses with the appropriate tone (1, 2, 3, or 4) for* 啊. *Then read the sentences aloud.)*

1. A: 明天上课一定要告诉老师，啊（　　　　）。

   B: 知道了。

2. A: 你记得老师今天说的话吗，啊（　　　　）？

   B: 老师让我们先做作业再去看电影。

3. A: 啊（　　　　）？五月还下雪？

   B: 就是，以前没有过。

4. 啊（　　　　）!你原来去酒吧玩儿了，所以我没找到你。

5. A: 啊（　　　　）？张小妹生病了？你怎么知道的？

   B: 她今天没来上课。

6. 今天天气不好，明天再去吧，啊（　　　　）。

三、用疑问词"什么+呀"完成下列句子，然后朗读。*(Use the question word "what + ya" after an adjective to create rhetorical questions indicating disagreement and complete the following sentences. Then read the dialogues aloud).*

Example:

A: 邮局离这儿很近。

B: 近什么呀，那天我走了半个小时才到。(That day, I walked for half an hour to get there.)

1. A: 我觉得学中文很容易。

   B: _____。

   (Learning to write characters gives me a headache.)

2. A: 从学校坐地铁到JFK机场很方便，是不是？

   B: _____。

   (One has to change bus and subway three or four times.)

3. A: 波士顿的天气很好，对不对？

   B: _____。

   (There is too much snow in winter and the summer is not long enough.)

4. A: 这件运动服你穿很合适。

   B: _____。

   (It is too big.)

四、用相邻的数字回答下列问题。(Use a combination of adjacent numbers to answer the following questions orally.)

1. 大学一年级学生一般多大年龄？

2. 从纽约寄一封信到波士顿要几天？

3. 波士顿的冬天多少度？

4. 中文班一般有多少学生？

5. 你一个星期运动几次？

五、作文 *(5. Composition)*

Write a paragraph (200 characters and 10 sentences minimum) talking about the weather in the place where you live. Make sure to use the given words and phrases.

1. 只是　 2. 比较　 3. 一定　 4. 不如　 5. 除了……以外，还　 6. 又是……，又是……　 7. 是……还　 8. 有的……，有的……甚至(还)有的

六、翻译 *(6. Translation)*

Translate the following sentences orally in class. Then type your translations in Chinese using the words and phrases provided.

1. At Xiaonian Wang's birthday party, his friends were eating food and having fun. They ate a lot of Chinese food that Xiaonian Wang's mother cooked for them. (又是，又是)

2. Learning to pronounce the four tones accurately is relatively difficult. (比较)

3. Accurate? What do you mean the forecast is accurate? The forecast said it was going to be a sunny day, but the sun never came out. (什么 + 呀 to form a rhetorical question indicating disagreement)

4. The bus I took this morning broke down and made me twenty minutes late for class. (害得)

5. Living in the dorm is both safe and convenient. (又，又)

6. Whatever you want to say, say it! I'm not going to buy it anyway. (反正)

7. Did you say that you're not going? Fine, I'm going anyway. (反正)

8. Do you like the weather in Boston or Hawaii better? (是，还是)

9. The weather in Boston is not as good as the weather in Hawaii. (不如 as a comparison)

10. Taking a taxi is too expensive, let's take the subway instead. (不如 as a preference)

	bǔ	chōng	yuè	dú	liàn	xí
	补	充	阅	读	练	习

▶ Supplementary Reading Exercises

··

(1) Controlled Vocabulary

Read the following passage and answer the following questions either in Chinese or in English.

	Chinese	Pinyin	Part of Speech	English
1.	观众	guānzhòng	N	viewer; audience
2.	局部	júbù	Adj	part
3.	气温	qìwēn	N	air temperature
4.	级	jí	M	(degree for wind)
5.	播送	bōsòng	V	broadcast
6.	傍晚	bàngwǎn	TW	towards evening; at night fall; at dusk
7.	收看	shōukàn	V	receive; accept

EXERCISES

天气预报

各位观众，早上好，今天是2003年十二月五日星期五，下面是今天全天和今后三天的天气预报。

今天晴，有时阴，局部有阵雨，晚上可能转雪。最高气温零上三度到六度，最低气温零到零下四度。西北风三到四级。

明天多云转晴，气温零下二度到零上五度，阵风二级。后天晴，气温零度左右。大后天晴转多云，傍晚到夜间有小雪，气温零下一度到七度。

天气预报播送完了，谢谢大家收看，今天晚上再见。

Questions

1. 天气预报说星期五的天气怎么样？
   What will the weather be like on Friday?

2. 星期六会是晴天吗？

   Is Saturday going to be a rainy day?

3. 哪天可能会下雪？

   On which day is snow expected?

4. 哪天最冷？哪天最热？

   Which day is going to be the warmest and which the coldest?

5. 哪天的风最大？

   Which day is going to be the most windy?

(2) Open Vocabulary

(1) Read the following weather forecast from a Chinese newspaper and answer the questions.

1. 这个天气预报是哪天的？

   What day is the weather forecast for?

2. 今天的天气怎么样？

   How is today's weather?

3. 今天的最高温度是多少？

   What is the highest temperature today?

4. 什么时候不下雨？

   When will it not rain?

5. 明天比今天热还是凉快？

   Will tomorrow be hotter or cooler than today?

(2) Read the following joke with the help of a dictionary and answer the questions either in Chinese or English. You can also retrieve an electronic version of this text from the accompanying online materials, and use an online dictionary or translation program to help you read it. After answering the questions, try to tell the story to a classmate in your own words without looking at the original text.

	Chinese	Pinyin	Part of Speech	English
1.	幸好	xìnghǎo	Ad	fortunately; luckily
2.	正好	zhènghǎo	Ad	happen to; chance to; as it happens

幸好沒住在局部

　　晚上珊珊一家人在看电视，正好播放天气预报。播音员播完"局部有雨"，珊珊的奶奶高兴地接着说："幸好我们没住在'局部'，那地方老是下雨，没有晴的时候。"

Questions

1. 珊珊家的人在做什么？
   What were the people in Shanshan's family doing?

2. 他们在听什么？
   What were they listening to?

3. 为什么珊珊的奶奶很高兴？
   Why was Shanshan's grandmother very happy?

4. "局部" 是什么意思？
   What does the expression "局部" mean?

5. 珊珊的奶奶是怎么理解"局部"的意思的？
   What did Shanshan's grandmother think the meaning of "局部" was?

▶ Stone Forest in Yunnan, China.

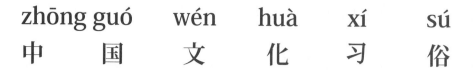

zhōng guó   wén   huà   xí   sú
中　国　文　化　习　俗

Chinese Customs and Culture

. . . .

èr shí sì jié qì
二　十　四　节　气

▶ The 24 Solar Terms

China has been an agricultural country for thousands of years, and climate changes have always been extremely important to Chinese farmers. Based on the practical needs of farmers, Chinese astronomers developed what are called the "twenty-four solar terms" toward the end of the Warring States Period (475–221 BC). The twenty-four solar terms were determined by changes in the sun's position along the ecliptic throughout the year. They were used to tell climate changes and help farmers decide when to plant or harvest crops. Each segment of the cycle is about half a month, corresponding to a full year of twenty-four segments. As a reflection of the regularity of the changes of the climate in the areas of the middle and lower reaches of the Yellow River, the twenty-four solar terms are still being used by farmers in China today.

The following is a brief chronological introduction of all the solar terms.

1. Lichun (立春 lìchūn): the Beginning of Spring, about February 4th, beginning of the first month in the Lunar Calendar.

2. Yushui (雨水 yǔshuǐ): the Beginning of Raining, about February 19th, middle of the first month in the Lunar Calendar.

3. Jingzhe (惊蛰 jīngzhé) : Waking of Hibernating Insects and Small Animals, about March 6, beginning of the second month in the Lunar Calendar.

4. Chunfen (春分 chūnfēn): the Spring Equinox, when day and night are of equal length, about March 20th, middle of the second month in the Lunar Calendar.

5. Qingming (清明 qīngmíng): Pure Brightness, about April 5th, beginning of the third month in the Lunar Calendar. The weather gets warmer. For the Han people, this is the time to honor the ancestors, one of the most important rituals in Confucian culture. Chinese families will gather to sweep the family graves, and to offer food and prayers to their deceased ancestors.

6. Guyu (谷雨 gǔyǔ): about April 20 in the middle of the third month in the Lunar Calendar. This is the time when millet and other vegetables are planted.

7. Lixia (立夏 lìxià): the Beginning of Summer, about May 6, in the beginning of the fourth month in the Lunar Calendar.

8. Xiaoman (小满 xiǎomǎn): Wheat becomes ripe, about May 21, in the middle of the fourth month in the Lunar Calendar.

9. Mangzhong (芒种 mángzhŏng): about June 6, at the beginning of the fifth month in the Lunar Calendar, indicating the ripeness of barley and wheat. It is time to start planting autumn crops.

10. Xiazhi (夏至 xiàzhì): the Summer Solstice. This day has the longest daytime of the year. It falls on about June 21, in the middle of the fifth month in the Lunar Calendar.

11. Xiaoshu (小暑 xiǎoshǔ): about July 7, at the beginning of the sixth month in the Lunar Calendar. This indicates the beginning of hot weather.

▶ The Three Pagodas Park in Dali, Yunnan, China.

12. Dashu (大暑 dàshǔ): about July 23, in the middle of the sixth month in the Lunar Calendar. This is the hottest day of the year.

13. Liqiu (立秋 lìqiū): the Beginning of Autumn, about August 8, at the beginning of the seventh month in the Lunar Calendar.

14. Chushu (处暑 chǔshǔ): about August 23, in the middle of the seventh month in the Lunar Calendar. This marks the end of summer, indicating the heat is over.

15. Bailu (白露 báilù): about September 8, in the beginning of the eighth month in the Lunar Calendar. This is the time when the weather starts to get drier.

16. Qiufen (秋分 qiūfēn): the Autumn Equinox, about September 23, in the middle of the eighth month in the Lunar Calendar. The days and nights are of equal length.

17. Hanlu (寒露 hánlù): about October 8, at the beginning of the ninth month in the Lunar Calendar. The weather gets distinctively colder, and leaves begin to fall.

18. Shuangjiang (霜降 shuāngjiàng): continuation of coldness and appearance of frost in the early mornings and late evenings, about October 23, in the middle of the ninth month in the Lunar Calendar.

19. Lidong (立冬 lìdōng): the beginning of Winter, about November 7, at the beginning of the tenth month in the Lunar Calendar.

20. Xiaoxue (小雪 xiǎoxuě): about November 22, in the middle of the tenth month in the Lunar Calendar. It starts snowing.

21. Daxue (大雪 dàxuě): about December 7, at the beginning of the eleventh month in the Lunar Calendar. In some areas, heavy snow begins.

22. Dongzhi (冬至 dōngzhì): the Winter Solstice, about December 22, in the middle of the eleventh month in the Lunar Calendar. This day has the shortest daytime of the year. It is on this day that the Chinese emperors went to the Temple of Heaven to worship and offer sacrifices to Heaven in ancient times.

23. Xiaohan (小寒 xiǎohán): about January 6, at the beginning of the twelfth month in the Lunar Calendar, indicating cold days, but not quite the coldest days.

24. Dahan (大寒 dàhán): about January 21, in the middle of the twelfth month in the Lunar Calendar. This is the coldest time of the year. After this, it will get gradually warmer as Spring approaches.

▶ Test Your Knowledge Can you identify the solar term for these events?

1. I plan to go home to pay tribute to my ancestors. When (during which solar term) should I go?

   A. Dongzhi (冬至 dōngzhì) B. Liqui (立秋 lìqiū) C. Qingming (清明 qīngmíng)

2. Which day has the shortest day time?

   A. Dongzhi (冬至 dōngzhì) B. Qingming (清明 qīngmíng) C. Lidong (立冬 lìdōng):

3. Which day has the longest day time?

   A. Qingming (清明 qīngmíng) B. Xiazhi (夏至 xiàzhì) C. Lixia (立夏 lìxià)

4. Which day and night are of equal length?

   A. Chunfen (春分 chūnfēn) B. Qingming (清明 qīngmíng) C. Liqui (立秋 lìqiū)

Answers:

1. C 2. A 3. B 4. A

▶ Students in China enjoy sightseeing despite the rain.

jié qì gē

节 气 歌

Song of the Solar Terms

Try reciting this rhyme, which Chinese children sing to remember the 24 solar terms and the climate changes associated with them.

lì	chūn	yáng	qì	zhuǎn		yǔ	shuǐ	yán	hé	biān
立	春	阳	气	转；		雨	水	沿	河	边；
jīng	zhé	wū	yā	jiào		chūn	fēn	dì	pí	gān
惊	蛰	乌	鸦	叫；		春	分	地	皮	干。
qīng	míng	máng	zhòng	mài		gǔ	yǔ	zhòng	dà	tián
清	明	忙	种	麦；		谷	雨	种	大	田；
lì	xià	é	máo	zhù		xiǎo	mǎn	niǎo	lái	quán
立	夏	鹅	毛	住；		小	满	鸟	来	全；
máng	zhǒng	wǔ	yuè	jié		xià	zhì	bù	ná	mián
芒	种	五	月	节；		夏	至	不	拿	棉；
xiǎo	shǔ	bù	suàn	rè		dà	shǔ	sān	fú	tiān
小	暑	不	算	热；		大	暑	三	伏	天。
Lì	qiū	máng	dǎ	diàn		chǔ	shǔ	dòng	dāo	lián
立	秋	忙	打	旬；		处	暑	动	刀	镰；
bái	lù	diǎn	yī	diǎn		qiū	fēn	wú	shēng	tián
白	露	点	一	点；		秋	分	无	生	田。
hán	lù	bù	suàn	lěng		shuāng	jiàng	biàn	le	tiān
寒	露	不	算	冷；		霜	降	变	了	天；
lì	dōng	xuě	máng	máng		xiǎo	xuě	jiāng	fēng	dòng
立	冬	雪	茫	茫；		小	雪	将	封	冻；
dà	xuě	dì	fēng	yán		dōng	zhì	shǔ	jiǔ	tiān
大	雪	地	封	严；		冬	至	属	九	天；
xiǎo	hán	dà	hán	yòu	yī	nián				
小	寒	大	寒	又	一	年。				

▶ Climbing the Great Wall.

春雨惊春清谷天，夏满芒夏暑相连。
chūn yǔ jīng chūn qīng gǔ tiān, xià mǎn máng xià shǔ xiāng lián

秋处露秋寒霜降，冬雪雪冬小大寒。
qiū chǔ lù qiū hán shuāng jiàng, dōng xuě xuě dōng xiǎo dà hán

每月两节不变更，最多相差一两天。
měi yuè liǎng jié bù biàn gēng, zuì duō xiàng chà yī liǎng tiān

上半年，六二一，下半年，八二三。
shàng bàn nián, liù èr yī, xià bàn nián, bā èr sān

附录一 APPENDIX 1

Answer Keys to Pinyin Review Exercise II

II. Foreign Words and Brand Names in Chinese

Since the 1980s, many foreign commodities and businesses have entered Chinese people's lives. In this part, we will practice pinyin with these foreign names.

A. Listen carefully to these names of fast food chains. Put tone marks over the correct syllables and write their English meanings.

	English	Pinyin	Characters
1.	McDonald's	Màidāngláo	麦当劳
2.	Burger King	Hànbǎo Wáng	汉堡王
3.	Kentucky Fried Chicken	Kěndéjī	肯德基
4.	Pizza Hut	Bǐsàwū	比萨屋 (必胜客)
5.	Taco Bell	Tǎkězhōng	塔可钟
6.	Subway	Sàibǎiwèi	赛百味
7.	Starbucks	Xīngbākè	星巴克
8.	Steak House	Pā Fáng	扒房
9.	Wendy's	Wēndì	温蒂
10.	Friday's	Xīngqīwǔ	星期五

B. Listen carefully to these food names and try to write down what you hear in pinyin. (Don't forget the tone marks!)

	English	Pinyin	Characters
1.	sandwich	sānmíngzhì	三明治
2.	hamburger	hànbǎobāo	汉堡包
3.	pizza	bǐsàbǐng	比萨饼
4.	chocolate	qiǎokēlì	巧克力
5.	cheese	zhīshì (nǎilào)	芝士 (奶酪)
6.	hot dog	règǒu	热狗
7.	croissant	niújiǎobāo	牛角包
8.	salad	shālā	沙拉
9.	sardine	shādīngyú	沙丁鱼

10.	fillet	fēilì	腓力
11.	cookie	qǔqí	曲奇

C. Listen carefully to these names of beverages and try to write the names in pinyin based on their English pronunciations.

	English	Pinyin	Characters
1.	Sprite	Xuěbì	雪碧
2.	Fanta	Fēndá	芬达
3.	7-Up	Qīxǐ	七喜
4.	coffee	kāfēi	咖啡
5.	Coca-Cola	Kěkǒu Kělè	可口可乐
6.	Pepsi	Bǎishì Kělè	百事可乐
7.	chocolate milk	qiǎokēlì nǎi	巧克力奶
8.	yogurt	yōugé	优格
9.	Whisky	Wēishìjì	威士忌
10.	Brandy	Báilándì	白兰地

D. The following are brand names of shoes and clothes. Can you figure out the English based on the pinyin spellings?

	English	Pinyin	Chinese Characters
1.	Nike	Nàikè	耐克
2.	Reebok	Ruìbù	锐步
3.	Adidas	Adídásī	阿迪达思
4.	Puma	Biāomǎ	彪马
6.	Levi's	Lǐwéi	李维
7.	Givenchy	Jìfánxī	纪梵希
8.	Louis Vuitton	Lùyìwēidēng	路易威登
9.	Victoria's Secret	Wéiduōlìyà Mìmì	维多丽亚秘密
10.	Tiffany	Tiěfūní	铁芙尼
11.	Hush Puppies	Xiábùshì	暇步士

E. Listen carefully to the names of cosmetics and add initials to form complete pinyin words.

	English	Pinyin	Chinese Characters
1.	Avon	Yǎfāng	雅芳
2.	Mary Kay	Méilínkǎi	玫琳凯
3.	Maybelline	Měibǎolián	美宝莲
4.	Lancôme	Lánkòu	兰蔻

	5.	L'Oreal	Ouláiyǎ	欧莱雅
	6.	Clinique	Qiànbì	倩碧
	7.	Elizabeth Arden	Yīlìshābái Yǎdùn	伊丽莎白雅顿
	8.	Chanel	Xiāngnài'er	香奈儿
	9.	Estee Lauder	Yǎshīlándài	雅诗兰黛
	10.	Almay	Aoměi	傲美
	11.	Christine Dior	Kēlǐsītīng Dí'ào	克里斯汀迪奥

F. Listen carefully to the skin care and health products, and add finals to form complete pinyin words.

	English	**Pinyin**	**Characters**
1.	Crest	Jiājiéshì	佳洁士
2.	Colgate	Gāolùjié	高露洁
3.	Pert	Piāoróu	飘柔
4.	Pantene	Pāntíng	潘婷
5.	Head & Shoulders	Hǎifēisī	海飞丝
6.	Lux	Lìshì	力士
7.	Dove	Duōfū	多芙
8.	Hazeline	Xiàshìlián	夏士莲
9.	Ponds	Pángshì	旁士
10.	Safeguard	Shūfújiā	舒肤佳
11.	Pampers	Bāngbǎoshì	帮宝适
12.	Kleenex	Shūjié	舒洁
13.	Johnson & Johnson	Qiángshēng	强生
14.	Victoria's Secret	Wéiduōlìyà Mìmì	维多丽亚秘密

G. Match English with the correct pinyin words. The Chinese characters are included for your reference.

	English	**Pinyin**	**Chinese Characters**
1.	T-shirt	(D.) tīxùshān	T 恤衫
2.	tank	(A.) tǎnkè	坦克
3.	cartoon	(I.) kǎtōng	卡通
4.	email	(H.) yīmèi'er	伊妹儿
5.	sofa	(B.) shāfā	沙发
6.	Internet cafe	(E.) wǎngbā	网巴
7.	Wal-Mart	(C.) Wò'ěrmǎ	沃尔玛
8.	Ikea	(F.) Yíjiā	宜家
9.	Tiffany	(J.) Tiěfúní	铁芙尼
10.	Fans	(G.) Fěnsī	粉丝

附录二 APPENDIX 2

Setting Up Your Computer to Type in Chinese

To Install Chinese in Microsoft® Windows® XP and Vista

Open the Windows Control Panel.

In the Control Panel, select "Date, Time, Language and Regional Options." (In Windows Vista, this may be called "Clock, Language, and Region.")

Open the "Regional and Language Options" icon.

Choose the "Languages" tab, and ensure the "Install Files for East Asian Languages" is checked. (In Windows Vista, choose the "Keyboards and Languages" tab, and then click "Change keyboards.")

Click the "Details" button to open the "Text Services and Input Languages" dialog.

If "Chinese" is not listed in the "Installed Services" box, click "Add."

In the "Input Language" list, if you are typing in simplified characters, choose "Chinese (PRC)." The "Keyboard Layout" should be set to "Chinese (Simplified) - Microsoft Pinyin IME 3.0." (If you want to type in traditional characters using a pinyin input method, you need to install a different input method editor, [also known as input method environment, IME], such as the Google Pinyin Input Method.)

In the "Text Services and Input Languages" dialog, under "Preferences," click the "Language Bar" tab. Make sure that "Show the Language bar on the desktop" is checked.

Click "OK" on both dialogs to return to the "Regional and Language Options.". You will probably need to insert your Windows XP operating system CD for the files to be installed.

The language bar should now have appeared in the bottom right of the taskbar. It should default to English, "EN."

Click on the "EN" button to show the available languages:

By changing the language to "CH", you can now type in pinyin. You can toggle between languages by pressing "CTRL" + "SHIFT" on your keyboard.

To Install Chinese in Apple® Mac® OS X

Open System Preferences. Select "International."

Select "Language" and choose "Edit List." On the screen that appears, check the box next to "Simplified Chinese" and/or "Traditional Chinese. Select "OK."

Select "Input Menu." Check the box next to the "Simplified Chinese" and/or "Traditional Chinese" input method. Mac OS X allows you to type in pinyin in both Simplified and Traditional Chinese.

Close the System Preferences window.

On the desktop, if you are using a US system, there should be a US flag icon in the upper right corner of your screen. Click on the icon to select your input method. You can now select Simplified Chinese or Traditional Chinese.

附录三 APPENDIX 3

Texts in Traditional Form

Lesson 1, Dialogue 1

格林：　　　　你好！

王老師：　　　你好！

格林：　　　　老師*，請問您貴姓？

王老師：　　　我姓王。你是新學生嗎？你叫什麼名字？

格林：　　　　是，我叫格林，是美國留學生。

王老師：　　　歡迎，歡迎。你吃飯了嗎？

格林：　　　　沒有。

王老師：　　　快去餐廳吃飯吧，再見。

格林：　　　　再見。

Lesson 1, Dialogue 2

格林：　　　　您好，王老師。好久不見，您好嗎？

王老師：　　　很好。我出差了，才回來。這位是誰？

格林：　　　　王老師，他是我的中國朋友，叫文國新。

王老師：　　　小文，你好。

文國新：　　　王老師好。

格林：　　　　小文給我起了一個中文名字，叫張學文。

王老師：　　　這個名字很好。哦，要上課了，一會兒見。

格林：　　　　一會兒見。

Lesson 1, Narration

　　　格林是美國留學生。他看見出差回來的王老師，告訴王老師，他有一個中國朋友，叫文國新。小文給他起了一個中文名字，叫張學文。

Lesson 2, Dialogue 1

中國學生：　請問，你是中國人嗎？

王小年：　　是啊。怎麼啦？

中國學生：你的中文怎麼說得不流利？

王小年：　我是華裔學生，有人叫我ABC。

中國學生：什麼是ABC？

王小年：　就是（American Born Chinese）在美國生的中國人。

中國學生：你的老家在哪兒？

王小年：　我是第三代移民，在美國長大。我的爺爺、奶奶是從中國廣東來美國的。

中國學生：我的老家也在廣東，可是爸爸、媽媽都在北京工作。

王小年：　那我們是老鄉了。我們去吃中國飯吧。

Lesson 2, Dialogue 2

中國學生：我很想家。

王小年：　你爸爸媽媽都是做什麼的呢？

中國學生：媽媽是醫生，爸爸是大學教授。你呢？

王小年：　我們家有五口人。爸爸、媽媽、一個哥哥和一個妹妹。爸爸、媽媽開了一家中餐館。

中國學生：我沒有兄弟姐妹。你哥哥和妹妹都上學嗎？

王小年：　他們不都上學，哥哥是中學老師，妹妹跟我都在紐約大學學習。我學電腦。妹妹在商學院學會計學。

中國學生：我才到紐約，英文不好，以後要多請教你。

王小年：　我們可以互相幫助。你可以教我學中文。

中國學生：那太好了。

Lesson 2, Narration

　　王小年是華裔大學生，在美國生，美國長。王小年的爸爸、媽媽開中餐館。哥哥是中學老師，妹妹跟王小年在紐約大學學習。王小年的中文不太好。一天王小年在學校見到一個中國學生，那個學生的媽媽是醫生，爸爸是大學教授。他才到紐約，英文不好。他跟王小年學英文，王小年跟他學中文。

Lesson 3, Dialogue 1

(Two freshmen at a Chinese college)

王家生：　張小妹，我們明天去看電影吧。

張小妹：　什麼電影？

王家生：　新到的美國大片兒。

張小妹：　嘿，真棒！在哪兒？

王家生： 大華電影院，坐14路公共汽車，在大新路下車。

張小妹： 14 路車站在哪兒？

王家生： 出北校門，往左拐，在第二個十字路口，紅綠燈旁邊。

張小妹： 我們幾點去？

王家生： 下午四點，怎麼樣？

張小妹： 好，明天下午，14路車站，不見不散。

王家生： 再見！

Lesson 3, Dialogue 2

(Two freshmen at an American college)

約翰： 蘇珊， 明天我們去看电電吧。

蘇珊： 對不起，我不喜歡看電影。(1)*

約翰： 那我們去體育館打球吧。

蘇珊： 打球太累了。(2)

約翰： 那我們去王小年的生日晚會，怎麼樣？

蘇珊： 那多沒意思。(3)

約翰： 去酒吧玩兒，好嗎？

蘇珊： 不去，我們還沒到喝酒的年齡。(4)

約翰： 那算了，你在家睡覺吧。

蘇珊： 不，我要跟我的男朋友去跳舞。

Lesson 3, Narration

　　王家生請張小妹去大華電影院看美國大片。張小妹很喜歡美國電影。他們說好明天下午四點在十四路汽車站見，一起去看電影，不見不散。

　　約翰 (John) 請蘇珊 (Susan) 看电影，可是蘇珊不喜歡看電影，她也不喜歡打球。約翰要請她一起去生日晚會和去酒吧，但是蘇珊都拒絕了。原來她要跟男朋友去跳舞。

Lesson 4, Dialogue 1

格林： 你好！請問你會說中文嗎？

王小年： 我會說一點兒。你怎麼會說中文？

格林： 我在中國學了一年中文。現在還在上中文課。

王小年： 你覺得中文難嗎？

格林： 語音和語法不太難，漢字最難。可是我用電腦學，就容易多了。

王小年： 中文的聲調也比較難，我都說不好。

格林： 在中國的時候，老師告訴我們，從開始就發准每一個音和聲調，下課以後還要多練。

王小年： 難怪你這個老外說得這麼准。

格林： 哪裏，哪裏。我說得還不好，不太流利。

王小年： 請告訴我怎麼用電腦學漢字，好嗎？

格林： 好。我從開始就用拼音輸入漢字，省了很多時間練習發音、會會話、閱讀和寫作。

王小年： 那你會不會寫漢字？

格林： 我也練習抄寫漢字，但是會寫的不太多。老師說等我們到了高年級，認識了幾千個漢字了，那時再學手寫漢字就不那麼難了。

王小年： 這個方法聽起來不錯，我以後也要試試。

Lesson 4, Dialogue 2

格林： 老師，我可以問您兩個問題嗎？

高老師： 什麼問題？

格林： 作業裏有一句話說：小王他們上課去了。"小王"是單數，為什麼用"他們"？

高老師： 這裏說的是小王和他的朋友們，也就是跟他一起的那組人。

格林： 我們以前在書裏學的"跟"是"和"的意思。可是在"跟他一起的那組人"這句話裏，"跟"好像不是"和"的意思。

高老師： 對，"跟"也可以作介词，意思是"同"(with)、"向"、"對"(to)。

格林： 懂了，謝謝老師，我走了。

高老師： 不客氣，再見。

Lesson 4, Narration

　　王小年和格林討論學習中文的問題。格林說中文語音和語法不太難，可是漢字比較難。王小年覺得中文的聲調也比較難，特別是四聲，因為他在家說廣東話。王小年說格林中文發音很好，可是格林說他說得不好，不流利。他還告訴王小年怎麼用電腦學習中文。他從開始就用拼音輸入漢字，省下來了很多時間練習發音、會話、閱讀和寫作。他也練習抄寫漢字，可是會寫的漢字不太多。老師說等他們到了高年級，認識了幾千個漢字了，那時再學手寫漢字就不那麼難了。格林說他現在覺得學中文不太難了。王小年說這個方法聽起來不錯，他以後也要試試。

Lesson 5, Dialogue 1

格林： 我們去超市，好嗎？

王小年： 好啊，我想買一些吃的東西和用的東西。

（在超級市場）

格林：　　我要買牛奶、麵包、奶酪和可樂。你呢？

王小年：除了吃的以外，我還要買洗衣粉、肥皂、洗髮液和紙巾。

格林：　　我們先去拿吃的吧。牛奶多少錢半加侖？

王小年：牛奶一塊七毛錢半加侖、麵包一塊八毛九一袋。哎，怎麼可樂比上星期貴了？上星期只要兩塊錢，今天要三塊七毛五分。

格林：　　上星期減價，所以便宜。這星期牛奶減價，還是拿牛奶吧。

王小年：你拿好了嗎？我們去那邊找用的東西吧。

格林：　　好，我要買一些刀、叉、杯子和餐巾紙什麼的。

王小年：哇，我今天買了一車東西。我們去付錢吧。

（付錢以後）

格林：　　我今天買的東西太多了，帶的現金不夠，用信用卡付的錢。

王小年：我也買了不少，我給售貨員八十塊，她只找了我三塊兩毛二分錢。

Lesson 5, Dialogue 2

格林：　　小姐，我想退這件衣服。

售貨員：請問您為什麼要退這件衣服呢？

格林：　　我不喜歡這件的顏色。你們要是有藍顏色的，我就換一件。

售貨員：這種衣服只有紅的、黃的、綠的，沒有藍的。您可以試試藍毛衣。

格林：　　我不想買毛衣，有藍運動衣嗎？

售貨員：運動衣只有黑的。

格林：　　那我買件藍西裝吧。小姐，便宜點兒好嗎？

售貨員：好，給您打九折。

格林：　　再便宜點兒吧。

售貨員：那給您打八折。請試試這件。

格林：　　這件很合適，謝謝。

Lesson 5, Narration

　　　王小年跟格林去超級市場買東西，他們要買一些吃的東西和日用品。他們拿了牛奶、麵包、奶酪和可樂，他們還買了洗衣粉、肥皂、洗髮液和紙巾。格林還買了一些刀、叉、杯子和餐巾紙等*。買可樂的時候，王小年覺得可樂比上星期貴了。上星期只要兩塊錢一瓶，今天要三塊七毛五分錢。格林告訴他上星期減價，所以便宜。這星期牛奶減價，王小年拿了牛奶。他們買了一車東西。格林帶的現金不夠，用信用卡付的錢。王小年花了七十六塊七毛八分錢。

Lesson 6, Dialogue 1

蘇珊： 約翰，你知道怎麼去肯尼迪機場嗎？

約翰： 當然知道。

蘇珊： 怎麼去最好？

約翰： 那要看你是要省錢還是要方便。

蘇珊： 先說怎麼省錢吧。

約翰： 那你可以坐地鐵。先坐6號車到大中央車站，然後換7號車，坐兩站到時代廣場，再坐A車到終點。

蘇珊： 地鐵不是紅線、藍線嗎？怎麼又是數字又是字母？

約翰： 你說的是波士頓的地鐵，那兒的地鐵用顏色。紐約地鐵線路多，所以又有數字又有字母。你下了地鐵還要換乘去機場的大巴。

蘇珊： 太麻煩了，聽說紐約的地鐵也很亂。你還是說說怎麼去方便吧。

約翰： 那當然是坐出租汽車了，又快又方便，只是貴了點兒，要五十塊錢左右。

蘇珊： 那也太貴了，就沒有別的辦法了嗎？

約翰： 你還可以坐地鐵到時代廣場的長途汽車站，那裏有到機場的大巴，只要十幾塊錢。

蘇珊： 這個辦法不錯，我就去長途汽車站吧。

Lesson 6, Dialogue 2

王小年： 中國有地鐵嗎？

格林： 北京、廣州和上海有，比紐約的地鐵漂亮多了，但線路很少，還在擴建。另外，南京等城市正在修建地鐵。

王小年： 你在中國的時候常坐什麼車？

格林： 我常常坐公共汽车。我们学校不通地铁。

王小年： 公共汽車上人多嗎？

格林： 上下班的時候人比較多，平時還好。

王小年： 在中國坐公共汽車跟美國一樣嗎？

格林： 差不多。從前門上車，後門下車，上了車先付錢，是往投幣箱投錢。可以是硬幣，也可以是紙幣，但不找錢。

王小年： 車上有空調嗎？

格林： 有的有，有的沒有。有空調的車比沒有空調的車貴一塊錢。

王小年： 你每次去城裏都坐公共汽車嗎？

格林： 不，我有的時候打的。

王小年： 什麼是"打的"？

格林： 就是坐出租汽車，現在在中國都叫"打的"。

王小年： 真有意思。我下次去中國也打的。

Lesson 6, Narration

　　蘇珊問約翰怎麼去肯尼迪機場，約翰告訴她可以乘地鐵，先乘6號車到大中央車站，然後換7號車坐兩站到時代廣場，再乘A車到終點。最後還要換去機場的大巴。可是蘇珊說太麻煩。約翰說可以坐出租汽車，可是蘇珊說太貴。最後蘇珊決定到時代廣場的長途汽車總站，去乘到飛機場的大巴。

　　在中國乘公共汽車和美國一樣，前門上車，後門下車。上車先買票，車上不找零，所以又叫無人售票車。格林在北京的時候，常常乘公共汽車去城裏。可是有的時候他也打的，也就是叫出租汽車。現在中國的城市出租汽車很多，也很方便。

Lesson 7, Dialogue 1

蘇珊：　你聖誕節回家嗎？

彼德：　不知道。回家要先坐五、六個小時的飛機到洛杉磯，再轉（飛）機，太累了。再說我感恩節才回去過。

蘇珊：　你家怎麼那麼遠，在哪兒？

彼德：　在夏威夷。

蘇珊：　在夏威夷過聖誕節，那多有意思。我跟你一起去，怎麼樣？

彼德：　真的？那太好了。我們馬上給旅行社打電話訂飛機票。

蘇珊：　你坐哪家航空公司的飛機？

彼德：　你坐哪家的我就坐哪家的。

蘇珊：　那好，就坐西北吧。我有西北航空公司的空中俱樂部會員證。

彼德：　行。可是我記得你爸爸、媽媽給你買了回家的飛機票，你不回去看他們嗎？

蘇珊：　沒關係。我叫他們給我改票，晚幾天回去。

彼德：　好，我們去訂票。

Lesson 7, Dialogue 2

蘇珊爸爸：　喂，請問是國際旅行社嗎？

旅行社：　　是。我可以幫助您嗎，先生？

蘇珊爸爸：　噢，我要改機票。

旅行社：　　沒問題。請您告訴我名字，航空公司，日期和航班號。

蘇珊爸爸：　是我女兒的，她叫 Susan White，12月18日坐西北航空公司，251航班從夏威夷到紐約肯尼迪機場。

（旅行社職員查電腦）

旅行社：　　找到了。因為您買的是便宜票，改票要付罰金100美元。請問您要怎麼改？

蘇珊爸爸：　那也只好付了。請改成12月24號，從夏威夷到波士頓。

旅行社：　　好。12月24號上午8點离開夏威夷，到洛杉磯轉機去芝加哥，再從芝加哥到紐約，再轉到波士頓，25號早上6點到。需要另付80美元，再加100美元罰金，一共180美元。

蘇珊爸爸：　可是要轉那麼多次，太麻煩了。有沒有快一點兒的？

旅行社：　　如果25號早上6點走，到舊金山轉機，美東時間當天晚10點可以到波士頓。

蘇珊爸爸：　那好。

旅行社：　　請問您怎麼付款？

蘇珊爸爸：　信用卡。

旅行社：　　好，請告訴我信用卡號碼和到期時間。

蘇珊爸爸：　5234-5678-9876-5432，2009年11月5日。

旅行社：　　謝謝。

Lesson 7, Narration

　　寒假蘇珊原來要回家，爸爸媽媽已經給她買了12月18日的飛機票。可是她要跟她的同學彼德去夏威夷玩兒。他們坐西北航空公司的飛機，因為苏珊是西北航空公司的空中俱樂部會員，可以積累飛行里程。

　　因为蘇珊要去夏威夷，她爸爸只好給她改飛機票。他得把12月18日的票改到25日，這樣蘇珊聖誕節就可以回家。從夏威夷回波士頓很麻烦，要先飛到舊金山，再轉機到波士頓，還要再付80美元的差价和100美元的罰金。可是蘇珊的爸爸只好這樣改。

Lesson 8, Dialogue 1

格林：　　　我要去郵局辦護照，你有事嗎？

王小年：　　我想去寄(一)個包裹，可是沒有東西包。

格林：　　　沒關系，到那兒買個紙盒就可以了。

王小年：　　那好，我們一起去吧。

(在郵局)

職員：　　　可以幫助您嗎？

王小年：　　我想買個紙盒寄東西。

職員：　　　怕壓嗎？

王小年：　　不怕，但我想知道對方收到沒有。

職員：　　　那好，你可以用這個信封，裏面有泡沫塑料，可以保護郵件。要是你寄特快專遞，你就可以查到對方什麼時候收到，又塊又安全，只要十三塊九毛五。

王小年：　　特快專遞好是好，就是太貴了。還可以寄什麼樣的郵件？慢一點沒關系。

職員：　　　如果不急，你可以寄這種挂號，對方收到後要在回執上簽字，然後回執會寄回给你，只要花差不多一半的錢 。

王小年：　　好，我就寄這種。

职员：　　　請填寫這份表，一共是五塊四毛五分錢。

Lesson 8, Dialogue 2

黃方： 對不起，我不會用這個現金機。你能教我怎麼用嗎？

格林： 哦，很容易。只要把你的銀行卡從這個口放進去，輸入你的密碼，再輸入要取的錢數，按OK就可以了。

黃方： 咦，怎麼錢不出來呢？

格林： 我看看。嗯，原來是機器壞了。那你到櫃台去取吧。

黃方： 可是我沒有存摺。

格林： 在美國銀行不用存摺。你只要知道你的賬號，填一張取款單，憑帶照片的證件就可以辦理了。

黃方： 真的，那存錢呢？

格林： 存錢跟取錢一樣，可以用現金機，也可以在櫃台辦理。

黃方： 原來這麼方便，那我試試。謝謝！

格林： 不客氣，再見。

Lesson 8, Reading

在中國郵局郵件的種類很多，有平信、掛號、航空、海運和快件等。平信就是一般信件，貼了郵票就可以寄。比較重要的信件一般寄掛號，因為每份信件郵局都要登記，收件人要簽字。國際郵件可以寄航空或海運。航空快，但是貴，而海運便宜得多。快件種類很多，有特快專遞、第二日投遞、三日到的優先郵件等。除了郵局，人們還常常使用中外私營郵遞公司寄快件和包裹。

Lesson 9, Dialogue 1

王家生： 高老師，張小妹生病了，今天不能來上課了。

高老師： 她得什麼病了？去看過病嗎？

王家生： 她咳嗽，流鼻涕、眼淚，好像有點發燒，可能感冒了。等會兒下了課我陪她去學校醫院看看。

高老師： 那好，告訴她安心休息，缺課我可以幫她補。

王家生： 好，謝謝老師。

（第二天）

高老師： 張小妹怎麼樣了？

王家生： 她昨天去看了醫生。醫生说是流感。

高老師： 吃藥了嗎？

王家生： 醫生開了些感冒藥、還有消炎和退燒的藥。她現在燒已經退了，就是還咳嗽、頭疼。

高老師： 得了流感一般都要一個星期才能好。告訴她要好好兒休息，多喝水，多吃水果和清淡的食物。

王家生： 我和同學們會好好兒照顧她，您放心。

Lesson 9, Dialogue 2

醫生： 哪兒不舒服？

格林： 大夫，我肚子疼得厲害，拉肚子，今天早上上吐下瀉。哎喲，哎喲……

醫生： 讓我來檢查一下。這裏疼嗎？

（醫生檢查格林的肚子。）

格林： 不疼。

醫生： 這兒呢？你昨天有沒有吃什麼不好的食物？

格林： 昨天夜裏睡覺前我餓了，吃了些冰箱裏的剩菜。

醫生： 那一定是菜壞了。你還要去化驗血和大便。

（過了大約半個小時。）

醫生： 化驗結果來了，你得了急性腸炎。我給你開點兒藥。這種藥一天吃三次，一次一片。要是過三天不好，你再來。

格林： 謝謝大夫，再見。

Lesson 9, Reading

　　在中國，很多大學都有醫院。要是學生和教師生了病，可以直接去看，不用預約。看病比較方便，先掛號，然後在候診區等着叫號。輪到了你，就可以進醫生診室看病，看完病去藥房取藥。學校醫院都是門診，只看一般的病，得了大病或者要住院得去校外的大醫院。得了急病要去醫院的急診室看病。

Lesson 10, Dialogue 1

王家生：啊，出太陽了，太好了。

張小妹：天氣預報說今天晴，真的出太陽了，真准。

王家生：准什麼呀？前天天氣預報也說是晴天，可是我踢足球的時候天變陰了，又是刮風，又是下雨，還打雷閃電，害得我淋成了落湯雞。

張小妹：那是陣雨。一片烏雲過了，天就好了。

王家生：反正天氣預報沒說有陣雨，我被淋濕了。

張小妹：好了。這個週末天氣怎麼樣？

王家生：星期六早上有霧，上午會轉晴。

張小妹：那我們去頤和園玩兒，怎麼樣？

王家生：太好了，我給你帶把太陽傘。

張小妹：我們9點半在宿舍樓前面見。

王家生：好，不見不散。

Lesson 10, Dialogue 2

黃方： 格林，你是哪裏人？

格林： 我是波士頓人。波士頓在新英格蘭地區，四季分明，非常美麗。

黃方： 聽說波士頓冬天很冷，雪很多．

格林： 對，冬天常常下雪，溫度一般是二三十度。

黃方： 你說的是華氏，那也就是攝氏零下了。夏天呢？一定比較涼快。

格林： 對，夏天白天熱，但早晚涼。春天和秋天不冷不熱，非常舒服。你是南京人吧？你們那兒氣候怎麼樣？

黃方： 我們那兒冬天不太冷，但夏天比較熱。過去人們常說南京象個火爐。

格林： 真的那麼可怕嗎？

黃方： 其實也不是，夏天溫度跟北京差不多。六月有兩三個星期的黃梅雨季，差不多天天下雨，因為潮濕，人覺得很不舒服。不過南京的氣候一般說來還是不錯的。

Lesson 10, Reading

　　現在人們都很注意天氣。每天電視、廣播、報紙和互聯网都有天氣預報，還有專門的天气預報電視頻道和网站。你可以知道當天的天氣怎麼樣，是陰天還是晴天、刮風還是多雲等。天氣預報除了報當天的天氣以外，還預報兩三天的天氣，有的電視台還報五天或者一個星期的天氣，甚至有的网站還報半個月的天氣，但一般不如近期的准。

总词汇表 GLOSSARY

A

Pinyin	Traditional	Simplified	Part of Speech	English	Lesson
a	啊	啊	Par	(a tone softener)	2
a	啊	啊	Int	ah, oh	10
āi	哎	哎	Int	hey!; look out!	5
āiyōu	哎哟	哎哟	Int	hey; ouch; ow	9
ānquán	安全	安全	Adj	safe; secure	8
ānxīn	安心	安心	VO	feel at ease; be relieved; set one's mind at rest	9
àn	按	按	V	press; push down	8

B

Pinyin	Traditional	Simplified	Part of Speech	English	Lesson
ba	吧	吧	Par	(here, a particle used for making suggestions)	1
bā	吧	吧	N	bar	3
bǎ	把	把	M	measure word for umbrella	10
bàba	爸爸	爸爸	N	papa; dad; father	2
báitiān	白天	白天	N	daytime; day	10
bàn	半	半	Adj	half; semi-	5
bàn	辦	办	V	do; handle; manage; attend to	8
bànfǎ	辦法	办法	N	way; means; measure	6
bànlǐ	辦理	办理	V	handle; conduct; transact	8
bāng	幫	帮	V	help; assist	9
bāngzhù	幫助	帮助	V	help; assist	2
bàng	棒	棒	Adj	(colloquial) good; excellent; awesome	3
bāo	包	包	V/N	wrap; bundle; bag	8
bāoguǒ	包裹	包裹	N	package; bundle; wrap up; bind up	8
bǎohù	保護	保护	V	protect; safeguard	8
bào	報	报	V	report; announce; declare	10
bàozhǐ	報紙	报纸	N	newspaper; newsprint	10
bēizi	杯子	杯子	N	cup; glass	5
běi	北	北	N	north	3
Běijīng	北京	北京	PN	Beijing (formerly called "Peking")	2

bítì	鼻涕	鼻涕	N	nasal mucus	9
bǐ	比	比	Prep	compare; contrast; than	5
bǐjiào	比較	比较	Ad	fairly; comparatively; quite; compare	4
Bǐdé	彼德	彼德	PN	Peter (a name)	7
bì	幣	币	N	money, currency	6
biàn	變	变	V	change; become different; become	10
biǎo	表	表	N	table; form; list; meter; watch	8
biéde	別的	别的	Adj	other; another	5
bīngxiāng	冰箱	冰箱	N	refrigerator; freezer	9
bìng	病	病	N	ill; sick; disease	9
Bōshìdùn	波士頓	波士顿	PN	Boston	6
bǔ	補	补	V	mend; patch; repair; make up for	9
bù	不	不	Ad	no; not	2
bùcuò	不錯	不错	Ad	not bad; pretty good; correct; right	6
bùjiànbùsàn	不見不散	不见不散	CE	(If we) do not see (each other), (we) should not leave.	3
bùrú	不如	不如	Conj	not equal to; not as good as; inferior to; it would be better to	10

C

Pinyin	Traditional	Simplified	Part of Speech	English	Lesson
cái	才	才	Ad	just	1
cài	菜	菜	N	vegetable; food; dish	9
cānjīnzhǐ	餐巾紙	餐巾纸	N	napkin	5
cāntīng	餐廳	餐厅	N	dining room; restaurant, dining hall	1
chā	叉	叉	N	fork	5
chá	查	查	V	check; examine; look into; investigate	7
chàbùduō	差不多	差不多	Adj	almost; nearly; about the same; similar	6
cháng	長	长	Adj	long	6
chángtú	長途	长途	Adj	long-distance	6
cháng	常	常	Ad	frequently; often; usually	6
chángyán	腸炎	肠炎	N	enteritis; intestinal inflammation	9
chāo(jí)shì (cháng)	超(級)市(場)	超(级)市(场)	N	supermarket	5
chāoxiě	抄寫	抄写	V	copy; transcribe.	4
cháoshī	潮濕	潮湿	Adj	moist; damp	10
chē	車	车	N	vehicle; car	5
chéng	成	成	V	accomplish; succeed; become	7
chéngshì	城市	城市	N	city; town	6

chéng	乘	乘	V	ride; multiply	6
chīfàn	吃飯	吃饭	VO	eat; have a meal	1
chū	出	出	V	go out; come out	3
chūchāi	出差	出差	V	be away on official business; be on a business trip	1
chūzū	出租	出租	V	rent, lease (out)	6
chūzūqìchē	出租汽車	出租汽车	N	taxi	6
chúle…yǐwài	除了…以外	除了…以外	Conj	except; besides; in addition to	5
chūntiān	春天	春天	N	spring; springtime	10
cì	次	次	M	(a measure word used for action, time(s))	6
cóng	從	从	Prep	from; through	2
cún	存	存	V	deposit	8
cúnqián	存錢	存钱	VO	deposit money	8
cúnzhé	存摺	存折	N	deposit book; bankbook	8

D

Pinyin	Traditional	Simplified	Part of Speech	English	Lesson
dǎ	打	打	V	play; strike; hit; break	3
dǎdí	打的	打的	V	take a taxi; take a cab	6
(dǎ)léi	(打)雷	(打)雷	V	thunder	10
dǎzhé	打折	打折	V	sell at a discount; give a discount	5
dà	大	大	Adj	big; large; great	2
dàbā	大巴	大巴	N	bus	6
dàbiàn	大便	大便	N	defecate; have a bowel movement; stool	9
Dàhuá Diànyǐngyuàn	大華電影院	大华电影院	PN	Dahua Movie Theater	3
dàpiānr	大片兒	大片儿	CE	well-known movie (especially referring to American movies)	3
dàxué	大學	大学	N	university	2
dàyuē	大約	大约	Ad	approximately; about; probably	9
Dàzhōngyāng Chēzhàn	大中央車站	大中央车站	PN	Grand Central Station (in New York)	6
dài	代	代	N	generation; era	2
dài	帶	带	V	take; bring; carry; belt; ribbon; tape	5
dài	袋	袋	N	bag; sack; pocket	5
dàifu	大夫	大夫	N	doctor	9
dān	單	单	N	sheet; bill; list	8
dānshù	單數	单数	N	single number	4
dàn	但	但	Conj	but; yet; still; nevertheless	6
dāngrán	當然	当然	Ad	certainly; of course; to be sure	6

dāngtiān	當天	当天	N	the same day; that very day	7
dāo	刀	刀	N	knife; sword	5
dào	到	到	V	arrive; reach	3
dàoqī	到期	到期	V	become due; mature; expire	7
de	的	的	Par	(a structural particle, used before noun)	1
de	得	得	Par	(a structural particle, used after verb)	2
de	地	地	Par	(a structural particle, used before verb)	6
débìng	得病	得病	VO	become sick	9
dēng	燈	灯	N	lamp; lantern; light	3
dēngjì	登記	登记	V	register; check in; enter one's name	8
děng	等	等	V	wait; await; when; till	4
děng	等	等	Par	and so on; and so forth; etc.	8
dì	地	地	N	ground, land	6
dìqū	地區	地区	N	area; district; region	10
dìtiě	地鐵	地铁	N	subway = 地下鐵路	6
dì-èr	第二	第二	Num	second	3
dì-sān	第三	第三	Num	third	2
diǎn	點	点	N	drop (of liquid); spot; dot; point; o'clock	3
diànhuà	電話	电话	N	telephone; phone; phone call	7
diànnǎo	電腦	电脑	N	computer	2
diànshì	電視	电视	N	television; TV	10
diànyǐng	電影	电影	N	film; movie; motion picture	3
diànyǐng yuàn	電影院	电影院	N	cinema; movie theatre	3
dìng	訂	订	V	subscribe to (a newspaper, etc.); book (seats, tickets, etc.); order (merchandise, etc.)	7
dōngtiān	冬天	冬天	N	winter	10
dōngxi	東西	东西	N	thing; creature	5
dǒng	懂	懂	N	understand; know	4
dōu	都	都	Ad	all; both	2
dù	度	度	M	degree; a unit of measurement for angles, temperature, etc.	10
dùzi	肚子	肚子	N	belly; abdomen; stomach	9
duì	對	对	Adj	right	4
duìbùqǐ	對不起	对不起	CE	I'm sorry; sorry, excuse me; I beg your pardon	3
duìfāng	對方	对方	N	the other (or opposite) side; the other party	8
duō	多	多	Adj	many; much	4
duō	多	多	Adj/Ad	many; much; more; far more	7
duōshǎo	多少	多少	QW	how much, how many	5
duōyún	多雲	多云	Adj	cloudy	10

E

Pinyin	Traditional	Simplified	Part of Speech	English	Lesson
è	餓	饿	Adj	hungry; starve	9

F

Pinyin	Traditional	Simplified	Part of Speech	English	Lesson
fā	發	发	V	send out; issue; deliver; distribute; express	4
fāshāo	發燒	发烧	V	have (or run) a fever; have (or run) a temperature	9
fájīn	罰金	罚金	N	fine; forfeit	7
fǎnzhèng	反正	反正	Ad	anyway; anyhow; in any case	10
fàn	飯	饭	N	cooked rice or other cereals; meal	1
fāngbiàn	方便	方便	Adj	convenient	6
fāngfǎ	方法	方法	N	method; way; means	4
fàng	放	放	V	let go; set free; put	8
fàngxīn	放心	放心	V	set one's mind at rest; be at ease; rest assured; feel relieved	9
fēicháng	非常	非常	Ad	extraordinary; unusual; special; very; extremely	10
fēijī	飛機	飞机	N	aircraft; airplane; plane	7
fēixíng	飛行	飞行	V	flight; flying	7
féizào	肥皂	肥皂	N	soap	5
fēn	分	分	M	(a measure word used for a unit of money; point; mark)	5
fēnmíng	分明	分明	Adj	clearly demarcated; sharply contoured; distinct; clear	10
fèn	份	份	M	share; portion	8
fēng	風	风	N	wind	10
fù	付	付	V	pay	5

G

Pinyin	Traditional	Simplified	Part of Speech	English	Lesson
gǎi	改	改	V	change; transform; alter; revise; correct	7
Gǎn'ēn Jié	感恩節	感恩节	PN	Thanksgiving	7
gǎnmào	感冒	感冒	V	common cold	9
gāngcái	剛才	刚才	Ad	just now; a moment ago	4
gāo	高	高	Adj	tall; high; of a high level or degree	4

gàosu	告訴	告诉	V	tell	1
gēge	哥哥	哥哥	N	(elder) brother	2
Gélín	格林	格林	PN	Green (a name)	1
gè	個	个	M	(a measure word used for counting objects, people, etc.)	1
gěi	給	给	Prep	for, to	1
gěi	給	给	Prep/V	to; for; give; grant	7
gēn	跟	跟	Conj/Prep	and; with; follow	2
gōnggòng	公共	公共	Adj	public; common; communal	3
gōnggòng qìchē	公共汽車	公共汽车	N	bus	3
gōngsī	公司	公司	N	company; corporation	7
gōngzuò	工作	工作	V/N	work; job	2
gòu	夠	够	Ad	enough; sufficient; adequate	5
guā	刮	刮	V	blow; scrape	10
guàhào	掛號	挂号	V	register (at hospital, etc.); send by registered mail	8
guǎi	拐	拐	V	turn	3
guǎn	館	馆	N	a place of accommodation for guests; a shop (often used in compound words)	2
guǎngbō	廣播	广播	N	broadcast; be on the air	10
Guǎngdōng	廣東	广东	PN	Guangdong Province (formerly called "Canton")	2
Guǎngzhōu	廣州	广州	PN	Guangzhou	6
guì	貴	贵	Adj	expensive; costly; noble	5
guìtái	櫃台	柜台	N	counter	8
guìxìng	(您)貴姓	(您)贵姓	CE	What is your honorable surname?	1
guójì	國際	国际	N	international	7
guò	過	过	V/Par	spend (time); celebrate a special occasion; an aspectual particle	7
guò	過	过	V	pass; beyond the limit	10
guòqù	過去	过去	TW	in the past; formerly	10

H

Pinyin	Traditional	Simplified	Part of Speech	English	Lesson
hái	還	还	Ad	still; yet; too; as well; in addition	4
háishì	還是	还是	Ad	still; nevertheless; all the same; had better; or	6
hǎiyùn	海運	海运	N	sea transportation; ocean shipping; by sea	8
hàide	害得	害得	V	cause; make (something unwelcome happen)	10
hánjià	寒假	寒假	N	winter vacation	7
hànzì	漢字	汉字	N	Chinese character	4

hángbān	航班	航班	N	scheduled flight; flight number	7
hángkōng	航空	航空	N	aviation	7
hǎo	好	好	Adj	good; fine; well	1
háojiǔbújiàn	好久不見	好久不见	CE	long time no see	1
hǎoxiàng	好像	好像	V/Ad	seem; be like	4
hào	號	号	N	sign; number; size; date	6
hàomǎ	號碼	号码	N	number	7
hē	喝	喝	V	drink; drink liquor	3
hé	和	和	Conj	and	2
hé	盒	盒	N	box, case	8
héshì	合適	合适	Adj	suitable; appropriate	5
hēi	嘿	嘿	Int	hey	3
hēi	黑	黑	Adj	black; dark	5
hěn	很	很	Ad	very	1
hóng	紅	红	Adj	red	3
hónglǜ dēng	紅綠燈	红绿灯	N	traffic light; traffic signal	3
hòu	後	后	Adj	back; behind; rear; after; afterwards	6
hòuzhěn	候診	候诊	V	wait to see the doctor	9
hòuzhěnqū	候診區	候诊区	N	waiting area	9
hùliánwǎng	互聯網	互联网	N	Internet; (also called 因特網 yīntèwǎng)	10
hùxiāng	互相	互相	Ad	mutual; each other	2
hùzhào	護照	护照	N	passport	8
huā	花	花	V	spend; expend	8
Huáshì	華氏	华氏	PN	Fahrenheit (temperature scale)	10
huáyì	華裔	华裔	N	foreign citizen of Chinese origin	2
huàyàn	化驗	化验	V	laboratory test	9
huài	壞	坏	Adj	bad; go bad; spoil; ruin	8
huānyíng	歡迎	欢迎	V	welcome	1
huàn	換	换	V	exchange; return; trade; change	5
huáng	黃	黄	Adj	yellow	5
Huángméiyǔ Jì	黃梅雨季	黄梅雨季	PN	the rainy season, usually in April, May or June, in the middle and lower reaches of the Changjiang River, China	10
huí	回	回	V	return; go back; turn around; answer; reply	7
huílái	回來	回来	V	return; come back	1
huízhí	回執	回执	N	a short note acknowledging receipt of something; receipt	8
huì	會	会	AV	be able to, can, know (how to)	4
huìhuà	會話	会话	N	conversation	4
huìyuán	會員	会员	N	member	7
huìyuánzhèng	會員證	会员证	N	membership card	7

huǒlú	火爐	火炉	N	(heating) stove	10
huò	貨	货	N	goods, commodity	5
huòzhě	或者	或者	Ad/Conj	or; either...or....	9

J

Pinyin	Traditional	Simplified	Part of Speech	English	Lesson
jīlěi	積累	积累	V	accumulate	7
jīchǎng	機場	机场	N	airport; airfield	6
jīqì	機器	机器	N	machine; machinery; apparatus	8
jí	急	急	Adj	impatient; anxious; worry;urgent; pressing	8
jíbìng	急病	急病	N	acute disease	9
jíxìng	急性	急性	Adj	acute	9
jízhěn	急診	急诊	N	emergency; emergency treatment	9
jízhěnshì	急診室	急诊室	N	emergency room	9
jǐ	幾	几	QW	how many; a few; several; some	3
jì	寄	寄	V	send; post; mail	8
jì	季	季	N	season	10
jìde	記得	记得	V	remember	7
jì	記	记	V	remember; bear in mind	7
jiā	家	家	N/M	family; home; (a measure word for stores and businesses)	2
jiālún	加侖	加仑	M	(a measure word used for gallon)	5
jiǎnchá	檢查	检查	V	check up; inspect; examine	9
jiǎnjià	減價	减价	V	mark down; reduce the price.	5
jiàn	見	见	V	see; catch sight of	1
jiàn	件	件	M	(a measure word used for for clothing)	5
jiāo	教	教	V	teach; instruct	2
jiào	叫	叫	V	call; to be named	1
jiàoshī	教師	教师	N	teacher	9
jiàoshòu	教授	教授	N	professor	2
jiéguǒ	結果	结果	N	result; outcome	9
jiècí	介詞	介词	N	preposition	4
jìnqī	近期	近期	N	in the near future	10
jìnqù	進去	进去	V	go in; get in; enter	8
jiǔ	酒	酒	N	alcoholic drink; wine; liquor; spirits	3
jiǔbā	酒吧	酒吧	N	bar	3
jiù	就	就	Ad	right away; already; as soon as; only; merely; exactly; precisely	4
Jiùjīnshān	舊金山	旧金山	PN	San Francisco	7
jiùshì	就是	就是	CE	that is...	2

jùlèbù	俱樂部	俱乐部	N	club	7
jù	句	句	N	sentence	4
jùjué	拒絕	拒绝	V	refuse; reject; turn down; decline	3
juéde	覺得	觉得	V	feel; think	4
juédìng	決定	决定	V	decide; make up one's mind; decision; resolution	6

K

Pinyin	Traditional	Simplified	Part of Speech	English	Lesson
kǎ	卡	卡	N	card	8
kāi	開	开	V	open; open up; run; drive	2
kāi	開	开	V	write out (a prescription); open	9
kāishǐ	開始	开始	V/N	begin; start; initial stage; beginning	4
kàn	看	看	V	see; look at; watch; read	3
kànbìng	看病	看病	VO	(of a doctor) see a patient; (of a patient) see (or consult) a doctor	9
kànjian	看見	看见	V	see	1
késou	咳嗽	咳嗽	V	cough	9
Kělè	可樂	可乐	N	cola	5
kěpà	可怕	可怕	Adj	fearful; frightful; terrible; terrifying	10
kěshì	可是	可是	Conj	but; yet; however	2
kěyǐ	可以	可以	AV	can; may	2
kè	課	课	N	class, lesson	1
kèqi	客氣	客气	Adj	polite; courteous; modest	4
Kěnnídí Jīchǎng	肯尼迪機場	肯尼迪机场	PN	John F. Kennedy (JFK) Airport (in New York)	6
kōngtiáo	空調	空调	N	air-conditioning, AC	6
kōngzhōng	空中	空中	N	in the sky; in the air	7
kǒu	口	口	M	(a measure word for people)	2
kǒu	口	口	N	mouth; opening; entrance	3
kuài	快	快	Ad	fast; quick; hurry up	1
kuài	塊	块	M	(a measure word used for a piece; lump; chunk; yuan)	5
kuàijì	會計	会计	N	accounting; bookkeeper; accountant	2
kuàijiàn	快件	快件	N	express mail; priority mail	8
kuǎn	款	款	N	a sum of money; fund	7
kuòjiàn	擴建	扩建	V	to expand; extend (a factory, mine, or other large infastructure)	6

L

Pinyin	Traditional	Simplified	Part of Speech	English	Lesson
la	啦	啦	Par	(a tone softener)	2
lādùzi	拉肚子	拉肚子	V	suffer from diarrhea; have loose bowels	9
lái	來	来	V	come	1
lán	藍	蓝	Adj	blue	5
lǎojiā	老家	老家	N	native place; old home	2
lǎoshī	老師	老师	N	teacher	1
lǎowài	老外	老外	CE	(used in Mainland China) refers to foreigners	4
lǎoxiāng	老鄉	老乡	N	person from the same hometown; fellow villager	2
le	了	了	Par	(an aspectual particle)	1
lèi	累	累	Adj	tired; fatigued; weary	3
lěng	冷	冷	Adj	cold	10
lǐchéng	里程	里程	N	mileage	7
lìhài	屬害	厉害	Adj	severe; sharp; terrible	9
liàn	練	练	V	practice; train; drill	4
liànxí	練習	练习	V	practise; exercise	4
liángkuài	涼快	凉快	Adj	nice and cool; pleasantly cool	10
lín	淋	淋	V	pour; drench	10
líng	零	零	Num	zero; nought; -odd	10
língqián	零錢	零钱	N	small change; pocket money	6
lìng	另	另	Adj	other; another	7
lìngwài	另外	另外	Ad	in addition to; moreover; besides	6
liú	流	流	V	flow; move from place to place; drift	9
liúgǎn	流感	流感	N	flu	9
liúlì	流利	流利	Adj	fluent; smooth	2
liúxuéshēng	留學生	留学生	N	foreign student	1
lóu	樓	楼	N	building	10
lù	路	路	M	road; route	3
lùkǒu	路口	路口	N	crossing; intersection	3
lǚxíng	旅行	旅行	N/V	travel; journey; tour; to travel	7
lǚxíngshè	旅行社	旅行社	N	travel agency	7
lǜ	綠	绿	Adj	green	3
luàn	亂	乱	Adj/N	in disorder; a mess; in confusion; disorder	6
lún	輪	轮	V	take turns	9
Luòshānjī	洛杉磯	洛杉矶	PN	Los Angeles	7
luòtāngjī	落湯雞	落汤鸡	CE	like a drenched chicken; soaked through; soaking wet	10

M

Pinyin	Traditional	Simplified	Part of Speech	English	Lesson
ma	嗎	吗	Par	(a particle used for making questions)	1
māma	媽媽	妈妈	N	mom; mother	2
máfan	麻煩	麻烦	Adj/V	troublesome; inconvenient; to trouble; trouble somebody; bother	6
mǎshàng	馬上	马上	Ad	at once; immediately; right away	7
mǎi	買	买	V	buy; purchase	5
màn	慢	慢	Adj	slow	8
máo	毛	毛	M	(a measure word used for a fractional unit of money)	5
máoyī	毛衣	毛衣	N	woollen sweater; sweater	5
méiguānxì	沒關系	没关系	CE	it doesn't matter; it's nothing; that's all right; never mind	7
méiyǒu	沒有	没有	Ad	not, not have	1
méi(yǒu) yìsī	沒(有)意思	没(有)意思	CE	not interesting	3
měi	每	每	Adj	every; each; per; often	4
Měidōng (shíjiān)	美東(時間)	美东(时间)	PN	American Eastern (Time)	7
Měiguó	美國	美国	PN	the United States of America	1
měilì	美麗	美丽	Adj	beautiful	10
měiyuán	美元	美元	N	American dollar; U.S. dollar	7
mèimei	妹妹	妹妹	N	younger sister; sister	2
men	們	们	Par	(a plural marker for pronouns and some animate nouns)	2
mén	門	门	N	entrance; door; gate; valve	3
ménzhěn	門診	门诊	N	outpatient service	9
mìmǎ	密碼	密码	N	secret code; password	8
miànbāo	麵包	面包	N	bread	5
míngtiān	明天	明天	TW	tomorrow	3
míngzi	名字	名字	N	(given or full) name	1

N

Pinyin	Traditional	Simplified	Part of Speech	English	Lesson
ná	拿	拿	V	hold; take; seize	5
nǎ	哪	哪	QW	which	4
nǎr	哪兒	哪儿	Pron	where	2
nǎli	哪裏	哪里	QW	where; (a polite response to decline a compliment)	4
nà/nèi	那	那	Pron	that; (a discourse connector)	2

nàme	那麼	那么	Conj	then; in that case; such being the case	7
nǎilào	奶酪	奶酪	N	cheese	5
nǎinai	奶奶	奶奶	N	grandmother; grandma; a respectful form of address for an elderly woman	2
nán	男	男	Adj	man; male	3
Nánjīng	南京	南京	PN	Nanjing	6
nán	難	难	Adj	difficult; hard	4
nánguài	難怪	难怪	Ad	no wonder; understandable; pardonable	4
ne	呢	呢	Par	(a question particle)	2
néng	能	能	AV	can; be able to; be capable of	9
nǐ	你	你	Pron	you	1
niánjí	年級	年级	N	grade; year	4
niánlíng	年齡	年龄	N	age	3
nín	您	您	Pron	you (polite)	1
niúnǎi	牛奶	牛奶	N	milk	5
Niǔyuē	紐約	纽约	PN	New York	2
Niǔyuē Dàxué	紐約大學	纽约大学	PN	New York University, NYU	2

O

Pinyin	Traditional	Simplified	Part of Speech	English	Lesson
ō	噢	噢	Int	Oh!	7
ò	哦	哦	Int.	(indicates realization or recollection)	1

P

Pinyin	Traditional	Simplified	Part of Speech	English	Lesson
pà	怕	怕	V	fear; dread; be afraid of; I'm afraid	8
pángbiān	旁邊	旁边	N	side; by; next to	3
pàomò	泡沫	泡沫	N	foam	8
pàomò sùliào	泡沫塑料	泡沫塑料	N	foam plastics	8
péi	陪	陪	V	accompany; keep somebody company	9
péngyǒu	朋友	朋友	N	friend	1
piányí	便宜	便宜	Adj	cheap	5
piào	票	票	N	ticket; ballot	6

pīān piàn	片	片	N/M	a flat, thin piece (here refers to a movie 電影片); (a measure word for a slice)	3
pīndào	頻道	频道	N	(of TV) frequency channel	10
pīnyīn	拼音	拼音	N	pinyin, combine sounds into syllables; spell	4
píng	憑	凭	Prep	depending on; go by; base on	8
píngxìn	平信	平信	N	ordinary mail	8
píng	瓶	瓶	N	bottle	5
píngshí	平時	平时	Ad	at ordinary times; in normal times; usually	6

Q

Pinyin	Traditional	Simplified	Part of Speech	English	Lesson
qíshí	其實	其实	Ad	actually; in fact; as a matter of fact	10
qǐmíngzi	起名字	起名字	VO	to give a name	1
qǐfēi	起飛	起飞	V	(of an aircraft) take off	7
qìhòu	氣候	气候	N	climate	10
qìchē	汽車	汽车	N	automobile; motor vehicle; car	3
qiān	千	千	Num	thousand	4
qiānzì	簽字	签字	VO	sign	8
qián	錢	钱	N	cash; money	5
qián	前	前	Adj	front; forward; ahead; before; preceding; former	6
qiántiān	前天	前天	TW	the day before yesterday	10
qīngdàn	清淡	清淡	Adj	light; weak; delicate; not greasy or strongly flavored	9
qíng	晴	晴	Adj	fine; clear	10
qíngtiān	晴天	晴天	N	fine day; sunny day	10
qǐng	請	请	V	please	1
qǐngjiào	請教	请教	V	ask for advice; consult	2
qiūtiān	秋天	秋天	N	autumn	10
qiú	球	球	N	ball; the globe; anything shaped like a ball	3
qū	區	区	N	area, district	9
qǔ	取	取	V	take; get; fetch	8
qù	去	去	V	go	1
qù	去	去	V	go	2
quē	缺	缺	V	be short of; lack be absent; vacancy; incomplete	9

R

Pinyin	Traditional	Simplified	Part of Speech	English	Lesson
ránhòu	然後	然后	Ad	then; after that; afterwards	6
ràng	讓	让	V	let; allow; make	9
rè	熱	热	Adj	heat; hot; heat up; warm up; popular	10
rén	人	人	N	human being; man; person; people	2
rènshí	認識	认识	V	know; understand; recognize	4
rìyòngpǐn	日用品	日用品	N	daily necessities	5
róngyì	容易	容易	Adj	easy; likely; liable	4
rúguǒ	如果	如果	Conj	if; in case; in the event of	7

S

Pinyin	Traditional	Simplified	Part of Speech	English	Lesson
sǎn	傘	伞	N	umbrella; something shaped like an umbrella	10
sàn	散	散	V	break up; disperse	3
shǎndiàn	閃電	闪电	V	lightning	10
shāngxuéyuàn	商學院	商学院	N	business school	2
shàng	上	上	Adj	upper; up; upward; superior; last (week)	5
shàngbān	上班	上班	V	go to work; start work	6
Shànghǎi	上海	上海	PN	Shanghai	6
shàngkè	上課	上课	V	attend class; go to class; give a lesson	1
shàngtù xiàxiè	上吐下瀉	上吐下泻	CE	vomit and diarrhea; suffer from vomiting and diarrhea	9
shàngwǔ	上午	上午	TW	morning	9
shàngxué	上學	上学	V	go to school; attend school	2
Shèshì	攝氏	摄氏	PN	Centigrade (temperature scale)	10
shéi	誰	谁	QW	who	1
shénme	什麼	什么	QW	what	1
shènzhì	甚至	甚至	Ad	even; (go) so far as to; so much so that	10
shēng	生	生	V	give birth to; be born	2
shēngbìng	生病	生病	VO	fall ill; get sick	9
shēngrì	生日	生日	N	birthday	3
shēngdiào	聲調	声调	N	tone; the tone of a Chinese character	4
shěng	省	省	V	save; omit	4
shèng	剩	剩	V	surplus; remnant; leave (over)	9
shèngcài	剩菜	剩菜	N	leftover food; leftovers	9

Shèngdàn Jié	聖誕節	圣诞节	N	Christmas	7
shī	濕	湿	Adj	wet; damp; humid	10
shí	十	十	Num	ten	3
shízì lùkǒu	十字路口	十字路口	N	four-way intersection	3
Shídài Guǎngchǎng	時代廣場	时代广场	PN	Times Square (in New York)	6
shíhòu	時候	时候	N	time; moment	4
shíjiān	時間	时间	N	time	4
shíwù	食物	食物	N	food; edible items	9
shǐyòng	使用	使用	V	make use of; use; employ; apply	8
shì	是	是	V	to be; yes	1
shì	試	试	V	try	4
shì	事	事	N	matter; affair; thing	8
shōudào	收到	收到	V	receive; get; achieve; obtain	8
shōujiànrén	收件人	收件人	N	addressee; consignee	8
shǒu	手	手	N	hand	4
shòu	售	售	V	sell	5
shòuhuòyuán	售貨員	售货员	N	cashier, shop assistant; salesclerk	5
shūfu	舒服	舒服	Adj	comfortable; well	9
shū	書	书	N	book	4
shūrù	輸入	输入	V	input; import	4
shùzì	數字	数字	N	numeral; figure; digit	6
shuǐ	水	水	N	water	9
shuǐguǒ	水果	水果	N	fruit	9
shuìjiào	睡覺	睡觉	V	sleep	3
shuō	說	说	V	speak; say	2
sīyíng	私營	私营	Adj	privately owned; privately operated; private	8
sìshēng	四聲	四声	N	the four tones	4
Sūshān	蘇珊	苏珊	PN	Susan (a name)	3
sùliào	塑料	塑料	N	plastics	8
sùshè	宿舍	宿舍	N	dorm	10
sùshèlóu	宿舍樓	宿舍楼	N	dormitory building	10
suànle	算了	算了	CE	let it be; let it pass; forget it	3
suǒyǐ	所以	所以	Conj	so; therefore; as a result	5

T

Pinyin	Traditional	Simplified	Part of Speech	English	Lesson
tā	他	他	Pron	he	1
tái	臺	台	N	broadcasting station	10
tài	太	太	Ad	excessively; too	3
tàiyáng	太陽	太阳	N	the sun; sunshine; sunlight	10
tǎolùn	討論	讨论	V	discuss	4

tèbié	特別	特别	Adj/Ad	special; particular; especially; particularly	4
tèkuài zhuāndì	特快專遞	特快专递	CE	Express Mail	8
téng	疼	疼	Adj/V	ache; pain; sore; love dearly	9
tī	踢	踢	V	kick; play (football)	10
tǐyùguǎn	體育館	体育馆	N	gym	3
tiānqì	天氣	天气	N	weather	10
tián	填	填	V	fill; stuff; write; fill in	8
tiàowǔ	跳舞	跳舞	V	dance	3
tīng	聽	听	V	listen	4
tīngqǐlái	聽起來	听起来	V	sound like	4
tīngshuō	聽說	听说	V	be told; it is said that...	6
tōng	通	通	V	open; through; get through	6
tóng	同	同	Prep/Adj	with; same	4
tóu	投	投	V	throw; cast; send	6
tóubìxiāng	投幣箱	投币箱	N	cash box; cash register	6
tóudì	投遞	投递	V	deliver	8
tuì	退	退	V	return; move back	5
tuìshāo	退燒	退烧	VO	bring down a fever	9

W

Pinyin	Traditional	Simplified	Part of Speech	English	Lesson
wā	哇	哇	Int	wow	5
wài	外	外	Adj	outside; foreign; external	4
wán	完	完	V	finish; complete	9
wánr	玩兒	玩儿	V	play; have fun; amuse oneself	3
wǎn	晚	晚	Adj/N	evening; night; late; later	7
wǎnhuì	晚會	晚会	N	an evening of entertainment; evening party	3
Wáng	王	王	PN	a surname	1
Wáng Jiāshēng	王家生	王家生	PN	Jiasheng Wang (a name)	3
Wáng Xiǎonián	王小年	王小年	PN	Xiaonian Wang (a name)	2
wǎng/wàng	往	往	Prep	in the direction of; toward	3
wǎngzhàn	網站	网站	N	web site	10
wèi	位	位	M	(a measure word for people)	1
wèi	喂	喂	Int	hello; hey	7
wēndù	溫度	温度	N	temperature	10
Wén Guóxīn	文國新	文国新	PN	Guoxin Wen (a name)	1
wèn	問	问	V	ask	1
wèntí	問題	问题	N	question; problem	4
wǒ	我	我	Pron	I; me	1
wūyún	烏雲	乌云	N	black clouds; dark clouds	10

Pinyin	Traditional	Simplified	Part of Speech	English	Lesson
wúrén	無人	无人	Adj	unmanned; self service	6
wù	霧	雾	N	fog; mist; fine spray	10

X

Pinyin	Traditional	Simplified	Part of Speech	English	Lesson
Xīběi Hángkōng Gōngsī	西北航空公司	西北航空公司	PN	Northwest Airlines	7
xīzhuāng	西裝	西裝	N	Western-style suit	5
xǐfàyè	洗髮液	洗发液	N	shampoo	5
xǐhuān	喜歡	喜欢	V	like; love; be fond of	3
xǐyīfěn	洗衣粉	洗衣粉	N	detergent	5
xià	下	下	V	get off; exit; below; down; under	3
xiàbān	下班	下班	V	to finish work; to get off work	6
xiàkè	下課	下课	V	get out of class; finish class	9
xiàwǔ	下午	下午	TW	afternoon	3
xiàyǔ	下雨	下雨	V	rain	9
xiàtiān	夏天	夏天	N	summer	10
Xiàwēiyí	夏威夷	夏威夷	PN	Hawaii	7
xiān	先	先	Ad	first; earlier; before	5
xiānsheng	先生	先生	N	mister (Mr.); gentleman; sir	7
xiànjīn	現金	现金	N	cash	5
xiànjīnjī	現金機	现金机	N	cash machine; ATM	8
xiànzài	現在	现在	N	now; at present	4
xiàn	線	线	N	route; line; thread; string; wire; clue	6
xiànlù	線路	线路	N	route; line	6
xiāng	箱	箱	N	box; case; trunk; anything in the shape of a box	6
xiǎng	想	想	V	think; miss	2
xiǎngjiā	想家	想家	VO	be homesick; miss home	2
xiàng	向	向	Prep	face; turn towards	4
xiāoyán	消炎	消炎	VO	diminish inflammation; counteract inflammation	9
xiǎo	小	小	Adj	small; little; young	1
xiǎojie	小姐	小姐	N	miss; young lady	5
xiǎoshí	小時	小时	N	hour	7
xiě	血	血	N	blood; related by blood	9
xiě	寫	写	V	write; compose	4
xiězuò	寫作	写作	N	writing	4
xièxiè	謝謝	谢谢	V	thanks; thank you	4
xīn	新	新	Adj	new	1
Xīn Yīnggélán	新英格蘭	新英格兰	PN	New England	10

xìnfēng	信封	信封	N	envelope	8
xìnjiàn	信件	信件	N	letters; mail	8
xìnyòngkǎ	信用卡	信用卡	N	credit card	5
xīngqī	星期	星期	N	week; Sunday	5
xíng	行	行	V	go; travel; all right; O.K.	7
xìng	姓	姓	V/N	surname; family name	1
xiōngdì jiěmèi	兄弟姐妹	兄弟姐妹	N	brothers and sisters	2
xiūjiàn	修建	修建	V	build; construct; erect	6
xiūxi	休息	休息	V	have (or take) a rest; rest	9
xūyào	需要	需要	V	need; want; require; needs	7
xué	學	学	V/N	study; subject of study	2
xuésheng	學生	学生	N	student	1
xuéxí	學習	学习	V	study	2
xuéxiào	學校	学校	N	school; educational institution	2
xuě	雪	雪	N	snow	10

Y

Pinyin	Traditional	Simplified	Part of Speech	English	Lesson
yā	壓	压	V	press; push down; hold down; weigh down	8
yā	呀	呀	Par	(particle indicating surprise, admiration or query)	10
yánsè	顏色	颜色	N	color; countenance; facial expression.	5
yǎnlèi	眼淚	眼泪	N	tears	9
yào	要	要	AV	must; should; will; be going to	1
yào	藥	药	N	medicine; drug	9
yàofáng	藥房	药房	N	drugstore; pharmacy	9
yéye	爺爺	爷爷	N	grandfather	2
yě	也	也	Ad	also	2
yèlǐ	夜裏	夜里	TW	at night	9
yī	衣	衣	N	clothes; clothing	5
yīfu	衣服	衣服	N	clothing; clothes	5
yīdìng	一定	一定	Ad	definitely; certainly; surely; necessarily	9
yībān	一般	一般	Adj	general; ordinary; common	8
yīdiǎnr	一點兒	一点儿	CE	a bit; a little	4
yīgòng	一共	一共	Ad	altogether; in all	7
yīhuìr	一會兒	一会儿	CE	a little while; in a moment	1
yīqǐ	一起	一起	Ad	together; in company	3
yīxiē	一些	一些	M	(a measure word used for some; a few; a little)	5
yīyàng	一樣	一样	Adj	the same; equally; alike; as...as....	6

yīshēng	醫生	医生	N	doctor	2
yīyuàn	醫院	医院	N	hospital	9
yí	咦	咦	Int	well; why.	8
Yíhéyuán	頤和園	颐和园	PN	the Summer Palace (in Beijing)	10
yímín	移民	移民	N	emigrant; immigrant	2
yǐjīng	已經	已经	Ad	already	7
yǐqián	以前	以前	TW	before; formerly; previously	4
yìsī	意思	意思	N	meaning, idea	4
yīn	音	音	N	sound	4
yīn	陰	阴	Adj	overcast; shade	10
yīnwèi	因為	因为	Conj	because; for	7
yínháng	銀行	银行	N	bank	8
Yīngwén	英文	英文	N	English (language)	2
yìng	硬	硬	Adj	hard; stiff; tough; firm	6
yòng	用	用	V	use; employ; apply	4
yōuxiān	優先	优先	Adj	have priority; take precedence	8
yóudì	郵遞	邮递	V	send by post (or mail); postal (or mail) delivery	8
yóujì	郵寄	邮寄	N	send by post; post; mail	8
yóujiàn	郵件	邮件	N	postal matter; post; mail	8
yóujú	郵局	邮局	N	post office	8
yóupiào	郵票	邮票	N	postage stamp; stamp	8
yǒu	有	有	V	have	1
yǒu yìsī	有意思	有意思	CE	interesting	3
yòu… yòu	又…又	又…又	Conj	both...and...	6
yǔ	雨	雨	N	rain	10
yǔfǎ	語法	语法	N	grammar	4
yǔyīn	語音	语音	N	speech sounds; pronunciation	4
yùbào	預報	预报	N	forecast	10
yùyuē	預約	预约	V	make an appointment	9
yuánlái	原來	原来	Adj	original; former	3
yuán	員	员	N	a person engaged in some field of activity	5
yuǎn	遠	远	Adj	far; distant; remote	7
Yuēhàn	約翰	约翰	PN	John (a name)	3
yuèdú	閱讀	阅读	N	reading	4
yùndòng	運動	运动	N	sports	5
yùndòngyī	運動衣	运动衣	N	sports wear	5

Z

Pinyin	Traditional	Simplified	Part of Speech	English	Lesson
zài	在	在	Prep	at	2
zài	再	再	Ad	another time; again; once more	6
zàijiàn	再見	再见	CE	goodbye	1
zàishuō	再說	再说	Conj	what's more; besides	7
zǎoshang	早上	早上	N	(early) morning	7
zěnme	怎麼	怎么	Ad	how; why	2
zěnmeyàng	怎麼樣	怎么样	CE	how about	3
zhàn	站	站	N	stand; (bus or train) stop; station	3
Zhāng Xiǎomèi	張小妹	张小妹	PN	Xiaomei Zhang (a name)	3
Zhāng Xuéwén	張學文	张学文	PN	Xuewen Zhang (a name)	1
zhǎng	長	长	V	grow	2
zhànghào	賬號	账号	N	account number	8
zhǎo	找	找	V	look for; try to find; seek; want to see; give change	5
zhàogù	照顧	照顾	V	look after; care for; attend to; show consideration for	9
zhàopiàn	照片	照片	N	photograph; picture	8
zhe	著	着	Par	(a particle indicating an action in progress)	9
zhé	摺	折	N	booklet	8
zhè/zhèi	這	这	Pron	this	1
zhème	這麼	这么	Pron	so	4
zhèyàng	這樣	这样	Pron	so; such; like this; this way	7
zhēn	真	真	Ad	true; real; genuine; really	3
zhēnde	真的	真的	Ad	really	7
zhěnshì	診室	诊室	N	(doctor's) consulting room	9
zhènyǔ	陣雨	阵雨	N	rain shower	10
zhèng	證	证	N	(ID) card; certificate	7
zhèng jiàn	證件	证件	N	credentials; papers; certificate;ID	8
zhèngzài	正在	正在	Ad	(used to indicate an action in progress) in the process of; be doing	6
Zhījiāgē	芝加哥	芝加哥	PN	Chicago	7
zhīdào	知道	知道	V	know; realize; be aware of	6
zhíjiē	直接	直接	Adj	direct; immediate	9
zhíyuán	職員	职员	N	office worker; staff member	7
zhǐ	只	只	Ad	only; merely	5
zhǐhǎo	只好	只好	Ad	have to	7
zhǐshì	只是	只是	Ad	merely; only; just; simply; however; but then	6
zhǐ	紙	纸	N	paper	8
zhǐhé	紙盒	纸盒	N	cardboard box	8

zhǐjīn	紙巾	纸巾	N	tissue, napkin	5
Zhōngguó	中國	中国	PN	China	1
Zhōngwén	中文	中文	N	the Chinese language	1
zhōngxué	中學	中学	N	middle school	2
zhōngdiǎn	终点	终点	N	terminal point; destination; finish	6
zhǒng	種	种	M	(a measure word used for kind; sort; type)	5
zhǒnglèi	種類	种类	N	kind; type; variety	8
zhòngyào	重要	重要	Adj	important; significant; major	8
zhōumò	週末	周末	N	weekend	10
zhùyì	注意	注意	V	pay attention to; take note (or notice) of	10
zhù	住	住	V	live	9
zhùyuàn	住院	住院	VO	be hospitalized	9
zhuānmén	專門	专门	Adj	special; specialized	10
zhuǎn	轉	转	V	turn; transfer	7
zhǔn	准	准	V/Adj	accurate; exact; allow; permit; standard	4
zì	字	字	N	word; character	3
zìmǔ	字母	字母	N	letters of an alphabet; alphabet	6
zǒng	總	总	Adj	general; overall; total;chief	6
zǒu	走	走	V	walk; go, leave	4
zúqiú	足球	足球	N	soccer; football	10
zǔ	組	组	N	group; set; series	4
zuì	最	最	Ad	most, -est	4
zuǒ	左	左	N	left, the left side; the left	3
zuò	做	做	V	do; make	2
zuò	坐	坐	N	sit; travel by (a car, plane, vehicle, etc.)	3
zuòyè	作業	作业	N	school assignment; homework	4

语言应用注释目录 List of Notes on Language Usage

Note: Items marked with an asterisk are those that students are required to master.

Lesson 1

1. 老师
2. 请问您贵姓
3. 什么
4. 了 (as a particle indicating completion of action)
5. 没有
6. 吗
7. 你吃饭了吗？(as a greeting)
8. 吧
*9. 你好吗？(吗 question)
10. 小文
*11. 这个名字很好。(adjectives used as verbs)

Lesson 2

1. 啊
*2. 得 + adjective (the complement of degree)
3. 华裔
4. 哪儿
*5. 是……的
*6. 都 (all, both)
7. 那 (as a discourse connector meaning "then")
*8. 们
9. 呢
*10. 不
*11. 不都

Lesson 3

1. 美国大片
2. 路
*3. 怎么样？ (tag questions)
4. 不见不散
5. 那 (as a discourse connector meaning "then")

Lesson 6

*1. 要看

*2. 是……还是

*3. 又……又

 3. 大巴 (bus)

 4. 说说 (reduplication of a verb)

 5. 只是

 6. 了 in 贵了 (indicating excess)

 7. 点儿

*8. 左右

 9. 也 in 那也太贵了。

10. 多了 in 漂亮多了。

11. 另外

12. 通 in 我们学校不通地铁。

13. 公共汽车上

14. 还好

*15. 差不多

*16. 有的有，有的没有。

17. 比

18. 打的

19. 不找零

20. 无人售票车

Lesson 7

*1. 先……再……

 2. 五、六个

 3. 过 (to indicate past experience)

*4. 怎么那么

*5. 过 (verb)

*6. 多 (adverb)

 7. 真的？

 8. 哪……哪 (question word…question word…) in 你坐哪家的我就坐哪家的。

 9. 行

10. 记得

11. 晚

12. 喂

13. 我可以帮助您吗，先生？

14. 噢

14. 找到 (resultative complement)

*15. 只好

16. 积累飞行里程。

*17. 得 (děi, as an auxiliary verb)

18. 把

Lesson 8

1. 你有事吗？

2. 个 (a measure word without a number before it)

3. 那好

*4. 好是好，就是/可是 (Adj. + 是 + Adj., 就是/可是……)

5. 还 (as well, in addition)

6. 什么样的

*7. 只要

8. 就 (an emphatic expression)

*9. 把

10. 咦

11. 嗯

*12. 原来

*13. 每份信件邮局都要登记 (topic-comment sentence)

14. 而

Lesson 9

*1. Change of status or new situation with 了

2. 能

3. 会儿

*4. 了 indicating future action

5. 我陪她去学校医院看看 (pivotal sentence)

6. 看医生

7. 开 (write a prescription)

*8. 就是 (only)

*9. 来 (come and do)

*10. 一下

*11. 有没有 (A-not-A question)

*12. 什么 as a general referral

*13 一天吃三次 (complement of frequency)

*14. 不用

15. 着

*16. 或者

Lesson 10

1. 啊

2. 出太阳了

*3. 准什么呀？(rhetorical question)

*4. 害得

5. 淋成了落汤鸡

6. 反正

*7. 被 (passive voice)

8. 好了

9. 哪里人？

10. 二、三十度

11. 那也就是摄氏零下了。(the Centigrade temperature scale)

*12. 比较 in 一定比较凉快。

*13. 吧 in 你是南京人吧？

*14. 是……还是……

15. 不如

ABOUT THE AUTHORS

Dr. Wayne Wenchao He has been teaching Chinese as a foreign language for more than twenty years. After more than twelve years of teaching at New York University, he has recently joined the faculty of the U.S. Military Academy at West Point. The Chinese for Tomorrow series is the result of his research and application of the Computer Chinese (CC) approach to Chinese language learning.

Dela Jiao is a senior lecturer in Chinese language. She has been teaching Chinese full-time in the East Asian Studies Department at New York University since 1994. Her teaching fields include Chinese language at all levels, Chinese culture, Chinese poetry, and modern Chinese literature.

Qiuxia Shao earned her B.A. at the Dalian Institute of Foreign Languages, and her Ed.M. and Ph.D. degrees at University at Buffalo, SUNY. She has been teaching Chinese at all levels in the United States since 1997, and is the proud mother of two children, Zhang Yancheng and Zhang Xiaolin.

Christopher Livaccari teaches the Chinese and Japanese languages and East Asian history at the College of Staten Island High School for International Studies; and serves on the board of directors of the Chinese Language Teachers Association of Greater New York. He is a former U.S. Foreign Service officer and a graduate of Columbia University, New York University, and the University of Chicago.